How to Read the Gospels

An Introduction

Yung Suk Kim

ROWMAN & LITTLEFIELD
Lanham • Boulder • New York • London

Senior Executive Editor: Richard Brown
Assistant Acquisitions Editor: Elizabeth Von Buhr
Sales and Marketing Inquiries: textbooks@rowman.com

Credits and acknowledgments for material borrowed from other sources, and reproduced with permission, appear on the appropriate pages within the text.

Published by Rowman & Littlefield
An imprint of The Rowman & Littlefield Publishing Group, Inc.
4501 Forbes Boulevard, Suite 200, Lanham, Maryland 20706
www.rowman.com

86-90 Paul Street, London EC2A 4NE

Copyright © 2024 by The Rowman & Littlefield Publishing Group, Inc.

All rights reserved. No part of this book may be reproduced in any form or by any electronic or mechanical means, including information storage and retrieval systems, without written permission from the publisher, except by a reviewer who may quote passages in a review.

British Library Cataloguing in Publication Information Available

Library of Congress Cataloging-in-Publication Data

Names: Kim, Yung Suk, author.
Title: How to read the Gospels : an introduction / Yung Suk Kim.
Description: 1st Edition. | Lanham : Rowman & Littlefield, [2024] | Includes bibliographical references and index.
Identifiers: LCCN 2024014933 (print) | LCCN 2024014934 (ebook) | ISBN 9781538186077 (cloth) | ISBN 9781538186084 (paperback) | ISBN 9781538186091 (ebook)
Subjects: LCSH: Bible. Gospels—Criticism, interpretation, etc.
Classification: LCC BS2555.52 .K544 2024 (print) | LCC BS2555.52 (ebook) | DDC 226/.061—dc23/eng/20240414
LC record available at https://lccn.loc.gov/2024014933
LC ebook record available at https://lccn.loc.gov/2024014934

Contents

Acknowledgments	ix

PART I: A Historical, Literary Introduction

1	Introduction	3
	What Is a Gospel?	4
	How to Read the Gospels	7
	As the Story of Jesus	7
	As the Story of the Evangelists Reflecting on the Significance of Jesus	9
	As the Story of Jesus and Evangelists for Contemporary Readers	12
	Transmission of the Story of Jesus	13
	The Synoptic Problem	14
	Two-Source Hypothesis	14
	What Is Q?	15
	Redaction Criticism	16
2	The Gospel of Mark	21
	Outline	24
	The Markan Jesus	25
	Distinctive Theological Themes	25
	Parables in Mark	26
	Notable Interpretation Issues	27
	A Close Reading of Mark	28
	1:1–13, Prologue	28
	1:14–8:26, Public Ministry	30

8:27–10:52, Jesus on the Way to Jerusalem	32
11:1–13:37, Ministry in Jerusalem	36
14:1–15:47, Passion Narrative: Last Supper, Trials, and the Crucifixion	38
16:1–8, The Resurrection of Jesus	40
Questions for Reflection	41
Further Reading	41

3 The Gospel of Matthew — 45
Outline — 48
The Matthean Jesus — 49
Distinctive Theological Themes — 50
Parables in Matthew — 50
Notable Interpretation Issues — 51
A Close Reading of Matthew — 52

1:1–2:23, Infancy Narrative	52
3:1–4:25, Ministry of Jesus	54
5:1–7:29, First Discourse: Sermon on the Mount	56
8:1–9:38, Jesus Heals Many People	60
10:1–10:42, Second Discourse: Missionary Instructions	61
11:1–12:50, Jesus's Ministry Continues while Opposition Arises	63
13:1–53, Third Discourse: Collections of Parables	64
13:54–17:27, Jesus Continues with His Mission and Foretells His Death and Resurrection	64
18:1–35, Fourth Discourse: Community Instructions	67
19:1–20:34, Jesus Continues to Teach on the Way to Jerusalem	67
21:1–23:39, Jesus Enters Jerusalem and Confronts Leaders	69
24:1–25:46, Fifth Discourse: Sermon on Eschatology	70
26:1–27:66, Passion Narrative	70
28:1–20, The Resurrection of Jesus	71

Questions for Reflection — 72
Further Reading — 72

4 The Gospel of Luke — 75
Outline — 79
The Lukan Jesus — 79
Distinctive Theological Themes — 80
Parables in Luke — 81
Notable Interpretation Issues — 82
A Close Reading of Luke — 83

1:1–4, Preface	83
1:5–2:52, Birth and Childhood of Jesus	84

3:1–4:13, Preparation for the Ministry of Jesus	86
4:14–9:50, Jesus's Ministry in Galilee	88
9:51–19:27, On the Way to Jerusalem	93
19:28–21:38, Jesus's Teaching in Jerusalem	99
22:1–23:56, The Suffering and Death of Jesus	99
24:1–53, The Resurrection of Jesus	102
Questions for Reflection	103
Further Reading	103
5 The Gospel of John	**105**
Outline	109
The Johannine Jesus	109
Distinctive Theological Themes	110
"I Am" Sayings of Jesus	111
Notable Interpretation Issues	112
A Close Reading of John	113
1:1–18, Prologue	113
1:19–5:47, Jesus's Ministry	114
6:1–12:50, Jesus's Ministry Grows and Faces Opposition	120
13:1–17:26, Farewell Discourses	124
18:1–20:31, Suffering and Glory	126
21:1–25, Addendum	129
Questions for Reflection	130
Further Reading	131

PART II: Reading the Gospels from Various Perspectives

6 Overview of Interpretive Approaches to the Gospels	**135**
Author-Centered, Historical Approach	137
Historical-Critical Method	137
Social-Science Criticism	138
Text-Centered, Literary Approach	139
Textual Criticism	139
Narrative Criticism	139
Reader-Centered, Comprehensive Approach	140
Reader-Response Criticism	140
Feminist Criticism	140
Womanist Interpretation	141
Ekklesia-Centered, Theological Interpretation	141
Jewish Interpretation	142
Inter(con)textual Interpretation	142
Queer Criticism	143
Postcolonial Criticism	143
Deconstruction Interpretation	143

Minoritized Criticism	144
Disability Studies	144
Ecological Criticism	144
7 The Gospel of Mark from Various Perspectives	**149**
Author-Centered, Historical Approach	149
Historical-Critical Method	149
Social-Science Criticism	150
Text-Centered, Literary Approach	151
Textual Criticism	151
Narrative Criticism	152
Reader-Centered, Comprehensive Approach	153
Reader-Response Criticism	153
Feminist Criticism	155
Womanist Interpretation	156
Ekklesia-Centered, Theological Interpretation	157
Jewish Interpretation	158
Inter(con)textual Interpretation	159
Queer Criticism	160
Postcolonial Criticism	161
Deconstruction Interpretation	163
Minoritized Criticism	164
Disability Studies	165
Ecological Criticism	166
8 The Gospel of Matthew from Various Perspectives	**171**
Author-Centered, Historical Approach	171
Historical-Critical Method	171
Social-Science Criticism	172
Text-Centered, Literary Approach	173
Textual Criticism	173
Narrative Criticism	174
Reader-Centered, Comprehensive Approach	175
Reader-Response Criticism	175
Feminist Criticism	176
Womanist Interpretation	177
Ekklesia-Centered, Theological Interpretation	179
Jewish Interpretation	181
Inter(con)textual Interpretation	182
Queer Criticism	183
Postcolonial Criticism	184
Deconstruction Interpretation	185
Minoritized Criticism	186
Disability Studies	188

	Ecological Criticism	189
9	The Gospel of Luke from Various Perspectives	195
	Author-Centered, Historical Approach	195
	Historical-Critical Method	195
	Social-Science Criticism	196
	Text-Centered, Literary Approach	197
	Textual Criticism	197
	Narrative Criticism	198
	Reader-Centered, Comprehensive Approach	200
	Reader-Response Criticism	200
	Feminist Criticism	201
	Womanist Criticism	202
	Ekklesia-Centered, Theological Interpretation	203
	Jewish Interpretation	204
	Inter(con)textual Interpretation	205
	Queer Criticism	206
	Postcolonial Criticism	207
	Deconstruction Interpretation	208
	Minoritized Criticism	209
	Disability Studies	211
	Ecological Criticism	212
10	The Gospel of John from Various Perspectives	217
	Author-Centered, Historical Approach	217
	Historical-Critical Method	217
	Social-Science Criticism	218
	Text-Centered, Literary Approach	219
	Textual Criticism	219
	Narrative Criticism	220
	Reader-Centered, Comprehensive Approach	221
	Reader-Response Criticism	221
	Feminist Criticism	222
	Womanist Interpretation	224
	Ekklesia-Centered, Theological Interpretation	225
	Jewish Interpretation	226
	Inter(con)textual Interpretation	227
	Queer Criticism	229
	Postcolonial Criticism	230
	Deconstruction Interpretation	231
	Minoritized Criticism	232
	Disability Studies	233
	Ecological Criticism	234

11	Conclusion	239
	The Importance of Various Readings of the Gospels	240
	Criteria for Solid Interpretation	242
	Readers' Critical, Imaginative Role	243
Bibliography		247
Index		267
About the Author		281

Acknowledgments

I thank God for allowing me to write and finish this book. During the peak time of my writing, I fell into a physical and mental infirmity like that which I'd never experienced before. I poured out my soul to the Lord like Hannah had done, exercised hard physically and spiritually, and thought again about myself and the world. I regained vitality and returned to the rhythm of my life. I am not alone and am surrounded by a cloud of witnesses who have supported me, whether directly or indirectly. I thank all my current students and the graduates of the Samuel DeWitt Proctor School of Theology at Virginia Union University. They are amazing souls who have impacted me in myriad ways. Through the ebb and flow, I have learned what they need most for their academic study, ministry formation, and ongoing ministry. My teaching and writing reflect their struggle, their yearning for justice and transformation in all aspects of life. I thank my dean, Dr. John Guns, who has never reduced his support for me and my projects. He trusted me as a scholar, teacher, and beloved brother. My colleagues at the Samuel DeWitt Proctor School of Theology are amazing. I appreciate their collegial support for my work.

I also give special thanks to the colleagues who read parts of the early stages of the manuscript and gave me feedback and suggestions: Dr. Susan Hylen at Candler School of Theology at Emory University; Dr. Nicholas Elder at the University of Dubuque Theological Seminary; Dr. Troy Troftgruben at Wartburg Theological Seminary; Dr. Ekaputra Tupamahu at George Fox University; and Dr. Robert Wafawanaka at Virginia Union University. Because of their encouragement and feedback, I was able to continue to develop and refine my manuscript.

I also want to thank the six anonymous peer reviewers chosen by my publisher for their critical, heartfelt review of my book proposal and a sample chapter. I could revise and restructure the manuscript satisfactorily because of their appreciation, encouragement, pungent evaluation, and suggestions for improvement.

Also, several other colleagues of mine read parts of the manuscript and gave me last-minute feedback. Dr. Troy Troftgruben at Wartburg Theological Seminary has been a constant supporter of my scholarship. He reviewed the chapters on Luke's Gospel and gave me very helpful feedback. Dr. Nicholas Elder at the University of Dubuque Theological Seminary helped me twice in reading chapters on Mark's Gospel. His affirmation of my work boosted my research and writing. Dr. Adele Reinhartz at the University of Ottawa gave me critical feedback on the chapters on John's Gospel. Finally, Dr. Ekaputra Tupamahu at George Fox University read a chapter on Matthew's Gospel and gave me important feedback along with warm support. Also, I won't forget about Dr. Michael Gorman at St. Mary's Seminary, who suggested adding the "Ekklesia-Centered, Theological Interpretation" sections to my book. His kind spirit and critical mind toward the church and real people are noteworthy.

Dr. Richard Brown, my editor at Rowman & Littlefield, took serious care with my book proposal and managed the peer review process well and patiently. Because of his trust and encouragement, I could focus on my research and writing.

Lastly, as always, my family inspires me and loves me. My deepest love goes to my wife, YongJeong, and my three daughters: Hyerim, HyeKyung, and HyeIn. I also recognize my sons-in-law: Jason, Jinho, and Stephen. They have never wavered in their love and support of my work. I also want to say "thank you" to my granddaughter, Hana, who is a joy to my life.

I
A HISTORICAL, LITERARY INTRODUCTION

Chapter 1

Introduction

This book features a twofold introduction to the four canonical Gospels: "A Historical, Literary Introduction" (part 1) and "Reading the Gospels from Various Perspectives" (part 2). Part 1 presents a bird's-eye view of the Gospels, including the characterization of Jesus; distinctive theological themes; parables; and a close reading. Often, readers jump into commentaries or other secondary sources without reading the primary source closely. Here, *close reading* means reading the text carefully from beginning to end, trying to understand what is going on in the story, and asking imaginative yet crucial questions about the text. Close reading is the first step toward critical interpretation because it enables readers to engage with the text wholeheartedly. Part 1 also provides consider-and-discuss textboxes with which readers may dive deep into the text to critically engage with the intricate interpretive issues. At the end of each chapter, it also includes a section entitled "Questions for Reflection" for further engagement.

Part 2 introduces readers to various readings of the Gospels that cover a wide array of interpretive methods ranging from historical-critical criticisms to reader-centered, comprehensive approaches. It includes traditional and emerging perspectives such as postcolonial criticism, minoritized criticism, womanist interpretation, queer criticism, disability studies, and Jewish interpretation. Here, the purpose is not to provide extensive illustrations of those criticisms but to showcase diverse ways of reading. Since there are two parts in this book, readers have an option: either to study them in sequence—that is, to read part 1 first and then part 2—or to read the two parts together. For example, if one is interested in Mark's Gospel, one can read the chapter on Mark in part 1 and the other on Mark in part 2, which deals with various readings of Mark. Before reading the main chapters, it is pivotal to ask some necessary questions: What is a gospel? How can we read the Gospels? What is the origin and development of the Gospel stories? In this introduction we explore these questions.

WHAT IS A GOSPEL?

The Greek term *euangelion* means "good news" or "gospel," which has frequently been used by the emperor when he's promoted his achievements or legitimated his imperial rule. This same term is also extensively used by the New Testament writers, especially in the four Gospels and Paul's letters. For example, Jesus proclaims "the good news of God" (Mark 1:14), which means the good news about or from God. Paul also refers to "the good news of God" for which he is set apart (Rom 1:1; cf. Rom 15:16; 2 Cor 11:7; 1 Thes 2:2, 8–9). He also refers to "the good news of Jesus Christ" (1 Cor 9:12–13; Gal 1:7; Phil 1:27; 1 Thes 3:2), which includes at least two aspects of the good news: (1) the good news that Jesus proclaims, which is the good news of God, and (2) the good news about Jesus because of his grace and faithfulness.[1] But there is no genre of "gospel" in ancient literature. The four Gospels are close to a biography plus a novel-like theological story. In some sense, these Gospels are like the following ancient biographies: *The Lives the Twelve Caesars* (Suetonius) and *The Lives of the Roman Emperors* (Plutarch). In John's Gospel, Jesus is the one sent by God and does the work of God. In Matthew's and Luke's Gospels, Jesus is born miraculously with a purpose. In Mark's Gospel, Jesus proclaims God's good news, healing the sick and asking for *metanoia*—a change of mind toward God. Jesus's proclamation of the good news challenges the hierarchical patron-client system in the Roman Empire because God's rule embraces the poor and the marginalized. He is crucified because of that. On the cross he says the last word, "It is finished" (John 19:30). To tell stories about Jesus, early Christians depended on their memory and received traditions, and they edited the source material to fit their context. This editing has led to four portrayals of Jesus in the four Gospels.

To understand a Gospel, we need to see the term *euangelion* (good news) in the broad, political context of the Roman Empire where the idea of good news is constituted by the emperor's birthday, victory at war, or political achievements. In other words, in the Roman Empire, the good news was political propaganda cementing the imperial power. Caesar Augustus (63 BCE–14 CE) established the Roman Empire with a military might and retained that mighty power, which no one could challenge. He was called *divi filius* (the son of God), *princeps* (first person), and *pontifex maximus* (greatest priest). Virgil wrote the epic poem *Aeneid* to praise the heyday of the Augustan Roman Empire. In this poem Aeneas is the legendary Trojan hero who traveled to Italy and established Rome. This heroic figure represents Augustus, who boasted about his achievements and inscribed them on the monument called Res Gestae Divi Augusti (The Deeds of the Divine Augustus). In the end the good news of the Roman Empire has two faces: the good news seen as peace and security brought by the empire through military conquest and control, as well as the good news seen as a political slogan or propaganda that appealed to the people. Emperors tried to unify and control their subjects with the forced good news that they were divinely chosen rulers. To this sociopolitical world of the Roman Empire, Jesus proclaimed the good news of God (Mark 1:14) and revealed God through his words and deeds. After Jesus, early Christians brought to the world the good news of Jesus Christ, who proclaimed the good news of God. The four Gospels resulted from the early Christian communities' long, persistent journey of faith. They did not simply deliver the word of God or the message about Jesus. They believed in the good news, which brings the power of God for salvation as the apostle Paul writes: "For I am not ashamed of the gospel; it is the power of God for salvation to everyone who has faith, to the Jew first and also to the Greek" (Rom 1:16).

TEXTBOX 1.1   **Types of Gospels**

NARRATIVE GOSPELS

Narrative means a story about related events. Mark, Matthew, Luke, and John contain a story about Jesus's life, and their narratives are not identical, because the author/editor of the Gospel edited the text.[1] The four canonical Gospels also include other small stories within the larger narrative: the infancy narrative in Matthew and Luke, miracles, healing, the passion narrative, and the resurrection story.

SAYINGS GOSPELS

Sayings gospels contain Jesus's teachings without narrative. For example, the Gospel of Thomas has 114 sayings of Jesus, composed of wisdom teaching, parables, and proverbs. The Coptic version of this Gospel was discovered at Nag Hammadi, Egypt, between 1945 and 1946. The fragments of the original Greek version of Thomas go back to around 200 CE. Interestingly, the hypothetical source Q also has sayings of Jesus, the purported source for Matthew and Luke. Other similar types of sayings gospels were also discovered near Hammadi, in the form of fragments: *Dialogue of the Savior*, which contains Jesus's dialogues with three of his disciples, Judas, Matthew, and Miriam, and the *Apocryphon of James*, which includes Jesus's conversation with Peter and James. Other Gnostic Gospels, such as the Gospel of Philip (180–250 CE) and the Gospel of Mary (120–180 CE), belong to this category of the sayings gospel. In the Gospel of Philip and the Gospel of Mary, Jesus loves Mary more than any other disciples. The Gospel of Judah (130–170 CE) is another Gnostic Gospel, mentioned first by Irenaeus of Lyons in the second century CE. Irenaeus responded to the heretics in his time, referring to those who say that Judas is a hero: "They produce a fictitious history of this kind, which they style the Gospel of Judas."[2]

INFANCY GOSPELS

While Matthew and Luke include birth narratives, in later times, there were more embellished stories of Jesus's birth. For example, the Infancy Gospel of Thomas includes miraculous stories about Jesus's childhood before he reached the age of twelve; it is mainly about his magical work. We have the Syriac manuscript of the fourth century CE and the later Greek manuscripts of the fourteenth and sixteenth centuries CE. The Infancy Gospel of James (140–170 CE) contains the story of Mary's conception and the birth of Jesus.

PASSION GOSPELS

Passion gospels include Jesus's suffering and death. For example, the Gospel of Peter (70–160 CE) contains a passion narrative, a story about the empty tomb, and the beginning of the resurrection story. Acts of Pilate (150–255 CE) contains stories about Jesus's trial before Pilate, his death and burial, the empty tomb story, and his resurrection. The purported author of the Gospel of Peter is Nicodemus. Stories about Jesus's death began to be told early on and ended up in the canonical Gospels.

OTHER FRAGMENTARY GOSPELS

The Gospel of the Ebionites (100–160 CE) appears in a few quotations by Epiphanius in the fourth century CE. It represents the work of the Ebionites, who were Greek-speaking Jewish Christians flourishing in the second and third centuries CE. The Gospel of the Hebrews (80–150 CE) appears in the writings of Clement of Alexandria (second century CE), Origen (third century CE), and Cyril (fourth century CE). This gospel contains traditions of Jesus's preexistence and his baptism, as well as other stories about him. The Gospel of the Nazoreans (100–160 CE), which is an extended version of the Gospel of Matthew, is preserved in quotations and allusions by church fathers.

NOTES

1. For more about the types of the Gospels, see Robert Funk, Bernard Brandon Scott, and James Butts, *The Parables of Jesus: Red Letter Edition, The Jesus Seminar* (Sonoma, CA: Polebridge, 1988), xvii–xx. See also, *Early Christian Writings* for a comprehensive list of early Christian writings: https://www.earlychristianwritings.com (accessed May 23, 2023).

2. Alexander Roberts, ed. "Irenaeus: Against Heresies," The Gnostic Society Library, 1.31.1, accessed February 23, 2021, http://gnosis.org/library/advh1.htm.

HOW TO READ THE GOSPELS

As the Story of Jesus

The four canonical Gospels are not eyewitness accounts of Jesus. They are neither pure biographies nor novels but stories about Jesus that are based on oral or written traditions about him. Indeed, they are the oldest Gospels written about forty to sixty years after Jesus died. So if we are interested in the real historical Jesus, we must depend on these writings because there are no earlier gospels than these. But still, the difficulty is as to how we can pull a secure image of Jesus since there are four versions of the story of Jesus as well as irreconcilable discrepancies among the four Gospels. The four evangelists (Mark, Matthew, Luke, and John) are theologians, not historians or biographers in a modern sense. They were more interested in the significance of Jesus and applying the story of Jesus to their religious life. For example, in Mark and Matthew, Jesus instructs the disciples to gather in Galilee after his resurrection because Galilee is Jesus's hometown and mission base. But in Luke, they are asked to gather in Jerusalem because, for Luke, Jerusalem must be the new mission starting place for the Gentiles. Jerusalem is the center of Judaism, but because the Jews rejected Jesus, the gospel then moved to the gentile areas. Historically speaking, concerning the disciples' gathering place, either Galilee or Jerusalem can be correct, but they cannot both be correct. Or both of them may be wrong, because there is no information about the place of their gathering outside the Gospels. In Matthew, Jesus's hometown is Bethlehem, and he was born there to fulfill the Old Testament prophecy in Micah 5:2, as quoted in Matthew 2:6. But according to Luke, Jesus's hometown is Nazareth. Here, the question is, Which place is his hometown? Matthew intends to connect Jesus's birth in Bethlehem with the Old Testament prophecy because he is the Jewish Messiah who came to fulfill the law and prophets. In John, Jesus was crucified on the day of preparation for Passover. So he did not eat the Passover meal; the implication is that he became a paschal lamb. But in Mark, Jesus ate the Passover meal and died after the event, which makes smoother sense than John. But John's theological claim seems clear that Jesus provided himself as a new paschal lamb.

Even with the above difficulties, we can draw some bare facts about Jesus from the accounts of the Gospels. All four Gospels confirm that Jesus was a Galilean or a Nazarean. He was a *tekton* (carpenter or builder) and lived with a poor family, born in tumultuous times under the Roman Empire. At some point in his adult life, he went to John the Baptist and was baptized by him in the Jordan. After that baptism, he began his public ministry by proclaiming the good news of God, which is none other than "the good news of the kingdom of God" (Mark 1:14–15; Luke 4:43; 8:1; 16:16). His initial preaching appears in Mark 1:15, which is about God's time (*kairos*), God's rule (*basileia tou theou*), and repentance (change of mind, *metanoia*). In these verses, Jesus declares that now is God's time and that people must accept it by changing their minds toward God. Now is the time for God to rule the world with justice and love. Therefore, people must seek God's will. To exemplify the good news of God, Jesus heals the sick, exorcises demons, feeds the hungry and thirsty, and tells parables about the new humanity and community. He also challenges wicked people and authorities and is crucified because of what he has said and done.

However, the above minimalist view of the historical Jesus does not let us know who he was or what he tried to achieve, because his work must be put into context. So scholars have proposed diverse opinions about the historical Jesus: "Jesus the Myth, Jesus the Hellenistic Hero, Jesus the Revolutionary, Jesus the Wisdom Sage, Jesus the Man of the Spirit, Jesus the Prophet of Social Change, Jesus the Apocalyptic Prophet, and Jesus the Savior."[2] Indeed, the historical Jesus studies comprise diverse methodologies and approaches. Suffice it to say, the Gospels may be a substantial source for the studies of the historical Jesus, but to nail down who he was and what he tried to achieve is a matter of debate. Even if we have earlier writings than the current Gospels, reconstruction is still a far cry, as it is a matter of interpretation. In the end we must acknowledge the reconstruction of Jesus is hard not merely because the Gospels are not eyewitness accounts but also because interpreting them is ambiguous or multifaceted. So the search for the historical Jesus must be done carefully with a sense of flexibility and rigor alike.

TEXTBOX 1.2 **Which Jesus?**

Often scholars perceive different kinds of Jesus. One possibility is to see Jesus as the Jesus of history versus the Christ of faith. The former refers to the real Jesus, who existed and lived and died. The interest is to know about him as objectively as possible. The latter is about the Christ/Messiah who was understood and confessed by the church or Christians. The above division makes sense because there is an unbridgeable gap between Jesus (history) and knowing about him (interpretation). However, this division is not always helpful or constructive because faith is also based on historical facts or testimonies about Jesus. Our methodology or perspectives in dealing with history are not perfect enough to tell who Jesus was. While honoring the gap between history and interpretation, we must not demonize one or the other, because faith also needs historical reasoning. A distrust between academia and the church is unnecessary; rather, there must be mutual critique and strengthening between them. For example, the historical Jesus study needs to consider the religious experience of Christians/the church because the Jesus of history does not exist apart from his religious experience. Likewise, Christians must be mindful of Jesus in history beyond their tradition. Besides the above opposing views of Jesus, we may consider the evangelists' Jesus—the Markan Jesus, the Matthean Jesus, the Lukan Jesus, and the Johannine Jesus. We will see about this in the next section. Also, we may perceive the real Jesus in the sense that he is understood and confessed by individuals in their personal contexts.[1]

NOTE

1. Richard Soulen, *Defining Jesus: The Earthly, the Biblical, the Historical, and the Real Jesus, and How Not to Confuse Them* (Eugene, OR: Cascade Books, 2015).

To understand the historical Jesus to a certain degree, interpreters may use various methods or approaches to the text. They may adopt them eclectically to explore him in context, and potential criticisms include but are not limited to textual criticism, historical-critical methods, social-scientific criticism, feminist criticism, or postcolonial criticism. But even before using this methodological approach to the text, interpreters must be informed of the first-century Palestine situation under the Roman Empire and the historical and literary context of the Gospels. In part 2, readers may see a variety of readings of the Gospels, and some of them are more historically minded than others. For example, textual criticism, the historical-critical method, and social-scientific criticism may be more helpful than others to explore the historical Jesus to some degree. But the bottom line is the historical Jesus is not limited by any methods. With an open mind, readers must be flexible and rigorous when using these methods.

As the Story of the Evangelists Reflecting on the Significance of Jesus

Stories about Jesus had circulated from the beginning of his ministry and then more widely after he died. His followers spread good news about him wherever they went. As time passed, multitudes of other Christians received the traditions about Jesus and passed them on to others. There were diverse/divergent stories about him: oral traditions, some from eyewitnesses and others from stories retold by generations of Christian witnesses who came after that. Four evangelists (Mark, Matthew, Luke, and John) looked back on Jesus's life and his faithful work of God. In this sense, the Gospels are the product of how early Christian communities interpreted the Jesus event in their contexts. Mark portrays Jesus as the suffering Son of God, who gives his life as a ransom for many (Mark 10:45).

The Messiah's suffering is predicted and necessary not because suffering has in it an intrinsic value but because his bold proclamation of the kingdom of God is against the kingdom of Rome's and Jerusalem's leadership. The cross is the cost of God's righteousness. Anyone who embraces God's rule and righteousness must face hardships and suffering. Jesus as the suffering Son of God shows the vulnerability of humanity, as he is agitated before the impending trials and suffering. He does not want to go through the difficult paths leading to the cross but submits to God's will. This portrayal of Jesus reflects the Markan community's struggle over the harsh conditions of life, such as persecution or trials. The community must decide to keep their faith or give up on it in a world where following Jesus leads to a cross-like life. The message is that God will prevail in the end, but until that time, the disciples are expected to undergo hard times because the good news is opposed by the authorities.

Matthew portrays Jesus as the Jewish Messiah who came to fulfill the law and the prophets (Mt 5:17). He reinterprets the Jewish law with a focus on integrity. Loving neighbors is not enough, and loving enemies is required. The law must be focused on benefiting others and be kept wholeheartedly. Murder is prohibited, and hating someone is also a serious matter, comparable to murder. Adultery is judged, and seeing a person with lust is also a sin. The Sabbath is a holy day and is important; it must be kept with integrity. But according to Jesus, even on the Sabbath, when someone is sick, he or she must be taken care of. The law must be flexible, depending on the context. On the other hand, Jesus presents himself as a narrow-minded Jewish Messiah who prohibits the disciples from entering a Samaritan town, asking them to go to the lost sheep of the house of Israel (Mt 10:5–6). Consistently, in Matthew 15:21–28, Jesus rejects the Canaanite woman's request for healing her daughter. The reason is the same: that his mission is for the lost sheep of the house of Israel. In the end he acknowledges her faith. Nevertheless, his initial rejection and derogatory words will not disappear with a final yes to her. This episode reflects the Matthean community's struggle with the mission policy for the Gentiles. The issue is whether the community must be inclusive of the Gentiles. If the community accepts them, what must be the condition for them? What kind of faith or practice of the law will be required for them?

Luke characterizes Jesus as the savior who seeks out and saves the lost (Luke 19:10). The motif of *the lost* and *saving* are great themes in Luke. Peter was lost in the sea, figuratively speaking, and is saved from a boat sinking in storms, and he is called to become a disciple amid the stormy sea (Luke 5:1–11). Zacchaeus is lost and saved from his hellish life because of his repentance. He was disgraced due to his tax collector job, but his family was saved on that day of repentance (Luke 19:1–10). In the parable of the father and two sons (Luke 15:21–34), the younger son/brother returns home after wasting the property. The compassionate father welcomes him because his lost son came home alive. The savior Jesus reflects the community's vision for empowering the downtrodden and marginalized, possibly under the auspices of the Roman Empire. On the one hand, Jesus died a prophetic death and never lamented over his suffering. He was ready to die as a prophet from the beginning of his ministry. But on the other hand, Luke portrays Jesus as an innocent prophet, who is considered not dangerous to the empire, as Pilate insists that he cannot find faults with Jesus and a Roman centurion says that he is innocent. (Luke 23:47). This portrayal of Jesus has to do with Luke's overriding concern that the gospel must be proclaimed to the Roman world without danger. Likewise, the Lukan Jesus is presented as the savior of the world who goes beyond Jewish boundaries and prefers the mission of the Gentiles to that of Jews (Luke 4:16–30). This mission strategy reflects Luke's community—mainly composed of the Gentiles—that seeks to spread the gospel among the Gentiles.

John depicts Jesus as the Son of God who is sent from heaven. Jesus repeatedly says that the Father sent him and that he does the works of God (John 3:17; 4:34; 6:38). He also says, "If I am not doing the works of my Father, then do not believe me. But if I do them, even though you do not believe me, believe the works, so that you may know and understand that the Father is in me and I am in the Father" (John 10:37–38). Jesus's work is to do God's will, which is stated in John 3:16: "God so loved the world." He embodies the divine Logos (Word) in a world replete with chaos and injustices. He shows the world that he came to bring the light, revealing God's love and testifying to the truth (John 3:19). The light came into the world through Jesus, but "people loved darkness rather than light because their deeds were evil" (3:19). So he says, "For all who do evil hate the light and do not come to the light, so that their deeds may not be exposed. But those who do what is true come to the light, so that it may be clearly seen that their deeds have been done in God" (John 3:20–21). Jesus is the light of the world not merely because he is the Son of God but because he does the works of God, which are to accept the light, to love people, and to hate evil. So he says, "Whoever follows me will never walk in darkness but will have the light of life" (John 8:12). Discipleship is not about believing but staying in his teaching (8:31). All of the above picture of the Johannine Jesus markedly differs from that in the Synoptic Gospels, especially concerning the language of the heavenly son sent by God, which reflects the Johannine community's confrontation with the synagogue. The Gospel of John claims that Jesus is the true Son of God who is sent by God and that he is "the way and the truth and the life" (14:6).

To explore the four evangelists' stories of Jesus, one indispensably must follow a close reading of each Gospel as this book features it. By paying attention to what is going on in the narrative, readers may better understand the evangelist's context and theology. While there are close readings of the Gospels in this book, readers need to engage with those readings and explore their own close reading along the way. Besides, readers can use textual criticism or redaction criticism to understand and clarify the evangelist's context and issues.

As the Story of Jesus and Evangelists for Contemporary Readers

By and large, we may consider two categories of contemporary readers: personal or individual readers and *ekklesia* (church) reading by the community. Church-centered reading has been dominant for most periods of Christianity, from the first century to the early sixteenth century, before the Reformation, during which the church as a whole had the power or authority to interpret the Gospels. Only after the Reformation was the Bible freely translated, and it then came to be in the hands of everyday people. But still, the most powerful activity in interpreting the Gospels has come from religious communities. Priests, pastors, and religious leaders communicate the gospel with the world and/or their congregants, based on their denominational guidelines. In limited but creative ways, they may exercise freedom of interpretation, but they are still under the supervision of the higher governing body. Sometimes reform is accepted by the church by reinterpreting the scripture. For example, some Christian Protestant denominations, such as the Presbyterian Church (USA), Episcopal Church, and the Evangelical Lutheran Church in America, have affirmed LGBT people by changing their denominational policy after rounds of discussion and interpretation concerning scripture and their Christian tradition. Theological debates and struggles are still ongoing within various religious organizations. In a world where climate change is a real threat and Christian good news gradually loses its taste for the real people in struggle, some may raise questions: What does it mean to form a community (ekklesia) in Jesus? What is the urgent message to bring forth to the world?

In addition to ekklesia-led reading, the Gospels are enjoyed and greatly read among various individuals from diverse cultures and backgrounds across the globe. While some engage in the Gospels to devote their lives to God and Jesus, others delve into the Gospels for moral guidance. Some researchers dig into the Gospels to excavate social-historical aspects of the text. While modern-day life strikingly differs from that of the first-century Roman, Mediterranean world, people still live on the same planet with the same need for some kind of salvation from or in their lives. It may be a recovery of a sense of meaning in life when people fall into despair and vanity. It may be a return to normal life when they are sick, destitute, insecure, lonely, and mentally ill. For some, salvation is more about the community and society rather than about individuals. They seek social justice, and for them, salvation means all people in the community or society may live peacefully with justice. For others, salvation means to live an ordinary life with God's blessing and without discrimination or prejudices against them. Across time and cultures, Christianity has played mixed roles in providing a sense of salvation to people. While it has been a crucial contributor to the balanced social fabric of human lives by awakening a sense of human dignity, freedom, and justice, it also has become a weapon for colonizing other countries or exploiting them. But the bottom line is that people still need good news that they may embrace when they go through the morass of their lives. Readers of diverse backgrounds and cultures still love to engage with the stories of Jesus to explore authentic faith or moral guidance.

As we've seen above, the Gospels are cherished by people for various reasons. At the same time, they are critiqued because of narrow or potentially harmful interpretations of the text. In part 2 readers will see a wide array of criticisms or interpretations in the sections entitled "Reader-Centered, Comprehensive Approach."

TRANSMISSION OF THE STORY OF JESUS

The four Gospels trace back to oral traditions, as Luke hints in the preface: "Since many have undertaken to compile a narrative about the events that have been fulfilled among us, just as they were handed on to us by those who from the beginning were eyewitnesses and servants of the word. I, too, decided, as one having a grasp of everything from the start, to write a well-ordered account for you" (Luke 1:1–3). Jesus and his disciples did not leave any writings, and stories about Jesus were spread orally. The followers of Jesus retold the stories of Jesus to others, who again retold them to others. This process continued throughout the first two centuries while some evangelists wrote them down. Why do we not have earlier writings on Jesus? There are three main reasons for that. First, the most effective communication in ancient times was by mouth-to-mouth. Second, Jesus's disciples were illiterate and could not write anything about Jesus. Third, early Christians believed that Jesus would come back so soon. Therefore, they were busy preaching the good news of God, and Jesus and did not have the leisure to write books. Even if they could write, most people were illiterate. Jesus's sayings (from Q, a hypothetical source of Jesus's sayings found in Luke and Matthew, but not Mark) may have existed before the narrative Gospels, written down at least forty to sixty years after Jesus died. But in terms of the narrative Gospel, Mark is the first of its kind, written before or during the Jewish war (70 CE). Then about a decade later, Matthew and Luke were written separately (85–90 CE). John came down a little later than those Gospels (90–95). Even after this period, stories about Jesus continued to spread, and some Gnostic gospels were composed in the second and third centuries CE. In sum, since the Gospels are not eyewitness accounts, we must consider the layers of oral traditions about Jesus and the communities behind these Gospels.

The Synoptic Problem

Mark, Matthew, and Luke are called the Synoptic Gospels because they are very similar. *Synoptic* means "seeing together," which implies that the evangelists depended on the same literary sources. But these three Gospels are also different from each other. Both the similarities and differences between the three Gospels puzzle readers, so this reality is called the Synoptic problem. But we can explain this issue through source theory and redaction criticism. The former explains why the three Gospels are similar, and the latter helps explain differences in the Gospels.

Two-Source Hypothesis

Two-source hypothesis means Matthew and Luke used two sources in their composition: Mark and Q. Mark became a primary source to Matthew and Luke. Q—a hypothetical source of Jesus's sayings—became the other source for Matthew and Luke. Matthew and Luke share Q, which does not appear in Mark. Q derives from *quelle* (German), which means "source." Even though the two-source hypothesis does not explain the unique materials in the Synoptic Gospels, it is a convincing theory that helps explain the evangelists' theology and issues. Scholars believe that Mark is considered the primary source for Matthew and Luke, and this theory, called Markan priority, is supported by the following reasons:

- Mark may be the earliest of the three Synoptic Gospels.
- Matthew reproduces about 90 percent of Mark; Luke, about 50 percent. There are often verbatim agreements. When they do disagree, Matthew and Luke follow the sequence of Mark. That is, Mark is responsible for the chronological outline of the life of Jesus for Matthew and Luke.
- Patterns of the agreement show that Matthew and Luke used Mark independently. There are three kinds of agreement patterns: (1) all three agree; this happens because Matthew and Luke did not change Mark; (2) all three differ; this occurs because Matthew and Luke changed Mark; and (3) only one of them (either Matthew or

Luke) agrees with Mark. This case happens because only one of them changed Mark. In this third scenario, there are rare agreements between Matthew and Luke when only Matthew changed Mark or when only Luke changed Mark. This result implies that Matthew and Luke did not depend on each other; that is, they were unknown to each other, and they edited Mark independently.
- Characteristics of the changes support the Markan priority: the style of writing, difficult ideas, unusual words, and grammar in Mark are checked and corrected. For example, see Mark 10:17–18 and Matthew 19:16–17.
- Mark is the shortest gospel. It would have been so hard for Mark to omit so many excellent materials in Matthew if Matthew were a source for Mark.
- Q, a source shared by Matthew and Luke but not found in Mark, appears in different places in their narratives because Matthew and Luke did not depend on each other, and they arranged Q materials by their choice.

What Is Q?

Q consists of what Matthew and Luke have in common and what does not appear in Mark. It refers to the sayings or teachings of Jesus. Q is similar in form to the Gospel of Thomas (114 sayings). Unlike Thomas, however, most of the "sayings" in Q are scattered into gospel discourses. See the contents of Q in table 1.1 below:

Table 1.1. The Contents of Q[1]

Title	Luke	Matthew
Preaching of John the Baptist	3:7–9, 16–17	3:7b–12
Temptations of Jesus	4:1–13a	4:1–11a
Beatitudes	6:20b–23	5:3, 6, 4, 11–12
Love of enemies	6:27–33, 35b–36	5:44, 39b–40, 42; 7:12; 5:46–47, 45, 48
On judging others	6:37a, 38c, 39–42	7:1–2; 15:14; 10:24–25a; 7:3–5
On bearing fruit	6:43–45	7:16–20; 12:33–35
House built on rock	6:46–49	7:21, 24–27
Healing a centurion's servant	7:1–2, 6b–10	8:5–10, 13
John the Baptist's questions	7:18–23	11:2–6
Jesus speaks about John	7:24–28, 31–35	11:7–11, 16–19
On following Jesus	9:57–60	8:19–22
Missionary instructions	10:2–12	9:37–38; 10:7–16
Woes against Galilean cities	10:13–16	11:21–23; 10:40
Thanksgiving to the Father	10:21–24	11:25–27; 13:16–17

(continued)

Table 1.1. *(continued)*

Title	Luke	Matthew
Lord's Prayer	11:2–4	6:9–13
Asking and receiving	11:9–13	7:7–11
Beelzebul controversy	11:14–15, 17–23	12:22–30
Return of the evil spirit	11:24–26	12:43–45
Sign of Jonah	11:29–32	12:38–42
On light and seeing	11:33–35	5:15; 6:22–23
Woes against Pharisees	11:39–44, 46–52	23:25–26, 23, 6–7a, 27, 4, 29–31, 34–36, 13
Fearing humans and God	12:2–9	10:26–33; 12:32
Role of the Holy Spirit	12:10–12	12:32; 10:19
Anxiety; treasure in heaven	12:22–31, 33–34	6:25–33, 19–21
Watch and be ready	12:39–40, 42–46	24:43–51
Divisions in families	12:51–53	10:34–36
Signs of the times	12:54–56	16:2–3
Settling out of court	12:58–59	5:25–26
Mustard seed and leaven	13:18–21	13:31–33
Exclusion from the kingdom	12:23–30	7:13–14, 22–23; 8:11–12; 20:16
Lament over Jerusalem	13:34–35	23:37–39
Parable of the banquet	14:16–24	22:1–10
Carrying the cross	14:26–27	10:37–38
Parable of salt	14:34–35	5:13
Parable of the lost sheep	15:4–7	18:12–14
On serving two masters	16:13	6:24
On the law and divorce	16:16–18	11:12–13; 5:18, 32
On sin and forgiveness	17:1, 3b–4	18:7, 15, 21–22
Faith like a mustard seed	17:6	17:20
Coming of the Son of Man	17:23–24, 26–27, 30, 33–35, 37	24:26–27, 37–39; 10:39; 24:40–41, 28
Parable of the talents	19:12–27	25:14–30
Disciples will judge Israel	22:30	19:28

1. Richard A. Edwards, *A Theology of Q: Eschatology, Prophecy, and Wisdom* (Philadelphia, PA: Fortress Press, 1976), xi-xiii. See also, "Early Christian Writings," Early Christian Writings.com, accessed May 23, 2023, https://www.earlychristianwritings.com/q-contents.html.

Redaction Criticism

Redaction criticism deals with how and why the author/editor of the final composition changed the source material. By figuring out edited texts or changes, readers seek to explore the evangelist's context, issues, and/or theology. The baptism of Jesus appears in Mark 1:9–11, Matthew 3:13–17, and Luke 3:21–22 (See table 1.2).

According to the two-source hypothesis, Mark 1:9–11 is a source for Matthew and Luke. In other words, Matthew and Luke independently

Table 1.2. The Baptism of Jesus

Mark 1:9–11	Matthew 3:13–17	Luke 3:21–22
9 In those days Jesus came from Nazareth of Galilee and was baptized by John in the Jordan. 10 And just as he was coming up out of the water, he saw the heavens torn apart and the Spirit descending like a dove upon him. 11 And a voice came from the heavens, "You are my Son, the Beloved; with you I am well pleased." (New Revised Standard Version, Updated Edition)	13 Then Jesus came from Galilee to John at the Jordan, to be baptized by him. 14 John would have prevented him, saying, "I need to be baptized by you, and do you come to me?" 15 But Jesus answered him, "Let it be so now, for it is proper for us in this way to fulfill all righteousness." Then he consented. 16 And when Jesus had been baptized, just as he came up from the water, suddenly the heavens were opened to him and he saw God's Spirit descending like a dove and alighting on him. 17 And a voice from the heavens said, "This is my Son, the Beloved, with whom I am well pleased." (New Revised Standard Version, Updated Edition)	21 Now when all the people were baptized and when Jesus also had been baptized and was praying, the heaven was opened, 22 and the Holy Spirit descended upon him in bodily form like a dove. And a voice came from heaven, "You are my Son, the Beloved; with you I am well pleased." (New Revised Standard Version, Updated Edition)

edited the Markan material of Jesus's water baptism to fit their context. So when readers compare Matthew 3:13–17 with Mark 1:9–11, they find differences in Matthew such as John's hesitation to baptize Jesus; a didactic, conversational style; and a voice from heaven saying, "This is my Son" (Mt 3:17). With these differences, readers may wonder why Matthew needed to edit the source material in Mark, and they may explain it as much as they can, based on the historical context of the Matthean community and given the whole narrative. For example, since Matthew's audience is primarily a Jewish community, perhaps John's baptism of Jesus may have troubled some Jewish Christians with the following question: Why does Jesus, who is superior to John, need his baptism? Why does he need his baptism of "repentance for the forgiveness of sins? (Mark 1:4). Matthew answers these questions. It is Jesus who asked for baptism, while John was hesitating. He explained the purpose of baptism is to fulfill all righteousness (Mt 3:15). The other noticeable difference in Matthew is a heavenly voice difference. While in Mark, Jesus is called by a voice saying, "You are my Son" (Mark 1:11), in Matthew, it says, "This is my Son" (Mt 3:17). This difference reflects Matthew's overarching portrayal of Jesus in the whole Gospel of Matthew—that is, Jesus is a visible, public teacher; prophet; and Messiah.

In the same manner, compare Luke 3:13–17 with Mark 1:9–11. Luke's differences are in the omission of details about baptism, such as where he was baptized, who baptized him, and where he came from. While it is impossible to explain everything definitively, we can do our best, given these changes. Luke wanted to portray Jesus as the universal savior by removing the baptizer's name as well as the provincial information about Galilee and Jordan. Instead, Luke added Jesus's prayer and the presence of other people at the baptism because they are among the prevalent themes of Luke's Gospel.

Table 1.3. Comparison of Mark 7:24–30 and Matthew 15:21–28

Mark 7:24–30	Matt 15:21–28
24 From there he set out and went away to the region of Tyre. He entered a house and did not want anyone to know he was there. Yet he could not escape notice, 25 but a woman whose little daughter had an unclean spirit immediately heard about him, and she came and bowed down at his feet. 26 Now the woman was a gentile, of Syrophoenician origin. She begged him to cast the demon out of her daughter. 27 He said to her, "Let the children be fed first, for it is not fair to take the children's food and throw it to the dogs." 28 But she answered him, "Sir, even the dogs under the table eat the children's crumbs." 29 Then he said to her, "For saying that, you may go—the demon has left your daughter." 30 And when she went home, she found the child lying on the bed and the demon gone. (New Revised Standard Version, Updated Edition)	21 Jesus left that place and went away to the district of Tyre and Sidon. 22 Just then a Canaanite woman from that region came out and started shouting, "Have mercy on me, Lord, Son of David; my daughter is tormented by a demon." 23 But he did not answer her at all. And his disciples came and urged him, saying, "Send her away, for she keeps shouting after us." 24 He answered, "I was sent only to the lost sheep of the house of Israel." 25 But she came and knelt before him, saying, "Lord, help me." 26 He answered, "It is not fair to take the children's food and throw it to the dogs." 27 She said, "Yes, Lord, yet even the dogs eat the crumbs that fall from their masters' table." 28 Then Jesus answered her, "Woman, great is your faith! Let it be done for you as you wish." And her daughter was healed from that moment. (New Revised Standard Version, Updated Edition)

We may also apply redaction criticism to Matthew 15:21–28, which is an edited version of Mark 7:24–30. (See table 1.3.)

There are several major differences or changes in Matthew 15:21–28 compared with Mark 7:24–30. The most striking difference is the woman's ethnic identity. In Matthew the woman is a Canaanite as compared to her being a Syrophoenician in Mark. Her Canaanite identity, coupled with her residence in Tyre and Sidon, vis-à-vis Tyre in Mark, reinforces the image of her marginality because Canaanites were, from Jewish perspectives, among the most impure. The other major difference is the severity of Jesus's rejection of her daughter's healing. Initially, he did not answer her. Then the disciples intervened with him and asked him to send her away. Then he said, "I was sent only to the lost sheep of the house of Israel" (Mt 15:24; cf. Mt 10:5–6). He insinuated the following: "I am not for you, a Canaanite woman, a Gentile." He also said, "It is not fair to take the children's food and throw it to the dogs" (15:26). Calling her a dog is a glaring verbal attack on her soul. But she persisted in asking for a blessing. The last notable difference is her faith, which Jesus eventually commends, whereas, in Mark, the word "faith" does not appear. If Mark offers a simple healing story, Matthew extends the story to emphasize faith and the community's mission policy. With all the above differences in Matthew 15:21–28, we may infer that these changes reflect a predominantly Jewish community struggling to open up the mission to the Gentiles. Jesus's encounter with the Canaanite woman in Matthew 15:21–28 reflects the Matthean community's situations where, supposedly, the majority of people have kept the Jewish laws and cultural boundaries against the Gentiles. The Canaanite woman represents the most outlandish form of marginality, as she is a Canaanite woman whose daughter is tormented by a demon. For Matthew's community, the implied condition for accepting the Gentiles requires their absolute faith, which acknowledges Jewish prerogatives and cultural boundaries.

NOTES

1. For Paul's view of the Gospel, see Yung Suk Kim, *How to Read Paul: A Brief Introduction to His Theology, Writings, and World* (Minneapolis, MN: Fortress, 2021), 49–62.

2. For more about these views of the historical Jesus, see "Historical Jesus Theories," Early Christian Writings, accessed July 15, 2023, https://www.earlychristianwritings.com/theories.html.

Chapter 2

The Gospel of Mark

The Gospel of Mark has received increasing attention from modern readers, as it is considered an important literary source for Matthew and Luke, according to the Markan priority theory. Mark is the shortest among the canonical Gospels, and it provides the basic chronology and framework of Jesus's story for Matthew and Luke. It also contains the kernel of Jesus's teaching about the kingdom of God and indispensable episodes in Jesus's public ministry.[1] This point does not mean that Mark is more historical than the other Gospels. Mark also inherited oral traditions and edited them to fit his community context.[2] Mark's renewed attention also has to do with the orality of this gospel written in Koine Greek, which is intended not for reading but for hearing.[3] As such, the tempo and mood of the Markan narrative are swift, straightforward, and vivid. For example, in the baptism of Jesus (Mark 1:9–11), readers may follow the Markan narrator as if something happened right before their eyes. Mark narrates facts about the baptism in two verses. Beginning with "in those days" (Mark 1:9)—a technique of swift transition to the next scene—the narrator tells the readers that Jesus came from Nazareth of Galilee and was baptized by John in the Jordan. There is no need to explain Jesus's baptism like was done in Matthew 3:13–17 or to omit some information such as the baptizer's name and the place of the baptism, like in Luke 3:21–22. Mark also tells readers how the baptism happened: "And just as he was coming up out of the water, he saw the heavens torn apart, and the Spirit descending like a dove on him" (1:10). The narrator also implies the significance of Jesus's baptism with a voice coming from heaven: "You are my Son, the Beloved; with you I am well pleased" (Mark 1:11).

Mark is distinctive in several ways. First, it is a fast-paced narrative that moves from Galilee to Jerusalem. While the first seven chapters are about Jesus's Galilean ministry, the remaining chapters (8–15) are about the passion for which Jesus makes a quick journey to Jerusalem. Second, in the narrative, the suffering of the Messiah is a big theme, and Mark's community faces faith and suffering in difficult times under the Roman Empire. Third, Mark emphasizes imminent eschatology and the radical intervention of God in the world on the last day. This view differs from Luke, who emphasizes the present work of God or the Holy Spirit; for example, in Luke, "today" (*sēmeron*) appears frequently (Luke 2:11; 4:21; 19:9; 23:43).[4] Fourth, Mark does not have the infancy narratives like Matthew or Luke do, and he begins with a title or announcement of "the good news of Jesus Christ" (Mark 1:1). Mark seems not interested in Jesus's birth or childhood; instead, his focus is on Jesus's adulthood and his public ministry. Fifth, unlike Matthew or Luke, Mark does not end with the resurrection appearance stories, but he ends at 16:8 (called the shorter ending), where women visitors to the tomb are filled with terror and amazement without telling anyone about what they'd heard.[5] The above distinctive features of Mark's Gospel also come with difficult texts; for example, those dealing with the messianic secret idea (1:43–45; 4:11; 8:29–30), the time of the Parousia (9:1; 13:30), or Jesus's relationship with God (10:18).

TEXTBOX 2.1 *Mark's Gospel at a Glance*

DATE

Mark was likely written between 65–72 CE, shortly before, during, or slightly after the fall of Jerusalem in 70 CE. While Matthew refers to the fall of Jerusalem (Mt 22:1–14), Mark does not refer to that event. But implicit knowledge of it is embedded in Jesus's eschatological discourse in Mark 13.

AUTHOR

The author is anonymous because there is no internal or external evidence about the authorship. The tradition of authorship is either Mark (Peter's interpreter) or John Mark (Paul's companion, as in Acts 12:12; 15:37; Col 4:10; 1 Tm 4:11; Philm 24). Eusebius (the fourth-century church historian) quotes Papias (the early second-century bishop of Hierapolis in Asia Minor), who says Mark was the interpreter of Peter and wrote his Gospel.

PLACE

While the place of composition is unknown, the possible candidates are Rome, Galilee, or northern Syria. Galilee is the place where Jesus instructs his disciples to gather after his resurrection. Given the anticity atmosphere (1:38, 45; 5:14; and chapters 6, 8, 11, and 13), the Gospel may have originated in northern Syria.

SOURCE

While we cannot name the source of specific materials for Mark, a variety of oral traditions were transmitted to Mark: for example, stories about miracles, parables, and a passion narrative. Otherwise, the so-called Q (Jesus's sayings source, shared in Matthew and Luke) is not found in Mark.

AUDIENCE

Mark addresses the community of mixed Christians who were going through hardships or persecution due to Nero's persecution in 64 CE or other kinds of turmoil in Palestine on the eve of the Jewish revolt against Rome. Mark aims to empower them to continue their faith in tough times.

GENRE

There is no gospel genre in ancient literature. All four Gospels are close to a Greco-Roman biography, but it is also like a story. In ancient times there were these types of literary works: *The Life of Aristotle* by Andronicus in 70 BCE; *The Life of Moses* by Philo in 25 BCE.

HOW IT BEGINS

Mark begins with "the good news of Jesus Christ" (1:1), which is explored throughout the narrative. Jesus becomes the good news because he proclaims the good news of God, which is detailed in 1:15.

HOW IT ENDS

Mark ends at 16:8 (the shorter ending), where women are terrified and do not tell the good news of the resurrection to other disciples. Mark 16:9–20 (the longer ending) is considered an appended text in later times.

ESCHATOLOGY

Mark has imminent eschatology. The second half of Mark is a passion narrative (chapters 8–15). Yet Jesus's teaching in 1:14–15 emphasizes the ongoing reality of the kingdom of God, which has come and will continue to come.

JESUS

He is portrayed as the suffering Son of God, who must suffer as the Messiah (10:45; 14:36; 15:34; cf. Luke 23:34, 46; John 10:11). His humanity is also emphasized: 1:41; 3:5; 14:33–34.

DISCIPLES

The disciples of Jesus have a hard time understanding Jesus (8:17–18, 31–33), always seeking fame and power (10:35–45). They do not have faith (4:35–41; cf, Mt 14:22–33).

HUMAN CONDITION

In Mark the human condition is a self-centered life that seeks one's power or fame without caring for others (8:34–35).

TRANSFORMATION

In Mark transformation is difficult because it requires following Jesus, which is a path for trials and dangers (8:34–35; 10:45).

UNIQUE CONTENT

1:15, "The time is fulfilled, and the kingdom of God has come near"
3:17, Boanerges, sons of thunder (James and John)
2:27–28, "The Sabbath was made for humans"
4:11, "To you has been given the secret of the kingdom of God"
8:34–35, "For those who want to save their life will lose it, and those who lose their life for my sake, and for the sake of the gospel, will save it"
14:51, The young man left the linen cloth and ran away naked

UNIQUE HEALINGS

7:34, Deaf and dumb man, "Ephphatha, be opened"
8:22–26, The blind man of Bethsaida: "I see people, but they look like trees, walking"

NOTABLE PARABLES

4:3–9, The parable of the sower
4:26–29, The parable of the seed growing secretly (unique to Mark)
4:30–32, The parable of the mustard seed
12:1–11, The parable of the tenant

OUTLINE

1:1–13, Prologue
1:14–8:26, Public Ministry
8:27–10:52, Jesus on the Way to Jerusalem[6]
11:1–13:37, Ministry in Jerusalem
14:1–15:47, Passion Narrative: Last Supper, Trials, and Crucifixion
16:1–8, The Resurrection of Jesus

THE MARKAN JESUS

On the one hand, Jesus is the authorized Son of God who is teaching amazingly, healing the sick, driving out unclean spirits, and challenging religious leaders. On the other hand, he is the opposed Son of God who is arrested, tortured, and crucified. His primary image is that of the suffering Son of God who is deeply grieved, even to death (Mark 14:34), and cries out, "Eloi, Eloi, lema sabachthani?" ("My God, my God, why have you forsaken me?"; 15:34; cf, Ps 22:2). He is unlike the Lukan Jesus, who is not agitated but ready to die as a prophet, praying that God would forgive those who kill him because they do not know what they do (Luke 23:34), and who dies peacefully on the cross, praying, "Father, into your hands I commend my spirit" (23:46). Overall, the Markan Jesus knows that suffering is hard and it is unwanted. He knows that proclaiming the good news of God is costly and that if he continues his ministry, he will face the same fate as that of John the Baptist. He also knows torture is evil and wrong, and he does not believe God prepared him for his death. In his prayer at Gethsemane, his point is not simply whether he must die but whether he must continue to proclaim the costly gospel of God. In the end, he decides to follow the will of God, which means he takes on the risk of dying for the good news of God. So he says, "For the Son of Man came not to be served but to serve, and to give his life a ransom for many" (Mark 10:45).

DISTINCTIVE THEOLOGICAL THEMES

First, Mark interprets Jesus as a model of selfless service to others. Jesus advocates for the poor and the oppressed and is crucified at the hands of Rome because of his bold proclamation of God's rule on earth. But he is vindicated by God and raised from the dead. Second, Mark encourages fearful Christians to live faithfully in a harsh world because God will be with them. The Markan community must go through trials and suffering, walk with Jesus, and serve those who are weak and marginalized in the community and society (Mark 10:45). Third, likewise, faith and discipleship in Mark is to follow the way of the cross, which does not mean that one must accept needless suffering, violence, or abuse. It means that one must be willing to take on the cost of ministry, to serve the oppressed and demonstrate God's justice in the world. Fourth, Mark clarifies the good news of Jesus (1:1), which has to do with the good news of God (1:14–5). "The good news of Jesus Christ" in Mark 1:1 is linked with his proclamation of "the good news of God" in 1:15. He does not proclaim his good news; he *becomes* the good news because of his work with God. He demonstrates God's impartial love through teaching, healing the sick, and challenging authorities and leaders of society. His proclamation is poignantly perspicuous, as is seen in Mark 1:15: "The time is fulfilled, and the kingdom of God has come near; repent, and believe in the good news." His point is that because God rules the world and people, they must change their minds and seek the way of God. Fifth and lastly, Markan eschatology is imminent in that the Son of Man will come soon to judge the world. So the community members must be ready for that day, living faithfully and undergoing hardships and persecution. This eschatology does not mean that people would not work hard in the present to wait for the Son of Man. Rather, Jesus's teaching about the kingdom of God exhorts them to change their minds now and believe in the good news.

PARABLES IN MARK

In Mark the most representative parable of Jesus is the sower (4:3–8), which is the basis of other parables such as the mustard seed (4:30–32) and seed growing secretly (4:26–29). This parable includes the principle of the kingdom of God and its challenge to Jesus's audience. Using agricultural images and metaphors, Jesus compares the kingdom of God to the sower, who scatters seeds indiscriminately on the ground. He does it this way so that the ground would be given fair chances for receiving seeds—that is, he does not discriminate against the ground. He risks losing or wasting seeds but does not care, because his purpose is to throw seeds as widely as possible to the ground. The implication is that God's kingdom must be like the sower's behavior—an attitude of impartial love and care for the ground and seeds. Parable interpretation is subject to hearers, and Jesus never explains the meaning of the parables throughout his teaching. The exception is in this parable, where the parable proper is in Mark 4:3–8, while 4:14–20 appears to be extended verses by Mark, who interprets the parable allegorically.[7] Mark explains the meaning of the sower: the sower is an evangelist, the seed is the word of God, and the soil condition is a person's heart. In some sense, Mark contextualized the parable of the sower to evangelize people through the preaching of the word of God. But in Jesus's context, the story is wide-open and challenges people more broadly. The sower can be anyone who is working for the kingdom of God. As the sower scatters the seeds evenly and profusely, God's people must do the same, without discriminating against any conditions. The sower knows that some seeds will fall on unwanted places, such as on the path, on rocky ground, and among thorns, but he does not care, because he knows it. His goal is to give enough (or at least fair) chances to the ground, whether it was cultivated or not, because, after sowing, it will be plowed.

The parable of the seed growing secretly is unique to Mark and presents different aspects of the kingdom of God than the parable of the sower, where the sower's positive involvement is important. But in the parable of the seed growing secretly, the focus is not on the sower but on the seed itself and on nature. Here, the sower's job is limited to sowing seeds and waiting for the harvest. Otherwise, he must watch how the seed is growing and appreciate the power of nature. Likewise, no one can deter the growth of the kingdom of God.

The mustard seed is another seed parable in Mark, which also appears in Matthew 13:31–32 and Luke 13:18–19. The teaching of this parable reveals that it is unlikely that anyone can become whatever he or she wants to become. The point is that one should not ignore others' or one's potential. There is no gift too small that one can ignore it. All people have their distinctive gifts or potential to achieve. One can grow enough to do something great in one's context. That growth does not have to be like that of a cedar tree, a symbol of glory or splendor in the Old Testament. The mustard seed grows into a big plant that is like a tree, but it is not a huge tree like a cedar tree. The small mustard seed growing to the size of a tree is a miracle and serves others with shade. The place to which the mustard seed is sown is the ground (*ge* in Greek), which is compared with the words "field" (*argos*) in Matthew and "garden" (*kepos*) in Luke. Perhaps the different places reflect the different contexts of the evangelists. For Mark, the emphasis is on God's impartial love for all; for Matthew, training disciples is important; Luke seems to emphasize the urban ministry context.

NOTABLE INTERPRETATION ISSUES

Since there are many interpretation issues in Mark's Gospel, we will recognize only a few notable ones. First, the issue is how to understand Jesus's eschatology. In Mark 9:1 and 13:30, Jesus predicted the last day would come during his lifetime. Scholars are divided over this issue. While some argue that imminent eschatology is Mark's own, others say that it is Jesus's. While the former group believes that Jesus is a type of wisdom teacher, the latter group thinks that Jesus is an apocalyptic prophet. Second, the issue is how to understand Jesus's self-understanding: Did he think that he was the Messiah? In Mark he is baptized by John, receives the Spirit at his baptism, and hears the voice of heaven: "You are my Son, the Beloved; with you I am well pleased" (1:9–11). But throughout the narrative, Jesus tries to hide his identity from the public (1:43–45;

4:11; 8:29–30). While Peter confesses that Jesus is the Messiah (8:29), and a centurion at Jesus's crucifixion says, "Truly this man was God's Son!" (15:39), Jesus humbly says that God alone is good (10:18). In the end, the question is, Why does Jesus keep his messianic identity secret? Third, the issue is how to understand "the good news of Jesus Christ" in Mark 1:1. How does it relate to "the good news of God" that he proclaims in 1:14? In what sense is Mark's Gospel the gospel of Jesus? Fourth and lastly, we may consider the other issue: how to understand Mark's view of the Roman Empire and the kingdom of God. Is Mark imperialistic or mimicking the imperial way of Rome? What is the nature of the kingdom of God? In what way does Mark resist or negotiate with Rome? (Refer to Mark 12:13–17.)

A CLOSE READING OF MARK

1:1–13, Prologue

The way the narrator of Mark's Gospel begins the story is very different from Matthew or Luke. While Matthew begins with the genealogy of Jesus (Mt 1:1–17), Luke starts with a prologue that emphasizes the reliability of his account (Luke 1:1–4). But Mark begins with "the good news of Jesus Christ" (1:1), which sounds like the title of the book and does not include Jesus's genealogy or birth narrative.[8] The good news of Jesus Christ is a central theme of Mark's Gospel. The question is *how to understand* the good news of Jesus Christ.

TEXTBOX 2.2 *Consider and Discuss*

"THE GOOD NEWS OF JESUS CHRIST" (MARK 1:1)

"The good news of Jesus Christ" may be the title of the book, but at the same time, Mark's Gospel is about the good news of Jesus. It may be that it is the good news Jesus proclaimed, as he had done in Mark 1:14, after John was arrested. Then this good news is about or from God. The content of this good news is in 1:15, where Jesus declares that God rules the world now, and therefore, people must change their minds. Throughout the narrative, for example, he has taught the kingdom of God (God's rule or reign) and healed the sick to show the coming of God's reign. The good news of Jesus Christ is also about Jesus because of his grace and sacrifice for God's kingdom. Discuss Mark's view of the good news of Jesus Christ and its relation to the good news of God.

After "the beginning of the good news of Jesus Christ" (Mark 1:1), the narrator introduces the prophets' allusion to the one who cries in the wilderness—namely, John the Baptist (1:2–3). "Sending my messenger ahead of you, who will prepare your way" (Mark 1:2) is quoted from Malachi 3:1, and "the voice crying in the wilderness; prepare the way of the Lord; make his paths straight" (Mark 1:3) comes from Isaiah 40:3. Both quotes are not the same as the words of these prophets. However, Mark's allusion seems clear in that the voice crying in the wilderness refers to John, who is introduced right after this in 1:4–8. In the wilderness John prepares the way of the Lord for Jesus by baptizing people and helping them to repent of their sins. Their sins are forgiven through *metanoia*. But now John suddenly introduces Jesus, saying: "The one who is more powerful than I is coming after me; I am not worthy to stoop down and untie the thong of his sandals. I have baptized you with water; but he will baptize you with the Holy Spirit" (Mark 1:7–8).

Then, Jesus is baptized by John (1:9–11). But the fact that Jesus is baptized by John may be surprising to the hearers/readers for two reasons: (1) How could John baptize Jesus when he said earlier that Jesus is more powerful than he? (2) Why does Jesus need John's baptism anyway if his baptism is for the forgiveness of sins? However, the narrator does not explain why Jesus needs such a baptism by John. While Matthew explains it, Luke omits the information about the baptizer. Maybe Mark does not need to explain it, because Jesus continues the work of God with John. Even though Jesus is special and more powerful than John, both of them are doing the work of God, which is to proclaim the kingdom of God. John's role is to prepare for Jesus's ministry after him. To be baptized, "Jesus came from Nazareth of Galilee in those days"—that is, he came a long way to the River Jordan from his home in Nazareth, only to be baptized by John. The narrator tells the story of Jesus with a curious contextual referent about the time and place where Jesus came from—"in those days" (Mark 1:9). What happened in Nazareth of Galilee *in those days*? Nazareth was a small town with many oppressed people. By contrast, just a few miles north of Nazareth, there was Sepphoris, a rich, cosmopolitan city with wealthy people. There is no historical evidence of whether Jesus visited that city or worked there. But most likely, he may have heard about that city and the imperial presence there. So hearers of the Gospel must be intrigued by the phrase "in those days" and must come up with certain conclusions about those days. How much was Jesus shaped by his hometown people and their lives? What did he think about Sepphoris and the rich people there? What did he think about local wealthy people, Jerusalem leaders, religious elites, and the presence of the Roman Empire throughout the land? Why did he decide to leave his hometown for the Jordan River to be baptized by John? What drove him to make such a drastic decision? When Jesus was coming out of the water, the heavens were torn apart, and the Spirit descended like a dove on him. The heavens being torn apart overshadows the gloomy atmosphere in the unfolding story of Jesus, who suffers and dies because he has proclaimed the good news. The curtain of the temple is also torn in two (Mark 15:38) after his death, which symbolizes the judgment of the world and introduces a new rule of God. When he comes out of the water, a voice from heaven says, "You are my Son, the Beloved; with you I am well pleased" (1:11). God calls Jesus, saying, "You are my Son, the Beloved" (1:11). In the Hebrew Bible, God's calling is special and gives a new mission to his servants. For example, God called Abraham, Moses, Isaiah, and Jeremiah, and all of them took on their mission and performed it through faith. But here, at the baptism of Jesus, the voice of God is not about giving a new vocation to Jesus. Rather, God recognizes and calls Jesus his Son, the Beloved. Then God says he is well pleased with him. This means Jesus has already followed God and pleased him. Moreover, he continues to please God as the story goes on. For Jesus, the Son of God is not a title but his identity and his life devoted to God. This devotion to God is the same love that he has for his people. For this, he gives his life as a ransom for many (Mark 10:45).

After the baptism, the Spirit leads Jesus to the wilderness so that he may be tested for forty days, which is also a symbolic number reminiscent of Moses's staying on Mount Sinai for forty days (Ex 24:18), his intercession for Israel for forty days (Dt 9:18, 25) to receive the law, the Israelites' wandering in the wilderness for forty years (8:2–5), and Elijah's travel to Horeb as he fled from Jezebel (1 Kgs 19:8). While Jesus was in the wilderness, he was tempted by Satan and won all of the tests by focusing on God's word and his work. So he pleased God, not Satan.

1:14–8:26, Public Ministry

Then the narrator swiftly makes a transition to Jesus's preaching. This transition happens because John was arrested. In the absence of John, Jesus had to continue the work of God, and so he came to Galilee, his hometown, and proclaimed the good news of God. Earlier, the narrator pointed out the details about what the time in Galilee looked like "in those days" from which Jesus had left for the Jordan. Jesus remembered his hometown people in Nazareth; they were uncared for and dishonored by the rich and imperial system, and he came back to them to preach his sermon, which is in Mark 1:15: "The time is fulfilled, and the kingdom of God has come near; repent, and believe in the good news." Here, the word for "time" is *kairos* in Greek, which means the proper time or opportunity for salvation. That is, now is the time of salvation because the kingdom of God ("the rule/reign of God"; Mark 1:15) has come near (the perfect tense). Here, the kingdom of God is not a place that is realized in the future but is God's rule or activity in the present. This means that God—not the emperor—rules the world with justice and mercy here and now. But this rule of God will not be realized unless people change their minds toward God. So Jesus asks them to repent (*metanoeo*)! The last part of the brief sermon, "Believe in the good news" (Mark 1:15), is its conclusion. Jesus's initial preaching, even if short, is well structured with four parts: (1) fulfillment of time (*kairos*), (2) God's reign (*basileia tou theou*), (3) repentance (*metanoia*), and (4) belief (*pistis*) in the good news. The first three parts are the main arguments, and the last one is the conclusion. In sum, throughout the narrative, Jesus brings the good news of God to the world through his teaching and healing.

> TEXTBOX 2.3 **Consider and Discuss**
>
> **JESUS'S INITIAL PREACHING (1:15)**
>
> Read Mark 1:14–15: "14 Now after John was arrested, Jesus came to Galilee proclaiming the good news of God 15 and saying, 'The time is fulfilled, and the kingdom of God has come near; repent, and believe in the good news.'" Will you consider Mark 1:15 as Jesus's initial preaching since it includes kernels of his proclamation? What does the rest of the narrative have to do with this preaching?

After his initial preaching, Jesus call the disciples, teaches in parables, appoints the twelve, heals the sick, does miracles, and is involved in controversies (Mark 1:16–8:26). This part of the story begins with Jesus's call of the first disciples (1:16–20) and ends with his curing of a blind man at Bethsaida (8:22–26). In between these two brackets, Jesus's other works are interwoven: healing, teaching, and sending his disciples on a mission. In Mark 1:21–2:12, Jesus heals the man with an unclean spirit, a paralytic, and many at Simon's house, as well as cleanses a leper. Then he is involved in a controversy about the Sabbath, but he says, "The sabbath was made for humankind, and not humankind for the sabbath; so the Son of Man is lord even of the sabbath" (Mark 2:27–28). This saying reveals how he interprets the law—that is, that the law is for humanity and not vice versa. The law comes from God and, therefore, his purpose must be accomplished. God wants all of humanity to love him and to love their neighbors. After this, Jesus heals more people and orders them not to reveal his identity. It is hard to know why Jesus does not want his identity to be known. The most practical reason could be that he does not want to be misunderstood by others or authorities so that his ministry could continue without being stopped too early. The reality is that even his disciples did not understand him. So he tells them not to pretend to know about him prematurely. Or if they were to hear that prohibition, they might be more curious about him.

Later Jesus appoints the twelve for a mission and talks about his true family: "Whoever does the will of God is my brother and sister and mother" (Mark 3:35). Then Jesus tells several parables: the sower (4:1–20), the seed growing secretly (4:26–29), and the mustard seed (4:30–32). After his parable teaching, Jesus heals more: the Gerasene demoniac (5:1–21), a daughter of Jairus restored to life (5:21–24, 35–43), and a woman suffering from hemorrhages for twelve years (5:24–34). Out of his compassion for the crowds, Jesus feeds the five thousand and, later, the four thousand in a deserted place, and yet the disciples do not understand the meaning of this miracle. Then Jesus encounters a Syrophoenician woman who, due to her strong faith, receives healing for her daughter (7:24–30). This episode contrasts with the disciples' lacking faith. Jesus's curing a blind man at Bethsaida implies a gradual process of restoring sight for the disciples because the man did not see all at once (Mark 8:22–26).

8:27–10:52, Jesus on the Way to Jerusalem

Jesus is on the way to Jerusalem (Mark 8:27–10:52), and this section consists of Jesus's question about his identity to his disciples (8:27–30) and three occasions of passion prediction (8:31; 9:31; 10:32). To answer the question of Jesus's identity, people think that Jesus is John the Baptist, Elijah, or one of the prophets. But Peter answers, "You are the Messiah" (Mark 8:29), which means "the anointed one" (*Christos*, in Greek). Based on Peter's confession, Jesus, for the first time, foretells his suffering, death, and resurrection (8:31–9:1). But Peter rebukes Jesus because he thinks the Messiah should not die but be successful. In turn, Jesus rebukes him: "Get behind me, Satan! For you are setting your mind not on divine things but on human things" (Mark 8:33). To help the disciples understand why the Messiah must suffer, he calls to the crowd with them and says, "If any want to become my followers, let them deny themselves and take up their cross and follow me. For those who want to save their life will lose it, and those who lose their life for my sake, and for the sake of the gospel, will save it" (Mark 8:34–35). Life can be enriched by following the way of Jesus, the Messiah, which means risking life for the kingdom of God in "this adulterous and sinful generation" (8:38). They think that if the people follow the Messiah's way, the kingdom of God will be coming soon, even before they die (9:1).

A few days later, Jesus takes with him three disciples (Peter, James, and John) and goes up to a high mountain (Mark 9:2–8). Suddenly, he is transfigured; his clothes become dazzling white. Elijah and Moses appear and talk with him. With such a mysterious experience, Peter is terrified and says, "Rabbi, it is good for us to be here; let us make three dwellings [tents], one for you, one for Moses, and one for Elijah" (Mark 9:5). Then a cloud overshadows them, and a voice from the cloud says, "This is my Son, the Beloved; listen to him!" (9:7). This voice refers to the same voice from heaven heard at Jesus's baptism (1:11). "Listen[ing] to him" means that Jesus's followers are to see the importance of the Messiah's work and his suffering. Suddenly, Moses and Elijah are gone, and Jesus alone remains. Coming down the mountain, Jesus answers the disciples' question about Elijah and who is supposed to come first before the kingdom of God (Mark 9:9–13). He implies that what he does as the Messiah continues the work of Elijah, whose job is to restore all things. But he says that he must go through suffering and contempt (9:12).

After this, Jesus comes to the other disciples, and he is surrounded by a great crowd (Mark 9:14–29). He heals a boy with a spirit and teaches the importance of faith and prayer. In Mark 9:31, Jesus again foretells his suffering and death. But the disciples do not understand what he means and are afraid even to ask him (9:32). Rather, the disciples argue with one another concerning who is the greatest. Jesus teaches them the following: "Whoever wants to be first must be last of all and servant of all" (Mark 9:35). Then he takes a little child in his arms, saying, "Whoever welcomes one such child in my name welcomes me, and whoever welcomes me welcomes not me but the one who sent me" (9:37). In a subsequent episode (9:38–41), the disciples try to stop someone from casting out demons in Jesus's name. But Jesus says, "Do not stop him; for no one who does a deed of power in my name will be able soon afterward to speak evil of me. Whoever is not against us is for us. For truly I tell you, whoever gives you a cup of water to drink because you bear the name of Christ will by no means lose the reward" (Mark 9:39–41). This saying of Jesus's echoes the Matthean Jesus: "Truly I tell you, just as you did it to one of the least of these who are members of my family, you did it to me" (Mt 25:40). After this, Jesus warns them not to sin by putting "a stumbling block before one of these little ones who believes" (Mark 9:42–50). They must treat others as brothers and sisters. They must be salt in the world. But before that, they must be salted themselves, which means to know the Messiah correctly and to follow him. The ultimate goal of their lives is to make peace with one another.

TEXTBOX 2.4 *Consider and Discuss*

MULTIPLE ASPECTS OF FAITH

There are multiple aspects of faith (*pistis*) in the New Testament: (1) faith as knowledge (*fides quae creditur*: faith which is believed);[1] (2) faith as assurance or conviction (*fides qua creditur*: faith by which it is believed); (3) faith as trust (as in Abraham's faith as quoted by Paul); and (4) faith as fidelity, loyalty, or faithfulness. The theme of faith as knowledge appears frequently in the Deutero-Pauline and pastoral letters (Col 1:4; 1 Tm 1:4; 3:13; 2 Tm 1:13; 3:15). Faith as assurance or conviction is emphasized in Hebrews (11:1–3). The themes of faith as trust and faith as fidelity, loyalty, or faithfulness are prevalent in Paul's undisputed letters and in the Gospels (Gal 3:6–18; Rom 4:1–12; 3:21–26; Gal 2:16–20). The concept of *pistis* in the Greco-Roman world, which is close to fidelity or trust, continues in the Gospels and in Paul's undisputed letter. As God is faithful, Jesus is also faithful. Likewise, the people of God must be faithful as Christ is. With all these diverse aspects of faith, consider and discuss faith in Mark's Gospel. Refer to the whole Gospel and specific verses referring to faith; for example, see Mark 2:5; 4:40; 5:34; 9:23–24, 42; 10:52; and 11:22. Overall, how is God or Jesus understood in Mark's Gospel concerning faith? What aspects of faith are recommended for the disciples?

NOTE

1. The classical distinction between *fides quae creditur* and *fides qua creditur* is found in Catholic theology.

Jesus's journey continues with his teaching about divorce (Mark 10:1–12). Concerning divorce, he prohibits it regardless of a certificate of dismissal by Moses because, he argues, marriage means for the two to be one flesh, according to Genesis 2:24 (cf. Mt 19:5; Eph 5:31). Furthermore, Jesus says remarriage is adultery (Mark 10:10–12). Holding the value of inseparable marriage as intended by God, Jesus is confident about marriage and human transformation as God's way. Then he teaches about children and uplifts them, saying, "Let the little children come to me; do not stop them; for it is to such as these that the kingdom of God belongs. Truly I tell you, whoever does not receive the kingdom of God as a little child will never enter it" (Mark 10:14–15). As he is still on his journey, a rich man comes to ask him, "Good Teacher, what must I do to inherit eternal life?" (10:17). Jesus rebukes him and says, "Why do you call me good? No one is good but God alone" (10:18; cf. Mt 19:17; Luke 18:19). Unlike Matthew, Mark says bluntly that no one is good but God alone. In Mark, Jesus is the Messiah who works for God. In this story of a rich man, it is also interesting that this man seeks eternal life, while many poor people seek shelter and food. He is very detached from the lives and daily realities of others. He says he's kept all the commandments well. But Jesus says, "You lack one thing; go, sell what you own, and give the money to the poor, and you will have treasure in heaven; then, come, follow me" (Mark 10:21). When the rich man hears this, he is "shocked and [goes] away grieving, for he [has] many possessions" (10:22; Matt 19:22; Luke 18:23). Then Jesus tells his disciples, "How hard it will be for those who have wealth to enter the kingdom of God!" (Mark 18:23). He goes on to say, "It is easier for a camel to go through the eye of a needle than for someone who is rich to enter the kingdom of God" (10:25). The disciples are astounded and say to one another, "Then who can be saved?" (10:26). Jesus's answer is those who have faith in God can be saved (10:27). He also confirms to Peter that those who give up their house or other material things for the sake of the good news will be rewarded (10:28–31).

A third time Jesus foretells his death and resurrection (Mark 10:32–34), followed by two episodes: one is about the request of James and John (10:35–45); the other, about the healing of blind Bartimaeus (10:46–52). James and John ask for a high-ranking seat and say, "What is it you want me to do for you? Grant us to sit, one at your right hand and one at your left, in your glory" (Mark 10:36–37). Then Jesus teaches the importance of each one's task and a new way of life, which is based on selfless service for the poor and oppressed. One's job is not to stand over others or rule them, but it is to serve them. Jesus says rewarding is God's business (Mark 10:40). The disciples' task is to do the work of Jesus with the spirit of the Messiah, as is summarized in Mark 10:43–45: "But it is not so among you; but whoever wishes to become great among you must be your servant, and whoever wishes to be first among you must be slave of all. For the Son of Man came not to be served but to serve, and to give his life a ransom for many."

The last episode is about the healing of blind Bartimaeus (Mark 10:46–52). This episode refers back to Peter's declaration about Jesus at the beginning of this section, Mark 8:27–10:52. The blind man seeks to regain his sight, cries out to Jesus, and says, "Jesus, Son of David, have mercy on me" (10:47–48). Jesus asks him, "What do you want me to do for you?" (10:51). Then the blind man says, "My teacher, let me see again" (10:51). Jesus says, "Go; your faith has made you well" (10:52). This episode contrasts Peter's confession about Jesus. Peter sees Jesus but does not understand him, because he seeks to be great with him. But the blind man was blind before, and now he sees Jesus because he had humble faith.

> **TEXTBOX 2.5** *Consider and Discuss*
>
> **"FOR THE SON OF MAN CAME NOT TO BE SERVED BUT TO SERVE AND TO GIVE HIS LIFE A RANSOM FOR MANY" (MARK 10:45).**
>
> Jesus refers to himself as the Son of Man in the sense of a human or a divine figure coming to judge in the future (Daniel 7:13 and 1 Enoch 37–71). He says, "The Son of Man came not to be served but to serve and to give his life a ransom for many" (Mark 10:45). Whom does Jesus serve? Does this saying refer to his crucifixion or his embracing of the marginalized? What is the significance of Jesus's death in Mark?

11:1–13:37, Ministry in Jerusalem

Jesus makes a triumphal entry into Jerusalem and does his last week's ministry before he is arrested, tried, and crucified. Since he is in Jerusalem, his topics cover the temple, Israel, the law, offerings, and taxes. For his entry into Jerusalem, Jesus rides on a colt as a humble king. People shout, "Hosanna! Blessed is the one who comes in the name of the Lord! Blessed is the coming kingdom of our ancestor David!" (Mark 11:9–10). Entering Jerusalem, he goes into the temple first, but because it is already late, he goes out to Bethany with the twelve. The following day, he sees a fig tree covered in leaves, but there is nothing to eat but those leaves. There is nothing wrong with the tree, because it is not the season for figs. Nevertheless, Jesus curses the fig tree. Then he enters the temple and cleanses it by driving out money changers (or other sellers), turning over their tables, and quoting from Isaiah 56:7 and Jeremiah 56:7, saying, "Is it not written, 'My house shall be called a house of prayer for all the nations?' But you have made it a den of robbers" (cf. Mt 21:13; Luke 19:46). Then the chief priest and the scribes hear it and try to find a way to kill him, but they cannot do so, as "the whole crowd [is] spellbound by his teaching" (Mark 11:18). In Jerusalem Jesus's authority is questioned (11:27–33). As he is walking in the temple, the religious leaders, such as the chief priests, the scribes, and the elders, come to him and say, "By what authority are you doing these things? Who gave you this authority to do them?" (Mark 11:28). Jesus asks them about John's authority, and they do not answer him, saying, "We do not know" (11:33). Jesus says to them, "Neither will I tell you by what authority I am doing these things" (11:33).

Now the narrator introduces a parable of allegory about the wicked tenants (Mark 12:1–12). The owner of the vineyard asked his tenants to work for him and left. Every season, he would send a slave, but each time, the slave was beaten and sent away empty-handed. More slaves were sent again, but they were killed. Even the beloved son of the owner was sent but killed. Then the owner said he would destroy the tenants and give the vineyard to others. Finally, when Jewish leaders "realized that he had told this parable against them, they wanted to arrest him, but they feared the crowd. So they left him and went away" (Mark 12:12). Here, Markan Jesus's point is not that God gave all prerogatives to the Gentiles and abandoned the Jews but that Gentiles or other Jewish tenants may fill in for the work of those who are wicked. Depending on where the parable proper ends, two meanings are possible from Jesus's context: (1) if the original parable ends at Mark 12:8, "they seized him, killed him, and threw him out of the vineyard," the tenants'/peasants' violent resistance is a viable option, or (2) if it ends at Mark 12:9a, the question is asked, "What then will the owner of the vineyard do?" and the punishment of the wicked tenants is expected.

In Jerusalem Pharisees and some Herodians ask Jesus about tax: "Is it lawful to pay taxes to the emperor, or not? Should we pay them, or should we not?" (Mark 12:14–15). Jesus answers them wisely, showing them a denarius: "Give to the emperor the things that are the emperor's, and to God the things that are God's" (12:17). Jesus also encounters Sadducees, who are the rich elites running the temple. They ask him about the resurrection: "In the resurrection whose wife will she be? For the seven had married her" (Mark 12:23). Jesus says: "When they rise from the dead, they neither marry nor are given in marriage, but are like angels in heaven" (12:25). Then he emphasizes the God of the living who works with his people in the present.

Jesus's encounter with religious leaders continues. Now one of the scribes comes to ask Jesus, "Which commandment is the first of all?" (Mark 12:28). Jesus cites the Shema in Deuteronomy 6:5 and the love of neighbor in Leviticus 19:18. Then the scribe, unlike other leaders, commends Jesus. So Jesus also says to him, "You are not far from the kingdom of God" (Mark 12:34). Jesus continues to teach in the temple and responds to the question about David's son. He says David's son is not the Messiah, because David himself calls him the Lord. He is also critical of some scribes who "like to walk around in long robes, and to be greeted with respect in the marketplaces, and to have the best seats in the synagogues and places of honor at banquets!" (Mark 12:38–39). He also says, "They devour widows' houses and for the sake of appearance say long prayers. They will receive the greater condemnation" (12:40). Then Jesus goes on to talk about the widow's offering. She puts in two small copper coins, but Jesus says she "has put in more than all those who are contributing to the treasury" (Mark 12:43). The reason is this: "For all of them have contributed out of their abundance; but she out of her poverty has put in everything she had, all she had to live on" (12:44).

Having enough teachings and encounters with religious leaders, Jesus now begins to talk about the last things: "the destruction of the temple foretold" (Mark 13:1–8), "persecution foretold" (13:9–13), "the desolating sacrilege" (13:14–23), "the coming of the Son of Man" (13:24–27), "the lesson of the fig tree" (13:28–31), and "the necessity for watchfulness" (13:32–37). The last day is not revealed to anyone. No one knows about that day—neither the angels in heaven nor the Son but only the Father. The end will come soon; therefore, Mark alerts his members to be ready for that day (13:32–33).

14:1–15:47, Passion Narrative: Last Supper, Trials, and the Crucifixion

As Jesus foretold three times before, he now goes through the most difficult times, when he is captured, tortured, and crucified. The religious leaders had planned to arrest Jesus, but they could not succeed, because they feared a riot during the festival (Mark 14:1–2). After this comes the episode of the anointing of the woman at Bethany (14:3–9). A woman pours the expensive ointment on Jesus's head in an act of appreciation for his work. Jesus commends her because she prepared him for his burial: "Wherever the good news is proclaimed in the whole world, what she has done will be told in remembrance of her" (Mark 14:9).

After a while the disciples prepare the Passover meal, and Jesus eats the meal with the twelve. But at this point, he reveals who will betray him and says, "It would have been better for that one not to have been born" (Mark 14:21). Then Jesus institutes the Lord's Supper (14:22–25): "'Take; this is my body.' Then he [takes] a cup, and after giving thanks he [gives] it to them, and all of them [drink] from it. . . . 'This is my blood of the covenant, which is poured out for many'" (Mark 14:22, 24). After the meal, they sing the hymn, but Jesus says that they will deny him. When Peter says he will not deny Jesus even though all deny him, Jesus tells Peter that he will deny Jesus three times before the cock crows twice (Mark 14:30). Peter denies it vehemently: "Even though I must die with you, I will not deny you" (14:31). "And all of them [say] the same" (14:31).

Then Jesus goes to Gethsemane to pray, and he takes with him Peter, James, and John (Mark 14:32–42). These three disciples are the ones who saw the transfiguration of Jesus before. Jesus begins to be distressed and agitated, showing emotional difficulties (Mark 14:33–34). His prayer is heavy, gloomy, realistic, and theological: "Abba, Father, for you all things are possible; remove this cup from me; yet, not what I want, but what you want" (14:36). During all this time of Jesus's struggle and determination, the disciples are indifferent. "They [do] not know what to say to him" (Mark 14:40). Finally, he says, "Enough! The hour has come; the Son of Man is betrayed into the hands of sinners. Get up, let us be going. See, my betrayer is at hand" (Mark 14:41–42). Then he is arrested (14:43–52). Suddenly, a certain young man wearing nothing but a linen cloth follows Jesus. Eventually, he leaves the linen cloth and runs off naked (Mark 14:51–52). It is hard to know what this incident means. After this, Jesus stands before the council (Mark 14:53–65). When all sorts of testimony against Jesus does not work out, the high priest stands up and asks Jesus, "Have you no answer? What is it that they testify against you?" (14:60). But Jesus does not answer him. So, again, the high priest asks, "Are you the Messiah, the Son of the Blessed One?" (Mark 14:61). Finally, Jesus says, "I am" (14:62). He also says, "You will see the Son of Man seated at the right hand of the power, and coming with the clouds of heaven" (14:62). Then he is charged with blasphemy (14:63). All members at the council decide that Jesus deserves death. While Jesus begins to be molested and tried, Peter is below in the courtyard. He denies Jesus three times as Jesus had foretold (Mark 14:66–72). A servant girl of the high priest insists that Peter knows Jesus. But each time, Peter denies him and even curses him by swearing an oath. When the cock crows twice, Peter remembers Jesus's saying, then "he [breaks] down and [weeps]" (Mark 14:72).

Jesus stands before Pilate because he has been sent by the Jewish leaders to the council (Mark 15:1–5). Pilate asks him, "Are you the King of the Jews?" (15:2). Jesus answers him, "You say so" (15:2). Then he makes no further reply when he is asked again (15:4–5). Pilate finally hands Jesus over to be crucified because the stirred crowd has requested the release of Barabbas instead of Jesus, wanting Jesus to be crucified (15:6–15). Then Jesus is mocked by the soldiers and led to the crucifixion (15:16–20). On the way to Golgotha, a passerby, Simon of Cyrene, the father of Alexander and Rufus, is picked out to carry the cross of Jesus (15:21). The narrator does not tell readers directly who this man is or why he is picked out. The only information about this man is that he comes from Cyrene, a city in North Africa. The soldiers crucify Jesus there, at Golgotha, at nine o'clock in the morning, and the inscription of the charge is written: "The King of the Jews," a political title (Mark 15:25–26). So he is accused of the crime of treason, not simply of blasphemy. Many passersby deride Jesus, saying: "Aha! You who would destroy the temple and build it in three days, save yourself, and come down from the cross!" (Mark 15:30). Likewise, the chief priests and the scribes also mock him, saying: "He saved others; he cannot save himself. Let the Messiah, the King of Israel, come down from the cross now, so that we may see and believe" (Mark 15:31–32). Even "those who [are] crucified with him also [taunt] him" (15:32).

When it is noon, "darkness [comes] over the whole land until three in the afternoon" (Mark 15:33). Then, at three o'clock, "Jesus [cries] out with a loud voice: 'Eloi, Eloi, lema sabachthani?' (which means, 'My God, my God, why have you forsaken me?' [in Aramaic])" (Mark 15:34). This is utter dereliction on the part of Jesus; there is no hope for him. Then, "Jesus [gives] a loud cry and [breathes] his last" (Mark 15:37). This ending of Jesus's last moment is very different from that of Luke's, where he peacefully commits his spirit into God's hands (Luke 23:46). Suddenly, "the curtain of the temple [is] torn in two, from top to bottom" (Mark 15:38), which signifies God's radical judgment of the unjust power/world, as the temple curtain's being torn in two follows Jesus's death. When the centurion sees Jesus's crucifixion, he says: "Truly this man was God's Son" (Mark 15:39). Here, "God's Son" implies a political connotation in which the centurion acknowledges Jesus—not the Roman emperor—as the true Son of God.

When evening comes on the day of Preparation, the day before the Sabbath (maybe this Sabbath refers to Thursday Passover, not the weekly Sabbath), Joseph of Arimathea, "a respected member of the council, who [is] also himself waiting expectantly for the kingdom of God," goes to Pilate and asks for the body of Jesus (Mark 15:42–43). He wraps the body in a linen cloth and lays it in a tomb.

> TEXTBOX 2.6 *Consider and Discuss*
>
> **"MY GOD, MY GOD, WHY HAVE YOU FORSAKEN ME?" (MARK 15:34)**
>
> In Mark, Jesus's death is not described as the noble death of heroes, like that of Socrates (*Plato's Phaedo*, 115b–118b) or the Jewish martyr Eleazar during the Maccabean Revolt (2 Macc 6:30), but his death is a difficult one. Jesus's cry of dereliction echoes Psalm 22:1–2: "My God, my God, why have you forsaken me? Why are you so far from helping me, from the words of my groaning? O my God, I cry by day, but you do not answer; and by night but find no rest." This Psalm is part of lament traditions in which people express their bitter feelings and look for their salvation. How can we understand Jesus's despair and his cry? Did he cry for help from God?

16:1–8, The Resurrection of Jesus

The irony is that "the good news of Jesus Christ" (Mark 1:1) ends with women fleeing from the tomb. Mary Magdalene and Mary the mother of James and Salome visit the tomb to anoint Jesus with spices. Then a young man dressed in a white robe, sitting on the right side of the tomb, tells them that Jesus was raised. The risen Lord does not appear directly. He also tells them, "But go, tell his disciples and Peter that he is going ahead of you to Galilee; there you will see him, just as he told you" (Mark 16:7). Galilee is Jesus's home district and the place he started the ministry with the disciples. Compare this with Luke, where the disciples are instructed to gather in Jerusalem because the good news must start from Jerusalem and spread to the Gentiles. This sequence represents Luke's concern for appealing to the Gentiles who'd heard about Judaism and/or Jerusalem. But Mark's audience is open to anyone, and there is no particular emphasis on Jerusalem. Hearing the good news of Jesus's resurrection, the women are supposed to be joyful. But they are afraid of telling this good news because they could be misunderstood or persecuted by the authorities. So they flee from the tomb and say nothing to anyone (Mark 16:8). If the story ends at 16:8 (shorter ending), not at 16:20 (longer ending), does Mark's Gospel sound hopeless? The answer is no, because the audience is given the rhetorical challenge of considering if they were like the women visiting the tomb and hearing the good news of Jesus's resurrection. Fear-stricken women reflect the Markan community's fear-ingrained life in the hostile Roman world. Mark implies that the good news of Jesus Christ is costly, and yet it is the good news that God prevails in the end.

QUESTIONS FOR REFLECTION

1. How does Mark portray Jesus? What kind of messiah or Son of God is he?
2. Why does Mark not include a birth/infancy narrative? Why does it begin with Jesus as an adult?
3. Why does Mark portray the disciples of Jesus negatively (4:35–41; 8:31–10:46)?
4. What should we think about the unnamed or minor characters in Mark? For example, consider the anointing woman at Bethany (Mark 14:3–9), the unnamed women followers of Jesus (15:40–41), Simon of Cyrene (15:21), and Joseph of Arimathea (15:43–47).
5. What is the cause of Jesus's death in Mark? What does it have to do with the good news of God?
6. Does the shorter ending of Mark at 16:8 make better sense than the longer ending at 16:20? In what way do you think so? If you do not agree, why?

FURTHER READING

Black, C. Clifton. *Mark's Gospel: History, Theology, Interpretation*. Grand Rapids, MI: Eerdmans, 2023.

Blount, Brian. *Go Preach! Mark's Kingdom Message and the Black Church Today*. Maryknoll, NY: Orbis, 1998.

Bovon, François. *The Last Days of Jesus*. Louisville, KY: Westminster John Knox, 2006.

Cartlidge, David, and David Dungan. *Documents and Images for the Study of the Gospels*. Minneapolis, MN: Fortress, 2015.

Choi, Jin Young, *Postcolonial Discipleship of Embodiment. An Asian and Asian American Feminist Reading of the Gospel of Mark*. New York: Palgrave Macmillan, 2015.

Collins, Adela Yabro. *Mark: A Commentary*. Minneapolis, MN: Fortress, 2007.

Dube, Musa W. "Mark's Healing Stories in an AIDS Context." In *Global Bible Commentary*, edited by Daniel Patte, 379–384. Nashville, TN: Abingdon Press, 2005.

Jebaraj, Edwin, and Johnson Thomaskutty. "The Gospel of Mark." In *An Asian Introduction to the New Testament*, edited by Johnson Thomaskutty, 75–101. Minneapolis, MN: Fortress, 2022.

Kim, Yung Suk. *Jesus's Truth: Life in Parables*. Eugene, OR: Resource, 2018.

Kinukawa, Hisako. "Luke." In *Global Bible Commentary*, edited by Daniel Patte, 367–378. Nashville, TN: Abingdon Press, 2005.

Levine, Amy-Jill. *A Feminist Companion to Mark*. Sheffield, England: Sheffield Academic Press, 2001.

Liew, Tat-siong Benny. *Politics of Parousia: Reading Mark Inter(con)textually*. Brill, 1999.

Malbon, Elizabeth Struthers. *Hearing Mark: A Listener's Guide*. Harrisburg, PA: Trinity Press International, 2002.

Marcus, Joel. *Mark 1–8*. New Haven, CT: Yale University Press, 2002.

———. *Mark 8–16*. New Haven, CT: Yale University Press, 2009.

Myers, Ched. *Binding the Strong Man: A Political Reading of Mark's Story of Jesus*. Maryknoll, NY: Orbis, 1988.

Powery, Emerson. "The Gospel of Mark." In *True to Our Native Land: An African American New Testament Commentary*, edited by Brian K. Blount, Cain H. Felder, Clarice J. Martin, and Emerson B. Powery, 151–157. Minneapolis, MN: Fortress, 2007.

Rhoads, David, Joanna Dewey, and Donald Michie. *Mark as Story: An Introduction to the Narrative of a Gospel*. Minneapolis, MN: Fortress, 2012.

Sánchez, David Arthur. "Ambivalence, Mimicry, and the Ochlos in the Gospel of Mark." In *Reading Minjung Theology in the Twenty-first Century*, edited by Yung Suk Kim and Jin-Ho Kim, 134–47. Eugene, OR: Pickwick, 2013.

Smith, Mitzi J. *Womanist Sass and Talk Back: Social (In)justice, Intersectionality, and Biblical Interpretation*. Eugene, OR: Cascade Books, 2018.

Smith, Mitzi J., and Yung Suk Kim. *Toward Decentering the New Testament: A Reintroduction*. Eugene, OR: Cascade Books, 2018.

St. Clair, Raquel. *Call and Consequences: A Womanist Reading of Mark*. Minneapolis, MN: Fortress, 2008.

Vena, Osvaldo D. "Mark: A Disabled Gospel for a Disabled Community." In *Latinx Perspectives on the New Testament*, edited by Osvaldo D. Vena and Leticia A. Guardiola-Saenz, 33–60. Lanham, MD: Lexington Books, 2022.

Wills, Lawrence. "The Gospel According to Mark." In *The Jewish Annotated New Testament*, edited by Amy-Jill Levine and Marc Zvi Brettler, 67–106. New York: Oxford University Press, 2017.

NOTES

1. Mitzi J. Smith and Yung Suk Kim, *Toward Decentering the New Testament: A Reintroduction* (Eugene, OR: Cascade Books, 2018), 84–102.

2. Oral traditions extend the "old, old story," in Joel Marcus's terms. Whereas Marcus limits the tradition to Jesus, Daniel Boyarin argues, for example, that Christology in Mark existed before Jesus in the sense that the idea of a messiah was prevalent among Jewish traditions. Joel Marcus, *The Way of the Lord: Christological Exegesis of the Old Testament in the Gospel of Mark* (Louisville, KY: Westminster John Knox, 1992), 203. See also, Daniel Boyarin, "The Sovereignty of the Son of Man: Reading Mark 2," in *The Interface of Orality and Writing: Speaking, Seeing, Writing in the Shaping of New Genres*, eds. Annette Weissenrieder and Robert B. Coote (Tübingen, Germany: Mohr Siebeck, 2010), 353–62.

3. Mark uses more historic present tense than Matthew or Luke, which implies the importance of colloquialism in the narrative. Nicholas Elder argues that "oral proclamation is thus the content of Mark's written medium." See Nicholas Elder, "The Synoptic Gospels as the Mixed Media," *Biblical Research* 64 (2019), 49. See also, David Rhoads, Joanna Dewey, and Donald Michie, *Mark as Story: An Introduction to the Narrative of a Gospel* (Minneapolis, MN: Fortress, 2012).

4. Troy Troftgruben, "Salvation 'Today' in Luke's Gospel," *Currents in Theology and Mission* 45, no. 4 (2018): 6–11. http://currentsjournal.org/index.php/currents/article/view/144.

5. The so-called longer ending (16:9–20) is considered an addendum inserted by later copyists.

6. "The way to Jerusalem" is highlighted by some scholars who find a chiasm in the Gospel. The central unit is Jesus's way to Jerusalem in 8:27–10:52. See Augustine Stock, *The Method and Message of Mark* (Wilmington, DE: Michael Glazier, 1989). See also, Joanna Dewey, *Markan Public Debate: Literary Technique, Concentric Structure, and Theology in Mark 2:1–3:6* (Chico, CA: Scholar's Press, 1980).

7. The other exception when a parable is explained is in the parable of wheat and weeds (Matthew 13:24–43).

8. "The good news of Jesus Christ" is not exactly the title of the book, but it "serves as a meta- or paratextual title for the entire narrative." See Elder, "The Synoptic Gospels as Mixed Media," 45–46.

Chapter 3

The Gospel of Matthew

The Gospel of Matthew shows fully developed narratives and well-structured discourses. The Gospel begins with the genealogy of Jesus and his birth story, contains stories of dynamic teachings and the ministry of Jesus, reaches its climax through a passion narrative, and ends with a glorious resurrection narrative, followed by his commissioning of the disciples and his promise of his presence until the end. The Gospel also includes five distinct discourses: the Sermon on the Mount (Mt 5–7), missionary discourse (Mt 10), parables (Mt 13), community discourse (Mt 18), and eschatological discourse (Mt 24–25). According to the Markan priority, Mark is a literary source for Matthew and Luke. Indeed, Matthew reproduces about 90 percent of Mark; of Luke, about half. If Mark had used Matthew as a source, how could Mark have omitted so many excellent materials in Matthew? Matthew also uses a third source, Q (Jesus's sayings), which does not appear in Mark, as well as other unique materials not found elsewhere, such as the birth narrative, the Sermon on the Mount, and parables like that of the laborers in the vineyard and the unforgiving servant. Using all available sources, written or oral, Matthew edits them and retells the story about Jesus to his community.

Matthew's Gospel is distinctive in several ways. First, it portrays Jesus as the Jewish Messiah and the Son of God who fulfills the law and the prophets: "Do not think that I have come to abolish the law or the prophets; I have come not to abolish but to fulfill" (Mt 5:17). Likewise, the genealogy of Jesus emphasizes his Jewishness. Second, Jesus is called Emmanuel, which means "God is with us." He promises his ever presence with his disciples after the resurrection: "I am with you always, to the end of the age" (Mt 28:20). Third, Jesus as a New Moses reinterprets the law (Sermon on the Mount in Mt 5–7) with integrity and emphasizes God's righteousness (6:33; 20:1–16). Fourth, Matthew emphasizes the importance of forgiveness in the *ekklēsia* (only Matthew says that Jesus will build his church [16:18]). In his community discourse, Jesus tells Peter to forgive anyone endlessly: "Not seven times, but, I tell you, seventy-seven times" (Mt 18:22). The parable of the unforgiving servant also highlights this teaching of forgiveness (18:23–35). Fifth, on two occasions in the narrative, Jesus represents Jewish exclusivism (10:5–6; 15:21–28). Jesus sends out his disciples and warns them, "Go nowhere among the Gentiles, and enter no town of the Samaritans, but go rather to the lost sheep of the house of Israel" (10:5–6). Later in his encounter with a Canaanite woman, Jesus repeats his Jewish exclusivism, saying, "I was sent only to the lost sheep of the house of Israel" (15:24), and "It is not fair to take the children's food and throw it to the dogs" (15:26). Jesus's disciples also intervened: "Send her away, for she keeps shouting after us" (15:23). The Matthean Jesus is very different from the Lukan Jesus, who says in his initial preaching that God prefers the Gentiles (Luke 4:16–30). But eventually, at the end of the episode, Jesus allows for her daughter's healing because of the Canaanite woman's faith. At the end of Matthew, Jesus sends out his disciples to "all nations" (*ethnē*; 28:19). Overall, Matthew's theology embraces God's impartial love (5:43–48), forgiveness (18:1–35), economic justice for all (20:1–16), and care for the marginalized (25:31–46).

TEXTBOX 3.1 **Matthew's Gospel at a Glance**

DATE

Matthew was likely written in 85–90 CE, fifteen or twenty years after Mark. There is a reference to the fall of Jerusalem that took place in 70 CE (Mt 22:1–14).

AUTHOR

According to the church tradition, the author is Matthew, a tax collector (Mt 9:9–13; 10:3). But there is no internal or external evidence that Matthew is the author.

PLACE

The place of composition is unknown. One possibility is Antioch in Syria because Ignatius, bishop of Antioch, wrote several epistles and seemed to depend partially on Matthew. For example, Jesus's baptism by John is explained in his letter to the Smyrnaeans 1:1 (Mt 3:15). Also, the Didache—an early second-century Christian writing with a purported origin in Syria—shares some contents of Matthew; for example, Didache 8 is similar to Matthew 6:5–13 (the Lord's Prayer).

SOURCE

Matthew used Mark as one primary source and then Q as a third source. Also, there are some unique materials (M). Matthew follows the storyline of Mark. Where Mark begins, Matthew also begins (Jesus's baptism), and where Mark ends, Matthew also ends (Jesus's resurrection). But Matthew contains much more materials than Mark, and its structure is much more complicated.

AUDIENCE

Matthew addresses the mixed community of Jews and Gentiles, but predominantly, he is addressing a Jewish community facing two issues at the same time: externally, confrontation with the Pharisees (for example, "synagogue" is mentioned frequently: 4:23; 9:35; 10:17; 12:9; 13:54; and 23:34), and internally, tension with Jewish-exclusive theology (10:5–6; 15:21–28).

HOW IT BEGINS

Matthew begins with a genealogy from Abraham and continues with the birth narrative. Five women appear in Jesus's genealogy. Jesus is a royal king (Son of David) and a son of Abraham (Jewish lineage). He is named Emmanuel.

HOW IT ENDS

Jesus gathers his disciples in Galilee and commissions them to the world. Jesus promises, "I am with you always, to the end of the age" (Mt 28:20).

ESCHATOLOGY

Matthew's eschatology is also imminent, similar to Mark's.

JESUS

Jesus portrayed as the Jewish Messiah fulfills the Scriptures (Mt 5:17–21). The righteousness of God is a dominating theme (6:33). He is also a New Moses: a great prophet, teacher, and lawgiver. Jesus is publicly known (unlike *the messianic secret* in Mark). Matthew is the only Gospel in which Jesus says, "I will build my church" (16:18).

DISCIPLES

Disciples are trusted, taught, and commissioned (Mt 7:21–27; 13:9, 23; 14:22–33; 21:6; 26:19; and 28:16–20).

HUMAN CONDITION

The human condition in Matthew is blind hypocrisy (23:3): "Therefore, do whatever they teach you and follow it; but do not do as they do, for they do not practice what they teach."

TRANSFORMATION

Follow the law with integrity, and strive for God's kingdom and his righteousness (Mt 6:33).

UNIQUE CONTENT

5:1–12, Beatitudes (part of the Sermon on the Mount)
14:28–33, Peter on the water
16:16–19, Peter's confession at Caesarea Philippi: "I will build my church on the rock"
25:31–46, The last judgment: sheep and goats
27:3–10, Death of Judas

UNIQUE PARABLES

13:24–30, Weeds and the wheat
13:31–50, Treasure, pearl of great value, net thrown into the sea
18:23–35, The unforgiving servant
20:1–16, The laborers in the vineyard
21:28–32, Two sons
22:1–14, Wedding banquet
25:1–13, Ten bridesmaids
25:14–30, Talents

OUTLINE

1:1–2:23, Infancy Narrative
3:1–4:25, Ministry of Jesus
5:1–7:29, First Discourse: Sermon on the Mount
8:1–9:38, Jesus Heals Many
10:1–10:42, Second Discourse: Missionary Instructions
11:1–12:50, Jesus's Ministry Continues while Opposition Arises
13:1–53, Third Discourse: Collections of Parables
13:54–17:27, Jesus Continues with His Mission and Foretells His Death and Resurrection
18:1–35, Fourth Discourse: Community Instructions
19:1–20:34, Jesus Continues to Teach on the Way to Jerusalem
21:1–23:39, Jesus Enters Jerusalem and Confronts Leaders

24:1–25:46, Fifth Discourse: Sermon On Eschatology
26:1–27:66, Passion Narrative
28:1–20, The Resurrection of Jesus

THE MATTHEAN JESUS

Because Jesus is the Jewish Messiah, his genealogy goes back to David and Abraham. He is the son of David and the son of Abraham. His birth fulfills Isaiah 7:14: "Therefore the Lord himself will give you a sign. Look, the young woman is with child and shall bear a son and shall name him Immanuel." The fourteen generations in his genealogy represent Jesus's perfect birth because the number fourteen reinforces holiness. There are also fourteen formula citations.[1] Jesus's birth story echoes Moses's. As Moses was saved from the river when Pharaoh has all the boys killed (Ex 1:22–2:10), Jesus was saved from massacre when Herod has all the male boys killed in Bethlehem (Mt 2:13–18). Moses climbs a mountain to receive the law from God (Ex 19:3), and similarly, Jesus teaches the law/sermon on the mountain. As Moses fasts for forty days and nights to record God's law (Ex 34:28), Jesus also fasts for forty days and nights in the desert. Like in the five books of Moses, Jesus delivers five discourses (in chapters 5–7, 10, 13, and 18, 22–25). In Matthew, Jesus appears as a great teacher, prophet, and lawgiver.

As the Jewish Messiah, Jesus says, "Do not think that I have come to abolish the law or the prophets; I have come not to abolish but to fulfill" (Mt 5:17). He also says, "Unless your righteousness exceeds that of the scribes and Pharisees, you will never enter the kingdom of heaven" (5:20). Jesus is baptized for fulfilling the righteousness of God. So he also says, "Strive first for the kingdom of God and his righteousness" (Mt 6:33). As the Jewish Messiah, he reinterprets the law, leading to the golden rule: "In everything do to others as you would have them do to you; for this is the law and the prophets" (7:12). This rule is reminiscent of Rabbi Hillel's saying: "What is hateful to you do not do to your neighbor; that is the whole Torah, while the rest is commentary. Go and learn it."[2]

On the other hand, the Matthean Jesus appears as a Jewish exclusivist who limits his mission to Jews only. But this happens only on two occasions. First, when he sends out his disciples for a mission, he gives these instructions: "Go nowhere among the Gentiles, and enter no town of the Samaritans, but go rather to the lost sheep of the house of Israel" (Mt 10:5–6). Second, when Jesus meets a Canaanite woman, he treats her like a no one and says, "I was sent only to the lost sheep of the house of Israel" (15:24), and "It is not fair to take the children's food and throw it to the dogs" (15:26). But at the end of the story, Jesus acknowledges her faith. Also, at the end of the narrative, he sends out his disciples to all nations (Mt 28:16–20). Matthew 10:5–6 and 15:21–28 reflect the Matthean community's struggle with opening the mission for Gentiles.

DISTINCTIVE THEOLOGICAL THEMES

Matthew, first of all, characterizes God as compassionate and impartial, as Jesus says: "For he makes his sun rise on the evil and on the good, and sends rain on the righteous and on the unrighteous" (Mt 5:45). To ensure God's impartial love for all, equal opportunities are given to all. For example, in the parable of wheat and weeds, the desired attitude is to avoid the premature judgment of other people because they may change in their remaining time. Second, Matthew emphasizes God's judgment on the last day. God is loving and merciful until the Parousia. Throughout Matthew's narrative, there is a consistent emphasis on a balance between God's love and God's judgment. Matthean parables such as the unforgiving servant (18:21–35) or the talents (25:14–30) maintain this stance. Third, Matthew emphasizes the importance of forgiveness for all to maintain a Christ-built church (16:16–18; 18:17–35). Because God is loving, the community members must love others, even enemies, and forgive one another. Fourth, Matthew emphasizes the righteousness of God, which is the central theme of the Hebrew Bible. Jesus came to fulfill it as the Son of God (Mt 5:17). His baptism is also for that purpose (3:13–17). He teaches that people must strive for God's rule and his righteousness first (6:33). He reinterprets the law with integrity (5:17–48). What matters more is a matter of the heart seeking the love of God and neighbor. Hypocrisy occurs when one does not do what one teaches or knows (Mt 23:2). Fifth and lastly, Matthew emphasizes the importance of serving the marginalized, as in 25:31–46. They should not judge others but do what Jesus taught them (28:16–20), following him (7:21–27; 13:9, 23; 21:6; 26:19).

PARABLES IN MATTHEW

Matthew uses some parables in Mark and edits them to fit his context. For example, the Matthean version of the parable of the mustard seed shows the importance of the place where the seed is sown; it is in the field (*argos*), a cultivated place. Matthew's community must prepare for such a field by following Jesus and doing the work of God. The community members must learn from him, as he invites them to the following: "Come to me, all you that are weary and are carrying heavy burdens, and I will give you rest. Take my yoke upon you, and learn from me; for I am gentle and humble in heart, and you will find rest for your souls. For my yoke is easy, and my burden is light" (Mt 11:28–30). They also have to build their house on the rock, not on sand (7:24–27). In other words, the hearing must cohere with action.

Matthew also includes parables that are unique to him to strengthen his theology for the community. The parable of the wheat and weeds (Mt 13:24–30) challenges the community members to rethink their view of others and their enemies and to love them unconditionally. Judgment or punishment happens only in the Parousia. So their task is to love even their enemies (Mt 5:44). The parable of the unforgiving servant (18:23–35) emphasizes God's incalculable grace and mutual forgiveness in the community. But there will be a consequence on the last day. The parables of the treasure and pearl (13:44–46) emphasize a radical decision about the kingdom of God. There is a time one must decide quickly and participate in God's work without hesitation. The parable of the vineyard laborers (Mt 20:1–16) deals with economic justice for all. The landowner in this parable is an atypical owner who is concerned with distributive justice for all workers. He pays the usual daily wage to all because he knows they need such a basic wage or "whatever is right" (Mt 20:4). Those who join the vineyard late could not find earlier work, because no one hired them. They are probably weak or ill, or some may have come to the labor market late due to personal or family issues. The parable of talents (Mt 25:14–30) shows the importance of working hard without wasting one's God-given talents, such as time, resources, and any gifts from God. This parable is not about whether one makes a big success but whether one tries hard, trusting God. This point is also seen in the parables of the wedding banquet (Mt 22:1–14) and of the ten bridesmaids (25:1–13). Lastly, the last judgment parable in Matthew 25:31–46 emphasizes serving "one of the least of these" (cf. 10:42; 18:6, 10, 14).

NOTABLE INTERPRETATION ISSUES

One of the crucial issues in Matthew is Christology. On the one hand, he is the Jewish Messiah who came to fulfill the law and the prophets. On the other hand, he commissions his disciples to all nations after the resurrection. He asks his disciples to love their enemies. But on other occasions, he rejects the Canaanite woman's request for her daughter's healing (Mt 15:21–28) and prevents his disciples from entering the Gentile regions (10:4–5). So he limits his mission to the lost sheep of the house of Israel and rejects the Canaanite woman's plea for healing for her daughter. Matthew also protects Jesus's image on several occasions. Jesus is said to be the carpenter's son, not a carpenter himself (Mt 13:55–56), but in Mark, he is the carpenter (Mark 6:3). In another place, Matthew changes Mark's wording of "Why do you call me good? No one is good but God alone" (Mark 10:17–18) to "Teacher, what good deed must I do to have eternal life? Why do you ask me about what is good?" (Mt 19:16–17).

The other issue is the Matthean community's historical context involving confrontation within the synagogue or Judaism. Matthew often uses the phrases "their synagogues" or "your synagogues" (4:24; 12:9; 13:54), which reflect Matthew's conflict with the Jewish synagogue.[3] Also consider the negative comments about Jewish leaders, especially in Matthew 23:27–29: "Woe to you, scribes and Pharisees, hypocrites! For you are like whitewashed tombs, which on the outside look beautiful but inside are full of the bones of the dead and of all kinds of uncleanness . . . but inside you are full of hypocrisy and lawlessness. . . . For you build the tombs of the prophets and decorate the graves of the righteous." In Matthew 27:25, the crowd says, "His blood be on us and on our children." Does the Gospel reflect Matthew's community that is separated from Judaism (an inter-community struggle)? Or does it reflect a struggle within Judaism? The other related issue is Matthew's position on Judaism and the law. Does the community keep the law as Jesus says, which is that not one stroke of a letter can be ignored (Mt 5:18)? Discipleship is also an important issue. Why are women not called disciples? Why are only male disciples commissioned? (Mt 28:16–20). Lastly, Matthew's view of the church/community needs discussion. Matthew is the only Gospel in which Jesus says, "I will build my church on the rock" (Mt 16:18). What does Matthew think about the Gentiles' joining the church, and on what conditions are they accepted into the community?

A CLOSE READING OF MATTHEW

1:1–2:23, Infancy Narrative

The narrator of Matthew's Gospel begins with the genealogy of Jesus, who is called the Messiah, the Son of David, and the son of Abraham (1:1). He is the anointed one (the Messiah) whose genealogy goes back to King David and Abraham, the forefather of Israel. Then the genealogy traces down to "Joseph the husband of Mary, of whom Jesus was born" (Mt 1:6). The fourteen generations in the genealogy symbolize the perfect birth of Jesus because the number fourteen represents such a double blessing. In the genealogy of Jesus, there are five women: Tamar, Rahab, Ruth, Bathsheba, and Mary. Four of the five women (excepting Mary) from the Hebrew Bible are Gentiles. Tamar deceived her father-in-law Judah and slept with him to secure her life because he did not give his third son to her after her two husbands died without sons. Rahab was a prostitute who helped the spies of Israel. Ruth was a Moabite woman who followed Naomi and, according to her scheme, married Boaz. Bathsheba was the wife of Uriah, but David took her and later killed him. Mary was found pregnant before her marriage to Joseph, which caused a great scandal. The five women were all involved in some kind of controversy. Again, except for Mary, the four women from the Hebrew Bible are Gentiles. So Matthew has emphasized the inclusion of the Gentiles in salvation history. Or, at least, Matthew has emphasized the inclusion of the marginalized, as all these women were marginalized. Or there are even other ways of interpreting Matthew's inclusion of these women. Some may see the importance of including women in the genealogy through a gender focus because, traditionally, they have not been part of genealogies. Others may recognize the importance of the "queer" in the genealogy because the five women were abnormal and yet paved a breakthrough.

In the genealogy, Joseph is mentioned not as the father of Jesus but as "the husband of Mary, of whom Jesus was born" (Mt 1:6). Joseph thought that Mary was pregnant by someone and wanted to cut off from his relationship with her. But he took Mary as his wife because an angel of the Lord told him in a dream that her child is from the Holy Spirit. The child is named Jesus, who "will save his people from their sins" (Mt 1:21). Matthew says, "All this took place to fulfill what had been spoken by the Lord through the prophet" (1:23), and he quotes Isaiah 7:14, where "the young woman" (*almāh* in Hebrew) bears a son, who will be named Emmanuel, which means "God is with us." Matthew 1:23 is the first among fourteen fulfillment citations in Matthew. But Matthew writes in Greek and uses the Greek word *parthenos* (1:23), which means a virgin. Matthew uses the Septuagint (the Greek translation of the Hebrew Bible), where *almāh* in Isaiah 7:14 is translated as *parthenos*. In Isaiah 7:14, Isaiah speaks to King Ahaz, who needs the Lord's assurance about the protection of Judah. As a sign, the young woman will bear a son. Matthew applies this text to the birth of Jesus, while the original context of Isaiah 7:14 is disparate. Matthew's point seems clear that Isaiah prophesied Mary's virgin birth.

The genealogy of Jesus followed by his birth story has a dramatic and fear-inspiring appearance. The wise men (astrologers) from the East came to Jerusalem to visit the child, the king of the Jews. But King Herod heard the news that Jesus would be born in Bethlehem, for Bethlehem was foretold as the land of Judah from which a ruler will come out (Mi 5:2), and so he tried to kill him. After paying homage to the child Jesus with gifts, the wise men returned to their home country without telling Herod when they'd found Jesus. Now an angel of the Lord told Joseph in a dream to flee to Egypt because Herod was trying to kill the baby. Joseph's family remained in Egypt until the death of Herod. Matthew quotes from Hosea

11:1, "Out of Egypt I have called my son." Herod knew that the wise men tricked him. Becoming furious, he "killed all the children in and around Bethlehem who were two years old or under, according to the time that he had learned from the wise men" (Mt 1:16; quoting Jer 31:15). The sorrow and laments over this massacre are expressed with a quote from Jeremiah 31:15, where Rachel was weeping over her children because they were no more. When Herod died, an angel of the Lord told Joseph in a dream to return to the land of Israel. Eventually, they went to Galilee and settled in a small town called Nazareth because Archelaus, the son of Herod, ruled over Judea. He was called a Nazorean, but the Old Testament does not mention such a name.

> TEXTBOX 3.2 *Consider and Discuss*
>
> ### THE GENEALOGY OF JESUS
>
> Matthew begins with the genealogy of Jesus, tracing it to Abraham and David. The former is the legendary figure with whom God made a covenant; the latter is the first king of a unified Israel. In this genealogy there are four women from the Old Testament: Tamar, Rahab, Ruth, and Bathsheba. Also, Mary, the mother of Jesus, is included. While she is called the mother of Jesus, Joseph is mentioned merely as the husband of Mary. While the four women, Tamar, Rahab, Ruth, and Bathsheba, are Gentiles, the common denominator for all of the five women is their sexually implicated image. What is the significance of the inclusion of these women in Matthew?

3:1–4:25, Ministry of Jesus

John the Baptist sets the stage for Jesus's public ministry and prepares the way of the Lord (Mt 3:1–12; cf. Is 40:3; Mark 1:2–8). He proclaims that people must prepare for the day of judgment by repenting, and he introduces Jesus as the one who will baptize people with the Holy Spirit and fire and complete his job as the last-day harvester (Mt 3:12). John is very critical of the Pharisees and Sadducees who are coming for baptism: "You brood of vipers! Who warned you to flee from the wrath to come? Bear fruit worthy of repentance. Do not presume to say to yourselves, 'We have Abraham as our ancestor'; for I tell you, God is able from these stones to raise up children to Abraham. Even now the ax is lying at the root of the trees; every tree therefore that does not bear good fruit is cut down and thrown into the fire" (Mt 3:7–10). John's harsh judgment against Jewish leaders reflects Matthew's tough relationships with the synagogue.

Then Jesus is baptized by John (Mt 3:13–17; cf. Mark 1:9–11). But the most striking difference in Matthew when compared to Mark is John's hesitation to baptize Jesus. This hesitation motif reflects two issues in Matthew's community—that is, why does Jesus need the baptism of John if he is superior to John? The other issue is why he needs John's baptism of repentance for the forgiveness of sins. Jesus explains that baptism is necessary so that they may fulfill all righteousness (Mt 3:15); that is, the baptism of Jesus is not about ranking or forgiveness of sins but about fulfilling all righteousness, which means they work together to demonstrate God's righteousness in the world. Indeed, righteousness is a central topic of Jesus's teaching in Matthew (3:15; 5:6, 10, 20; 6:33; 21:32). The other big difference in Matthew is that a voice from heaven says, "This is my Son" (3:17). In Mark a voice says, "You are my Son" (1:11). While Mark emphasizes Jesus's intimate relationship with God, Matthew presents Jesus as a public figure. In Matthew, Jesus does not try to hide his identity—unlike in Mark—and he appears to be a great teacher, prophet, and lawgiver who is publicly known.

In the temptation of Jesus (Mt 4:1–11), Matthew expands the Markan version of the temptation story (Mark 1:12–13) and includes three tests or temptations. The first temptation is about making bread out of stones, and Jesus's answer is "One does not live by bread alone, but by every word that comes from the mouth of God" (Mt 4:4). Here, the point is that one must seek God's righteousness first, as he explains to his disciples later in Matthew 6:25–34. The second temptation is about jumping off from the pinnacle of the temple, and Jesus answers, "Again it is written, 'Do not put the Lord your God to the test'" (4:7). His point is that one must be humble before God and that one should not seek to be great. The last temptation is about worshiping the devil. Jesus says, "Away with you, Satan! for it is written, 'Worship the Lord your God, and serve only him'" (Mt 4:10). Here, he emphasizes sole devotion to God, who is almighty and all-loving. Jesus went through all the tests successfully.

After the tests in the wilderness, Jesus begins his ministry, calls the first disciples, and ministers to various people (Mt 4:12–25). Matthew follows the Markan story of Jesus (Mark 1:14–45). Like Mark, Matthew says that Jesus started his ministry after John was arrested. But the difference is that Jesus "made his home in Capernaum by the sea, in the territory of Zebulun and Naphtali (Mt 4:13), which is the fulfillment of the words of the prophet Isaiah (Mt 4:15). From this region, "Jesus began to proclaim, "Repent, for the kingdom of heaven has come near" (Mt 4:17), which echoes John's preaching in Matthew 3:2 and Jesus's initial preaching in Mark 1:15. Here "the kingdom of heaven" is interchangeable with "the kingdom of God" because, in Matthew's Jewish version of the gospel, heaven represents God. Then Jesus called the first group of disciples from their workplace, where they were fishing: Simon (Peter) and Andrew his brother as well as James, son of Zebedee, and his brother John. Then, throughout Galilee, he taught in the synagogues, proclaimed the good news of the kingdom, and healed the sick. Here, "the good news of the kingdom" is interchangeable with "the good news of God" because the kingdom (*basileia*) comes from God. Because of Jesus's teaching and healing, his reputation had spread far to Syria, and "great crowds followed him from Galilee, the Decapolis, Jerusalem, Judea, and from beyond the Jordan" (Mt 4:25). This image of Jesus, as he was well known by many, coheres with a heavenly voice's saying, "This is my Son" (3:27).

TEXTBOX 3.3 **Consider and Discuss**

JESUS'S CALL OF THE FIRST DISCIPLES (MT 4:18–22)

During Jesus's time, Herod Antipas, the tetrarch, ruled Galilee and Perea as a puppet state of the Roman Empire (Matthew 14:1; Mark 6:14; Luke 3:1). He was involved in Roman-style building projects at Sepphoris and constructed his new capital, Tiberias, named for the current emperor Tiberius, on the shore of the Sea of Galilee. Galilean peasants and fishermen were devastated by his callous rule entailing higher taxes and flagrant corruption, among other things.[1] Jesus resided in the fishing village of Capernaum and had lots of ministry work around and across the Sea of Galilee. Jesus called two brothers, Simon and Andrew, who were fishing in the Sea of Galilee; they left their nets and followed him (Mt 4:18–20). He also called James, son of Zebedee, and his brother John (4:21–22). Consider and discuss the above sociopolitical and economic situations where Jesus called the first disciples. What does it mean to call them in such a world? What made them follow Jesus? What did they desire or envision?

NOTE

1. K. C. Hanson, "The Galilean Fishing Economy and the Jesus Tradition," *Biblical Theology Bulletin* 27, no. 3 (1997): 99–111.

5:1–7:29, First Discourse: Sermon on the Mount

The Sermon on the Mount in 5:1–7:29 is unique to Matthew, and Jesus reinterprets the law with integrity. He teaches his disciples, asks them to adopt the rule of God, demonstrates God's righteousness, and embraces the marginalized. In the Beatitudes, Jesus redefines who must be blessed by God: the poor in spirit, those who mourn, the meek, those who hunger and thirst for righteousness, the merciful, the pure in heart, the peacemakers, and those who are persecuted for righteousness' sake. See table 3.1, where we compare the Matthean beatitudes with the Lukan beatitudes.

Table 3.1. Beatitudes in Matthew and Luke

Matthew 5:1–12	Luke 6:17–23	Woes in Luke (6:24–26)
1 When Jesus saw the crowds, he went up the mountain, and after he sat down, his disciples came to him. 2 And he began to speak and taught them, saying:	17 He came down with them and stood on a level place with a great crowd of his disciples and a great multitude of people from all Judea, Jerusalem, and the coast of Tyre and Sidon. 18 They had come to hear him and to be healed of their diseases, and those who were troubled with unclean spirits were cured. 19 And everyone in the crowd was trying to touch him, for power came out from him and healed all of them. 20 Then he looked up at his disciples and said:	
3 "Blessed are the poor in spirit, for theirs is the kingdom of heaven."	20 "Blessed are you who are poor, for yours is the kingdom of God."	24 "But woe to you who are rich, for you have received your consolation."
4 "Blessed are those who mourn, for they will be comforted."	21 "Blessed are you who weep now, for you will laugh."	25 "Woe to you who are laughing now, for you will mourn and weep."
5 "Blessed are the meek, for they will inherit the earth."		
6 "Blessed are those who hunger and thirst for righteousness, for they will be filled."	21 "Blessed are you who are hungry now, for you will be filled."	
7 "Blessed are the merciful, for they will receive mercy."		
8 "Blessed are the pure in heart, for they will see God."		
9 "Blessed are the peacemakers, for they will be called children of God."		
10 "Blessed are those who are persecuted for the sake of righteousness, for theirs is the kingdom of heaven."		

(continued)

Table 3.1. *(continued)*

Matthew 5:1–12	Luke 6:17–23	Woes in Luke (6:24–26)
11 "Blessed are you when people revile you and persecute you and utter all kinds of evil against you falsely on my account. 12 Rejoice and be glad, for your reward is great in heaven, for in the same way they persecuted the prophets who were before you."	22 "Blessed are you when people hate you and when they exclude you, revile you, and defame you on account of the Son of Man. 23 Rejoice on that day and leap for joy, for surely your reward is great in heaven, for that is how their ancestors treated the prophets."	26 "Woe to you when all speak well of you, for that is how their ancestors treated the false prophets."

There are several differences between Matthew and Luke. First, in Matthew, Jesus goes up the mountain; sits down as a great teacher, like a new Moses; and teaches his disciples, whereas, in Luke, Jesus teaches on the plain with the presence of the disciples and a great multitude of people. This difference may be understandable because, first, whereas Matthew intends to portray Jesus as a great teacher/prophet like Moses, Luke paints him as a compassionate teacher and healer for real people (multitudes of people). Second, in Matthew, blessed are *they* (third-person plural) is used, whereas Luke uses blessed are *you* (second-person plural). It is hard to know the reason for this difference, but most likely, Matthew is emphasizing Jesus's public, objective ministry, as we've seen at his baptism, where a voice names him, saying, "This is my Son." By contrast, Luke underscores either Jesus's concern for his poor disciples, addressed in the second-person plural, or his immediate compassion for all others who are poor, being addressed in the second-person plural, to convey his intimacy with them. Likewise, Luke emphasizes "you who weep now" and "you who are hungry now" (6:21). Third, Matthew uses "blessed are those who are poor in spirit" (5:3), which seems ambiguous to those discerning what it means, but in Luke, the focus is on the poor people themselves: "Blessed are you who are poor, for yours is the kingdom of God" (6:20). But this difference alone does not tell us that Matthew is less concerned about the poor, because, for example, "one of the least of these" may be understood as Jesus's embracing the poor and marginalized (Mt 10:42; 18:14; 25:45). Fourth and lastly, in Matthew, the meek people will inherit the land, while Luke omits it altogether, which is puzzling given the Gospel's emphasis on the blessing of the poor who need the land.

After that, Jesus touches on various topics in daily life or the community: anger (Mt 5:21–26), adultery (5:27–30), divorce (5:31–32), oaths (5:33–

37), retaliation (5:38–42), and love for enemies (5:43–48). Even anger is liable to judgment (5:22). Reconciling with a brother or sister must precede one's offering at the altar (5:23). Adultery begins within one's heart when one looks at a woman with lust (5:27). Jesus's teaching about divorce in Matthew 5:31–32 is a bit different from Mark's depiction in the sense that divorce is allowed on the ground of unchastity. In Mark divorce is not allowed without exceptions (Mark 10:1–12). Otherwise, in both Matthew and Mark, remarriage is discouraged. Jesus also talks about oaths, which must be carefully made (Mt 5:33–37). Jesus reinterprets retaliation laws and asks the disciples to love their enemies (5:43–44). But "hating your enemy" (5:43) does not appear in the Old Testament. Probably, Jesus is referring to the cultural practice of retaliation laws with which people would think they have to love neighbors and hate enemies, based on Exodus 21:22–25. His ethical demand comes from God's character, which is impartial. God's righteousness spreads to all, the evil and the good (Mt 5:45–47). The disciples must be perfect as God is perfect (5:48).

The Sermon on the Mount continues. Jesus takes on the issues of religious life: almsgiving (Mt 6:1–4), prayer (6:5–15), fasting (6:16–18), treasures (6:19–21), the sound eye (6:22–23), serving two masters (6:24), seeking God's righteousness (6:25–34), judging others (7:1–5), and profaning the holy (7:6). Almsgiving must be done quietly, and prayer must come from one's heart without uttering many words. Jesus teaches the disciples how to pray (the Lord's Prayer in Mt 6:9–13). There are seven noticeable points in this prayer. First, the issue is knowing who God is. "Our father in heaven" (Mt 6:9) does not denote the place of God; the point is that God is beyond our thought. While we remain in our way, God is in the realm of heaven; that is, we must acknowledge God's sovereignty. But this God is *our* God. God is everywhere and loves everyone. His name is hallowed because of this. Second, "May your kingdom come" (Mt 6:10) means God must rule the world and people. In other words, we must accept God's rule, which requires us to be humble, embrace the marginalized, and seek God's righteousness. Third, we must realize God's will on earth, rejecting a dualism between heaven and earth. Also, it is not our will that we must execute here on earth. Fourth, we must pray for our daily bread, which means we must feel happy with what we have daily. Seeking more than we need is temptation and goes against God's righteousness (cf. Mt 6:25–34). Fifth, mutual forgiveness is a mandate because God already forgave us. The parable of the unforgiving servant touches on this point (Mt 18:23–35). Sixth, we must pray that we do not live through the time of trial, because we are so fragile and broken. Seventh, God is the one who rescues us from the evil one.

Jesus's teaching continues. Fasting should be quiet, and treasures must be stored in heaven, which means investing in God's righteousness. For this task, people need robust eyes: "The eye is the lamp of the body. So, if your eye is healthy, your whole body will be full of light" (Mt 6:22). To be sober, they must devote themselves to God and his righteousness. What they must seek first is not what to eat or what to wear but "the kingdom of God and his righteousness" (Mt 6:33). So Jesus says, "So do not worry about tomorrow, for tomorrow will bring worries of its own. Today's trouble is enough for today" (6:34). In seeking God's rule, one must not judge others fast, because there may be a log in one's eye (7:1–5). One must value what is holy and keep it carefully (7:6).

Jesus concludes the Sermon on the Mount by dealing with personal virtue and ethical life: the importance of endless trials and endeavors (Mt 7:7–11), the golden rule (7:12), the narrow gate (7:13–14), a tree and its fruit (7:15–20), self-deception (7:21–23), and hearers and doers (7:24–29). Jesus says, "Ask, and it will be given you; search, and you will find; knock, and the door will be opened for you" (7:7). The golden rule is as follows: "In everything do to others as you would have them do to you; for this is the law and the prophets" (7:12). This rule is reminiscent of Rabbi Hillel's saying, "Whatever is hateful to you, do not do to others; this is the whole Torah, and the rest is commentary, go and learn it."[4] To live an ethical life, one must enter the narrow gate, which is difficult to take, but it is the way of life (Mt 7:13–14). When one takes the difficult road, one may bear good fruit (7:15–20). An ethical person is not someone who says "Lord, Lord" (7:21), but it is the one who hears the words of the Lord and acts on them (7:24). Such a person is like "a wise man who built his house on rock" (7:24).

8:1–9:38, Jesus Heals Many People

After the Sermon on the Mount, Jesus comes down the mountain, and great crowds follow him. He heals many sick people and performs a miracle of stilling the storm. While most of these healing/miracle stories come from Mark, Jesus's healing of two blind men is unique to Matthew. Jesus heals some people because of their faith: a leper, a woman suffering from hemorrhages, and two blind men. In other cases, he heals the sick because of others' faith: a centurion's faith for his servant, four people's faith for the paralytic, and a synagogue leader's faith for her daughter. In particular, a centurion's faith stands out, as Jesus says that he has not found such faith in Israel. In Matthew, only two Gentiles receive praise from Jesus because of their faith: the centurion and a Canaanite woman (15:21–28). Jesus heals some people by his own initiative: Peter's mother-in-law, many at Peter's house, and two demoniacs, as opposed to one demoniac in Mark. We should not assume that Jesus's healing always takes place in one form.

In healing episodes, Matthew shortens the Markan stories on two occasions. While Mark tells a long story of a demoniac in Mark 5:1–20, Matthew tells it in only seven verses (8:28–34). While Mark spends much space on the healing of "a woman suffering from hemorrhages and a girl restored to life" (Mark 5:21–43), Matthew tells the story in only nine verses (9:18–26). In these two episodes, Matthew shortens and refines Mark; in doing so, Matthew loses Mark's vivid, dynamic story of healing. Matthew does not say that the woman suffering from hemorrhages tried everything and spent all her money for curing the disease or that she told the whole truth about touching Jesus's cloak. Also, in the case of demoniacs, Matthew simplifies a complex, dynamic Markan story of healing.

Besides healing, Jesus stills the storm and asks his trembling disciples, "Why are you afraid, you of little faith?" This saying differs from that in Mark, where Jesus says: "Why are you afraid? Have you still no faith?" (Mark 4:40). Also, Jesus calls a tax collector, Matthew, and eats with many tax collectors and sinners. Against the charge of the Pharisees, Jesus answers, "Those who are well have no need of a physician, but those who are sick. Go and learn what this means, 'I desire mercy, not sacrifice.' For I have come to call not the righteous but sinners" (Mt 9:11–13). The themes of mercy and righteousness are consistent throughout the narrative and confirm the Matthean Jesus, who has come to fulfill the righteousness of God (5:17; 25:31–46). Jesus also speaks to the disciples of John, who ask about the need for fasting. His point is that there is time for fasting, but now is not that time, because the wedding is going on with the guests. This means that Matthew's community members should do their best in the present. Likewise, Jesus asks "would-be-followers" to follow him in the present (Mt 9:20–22). After this, Jesus continues his work, teaching in their synagogues, proclaiming the good news of God, and curing more sick people (9:35). He sees many who are "harassed and helpless, like sheep without a shepherd" (9:36). So he says, "The harvest is plentiful, but the laborers are few; therefore ask the Lord of the harvest to send out laborers into his harvest" (9:37–38). Later, the parable of the vineyard laborers in Matthew 20:1–16 supports the idea that the Lord needs many laborers in his vineyard.

10:1–10:42, Second Discourse: Missionary Instructions

Jesus calls his twelve disciples and sends them out on a mission to cast out unclean spirits and cure the sick. But unlike Mark or Luke, Matthew adds these words: "Go nowhere among the Gentiles, and enter no town of the Samaritans, but go rather to the lost sheep of the house of Israel" (10:5–6). This instruction sounds like Jewish-exclusive theology, which appears again in Matthew 15:21–28 (a Canaanite woman's story). Jesus's missionary discourse reflects the Matthean community's struggle with the Gentile mission or inclusion. Sending out his disciples, Jesus asks his disciples not to take money or other items for travel (cf. Mark 6:8; Luke 9:3) but to depend on the town or village they enter. If they are welcomed, they may stay, and otherwise, they are to shake off the dust from their feet. Mission strategy is aggressive and reciprocal, as Jesus says: "If the house is worthy, let your peace come upon it; but if it is not worthy, let your peace return to you" (Mt 10:13). Jesus also warns the disciples that they will face persecution. Yet he affirms that the Spirit will help them in difficult times. They need endurance until they are saved. Meanwhile, they must continue to proclaim the good news of the kingdom to all the towns of Israel (Mt 10:16–23). Jesus encourages them not to fear persecutors but to trust God, who counts even the hairs of their heads (10:26–30). They are of "more value than many sparrows" (10:31). Therefore, they should boldly proclaim the kingdom of God as Jesus did. In Matthew 10:34–39, Jesus again warns that there will be difficult times for the disciples because of him, and he asks them to follow him even at the risk of life. So he says, "Whoever loves father or mother more than me is not worthy of me; and whoever loves son or daughter more than me is not worthy of me; and whoever does not take up the cross and follow me is not worthy of me. Those who find their life will lose it, and those who lose their life for my sake will find it" (Mt 10:37–39). But all the disciples' work must be focused on serving the marginalized, which is the same as welcoming Jesus or following him. So he says, "Whoever welcomes you welcomes me, and whoever welcomes me welcomes the one who sent me" (Mt 10:40) and "Whoever gives even a cup of cold water to one of these little ones" will not lose their reward (10:42). This phrase, "one of these little ones," appears in the parable of the lost sheep (18:14) and in the last judgment parable ("one of the least of these" in 25:40).

TEXTBOX 3.4 *Consider and Discuss*

"ONE OF THESE LITTLE ONES" (MT 10:42)

Matthew uses "one of these little ones" in 10:42 and 18:14 as well as "one of the least of these" in 25:40. Read these three instances where the notion of the little one appears. Who is this little one (or this group of people)? Does each instance point to a different group of people? Or do the three instances point to the same group? Are they marginalized members in the Christian community? Are they Christian missionaries? Or are they another form of marginalized people in society? How does "one of these little ones" relate to Matthew's theology or ethics?

11:1–12:50, Jesus's Ministry Continues while Opposition Arises

After teaching his twelve disciples, Jesus continues to proclaim the good news of the kingdom in many cities, and he confronts the world. John the Baptist, who is now in prison, sends his disciples to Jesus to check whether he is the Messiah. John's action is hardly understandable, because he earlier says, "I baptize you with water for repentance, but one who is more powerful than I is coming after me; I am not worthy to carry his sandals. He will baptize you with the Holy Spirit and fire" (Mt 3:11). He also baptizes Jesus (3:17) and hears the divine voice that says, "This is my Son" (3:17). But probably because John is in prison, he is fearful about his future. Jesus answers, "Go and tell John what you hear and see: the blind receive their sight, the lame walk, the lepers are cleansed, the deaf hear, the dead are raised, and the poor have good news brought to them. And blessed is anyone who takes no offense at me" (Mt 11:4–6). Then the story turns swiftly to Jesus's positive saying about John: "Among those born of women no one has arisen greater than John the Baptist" (11:11). Jesus commends him because John has done his best in teaching the kingdom of God, even though people did not change their minds. So he laments over unrepentant cities such as Chorazin, Bethsaida, and Capernaum, and compares them with Gentile cities: Tyre, Sidon, and Sodom (Mt 11:23–24).

Then Jesus invites people to take his yoke, which is paradoxical because the yoke must be heavy and difficult (Mt 11:28–30). But he says his yoke is easy because when people follow Jesus, they find peace and rest in him. It is easy because he is gentle and humble in heart. So they can learn from his embodiment of God's righteousness. But the Pharisee's yoke differs from Jesus's because the law is absolute without exceptions. Here, the point is not that all Pharisees are legalistic or hypocritical but that Jesus points out specific cases where some Pharisees have accused him of breaking the Sabbath. One day, the disciples of Jesus had gone through the grain fields on the Sabbath, plucked heads of grain, and eaten them (Mt 12:1–8). Jesus's point is the law must be flexible and contextual. He interprets scripture and says that David and his hungry companions entered the house of God and ate the bread, which was not for them to eat but only for the priests (Mt 12:3–4; cf. 1 Sm 21:6). Jesus also says that the priests in the temple on the Sabbath break the Sabbath and yet are guiltless (Mt 12:5; cf. Nm 28:9). The priests did not do wrong by preparing offerings and other works related to their priesthood. Jesus's point is that the true Sabbath means mercy and love. The Son of Man came for that purpose (Mt 12:8; cf. Mark 2:23; Luke 6:1). Later, Jesus enters their synagogue and finds a man with a withered hand. The Pharisees ask Jesus, "Is it lawful to cure on the Sabbath?" (Mt 12:10). He answers, "It is lawful to do good on the Sabbath," as saving a person out of the ditch is the purpose of the Sabbath (12:12). From this time onward, the Pharisees plot to kill him. Knowing this, Jesus departs, and many crowds follow him (Mt 12:15). Then the narrator quotes Isaiah 42:1–4 to confirm Jesus as God's chosen Messiah, who "will proclaim justice to the Gentiles. . . . He will not break a bruised reed or quench a smoldering wick until he brings justice to victory" (Mt 12:18–21). As the Messiah, Jesus, asks for repentance, Jewish leaders must repent and seek God's will (12:22–50). Ultimately, their true miracle must be repentance, which will bear fruit. The repentant persons will do the will of God in heaven, as they are the children of God (12:50).

13:1–53, Third Discourse: Collections of Parables

Most of the parables in Matthew are found in chapter 13. Matthew borrows some important parables from Mark: the sower and the mustard seed. In chapter 13, there are also unique parables—for example, those of the wheat and weeds, treasure, pearl, and net. There are also other important unique parables, such as the unforgiving servant (Mt 18:23–35) and the vineyard laborers (20:1–16). Since we reviewed parables in Matthew earlier, there is no need to reiterate what is there. However, we need to know that the Matthean parables reinforce Matthean theology—for example, the importance of serving the marginalized (lost sheep) and God's immense forgiveness (unforgiving servant).

13:54–17:27, Jesus Continues with His Mission and Foretells His Death and Resurrection

Jesus came to his hometown and taught the people in their synagogue (Mt 13:54; cf. Luke 4:16–30). They are amazed by his teaching and ask, "Is not this the carpenter's son? Is not his mother called Mary?" (Mt 13:55). Yet Matthew is careful about the image of Jesus. For example, in Mark, Jesus is called the carpenter, the son of Mary (Mark 6:3). But in Matthew, he is called the carpenter's son. Perhaps Matthew is bothered by Mark's description of Jesus being a carpenter since he was born as the Son of David. Also, unlike Luke, Matthew does not include harsh responses from Jesus's hometown people when he is teaching. In Luke 4:16–30, they are mad because of Jesus's preaching on Gentile preference. But Matthew does not include that part of the story. Simply, he says they take offense at him. Then Jesus says, "Prophets are not without honor except in their own country and in their own house" (Mt 13:57). He stops doing work there "because of their unbelief" (13:58).

After the rejection at his hometown and hearing of the death of John the Baptist (Mt 14:1–12), Jesus does more healing work (e.g., the sick at Gennesaret, the Canaanite woman's daughter, many at the Sea of Galilee). Among others, the Canaanite woman's story stands out (15:21–28). Unlike the Syrophoenician woman's story in Mark 7:24–30, this story of the Canaanite woman emphasizes the woman's faith and challenges Jewish exclusivism. Given Matthew's portrayal of Jesus as the Jewish Messiah, Jesus limits his mission to "the lost sheep of the house of Israel" (Mt 15:28; cf. 10:5–6) and refuses to heal the daughter of the Canaanite woman. His disciples also intervene and push Jesus to "send her away, for she keeps shouting after [them]" (15:23). Jesus even calls the Gentiles "dogs" (15:26). But this woman persists in her request because she believes that the Messiah must bless her and her daughter. In other words, she thinks she also deserves God's blessing. Finally, Jesus acknowledges her faith and exclaims, "O! Woman, great is your faith!" (Mt 15:28).

> TEXTBOX 3.5 *Consider and Discuss*
>
> **JESUS AND THE CANAANITE WOMAN (MT 15:21–28)**
>
> In Matthew 15:21–28, Jesus encounters a Canaanite woman who desperately seeks her daughter's healing. The disciples urge him not to bother and to send her away. He is adamant about his mission priority for the Jews and so is very harsh, rejecting her plea: "It is not fair to take the children's food and throw it to the dogs" (Mt 15:26). But the woman is persistent, and eventually, he allows for her daughter's healing. How can we respond to Jesus's demeanor in this story? In what way does the Matthean Jesus reflect Matthew's community? What is this faith of hers that Jesus acknowledges—namely, is it submissive faith or a challenging one? Is her faith in God or in Jesus or both? From Matthew's perspective, what community issues are dealt with here?

Jesus continues his work and feeds the crowds twice, one time with the five thousand, besides women and children (Mt 14:13–21; cf. Mark 6:34–44; Luke 9:10–17; and John 6:1–14); the other time, with the four thousand, besides women and children (Mt 15:32–39; cf. Mark 8:1–10). Only Matthew mentions the presence of women and children among those fed. Jesus has compassion for the crowds who are hungry in a deserted place. In the former miracle, five loaves and two fish are used for feeding the five thousand. The leftovers are twelve baskets full. But in the latter miracle, seven loaves and a few small fish are used for feeding the four thousand. The leftover is only seven baskets full. After feeding the five thousand, Jesus walks on the water to see how his disciples are doing in their boat

(Mt 14:22–33; cf. Mark 6:45–52). They think Jesus is a ghost, so they are terrified. Jesus encourages them not to fear him, because he is not a ghost. Then, all of a sudden, Peter wants to walk on the water just like Jesus, but he soon begins to sink because he is afraid. Jesus saves him, saying, "You of little faith, why did you doubt?" (Mt 14:31). This "little faith" is compared with Jesus's rebuking of the disciples in Mark 4:35–41, when he stills the storm: "Why are you afraid? Have you still no faith?" (Mark 4:40).

Jesus also engages the Pharisees and scribes who've asked him about purity laws (Mt 15:1–9). They complain about his disciples not washing their hands before eating. Jesus's answer is so simple that mere law keeping for the sake of one's tradition is hollow. The point is in whether one sincerely cares for others. So he quotes Isaiah 29:13: "This people honors me with their lips, but their hearts are far from me; in vain do they worship me, teaching human precepts as doctrines" (Mt 15:8–9). He also says, "It is not what goes into the mouth that defiles a person, but it is what comes out of the mouth that defiles" (15:11).

After engaging with the Pharisees and warning the disciples about their teaching, Jesus comes into Caesarea Philippi and asks the disciples, "Who do people say that the Son of Man is?" (Mt 16:13). Peter says it right: "You are the Messiah, the Son of the living God" (16:16). Peter's confession about Jesus is similar to that in Mark 8:27–33 and Luke 9:18–22. But in the details, Jesus's response to Peter differs here from in Mark or Luke. He blesses Peter and says, "For flesh and blood has not revealed this to you, but my Father in heaven" (Mt 16:17). Furthermore, he states, "You are Peter, and on this rock I will build my church, and the gates of Hades will not prevail against it" (16:18). The use of "my church" is seen only in Matthew. This saying shows Matthew's desire to build a community based on Jesus's teaching. Peter is given honor and authority: "I will give you the keys of the kingdom of heaven, and whatever you bind on earth will be bound in heaven, and whatever you loose on earth will be loosed in heaven" (Mt 16:19). But soon, when Jesus talks about his suffering (in 16:21 and again in 17:22), Peter rebukes him because he believes it should never happen to Jesus. In return, Jesus reproves Peter because he does not set his mind on divine things (16:23). So Jesus teaches his disciples, saying, "If any want to become my followers, let them deny themselves and take up their cross and follow me. For those who want to save their life will lose it, and those who lose their life for my sake will find it" (Mt 16:24–25).

Then, six days later, Jesus goes up a high mountain with Peter, James, and his brother John. There he is transfigured (Mt 17:1–13; cf. Mark 9:2–8; Luke 9:28–36). As in his baptism, a voice from the cloud says, "This is my Son, the Beloved; with him I am well pleased; listen to him!" (Mt 17:5). This means his disciples must listen to his passion prediction and get ready for the way of the cross. After the transfiguration, Jesus cures a boy with a demon (Mt 17:14–20). When his disciples come to ask why they cannot cast a demon out, Jesus answers, "Because of your little faith" (17:20).

18:1–35, Fourth Discourse: Community Instructions

Matthew 18 is called community discourse because it deals with community issues, such as the right ethical attitude toward others (Mt 18:1–5), the need for caring for the marginalized ("one of these little ones"; 18:6–14), correcting wrongs (18:15–20), and forgiveness (18:21–35). A wise person must be humble like children and should not "put a stumbling block before one of these little ones" (18:6), who includes the marginalized and children. A great person "[does] not despise one of these little ones" (Mt 18:10). The care of "one of these little ones" is indeed a dominating theme in Matthew's Gospel, as it appears frequently (10:42; 18:6, 10, 14; 25:40, 45). The same theme is also found in the parable of the lost sheep (18:12–14), where Jesus asks, "If a shepherd has a hundred sheep, and one of them has gone astray, does he not leave the ninety-nine on the mountains and go in search of the one that went astray?" (18:12). One sheep has not been merely lost but led astray. Therefore, the shepherd must put the lost sheep back into the fold. God in heaven does not want "one of these little ones" to be lost. To correct wrongs, a faulty person must be dealt with carefully; the conversation must begin with a one-on-one meeting, move to a group of witnesses, and finally, to the community/church (Mt 18:15–20). The other important community issue is forgiveness. Peter thinks forgiving seven times is enough, but Jesus asks him to do it seventy-seven times (Mt 18:21–22). To illustrate the importance of forgiveness, Jesus tells a parable about an unforgiving servant (18:23–35). A king forgives his servant, who owes him ten thousand talents, amounting to sixty million denarii. But this servant does not forgive his fellow, who owes him only a hundred denarii, a tiny amount by comparison. He even seizes his fellow by the throat, and this poor fellow servant pleads with him, "Have patience with me, and I will pay you" (Mt 18:29). In the end he is put into prison because of one hundred denarii. Later, the master/king knows what happened because the other servants have reported it to him. Then the forgiven-yet-unforgiving servant is punished because of his careless mind. This punishment reflects Matthew's theology that while God's compassion is abundant, there will be a judgment on the last day.

19:1–20:34, Jesus Continues to Teach on the Way to Jerusalem

Jesus engages some Pharisees because they've asked him, "Is it lawful for a man to divorce his wife for any cause?" (Mt 19:3). His answer is similar to what he says in Mark 2:1–12. Divorce is not allowed, because God makes two become one flesh. But Matthew allows for an exception in that a man divorces his wife for unchastity. Then children are brought to Jesus, and he blesses them, as he'd embraced them earlier, in 18:1–5. After this, someone approaches Jesus and asks, "Teacher, what good deed must I do to have eternal life?" (Mt 19:16; compare this with Mark 10:17 in which a young man begins his question with "Good teacher"). Jesus answers, "Why do you ask me about what is good?" (Mt 19:17; compare this with Mark 10:18, where he says, "Why do you call me good?"). This young man has kept all the commandments. But Jesus says he lacks one thing: selling all his possessions and giving the money to the poor. Then the man goes away grieving, for he was rich. Jesus explains to his disciples how hard it is for a rich person to enter the kingdom of heaven. The problem is in not sharing what one has with others. Then Jesus tells a story about economic justice in the parable of the vineyard laborers (Mt 20:1–16). This parable is about a vineyard landowner who is atypical in his treatment of laborers. He cares for full employment and adequate pay for all hired. See below for more about this parable, and discuss it.

TEXTBOX 3.6 *Consider and Discuss*

VINEYARD LABORERS (20:1–16)

One issue in the parable of the vineyard laborers is a matter of justice. Does this parable talk about attributive justice or distributive justice? The former operates with the principle that more work will get more pay. The latter considers economic justice for all by distributing a fair income. The proponents of the former would say the landlord is wrong and abusive to the workers because he pays the same, usual daily wage regardless of their work hours. But there is no guarantee that the early comers worked harder than the others. They agreed to work for a usual daily wage. Those who support the notion of distributive justice would say that the landlord is good (*agathos*) because he is concerned with the needs of all the workers. The landlord's concern is to give work opportunities to people who unfortunately did not get the job early. He probably understood why they were late to the market. Perhaps they were late because of taking care of family business, or they looked sick. With the above in mind, how do you understand the Greek adjective *agathos*, which means "good." Does it relate to God's character, as Jesus refers to God as good (Mark 10:18)? Or does it mean simply "generous," as most English translations, such as the NRSVue, NIV, and CEB, translate it?

On the way to Jerusalem, Jesus tells the disciples a third time that he must suffer and die (Mt 20:17–19), but they do not understand it. They are more interested in the rank or position they hold within the "Jesus movement." The mother of James and John comes to Jesus and asks for better places for her sons in the future kingdom. Here, we see Matthew saving the two disciples' reputations because he says those who'd come to Jesus were not James and John but only their mother. But in Mark, the two disciples do come to Jesus (Mark 10:35). In Matthew the other disciples are mad at these two brothers because their mother seeks out Jesus for her sons. Then Jesus tells them, "The Son of Man came not to be served but to serve, and to give his life a ransom for many" (Mt 20:28; cf. Mark 10:45). In contrast with the disciples' lack of faith in Jesus, two blind men are humble and seek mercy from Jesus (Mt 20:29–34). As a result, they regain their sight and follow him.

21:1–23:39, Jesus Enters Jerusalem and Confronts Leaders

Matthew reproduces most of Mark 11:1–12:40 for the story of Jesus in Jerusalem. Jesus triumphantly enters Jerusalem, sitting on a donkey and a colt (two animals). In Mark 11:1–6, Jesus rides on a colt (one animal), which is close to Zechariah 9:9, where a donkey is restated as a colt. The prophet says the future king is humble and is riding on a donkey—that is, on a colt, the foal of a donkey. Given Zechariah 9:9 in this context and the one donkey in Mark, Matthew's reference to two animals seems odd. Entering Jerusalem, Jesus cleanses the temple and cures the blind and the lame in the temple. After this he curses a fig tree because there is no fruit, only leaves. But Matthew omits the phrasing "for it was not the season for figs," which is found in Mark 11:13. This omission is understandable because the fig tree is not responsible for fruit if it is not in good season. In Jerusalem, Jesus's authority is questioned and challenged by the Pharisees and scribes. But he defends himself by answering about taxes, the resurrection, the greatest commandment, and David's son. Concerning tax, he says, what belongs to God is God's. Regarding resurrection, God is the God of the living. The greatest commandment is the love of God and the love of neighbor. David's son cannot be the Messiah, because David was the Messiah.

Then Jesus gives a long list of woes to the Jewish leaders (Mt 23:1–36). They are called hypocrites. Here, all kinds of hypocrisy are named. For example, they teach well, but they do not do what they teach (Mt 23:2). They offer money to God, but they do not care about justice, mercy, and faith (23:23). They "clean the outside of the cup and of the plate, but inside they are full of greed and self-indulgence" (23:25); they are "like whitewashed tombs, which on the outside look beautiful, but inside they are full of the bones of the dead and of all kinds of filth" (23:27). They "build the tombs of the prophets and decorate the graves of the righteous"

(23:29). All these vitriolic sayings about the scribes and Pharisees reflect Matthew's conflict/confrontation with the synagogue (cf. 23:37–39).

24:1–25:46, Fifth Discourse: Sermon on Eschatology

Jesus gives a variety of eschatological sermons, much of which come from the Markan passion narrative. He tells his disciples that the temple will be thrown down and there will be signs of the end of the age. False teachers will arise, and there will be rumors of wars. There will be persecutions for the followers of Jesus. There will also be the desolating sacrilege (Mt 24:15–28), "but the one who endures to the end will be saved" (24:13). The end will come only after "this good news of the kingdom will be proclaimed throughout the world" (24:14). The Son of Man will come shortly, so people must be ready for that day (24:29–31). People know that summer is near when the branch of the fig tree becomes tender. Likewise, they must know the Son of Man is near (Mt 24:32–35). So they should always be watchful because "about that day and hour no one knows, neither the angels of heaven, nor the Son, but only the Father" (24:36). Then Jesus tells three eschatological parables. In the parable of the ten bridesmaids, the point is that people should be ready for the last day. In the parable of the talents, they should do their best, using their talents. In the parable of the judgment of the nations, they must care for "one of the least of these" (Mt 25:45; cf. 10:42; 18:14).

26:1–27:66, Passion Narrative

Matthew uses the Markan passion narrative without much change. The exception is the death of Judas, which is unique to Matthew (Mt 27:3–10). The chief priests and elders have had the plot to kill Jesus since before the Passover. At Bethany a woman pours oil on the head of Jesus to show appreciation for his love and care for her. Then, soon after Judas agrees to betray Jesus, Jesus has a Passover meal with his disciples and institutes the Lord's Supper. Peter's denial is foretold. Jesus then prays at Gethsemane and asks God, "My Father, if it is possible, let this cup pass from me; yet not what I want but what you want" (Mt 26:39; cf. Mark 14:36). Soon, he is arrested and brought before the high priest. His charge is blasphemy because he is called the Messiah and the Son of God (Mt 26:63–68). He answers Pilate that he is the King of the Jews (27:11). Claiming kingship without Rome's approval is sedition, but Pilate does not charge him. Because of his wife's dream, Pilate wants to release Jesus (instead of Barabbas), but the Jews oppose him and want Jesus to be crucified. They shout, "His blood be on us and on our children" (Mt 27:25). Matthew implies that Jesus's crucifixion results not from Rome but from the Jews' charging of Jesus with blasphemy. But Jesus's political charge is hidden in the narrative because his words and deeds are against Rome. At his death, Jesus cries out with a loud voice: "My God, my God, why have you forsaken me?" (Mt 12:46; Mark 15:34). After Jesus dies, the curtain of the temple is torn in two. But Matthew tells more than Mark does: "The earth shook, and the rocks were split. The tombs also were opened, and many bodies of the saints who had fallen asleep were raised" (27:51-52). Then the centurion says, "Truly this man was God's Son!" (27:54). There were also many women, watching Jesus's crucifixion from a distance; "they had followed Jesus from Galilee and had provided for him. Among them were Mary Magdalene, and Mary the mother of James and Joseph, and the mother of the sons of Zebedee" (Mt 27: 55–56). Later, Jesus is buried by Joseph of Arimathea, who is a disciple of Jesus but otherwise unknown in the narrative. Matthew adds more to the Markan burial story of Jesus. The next day, the chief priests and Pharisees gather and worry that Jesus's body will be stolen by people who will say that he was raised. So they arrange for the guard to make the tomb secure by sealing the stone (Mt 27:66).

> TEXTBOX 3.7   **Consider and Discuss**
>
> **"HIS BLOOD BE ON US AND ON OUR CHILDREN!" (MT 27:25)**
>
> In Matthew 27:25, "all the people answered: 'His blood be on us and on our children!'" For a long time throughout Christian history, there has been a misunderstanding that all Jews at all times must be held accountable for Jesus's death. But here, "all the people" (*pas ho laos*) does not mean all Jews throughout history; this phrase refers to all those who were there, responding to Pilate. In the crucifixion narrative, those who were more directly involved in Jesus's death are identified as Pilate, the leaders of Jerusalem, and the Roman soldiers. Discuss the impact of Matthew 27:25 on Jewish-Christian relations.

28:1–20, The Resurrection of Jesus

After the Sabbath Mary Magdalene and the other Mary visit the tomb. With a great earthquake, an angel of the Lord comes from heaven and rolls back the stone. He tells the women, "Do not be afraid; I know that you are looking for Jesus who was crucified. He is not here; for he has been raised, as he said. Come, see the place where he lay" (Mt 28:5–6). The angel also tells them to report this good news to the disciples of Jesus. Unlike the resurrection account in Mark 16, Matthew says that "the women [leave] the tomb quickly with fear and great joy, and [run] to tell his disciples" (28:8). They also meet Jesus on the way, who says, "Greetings!" (28:9). Jesus encourages them, saying: "Do not be afraid; go and tell my brothers to go to Galilee; there they will see me" (28:10). After this, Matthew talks about the conspiracy theory being planned by the chief priests and the elders in which they'd spread the word that Jesus's body was stolen by his disciples. The final scene of Matthew's narrative is the commissioning of the disciples (28:16–20). Unlike his earlier position toward the Gentiles in Matthew 10:5–15 and 15:21–28, where Jesus has prevented the disciples from entering Gentile regions, the risen Lord now commissions them for all nations.

QUESTIONS FOR REFLECTION

1. How does Matthew portray Jesus? What is his primary work as the Jewish Messiah?
2. Talk about the genealogy of Jesus in Matthew's Gospel with a focus on its differences from Luke's.
3. Why does Matthew include the story about Jesus's escape to Egypt and return to Israel?
4. In what way does Jesus have parallels with Moses, and what is the significance of those parallels?
5. Is Matthew's Gospel against Judaism? If not, to what degree does Matthew and/or Matthew's community embrace Jewish laws and customs?
6. Is the so-called great commission in 28:16–20 conducive to colonialism? Why are women not included in the disciples of Jesus?

FURTHER READING

Aune, David E, ed. *The Gospel of Matthew in Current Study: Studies in Memory of William G. Thompson, S. J.* Grand Rapids, MI: William B. Eerdmans, 2001.

Brown, Michael J. "The Gospel of Matthew." In *True to Our Native Land: An African American New Testament Commentary*, edited by Brian K. Blount, Cain H. Felder, Clarice J. Martin, and Emerson B. Powery, 85–120. Minneapolis, MN: Fortress, 2007.

Carter, Warren. *Matthew: Storyteller, Interpreter, Evangelist.* 2nd ed. Peabody, MA: Hendrickson, 2004.

Cho, Jae Hyung. "The Gospel of Matthew." In *An Asian Introduction to the New Testament*, edited by Johnson Thomaskutty, 47–73. Minneapolis, MN: Fortress, 2022.

Culpepper, R. Alan. *Matthew: A Commentary.* Louisville, KY: Westminster John Knox, 2022.

Duarte, Alejandro Alberto. "Matthew." In *Global Bible Commentary*, edited by Daniel Patte, 350–60. Nashville, TN: Abingdon Press, 2005.

Dube, Musa. *Postcolonial Feminist Interpretation of the Bible*. St. Louis, MO: Chalice Press, 2000.
France, R. T. *The Gospel of Mark*. Grand Rapids, MI: William B. Eerdmans, 2014.
Gale, Aaron M. "The Gospel According to Matthew." In *The Jewish Annotated New Testament*, edited by Amy-Jill Levine and Marc Zvi Brettler, 9–66. New York: Oxford University Press, 2017.
Gench, Frances Taylor. *Wisdom in the Christology of Matthew*. Lanham, MD: University Press of America, 1997.
Glancy, Jennifer A. *Slavery in Early Christianity*. Minneapolis, MN: Fortress, 2006.
Kampen, John. *Matthew within Sectarian Judaism*. New Haven: Yale University Press, 2019.
Kim, Yung Suk. *Resurrecting Jesus: The Renewal of New Testament Theology*. Eugene, OR: Cascade Books, 2015.
Kingsbury, Jack Dean. *Matthew as Story*. Philadelphia, PA: Fortress, 1988.
Levine, Amy-Jill, ed. *A Feminist Companion to Matthew*. Sheffield, England: Sheffield Academic Press, 1998.
Luz, Ulrich. *The Theology of the Gospel of Matthew*. Cambridge, England: Cambridge University Press, 1995.
Overman, J. Andrew. *Church and Community in Crisis: The Gospel According to Matthew*. Harrisburg, PA: Trinity Press International, 1996.
Powell, Mark Allan. *God with Us: A Pastoral Theology of Matthew's Gospel*. Minneapolis, MN: Fortress, 1995.
Reid, Barbara. *The Gospel According to Matthew*. Vol. 1. New Collegeville Bible Commentary. Collegeville, MN: Liturgical Press, 2005.
Ruiz, Gilberto A. "Matthew: Negotiating Tradition and Identity in Matthean and Latinx Contexts." In *Latinx Perspectives on the New Testament*, edited by Osvaldo D. Vena and Leticia A. Guardiola-Saenz, 11–32. Lanham, MD: Lexington Books, 2022.
Senior, Donald. *What Are They Saying about Matthew?* Mahwah, NJ: Paulist Press, 1996.
Smith, Mitzi J., and Jayachitra Lalitha, eds. *Teaching All Nations: Interrogating the Matthean Great Commission*. Minneapolis, MN: Fortress, 2014.

NOTES

1. Matthew 1:23; 2:5b–6, 15b, 17–18, 23b; 3:3; 4:14–16; 8:17; 12:17–21; 13:14–15, 35; 21:4–5; 26:56; and 27:9–10.

2. Babylonian Talmud, *Shabbat*, 31a. On another note, Confucius, a Chinese philosopher in the sixth century BCE, also says this: "Do not do to others what you would not want others to do to you" (*Analects* 15:24).

3. See Dorothy Lee, "Matthew's Gospel and Judaism," Jewish Christian Relations, accessed May 23, 2023, https://www.jcrelations.net/article/matthews-gospel-and-judaism.html.

4. Babylonian Talmud, *Shabbat*, 31a.

Chapter 4

The Gospel of Luke

Historically, the Gospel of Luke has received mixed responses from its readers. While some appreciate the Gospel's social justice message, others point out its conservative reaction to the Roman Empire. On the one hand, the radical social gospel message is clear. For example, Mary's Magnificat in Luke 1:46–55 challenges the status of the Roman Empire and the elite patron-client system. Mary exalts the Lord: "He has shown strength with his arm; he has scattered the proud in the imagination of their hearts. He has brought down the powerful from their thrones and lifted up the lowly; he has filled the hungry with good things and sent the rich away empty" (Luke 1:51–53). Jesus also appears as a social prophet and reads Isaiah 61:1–2: "The Spirit of the Lord is upon me, because he has anointed me to bring good news to the poor. . . . to set free those who are oppressed, . . . to proclaim the year of the Lord's favor" (Luke 4:18–19). However, because of Luke's interest in the Gentile mission as well as his need for survival and growth under the Roman Empire, the Gospel tends to be like a blunt sword against the Empire.[1] For instance, in the parable of the rich man and Lazarus (Luke 16:19–31), the problem is not that the man was rich but that he did not take care of Lazarus. How he became rich is not the issue. In the episode of a young, rich ruler (Luke 18:18–23), when Jesus asks him to sell everything and share it all with the poor, the ruler does not go away even when he feels sad, whereas, in Mark, he goes away. The other aspects that are like a blunt sword are also noted. In the Lukan beatitudes (6:20–23), there is no beatitude saying, "Blessed are the meek, for they will inherit the earth," which appears in Matthew 5:5. Maybe it is because the land is an untouchable source of wealth and social status. Also, the Lukan Jesus is portrayed as an innocent prophet, who dies because of the Jews' misunderstanding, not because of his politically dangerous, revolutionary challenge to Rome. Pilate keeps saying he cannot find fault with Jesus, and a Roman centurion says he is innocent (Luke 23:47). Luke seems to appeal to the Roman elites and claims that Christianity is not antisocial or anti-imperial; it is an innocuous gospel. Seen from the above perspectives, it becomes apparent that Luke's Gospel was written to the Roman world to defend Christianity. In other words, the Gospel of Luke is an apology. But some scholars argue that Luke's Gospel was addressed to the internal members of the Lukan community, or Christians.[2] In other words, it was written to provide legitimation for their place in society and in the Christian faith. Legitimation theory explains the need for comforting and supporting Christians living in an unstable, harsh world. So the Gospel of Luke legitimates their Christian beliefs and practices, and it empowers them to stay in the faith.

Compared to Matthew, Luke deviates from Mark a great deal, and he edits Markan materials in his context. He also uses a third source, Q, and includes materials unique to the gospel of Luke, such as infancy narratives, parables, and healing materials. Using all the available sources, Luke writes to the Gentiles and presents Jesus as the savior of the world (1:69; 2:11). So the Lukan genealogy connects Jesus to Adam, son of God. This suggests that Jesus is the savior for all humans. This genealogy in Luke differs from the one in Matthew, where Jesus is connected with his Jewish lineage as the son of David and the son of Abraham. Likewise, in Luke, Jesus preaches that God sent Elijah and Elisha to help and heal the Gentiles first, even when there were many widows and lepers in Israel (4:25–27). The Lukan Jesus is very different from the Matthean Jesus, who is sent only to the lost sheep of the house of Israel (Mt 15:21–28). The Lukan Jesus emphasizes that he has come to seek and save the lost (Luke 19:10), who are sinners, tax collectors, and Gentiles. Three "lost" parables support this theme of saving the lost (15:1–32). The Lukan Jesus also preaches the good news to the poor and dies a prophetic death. He is never agitated or anguished about his suffering and death; he asks people in Jerusalem not to weep for him but to weep for themselves (Luke 23:28). He calmly prays, "Father, forgive them; for they do not know what they are doing" (23:34). He does not utter the "My God, my God, why have you forsaken me?" (Mark 15:34). Rather, he says, "Father, into your hands I commend my spirit" (Luke 23:46).

Luke brings some resolution to the delay of Parousia with an emphasis on "today" (*sēmeron*).[3] The kingdom of God is in the here and now. When the Pharisees ask about the kingdom of God, Jesus says, "The kingdom of God is not coming with things that can be observed; nor will they say, 'Look, here it is!' or 'There it is!' For, in fact, the kingdom of God is among you" (Luke 17:20–21). The solution to the delay of Parousia is not to focus on future eschatology but to redirect the community's attention and energy to the work of God or the Spirit "today." Indeed, the savior was "born today in the city of David" (Luke 2:11). "Today this scripture has been fulfilled in your hearing" (4:21). Salvation came to Zacchaeus's house "today" (19:9). Today a thief will be in paradise with Jesus (24:43).

TEXTBOX 4.1 *Luke's Gospel at a Glance*

DATE

Luke was likely written around 85–90 CE, after the fall of Jerusalem.

AUTHOR

The author is anonymous. According to the church tradition, the author of the Gospel of Luke is either Luke the physician (Col 4:14) or Paul's companion Luke (Phlm 24; 2 Tm 4:11; cf. Acts 16:10–17; 20:5–15; 21:1–18; 27:1–28:16).

PLACE

The place of composition is unknown; however, one possibility is Antioch. Eusebius and Jerome refer to Luke as a person of Antioch (see also, Acts 11:19–15:40; 18:22–23).

SOURCE

Mark is one primary source; Q is another important source. There are also a good number of unique materials in Luke. Luke's style of Greek is more elaborate than Mark's (cf. Mark 9:5; Luke 9:33).

AUDIENCE

The audience is predominantly Gentile Christians and Jewish Christians in the Diaspora.

HOW IT BEGINS

Luke begins with a historical preface, arguing that he examines the past and writes an orderly account. Later the Roman event is mentioned: Emperor Augustus's order of registration at their hometown. But there was no census at the time of Jesus's birth. The census was in 6 CE. Luke continues with an infancy narrative in which Jesus's genealogy is traced from the bottom up: Joseph to Adam, son of God. Luke emphasizes Jesus's lowly birth in a manger and the shepherds' announcement of the good news.

HOW IT ENDS

Luke ends with Jesus explaining the scriptures on the way to Emmaus and instructs his disciples to gather in Jerusalem.

ESCHATOLOGY

Luke's eschatology emphasizes "today," resulting from the delay of Parousia (Luke 17:21).

JESUS

Jesus, portrayed as the Jewish prophet, came to seek and save the lost (Luke 19:10).

DISCIPLES

The disciples are not perfect, but they are full of potential.

HUMAN CONDITION

The human condition in Luke is that people do not know who the Messiah is. Also, the human condition is that of a society without mercy and inequalities in wealth and power.

TRANSFORMATION

The solution to the problem is for the people to know that Jesus is the Messiah and repent of their sins. Also, people must seek a society of mercy, sharing wealth, and the equal opportunity to engage the power to serve.

UNIQUE CONTENT

3:23–38, Genealogy of Jesus: from Joseph to Adam
4:16–30, Jesus's initial preaching and his rejection at Nazareth
6:20–49, Sermon on the plain: "Blessed are you who are poor (not in spirit), blessed are you who hunger now, blessed who weep now, and Woe to you who are rich"
7:36–50, A woman sinner wets Jesus's feet with her tears
8:1–3, The ministering women: Mary Magdalene, Joanna, Susanna
10:1–12, Mission of the seventy
10:38–42, Mary and Martha: Mary listening to Jesus, Martha working in the kitchen
19:1–10, Zacchaeus at Jericho
23:28, Lamentation over Jerusalem: "Daughters of Jerusalem, do not weep for me"
23:43, "Today you will be with me in paradise"
24:13–53, The road to Emmaus

UNIQUE HEALINGS

5:1–11, Large catch of fish
7:11–17, The son of the widow of Nain, raised
17:11–19, Lepers healed, but only one returns and thanks

UNIQUE PARABLES

10:29–37, A Samaritan
11:5–8, Friends at midnight
12:13–21, Rich fool
13:6–9, Barren fig tree
14:16–24, Great banquet
15:8–10, Lost coin
15:11–32, Lost son (father and two sons)
16:1–13, Dishonest steward
16:19–31, Rich man and Lazarus
18:1–8, Unjust judge and widow
18:9–14, Pharisee and tax collector

OUTLINE

1:1–4, Prologue
1:5–2:52, Birth and Childhood of Jesus
3:1–4:13, Preparation for the Ministry of Jesus
4:14–9:50, Jesus's Ministry in Galilee
9:51–19:27, On the Way to Jerusalem
19:28–21:38, Jesus's Teaching in Jerusalem
22:1–23:56, The Suffering and Death of Jesus
24:1–53, The Resurrection of Jesus

THE LUKAN JESUS

There are several characteristics of the Lukan Jesus. First, he is portrayed as the savior of the world; he has come to seek and save the lost, especially the Gentiles. The genealogy of Jesus traces back to Adam, son of God, to indicate that he is the Messiah for the whole world and all people. The Lukan genealogy affirms the importance of the whole of humanity, which is in contrast with the Matthean genealogy that traces back to David and Abraham, two foundational figures for Judaism. The Lukan Jesus preaches a God with a more expansive global vision, including a preferential love for the Gentiles (Luke 4:25–27). This expansive vision will be made fully explicit in Luke's second volume, the Acts of the Apostles. He says God sent Elijah and Elisha to two Gentiles though there were many widows and lepers in Israel.

Second, the Lukan Jesus dies as a prophet (Luke 7:16; 23:28, 46), and he is adamant about his prophetic mission. He is not grieved for his death. Rather, he prays for those who kill him (Luke 23:34). He is anointed by the Spirit and brings good news to the poor (4:18; Is 61:1). The Lukan Jesus differs from the presentation of Jesus in Mark or Matthew, where he dies in despair (Mark 14:33–34; 15:34; Mt 27:46).

Third, the Lukan Jesus is characterized with Jewish roots and traditions to appeal to the Gentiles, as anything new in the Roman world is suspicious. He teaches often in the synagogues, as is his custom. He is circumcised on the eighth day and brought to the temple at the age of twelve for consecration. He is recognized by Simeon and Anna in the temple. In Luke, Jesus's last episode in the temptation occurs in the temple, whereas, in Matthew, the temple temptation occurs in the second episode. He instructs his disciples to gather in Jerusalem and wait for the power from on high there.

DISTINCTIVE THEOLOGICAL THEMES

Above all, Luke first emphasizes Christianity's universality. While Luke's Gospel portrays Jesus as the savior for the Gentiles, the book of Acts shows how the story of Jesus moves to the Gentile world. Luke-Acts is a two-volume set, which aims to position Christianity on the world stage. In doing so, Luke tends to portray the good news as innocuous, not as posing a threat to the system of the Roman Empire. Luke has more interest in spreading the gospel to the Gentiles, resulting in a blunt sword strike against the Roman Empire. In other words, Jesus is portrayed as an innocent savior, as the centurion says in Luke 23:47: "Certainly this man was innocent." Pilate keeps saying to Jewish leaders that he cannot find fault with Jesus; he does so three times (23:1–25). Second, however, the innocuous gospel does not exclude some aspects of social justice, because Luke includes radical prophetic messages from Jesus (4:18–19) and Mary's Magnificat (1:46–55). Some of Luke's unique parables emphasize the importance of justice, as seen in the widow and unjust judge (18:1–8) and the care for the marginalized in the Pharisee and tax collector (18:9–14).

Third, Luke likewise emphasizes the down-to-earth perspectives touching on real people's needs. For example, Luke highlights people's presence at the baptism of Jesus while they are also being baptized. They respond to Jesus's crucifixion by beating their breasts (Luke 23:48). The lost people, such as sinners and tax collectors, are found and saved. Zacchaeus, a chief tax collector, is found and saved (Luke 19:1–10). The prodigal son was dead and is alive again (15:24). A people-oriented ministry of Jesus is foreshadowed when he is baptized: "The Holy Spirit descended upon him in bodily form like a dove (3:22).

Fourth, Luke's eschatology is reoriented and emphasizes the importance of today in the global mission initiated by Jesus. It is today that Jesus is seen in the hearts of his followers and society. When women visit the tomb of Jesus, they hear that he is not in the tomb. He must be found in society and their community. Today the poor must be blessed. While the ultimate salvation is yet to come, the joy of a new life is beginning. This view of eschatology differs from that held by Mark and Matthew, who emphasize a more imminent eschatology. Along with his emphasis on today, Luke is on a mission to seek and save the lost, including the Gentiles and the marginalized.

Fifth and lastly, Luke seems more inclusive of women. Luke is positive toward women, as he includes unique stories about women (Luke 8:1–3;10:38–42). Mary seems to be a disciple of Jesus when she listens to him. But it is questionable whether Luke fully recognizes women's apostolic work, as Mary's work is limited to listening rather than teaching. Overall, Luke includes more women than other Gospels do. However, women's faith or potential is not fully recognized. For example, in the parable of the widow and unjust judge (18:1–18), Luke portrays her as a model of prayer. But in the parable proper, Jesus emphasizes the importance of her faith in seeking justice. The widow in this parable is bold and persistent in seeking justice, just like the Canaanite woman in Matthew 15:21–28. She does not stay at home to pray and wait for the result. She goes out to seek justice and does not give up until she is heard. She demands justice because she believes that God must hear her. Even though the judge is evil and careless about her, she keeps bothering him because she trusts in God.

PARABLES IN LUKE

Luke includes a variety of parables in his narrative. Luke borrows some seed parables from Mark and edits them (e.g., the sower and mustard seed). At other times, he uses the Q parables (e.g., the lost sheep and the leaven), shared between Matthew and Luke, and fits them in his context. For example, while Matthew emphasizes the importance of "one of these little ones" in the parable of the lost sheep (Mt 18:10–14), Luke elevates the theme of "the lost" (15:3–7). Luke also includes peculiar parables that complement his theology. The good Samaritan (Luke 10:25–37) calls for a radically new concept of neighbor, defined not by ethnicity or religion but by mercy and compassion. A neighbor is someone who can help others with compassion. Likewise, the parable of the father and two sons in Luke 15:11–32 also emphasizes the father's mercy and compassion for his lost son. While we may read Luke emphasizing repentance/return of the lost son, the more proper reading may be the father's unconditional, compassionate love. The father has forgiven him already and accepted him into his house. However, the true reconciliation among the three family members (father and two sons) is yet to be realized, as the story is open-ended. The parable of the dishonest manager (Luke 16:1–13) shows the importance of care and responsibility for the community. The parable of the rich man and Lazarus (16:19–31) stresses the responsibility of the rich for taking care of the marginalized. The parable of the widow and judge (18:1–8) is a story, from Luke's perspective, about ardent prayer. Lastly, the Pharisee and the tax collector (18:9–14) challenges self-satisfying religiosity that does not see the need of others, especially the marginalized.

NOTABLE INTERPRETATION ISSUES

First, the issue is how to characterize Luke's Gospel since it involves multifaceted meanings or implications. On the one hand, there are social gospel messages in Luke. For instance, Jesus's reading of Isaiah 61:1–2 is unique to Luke and speaks itself for the cause of social justice. But on the other hand, Luke does not seem to challenge Rome, portraying Jesus as an innocent prophet who is considered a victim of the Jews' misunderstanding of their Messiah. So in the end, the question is as follows: Is Luke a radical social gospel or an innocuous gospel? Also, the related issue asks, How we can explain the historical community behind this Gospel? Is it a conservative community that tones down the radical message of Jesus because of the community's survival under Rome? But if we read individual texts—for example, in Luke 4:17–18, as well as elsewhere—certainly, there are social gospel messages. Therefore, ultimately, understanding Luke is a matter of interpretation.

Second, the other interpretive issue is regarding Luke's stance toward Judaism. On the one hand, Jesus is placed within Jewish tradition, ranging from his birth to his synagogue teaching. His parents had taken him to the temple for dedication. But his message is often anti-Jewish, as seen in Luke 4:25–28, where Jesus rebuts the claim that God favors Israel. Also, in allegorical parables such as that of the tenants (Luke 20:9–19) or of the lost son (15:21–34), Luke replaces Israel with the church. How can one reconcile the difference between Jesus's Jewish roots and his anti-Jewish message?

Third, evaluating women characters in Luke is a hard task. Are they positive models of discipleship or objects of charity or models of domesticated faith? In the infancy narratives, Elizabeth, mother of John the Baptist, and Mary, mother of Jesus, appear and take on certain roles in the births of John and Jesus. Elizabeth is righteous along with her husband, Zechariah, a priest. Mary eventually accepts the conception by the Holy Spirit, saying to the angel Gabriel, "Here am I, the servant of the Lord; let it be with me according to your word" (Luke 1:38). Anna, a prophetess, blesses the child Jesus (2:36–38). Jesus heals Simon Peter's mother-in-law (4:38–39), a twelve-year old girl (8:41–42, 49–56), a woman with a twelve-year-long blood flow (8:43–48), and a woman who's been crippled for eighteen years (13:10–17). There are exemplary women: a sinful woman anointing Jesus (7:37–50), Mary listening to Jesus (10:38–42), a woman finding a lost coin (15:8–10), a widow's faith in seeking justice (18:1–5), and a poor widow giving two small coins to the temple (21:1–4). Women follow Jesus in his journey to Jerusalem (8:1–3), observe the crucifixion (23:27, 49), and witness the resurrection (24:1–3). As we see above, the characterizing of all these women's roles or potential is subject to interpretation.

Fourth and lastly, there is a debate on the purpose of the Gospel. Some see it as the gospel of apology, which means it was written to the Gentiles to explain the gospel's harmlessness to the Roman imperial system and to convert them to Christianity. This view is well taken by many because Luke has an interest in the Gentile mission and must defend the gospel for it to survive and grow under the Roman Empire. But others see it as the gospel of legitimation, which means it was written to Christians who struggled to keep faith in the Roman Empire. The gospel messages serve as a symbolic canopy under which those Christians are comforted and assured about their relationships with God and Jesus. This sense of protection from God legitimates their place in society and helps them to sustain their faith.

A CLOSE READING OF LUKE

1:1–4, Preface

The narrator of Luke's Gospel begins with a "historical" preface in which the narrator says the author writes an orderly account of Jesus after having examined all the traditions about him, be they oral or written. Theophilus, the recipient's name, is either a person or a group of Gentile Christians. Luke writes this gospel to Theophilus so that "[he] may know the truth concerning the things about which [he has] been instructed" (1:4). Luke has a clear purpose for writing the Gospel, which is to let readers know "the truth concerning the things about which [they] have been instructed" (1:4). So readers are expected to know the truth about Jesus—what he said and did.

1:5–2:52, Birth and Childhood of Jesus

After the preface the narrator goes on to talk about the birth of John the Baptist and that of Jesus. The birth narrative of Jesus is completely different from that found in the Gospel of Matthew. John's father was Zechariah, a priest, and his mother was Elizabeth. Both of them were righteous before God. They had no children, because Elizabeth was barren. This story sounds like the story of Abraham and Sarah in Genesis, as they also had no children. The angel Gabriel appears to Zechariah and tells him that his wife, Elizabeth, will bear a son, who will be named John. But Zechariah does not believe it, so he is muted until all things foretold come to occur. Elizabeth conceives and says, "This is what the Lord has done for me when he looked favorably on me and took away the disgrace I have endured among my people" (Luke 1:25). Her experience echoes Hannah's story in that she bears Samuel from her disgraceful experience (1 Sm 1:1–2:21). As Samuel was a great prophet, so too will John be a great prophet who prepares the way of the Lord.

Then, six months later, the angel Gabriel appears to Mary, a virgin engaged to Joseph, in Nazareth of Galilee. The angel tells her that she will bear a son and name him Jesus (Luke 1:30). In Matthew's birth account, Joseph has a dream in which an angel tells him that he will name his son Jesus. But here, in Luke, it is Mary who will name her son Jesus. Mary says to the angel, "How can this be, since I am a virgin?" (Luke 1:34). The angel says that the conception is by the Holy Spirit and that "nothing will be impossible with God" (1:37). Then Mary says, "Here am I, the servant of the Lord; let it be with me according to your word" (1:38), which sounds like Isaiah's saying: "Here am I; send me!" (Is 6:8). Her response reflects that of Isaiah to the voice of the Lord: "Whom shall I send, and who will go for us?" (Luke 6:8). Mary also says yes to the angel. Then Mary visits Elizabeth in a Judean town. Elizabeth is very excited about Mary's visit and says, "Blessed are you among women, and blessed is the fruit of your womb" (Luke 1:42). Then Mary gives a song of the fulfillment of the prophet (1:46–55), called the Magnificat, which may be read alongside Hannah's prayer/song in 1 Samuel 2:1–10. Hannah prays, "My heart exults in the Lord; my strength is exalted in my God. . . . Talk no more so very proudly, let not arrogance come from your mouth; The bows of the mighty are broken, but the feeble gird on strength. . . . The Lord makes poor and makes rich; he brings low; he also exalts. He raises up the poor from the dust" (1 Sm 2:1–8). Similarly, Mary says, "My soul magnifies the Lord, and my spirit rejoices in God my Savior, for he has looked with favor on the lowliness of his servant. . . . he has scattered the proud in the thoughts of their hearts. He has brought down the powerful from their thrones, and lifted up the lowly; he has filled the hungry with good things, and sent the rich away empty" (Luke 1:46–53).

After the birth of John (Luke 1:57–66), his father Zechariah is filled with the Spirit and speaks the prophecy about his son. The child will be called the prophet of the Most High and go before the Lord to prepare his ways (1:76). John will give knowledge of salvation by the forgiveness of their sins (1:77) and "guide our feet into the way of peace" (1:79). Here, John's guidance into the way of peace sounds interesting since his message is harsh: "You brood of vipers! Who warned you to flee from the wrath to come?" (Luke 3:7; cf. Mt 3:7). We wonder about "the way of peace" to which John guides people. Certainly, his harsh preaching for repentance will lead to the way of peace. But given the fact that Luke frequently uses the word "peace" throughout the narrative (2:14, 29; 7:50; 8:48; 10:6)—especially the one in Luke 2:14: "Glory to God in the highest heaven, and on earth peace among those whom he favors!"—we also wonder if it has to do with the so-called innocuous gospel, which does not challenge the system of the Roman Empire. On the one hand, Luke implies that peace is important to the lives of Christians, and on the other hand, we wonder if the emphasis on peace along with Luke's portrayal of Jesus as the innocent Messiah has to do with an appeal to Rome, connoting to the imperial power that Christianity is the religion of peace.

Then the narrator tells the birth of Jesus and insinuates that he is a well-versed historian who knows much about the Roman world (Luke 2:1–7). For example, he writes that Emperor Augustus ordered that all the world should be registered—that is, a census—and a census happened during the governorship of Quirinius in Syria. But there was no census at the time of Herod the King. Luke mistakes it, since the first census was taken in 6 CE. According to the imperial order, Joseph and Mary go to Bethlehem from Galilee to register there because he is a descendant of David—in Bethlehem. Then the time comes for her delivery of the child, but the couple cannot find a place for delivery. So she gives birth to her child and lays him in a manger, which signifies Jesus's lowly birth. Likewise, the good news of his birth is announced to the shepherds first. The good news is "To you is born *this day* (*sēmeron*) in the city of David a Savior, who is the Messiah, the Lord" (Luke 2:11). "Today" is important to Luke's eschatology in that the Holy Spirit is working with people *now*—that is, the good news occurs in the here and now because of Jesus, who comes from the city of David but saves the world. The angel sings, "Glory to God in the highest heaven, and on earth peace among those whom he favors!" (Luke 2:14). After the angels left, the shepherds bring the good news to Bethlehem and tell people there. They also go to Mary and Joseph and tell the couple what happened to them. Then "Mary [treasures] all these words and [ponders] them in her heart" (Luke 2:19).

After eight days Jesus is circumcised. Luke emphasizes the Jewishness of Jesus and tells the world that Jesus comes from Jewish origins. This Jewishness of Jesus legitimates Luke's Christian movement because Judaism has been well known; otherwise, all things new are suspicious in the Roman world. So he is presented to the temple, where his parents offer a sacrifice. Simeon, a righteous and devout man in Jerusalem, recognizes the special child of God and thanks God, saying, "Master, now you are dismissing your servant in peace, according to your word; for my eyes have seen your salvation" (Luke 2:29–30). He also says that the child is "a light for revelation to the Gentiles" (2:32). Another prophet, Anna, the daughter of Phanuel, also speaks well about the child. Luke describes this woman in detail: "She was of a great age, having lived with her husband seven years after her marriage, then as a widow to the age of eighty-four" (2:36–37a). She stays in the temple and "[worships] there with fasting and prayer night and day" (2:37b). After all the business in the temple, Mary and Joseph return to Galilee, to their town of Nazareth (2:39). In Luke, Nazareth is Jesus's hometown, whereas, in Matthew, Bethlehem is his hometown. According to Luke, Jesus is born in Bethlehem because Mary and Joseph had to register there by order of Emperor Augustus. But Matthew says Jesus is born in Bethlehem because it is his hometown. Because of Herod's plot to kill Jesus, Joseph and Mary flee to Egypt and later come to settle in Nazareth because they fear Archelaus, son of Herod the Great (Mt 2:1–12).

The narrator now talks about Jesus's childhood episode, which is unique to Luke. At the age of twelve years, Jesus follows his parents as they go to Jerusalem to observe the Passover. The parents think their child has gone with them, but they realize that he has not. They go back to the temple and find him there, talking with Jewish teachers. Mary says to the boy, "Child, why have you treated us like this? Look, your father and I have been searching for you in great anxiety" (Luke 2:48). But the child says, "Why were you searching for me? Did you not know that I must be in my Father's house?" (2:49). Jesus is devoted to the temple and God. Eventually, Jesus goes down to Nazareth with his parents and is obedient to them. Again, the narrator says, "His mother treasured all these things in her heart" (Luke 2:51). Jesus grows in wisdom and "in divine and human favor" (2:52).

3:1–4:13, Preparation for the Ministry of Jesus

Luke follows Mark in talking about John the Baptist's proclamation and ministry as well as the baptism and the temptation of Jesus. Luke emphasizes historical details about the time when John is active in preparing for the way of the Lord—that is, the word of God comes to John in the wilderness "in the fifteenth year of the reign of Emperor Tiberius [29 CE] when Pontius Pilate [is] governor of Judea, and Herod [is] ruler of Galilee, and his brother Philip ruler of the region of Ituraea and Trachonitis, . . . during the high priesthood of Annas and Caiaphas" (Luke 3:1–2). Luke uses these historical details to tell the audience that his Gospel is accurate. In this political world, John the Baptist works and goes into all the region around the Jordan to proclaim "a baptism of repentance for the forgiveness of sins" (Luke 3:3). Then, the prophet Isaiah is quoted as follows: "The voice of one crying out in the wilderness: 'Prepare the way of the Lord, make his paths straight. Every valley shall be filled, and every mountain and hill shall be made low, and the crooked shall be made straight, and the rough ways made smooth. And all flesh shall see the salvation of God'" (Luke 3:4–6; cf. Is 40:3–5). Luke gives an extended quote from Isaiah 40:3–5 but omits Malachi 3:1 ("See, I am sending my messenger ahead of you, who will prepare your way"), as seen in Mark, who conflates Malachi 3:1 with Isaiah 40:3. Luke has a focus on John the Baptist's prophetic work, which is to prepare the way of the Lord and make his paths straight. While in Matthew 3:7, John the Baptist is critical of many Pharisees and Sadducees who have come for baptism, in Luke 3:7, he is critical of the crowds and says, "You brood of vipers! Who warned you to flee from the wrath to come? Bear fruits worthy of repentance" (Luke 3:7–8; Mt 3:7–8). Then the crowds respond, "What should we do?" (Luke 3:10), which is unique to Luke. The crowds' response foreshadows the women's response to Jesus's suffering in Luke 23:27 and the same crowds' response to Jesus's crucifixion in Luke 23:48. In the former, women beat their breasts and wail for Jesus. In the latter, "all the crowds who [have] gathered there for this spectacle [see] what [has] taken place, they return[] home, beating their breasts." John answers, "Whoever has two coats must share with anyone who has none; and whoever has food must do likewise" (Luke 3:11). To tax collectors, he says, "Collect no more than the amount prescribed for you" (3:13). To soldiers, he says, "Do not extort money from anyone by threats or false accusation, and be satisfied with your wages" (3:14). As we see here, Luke emphasizes a charity gospel for everyday people—the crowds, tax collectors, and soldiers—rather than challenging the system of the Roman Empire. After this John the Baptist introduces Jesus to them and clarifies that he, John, is not the Messiah. In the end he is put into prison because he has accused Herod of doing evil acts (Luke 3:19). Jesus is baptized, and his baptism is very different from Mark's portrayal because Luke omits all important information in Mark, such as the baptizer's name, the place of baptism, and the place from which Jesus came. Instead, Luke adds a different texture to the story: people's presence and their baptisms, Jesus praying at his baptism, heaven opening (*aneōchthēnai*; cf. "torn apart" [*schizomenous*], used in Mark 1:10), and the Holy Spirit's coming in "bodily form" (Luke 3:22) like a dove. The above differences in Luke reflect Lukan theology, which is focused on the Gentile mission, everyday people, the Holy Spirit, and prayer.

The baptism of Jesus is followed by his genealogy. The narrator says Jesus is about thirty years old when he begins his work (Luke 3:23). Unlike in Matthew, Luke traces the genealogy of Jesus from the bottom up, ending with the "son of Enos, son of Seth, son of Adam, son of God" (3:38). The Lukan genealogy presents Jesus as the savior of the world because he is the son of Adam, son of God. This genealogy is different from the one in Matthew, who connects Jesus with David and Abraham, Jewish legendaries. The other notable thing in the Lukan genealogy is that Jesus is said to be the son of Joseph (Luke 3:23), whereas, in Matthew, he is merely "the husband of Mary, of whom Jesus was born, who is called the Messiah" (Mt 1:16). In the details there are more differences between Matthew's genealogy and Luke's. For example, in Matthew, Joseph's father is Jacob, whereas in Luke, his father is Heli. Many generations do not agree with one another on both accounts.

Being full of the Spirit after his baptism, Jesus is led by the Spirit into the wilderness (Luke 4:1–13). There he is tempted by the devil for forty days, and he eats nothing. There are three tests for him: making bread (Luke 4:3–4), worshiping the devil (4:5–8), and throwing himself off the pinnacle of the temple (4:9–13). Jesus passes these three tests with the word of God. In Luke the test ends with the temple-in-Jerusalem temptation, which indicates Luke's emphasis on Jesus's roots/origin in Judaism (cf. Luke 2:21–51).

4:14–9:50, Jesus's Ministry in Galilee

During his public ministry in Galilee, Jesus often teaches in the synagogues, heals the sick, calls his first disciples, performs miracles, and foretells his death and resurrection. After the temptation, Jesus is filled with the power of the Spirit and returns to Galilee. Then he begins to teach in the synagogues. One day, he comes to Nazareth, his hometown, and enters the synagogue on the Sabbath day, "as was his custom" (Luke 4:16). He preaches his initial sermon and engages with people in the synagogue (4:18–27). His initial sermon is about social justice as he reads Isaiah 61:1–2, which is quoted in Luke 4:18–19: "The Spirit of the Lord is upon me, because he has anointed me to bring good news to the poor. He has sent me to proclaim release to the captives and recovery of sight to the blind, to set free those who are oppressed, to proclaim the year of the Lord's favor." Then he says, "Today this scripture has been fulfilled in your hearing" (Luke 4:21). It is today (*sēmeron*) that God's work of liberation has been fulfilled. Jesus's hometown people are amazed at his gracious words. But soon after, they say, "Is not this Joseph's son?" (Luke

4:22). Seeing their condescending attitude toward him, Jesus says, "Truly I tell you, no prophet is accepted in the prophet's hometown" (4:24). Then, he shifts the topic to the times of Elijah and Elisha and turns the tables; he says that God sent Elijah to the widow at Zarephath in Sidon, even when there were many widows in Israel; likewise, he says that God sent Elisha to Naaman the Syrian, even when there were many lepers in Israel. Hearing such aggressive words, Jesus's hometown people become very angry and "[lead] him to the brow of the hill on which their town was built, so that they might hurl him off the cliff" (Luke 4:29). But they do not succeed, because Jesus "[passes] through the midst of them" (4:30).

> TEXTBOX 4.2 *Consider and Discuss*
>
> **JESUS'S PREACHING ON GENTILE PREFERENCE (LUKE 4:16–30)**
>
> In Luke 4:16–30, Jesus enters the synagogue on the Sabbath, as was his custom, and reads the prophetic texts in Isaiah 61. After reading the scripture, he talks to his hometown people and unsettles their minds because he says God cares for Gentiles first. The Lukan Jesus favors the Gentile mission, whereas the Matthean Jesus limits his mission to the lost sheep of the house of Israel (Mt 15:21–28). Why does the Lukan Jesus preach this way? How can we understand this difference between Matthew and Luke?

After this initial sermon, Jesus continues teaching and healing the sick. He goes to Capernaum and teaches in the synagogue (Luke 4:31–37). There he meets a man with an unclean spirit and heals him (cf. Mark 1:21–28). That evening, Jesus enters Simon's house and heals his mother-in-law and many more (Luke 1:38–41). He continues proclaiming the kingdom of God in the synagogues of Judea (4:42–44). Then he calls the first disciples (5:1–11). In this call story, Jesus gets into Simon's boat to teach the crowds from there. After teaching, he asks Peter to go to the deep water and let down nets for a catch (Luke 5:4). Peter hesitates a bit but listens to Jesus, and he "[catches] so many fish that their nets [are] beginning to break" (5:6). Even their boats begin to sink. Then, all of a sudden, Peter is afraid and falls down at Jesus's knees. He says, "Go away from me, Lord, for I am a sinful man!" (Luke 5:8). Then Jesus says to Peter, "Do not be afraid; from now on you will be catching people" (5:10). After this, "they [leave] everything and follow[] him" (5:11). But this call story is unique to Luke, which conveys the Lukan theology of mission. In Mark and Matthew, there is a simple call story in which Jesus calls the disciples and they follow him (Mark 1:17–18; Mt 4:19–20). But Luke extends the story to Peter's experiential transformation amid a sinking boat. Peter realizes that he is nothing before the presence of the Lord. Then Jesus calls him and gives him a new vocation of saving the lost, as Peter himself is saved from his loss.

Jesus's mission continues with cleansing a leper (Luke 5:12–16; cf. Mark 1:40–54; Mt 8:1–4), healing a paralytic (Luke 5:17–26; cf. Mark 2:1–12; Mt 9:2–8), calling a Levi (Luke 5:27–32; cf. Mark 2:13–17; Mt 9:9–13). All these healing stories are shared among all three of the Gospels. One day, the Pharisees and their scribes ask Jesus about fasting (Luke 5:33–39). Jesus says there is a time to fast, but it is not now, because now is the time to work. They also ask about the Sabbath (Luke 6:1–5; cf. Mark 2:23–28; Mt 12:1–8). Jesus answers, "The Son of man is lord of the Sabbath" (Luke 6:5). In the synagogue, he heals a man with a withered hand (6:6–11) and argues that it is lawful to do good on the Sabbath (6:9).

Then Jesus calls the twelve disciples: "Simon, whom he named Peter, and his brother Andrew, and James, and John, and Philip, and Bartholomew, and Matthew, and Thomas, and James son of Alphaeus, and Simon, who was called the Zealot, and Judas son of James, and Judas Iscariot, who became a traitor" (Luke 6:14–16). As Jesus continues to teach and heal, many follow him, including "a great crowd of his disciples and a great multitude of people from all Judea, Jerusalem, and the coast of Tyre and Sidon" (6:17). Then Jesus teaches his disciples (the sermon on the plain in Luke 6:20–49). The Lukan beatitudes ("blessings") are found in Luke 6:20–26 (cf. Mt 5:3–12). While Matthew has nine blessings, Luke has only four. More interestingly, Luke includes a series of woes: "Woe to you who are rich" (6:24), "Woe to you who are full now" (6:25), "Woe to you who are laughing now" (6:25), and "Woe to you when all speak well of you" (6:26). Also, some noticeable differences are as follows: (1) in Matthew 5:3, we see the beatitude "Blessed are the poor in spirit," while in Luke 6:20b, it is "Blessed are you who are poor," and (2) Matthew 5:6 says, "Blessed are those who hunger and thirst for righteousness," while in Luke 6:21, we see "Blessed are you who are hungry now." Luke's emphasis on the poor now is distinguished from Matthew's emphasis on the poor in spirit. In the sermon on the plain, there are also teachings such as "love for enemies" (Luke 6:27–36; cf. Mt 5:38–48), "judging others" (Luke 6:37–42; Mt 7:1–5), "a tree and its fruit" (Luke 6:43–45; Mt 7:16–19), and "the two foundations" (Luke 6:46–49; Mt 7:24–27).

Then Jesus enters Capernaum and heals a centurion's servant (Luke 7:1–10; cf. Mt 8:5–13). The centurion asks Jesus to speak the word without coming to his house. Jesus praises his faith and says, "I tell you, not even in Israel have I found such faith" (Luke 7:9). After this, Jesus goes to a town called Nain and meets a widow whose son has just died and "[is] being carried out" (7:11). Jesus has compassion for her and raises her son. This story at Nain is found only in Luke. Then Jesus's reputation spreads throughout Judea. The disciples of John see all these things and report them to him. John sends two of his disciples to Jesus to confirm that he is the Messiah. Jesus answers them, "Go and tell John what you have seen and heard: the blind receive their sight, the lame walk, the lepers are cleansed, the deaf hear, the dead are raised, and the poor have good news brought to them. And blessed is anyone who takes no offense at me" (Luke 7:22–23; cf. Mt 11:4–6). After John's disciples leave, Jesus speaks to the crowds about John and lifts up his work, which is to prepare the way of the Lord.

The narrator now talks about a sinful woman anointing Jesus (Luke 7:36–50). One of the Pharisees asks Jesus to eat with him. "A sinful woman" comes to the Pharisee's house. The narrator does not explain why she is called a sinful woman. Note her actions toward Jesus: "She [stands] behind him at his feet, weeping, and [begins] to bathe his feet with her tears and to dry them with her hair. Then she [continues] kissing his feet and anointing them with the ointment" (Luke 7:38). This episode is different from that in Matthew 26:6–13 and Mark 14:3–9, both of which show a woman—not a sinful woman—anointing Jesus on his head—not on his feet—to prepare for Jesus's burial. In Matthew and Mark, this occurs in Jesus's passion journey. But here, in Luke, the point is the woman's love for Jesus. The other difference is about whose house Jesus has entered. In Luke, Jesus enters the Pharisee's house, whose name is Simon. But in Matthew and Mark, the house belongs to Simon the Leper. In the end, in Luke, Jesus commends her because of her love for him. People in the house ask, "Who is this who even forgives sins?" (Luke 7:49). Then Jesus says to the woman, "Your faith has saved you; go in peace" (7:50). This story of a sinful woman in Luke is not about the preparation for Jesus's burial but her love and faith. The anointing woman story also appears in John 12:1–7 in which Mary, the sister of Lazarus, anoints Jesus's feet at Bethany, which is the same place where the anointing occurs in Mark and Matthew. All of the above differences have to do with the fluid nature of the story and the limited memories of the storytellers. After this event of a woman's anointing, Jesus goes through many cities and villages and proclaims "the good news of the kingdom of God" (Luke 8:1). He does not proclaim his good news but delivers God's good news. He shows God's love through his healing ministry. In his public ministry, Jesus is accompanied by devoted women followers: "Mary, called Magdalene, from whom seven demons had gone out, and Joanna, the wife of Herod's steward Chuza, and Susanna, and many others, who [provide] for them out of their resources" (Luke 8:2–3).

Jesus also teaches about the kingdom of God through parables. Luke simplifies the Markan version of the parable of the sower (Luke 8:4–8; cf. Mark 4:3–9) by phrasing it as "a hundredfold" production instead of as "yielding thirty and sixty and a hundredfold," like in Mark 4:8.

Like Mark, Luke also explains the meaning of the parable of the sower (8:11–15), but he refines Mark. For example, Luke says simply, "Now the parable is this: The seed is the word of God" (8:11), whereas Mark has two verses devoted to rebuking the disciples: "Do you not understand this parable? Then how will you understand all the parables? The sower sows the word" (Mark 4:13–14). This tendency between Luke and Mark is also maintained in the story of Jesus's calming a storm (Luke 8:22–25; Mark 4:35–41; Mt 8:23–27). Luke says to the disciples, "Where is your faith?" (8:25). But Mark says, "Why are you afraid? Have you still no faith?" (4:40). Mark is more negative toward the disciples. Meanwhile, Matthew changes the wording of "no faith" in Mark to "little faith" (Mt 8:26), implying that Matthew's disciples are considered hopeful in their work.

Then Jesus arrives at Gerasenes, the opposite of Galilee, and meets a man who has demons (Luke 8:26–27; Mark 5:1–20; Mt 8:28–34). Luke uses the Markan version and edits it. For example, while Mark mentions those who have witnessed the event (5:14–17), Luke emphasizes "all the people" who were there: "all the people of the surrounding country of the Gerasenes asked Jesus to leave them" (8:37). Luke's emphasis on "all the people" is also seen at Jesus's baptism: "Now when all the people were baptized, and when Jesus also had been baptized and was praying, the heaven was opened" (3:21). In Luke the presence of all the people or crowds has to do with how Lukan theology is focused on the down-to-earth perspective. Jesus also heals a woman who has suffered from hemorrhages for twelve years (Luke 8:43–48) and the daughter of Jairus, a leader of the synagogue (8:40–42; 49–56). In both of these healing stories, the point is clear: "Do not fear but believe it" (8:47–50). Jesus declares to the woman, "Daughter, your faith has made you well; go in peace" (8:48). The woman with the hemorrhages publicly professes her faith "in the presence of all the people why she [has] touched him" (8:47). Again, here, including "all the people" is important to Luke. Later on, Jesus calls the twelve disciples and sends them out to "proclaim the kingdom of God and to heal" (Luke 9:2). He gives these instructions: "Take nothing for your journey, no staff, nor bag, nor bread, nor money—not even an extra tunic" (9:3; cf. 10:4). Compare this verse with Mark 6:8, where a staff is allowed, or with Matthew 10:9–10, where the prohibited things include high-value items such as gold, silver, or copper. Jesus sends his disciples on a mission, which is to bring "the good news and cure diseases" (Luke 9:6). On their return, Jesus teaches and cures more people. Later, he feeds the five thousand men in a desert with five loaves and two fish. But Luke does not mention the presence of women or children, whereas Matthew mentions it (Mt 14:21).

One day, Jesus asks his disciples, "Who do the crowds say that I am?" (Luke 9:18). Note here that Luke uses *ochloi* (crowds), whereas Mark and

Matthew use *anthropoi* (people). What this difference makes is unclear, but it may have to do with Luke's focus on the down-to-earth perspective of a world where the crowds daily struggle to live. The disciples answer that he is "John the Baptist, Elijah, or one of the ancient prophets" (Luke 9:19). He says to them, "But who do you say that I am?" (9:20). Peter answers, "The Messiah of God" (9:20; cf. Mark 8:27–33; Mt 16:13–23). After this, Jesus foretells his death and resurrection (Luke 9:21–27) and says to them, "If any want to become my followers, let them deny themselves and take up their cross daily and follow me" (9:23). He also tells them, "There are some standing here who will not taste death before they see the kingdom of God" (9:27).

The next scene of the narrative moves to the transfiguration of Jesus. This episode is taken from Mark 9:2–8 (cf. Mt 17:1–8) and emphasizes that Jesus is the Son of God, who must suffer and continue to do his work. After this event Jesus does several things, including his healing a boy with a demon (Luke 9:37–43); foretelling his death again (9:44–45); talking about "true greatness," which is to welcome a little child, the least among them (9:47–48); and asking the disciples not to stop someone who casts out a demon in his name because "whoever is not against [them] is for [them]" (9:50).

9:51–19:27, On the Way to Jerusalem

Luke devotes eleven chapters to talk about Jesus's journey to Jerusalem, whereas Mark has only two chapters about that part of the story (Mark 8:31–10:52). For Mark, the last week in Jerusalem is important and a climax, and Jesus must face it soon. So the narrative moves fast and with tensions. But for Luke, Jesus has still lots of things to do before reaching Jerusalem. Even when he enters it, he still has many things to do. For Luke, Jerusalem is not the goal or end of Jesus's ministry, because his work *today* must be realized for real people in every moment of every day. This is so much so that it is necessary for Jesus to spend enough time with the people in need along his way to Jerusalem. He teaches and heals them, speaking parables, as well as engaging the Jewish leaders. Setting his face to go to Jerusalem (Luke 9:51–56), Jesus does not judge the people in a Samaritan village who do not accept him (an episode unique to Luke). On his way, he meets three people who want to follow him (Luke 9:57–62). Soon he appoints seventy and sends them so that they may proclaim the kingdom of God, which has come near (10:1–16; cf. Mark 6:6–13; Matt 9:35–10:16). The mission of the seventy is unique to Luke, and Jesus rejoices at the success of the seventy and thanks God.

All of a sudden, a lawyer comes up to Jesus to test him and says, "What must I do to inherit eternal life?" (Luke 10:25; cf. 18:18). Jesus says,

"What is written in the law?" (10:26). He answers well: "You shall love the Lord your God with all your heart, and with all your soul, and with all your strength, and with all your mind; and your neighbor as yourself" (10:27; cf. Dt 6:5; Lv 19:18). Jesus says, "You have given the right answer; do this, and you will live" (Luke 10:28). But the lawyer does not go home and asks, "Who is my neighbor?" (10:29). Then Jesus tells a parable of a Samaritan (10:30–37), a story which is found only in Luke. A man meets robbers on the way to Jericho from Jerusalem. When he is half dead, a priest and a Levite pass by him on the other side. But a Samaritan sees him and helps him because he is "moved with pity" (*splagchnizomai*, which means to be moved in the inward parts). So the Samaritan's action is not merely based on his cognitive thinking but on his bodily feeling. He's identified with the victim and done everything he could: "He [goes] to him and [bandageds] his wounds, having poured oil and wine on them. Then he [puts] him on his own animal, [brings] him to an inn, and [takes] care of him" (Luke 10:34). Jesus's final question to the lawyer is as follows: "Which of these three, do you think, was a neighbor to the man who fell into the hands of the robbers?" (10:36). The lawyer answers correctly: "The one who showed him mercy" (10:37). Jesus says, "Go and do likewise" (10:37). Since the parable stops here, readers wonder if the lawyer goes on to make some changes in his life.

TEXTBOX 4.3 *Consider and Discuss*

GOOD SAMARITAN (LUKE 10:25–37)

The parable of the Good Samaritan has often been read as a story of charity. In this view the moral lesson is to imitate the Samaritan, who did his best to help the victim. But this parable also has been read allegorically through the Christological lens of salvation. In the allegory, a certain man is Adam, Jerusalem is the heavenly city, and Jericho is this world, or our mortality. The priest and the Levite equate to the law. The Samaritan is Jesus, and the inn is the church. But this parable is about a neighbor: "Who is my neighbor?" (Luke 10:29). In this story Jesus redefines *neighbor* as someone willing to help. The question is not about who is worthy as a neighbor but who can help those in need. So the Samaritan is a neighbor to the one who needs help. Given all the above, what is your reading of this parable?

Then Jesus goes to a certain village, where Martha welcomes him into her home (Luke 10:38–42). Mary, her sister, listens to him, sitting at his feet. But Martha does not like Mary, because she is not helping her. Jesus says to Martha that she is worried too much. He also says that Mary did a good job because she has chosen the better part. Mary is considered a disciple, but she is never called a disciple. Mary's listening to Jesus is a matter of interpretation because it could be a sign of discipleship *or* a sign of obedience connoting gender and/or class hierarchy.

After this, Jesus teaches his disciples how to pray: "Father, hallowed be your name. Your kingdom come. Give us each day our daily bread. And forgive us our sins, for we ourselves forgive everyone indebted to us. And do not bring us to the time of trial" (Luke 11:2–4; cf. Matt 6:9–13). Then, he emphasizes the importance of "asking" and gives a story about a friend visiting at midnight, which is unique to Luke (11:5–8). At other times, Jesus defends himself when he is accused of casting demons via Beelzebul (11:14–23; Mark 3:23–30; Mt 12:25–37). He answers, "Every kingdom divided against itself becomes a desert, and house falls on house. If Satan also is divided against himself, how will his kingdom stand?—for you say that I cast out the demons by Beelzebul" (Luke 11:17–18).

Then Jesus denounces the Pharisees and lawyers (Luke 11:37–54). In Matthew, Jesus's severe denunciation occurs in the eschatological discourse (Mt 23:25–36), but in Luke, it happens long before the passion narrative. The story in Luke begins with a Pharisee's invitation to Jesus to eat with him. In Luke the Pharisees often invite Jesus to eat (cf. 7:36–50, a sinful woman's story at the Pharisee's house). The Pharisees complain that Jesus does not keep the tradition of washing before dinner. So Jesus gives a long list of woes to the Jewish leaders because of their hypocrisy (Luke 11:42–44). He also warns people that "one's life does not consist in the abundance of possessions" (12:15). After this, he tells the parable of the rich fool, found only in Luke (12:16–21) to teach the importance of sharing in the here and now. Likewise, he also tells his disciples that they should not worry about what to eat or what to wear (12:22–34; cf. Matt 6:25–34). The lilies and birds do not fight, and yet they live well. What people must do is to "strive for his kingdom" (Luke 12:31; cf. Matt 6:33). They also must be watchful and faithful because they do not know when the Son of Man will come back (Luke 12:35–48; Matt 24:43–51). People must know the time (Luke 12:54–56) and know "what is right" (12:57–59). Also, they must repent to avoid punishment (13:1–5), which is unique to Luke.

When Jesus teaches in the synagogues on the Sabbath, he sees "a woman with a spirit that [has] crippled her for eighteen years" (Luke 13:11). This episode is also unique to Luke. As Jesus heals her, the leader of the synagogue complains that he's done it on the Sabbath. Then Jesus says, "You hypocrites! Does not each of you on the Sabbath untie his ox or his donkey from the manger, and lead it away to give it water? And ought not this woman, a daughter of Abraham whom Satan bound for eighteen long years, be set free from this bondage on the Sabbath day?" (Luke 13:15–16). The phrase "a daughter of Abraham" affirms Luke's inclusion of women in the church. After this, Jesus tells two parables in a row: the mustard seed (Luke 13:18–19; cf. Mark 4:30–32; Mt 13:31–32), as well as the yeast (Luke 13:20–21; cf. Mt 13:33). The kingdom of God is like a mustard seed when it is sown in the garden; it grows and becomes a tree. Anyone, like a crippled woman with a spirit, may become a new person and grow with the rule of God. Everyone has potential and is precious. In the parable of the leaven, the kingdom of God is compared to the leaven that is taken by a woman and mixed with flour. Leaven is small and hidden in flour, but it is essential to make the bread tasty. Leaven, like a mustard seed, is small yet powerful when it is used in the right place.

On his way to Jerusalem, Jesus also talks about the narrow door, which is to seek God's will. But people desire to enter the wide, easy door to fill their bellies (Luke 13:22–30; cf. Mt 7:13–14). Then some Pharisees come to Jesus and say, "Get away from here, for Herod wants to kill you" (Luke 13:31). Jesus says, "Go and tell that fox for me, 'Listen, I am casting out demons and performing cures *today and tomorrow, and on the third day* I finish my work. Yet *today, tomorrow, and the next day* I must be on my way, because it is impossible for a prophet to be killed outside of Jerusalem'" (emphasis added, Luke 13:32–33). This story is found only in Luke, and Luke tells the importance of Jesus's work today, before reaching Jerusalem.

Then Jesus laments over Jerusalem (Luke 13:34–35; cf. Matt 23:37–39). At another time, Jesus heals a man with dropsy at the house of a Pharisee leader (Luke 14:1–6). He also is invited to eat with a Pharisee on the Sabbath, when he again defends himself about curing people on the Sabbath. Then he talks about humility and hospitality (Luke 14:7–14), found only in Luke. He says, "When you are invited by someone to a wedding banquet, do not sit down at the place of honor, in case someone more distinguished than you has been invited by your host" (14:8). Likewise, he says, "When you give a luncheon or a dinner, do not invite your friends or your brothers or your relatives or rich neighbors, in case they may invite you in return, and you would be repaid" (14:12). God's beloved community must include the marginalized. Likewise, in the parable of the great dinner (Luke 14:15–24; cf. Mt 22:1–14), the challenge is whether the community will include "the poor, the crippled, the blind, and the lame" (Luke 14:21). This emphasis on the marginalized is distinguishable from Matthew's description of the guests as "both good and bad," which connotes fair opportunities for people (Mt 22:1–14; see also, the parable of the wheat and weeds). Jesus gives a few important parables that are unique to Luke and reflect the Lukan context and theology. Three "lost" parables in Luke 15:1–32, including the lost sheep (shared with Matthew), emphasize an important theme of Luke, which is to seek and save the lost (cf. Luke 19:10). The parable of the dishonest manager emphasizes the importance of the community of care and love. Power must be used for community building. The dishonest manager corrects what he did wrong by lowering the borrowers' payments, so his master commends him on his shrewd act (Luke 16:8). In the parable of the rich man and Lazarus, the rich man's responsibility is to care for the marginalized. In the parables of the widow and the unjust judge, the problem is the judge's uncaring mind. Likewise, the issue in the parable of the Pharisee and the tax collector is the Pharisee's uncaring pride; he lacks mercy toward the marginalized.

> TEXTBOX 4.4 *Consider and Discuss*
>
> **THE PARABLE OF THE FATHER AND TWO SONS (LUKE 15:11–32)**
>
> The parable in Luke 15:11–32 is often called the prodigal son or the lost son, but it is about a dysfunctional family with a father and two sons. Traditional interpretation renders this parable a story of salvation and reads it allegorically. The father represents a compassionate God, the older son represents the Jews, and the younger son represents sinners and/or Gentiles who repent. But if we focus on the story as is told by Jesus in the original context, the issue is family disunity, which needs resolution. The younger son returns home after wasting all his resources, and his father welcomes him without conditions. But his older brother is upset because his father did not punish or scold his younger son. So the father explains why he has prepared a sumptuous welcome party for the younger son. He says, "[It is] because this brother of yours was dead and has come to life; he was lost and has been found" (Luke 15:32). The father insinuates that he does not simply condone what his son did wrong by wasting the money and being disloyal to him. The only reason he celebrates the return of his son is that he came home alive. The story ends here. Could the family members reach reconciliation eventually? If they were to do so, what process would they need?

In his journey to Jerusalem, Jesus also speaks on other things, such as hypocrisy, divorce, forgiveness, and faith (Luke 16:14–18; 17:1–10; 20–37). Among other things, his view of the kingdom of God is noteworthy (17:20–37) because he emphasizes the present reality of the kingdom, which is here in the world. He says, "The kingdom of God is not coming with things that can be observed; nor will they say, 'Look, here it is!' or 'There it is!' For, in fact, the kingdom of God is among you" (Luke 17:20–21). For more on this topic of the kingdom of God in Luke, see below.

TEXTBOX 4.5 *Consider and Discuss*

THE KINGDOM OF GOD (LUKE 17:20–21)

When the Pharisees ask Jesus when the kingdom of God is coming, Jesus answers, "The kingdom of God is not coming with things that can be observed, nor will they say, 'Look, here it is!' or 'There it is!' For, in fact, the kingdom of God is *among or within* you" (Luke 17:21). The Greek adverb *entos* has a double meaning: "among" or "within." Jesus's answer is radical because the majority of people believed in the future kingdom of God. But he argues it is already here, among the people or within their hearts. Here, the kingdom of God is not a place or time but a godly rule—that is, God is with people now. The Holy Spirit is working now in the community. Otherwise, this would not seem to mean that the kingdom of God has been realized already. Why does the Lukan Jesus emphasize the kingdom of God that is within or among the people? Does this emphasis have to do with Luke's focus on "today"? Does this emphasis reflect the delay of Parousia?

Jesus foretells his death and resurrection a third time, which means he soon will enter Jerusalem (Luke 18:31–34). But his disciples still do not get it. Then he meets a blind beggar and heals him because the man wants to see again (Luke 18:35–43). This event is comparable to the disciples' blindness. Then he enters Jericho and sees Zacchaeus sitting on a sycamore tree, as he is short in stature. He is a chief tax collector and is rich. He wants to see Jesus. Knowing his mind, Jesus says he will stay at his house *today* (*sēmeron*). But people complain that Zacchaeus is a sinner. Then Zacchaeus repents and says, "Look, half of my possessions, Lord, I will give to the poor; and if I have defrauded anyone of anything, I will pay back four times as much" (Luke 19:8). Then Jesus says, "*Today* [*sēmeron*] salvation has come to this house, because he too is a son of Abraham. For the Son of Man came to seek out and to save the lost" (Luke 19:9; emphasis added). For Luke, today is the day of salvation, and God is working today.

TEXTBOX 4.6 *Consider and Discuss*

"TODAY" (*SĒMERON*) IN LUKE

In Luke, "today" (*sēmeron*) is important. Today is the day of salvation (Luke 2:11). Today, scriptures are fulfilled in the hearing of the people (4:21). Today is the day of repentance and renewal (5:26). The lost are found and restored today (19:10). God's reign is in the here and now (17:21). A paradise is promised today (23:43). The importance of today is also linked with the kingdom of God in the here and now (17:21). Why does Luke emphasize "today"? On the one hand, Luke is practical and considers the importance of helping real people today. On the other hand, Luke stabilizes the community with a focus on today. But if Luke is not radical enough in embracing the marginalized or challenging the system of the Roman Empire, how would you respond?

19:28–21:38, Jesus's Teaching in Jerusalem

Jesus's teaching in Jerusalem follows Mark. He rides on a colt and enters Jerusalem triumphantly. People bless his entry into Jerusalem and shout, "Blessed is the king who comes in the name of the Lord! Peace in heaven, and glory in the highest heaven!" (Luke 19:38). "Peace in heaven" is found only in Luke, which coheres with the Lukan theme of peace in the world (cf. Mark 11:9–10). But Jesus weeps over Jerusalem and laments over people's inability to make peace, which is also found only in Luke (19:42). Then he enters the temple and cleanses it, saying that the temple is a house of prayer. Then Jewish leaders try to find a way to kill him. But Jesus engages with them, affirming his authority as coming from God (Luke 20:4), implying all things belong to God (20:24–25), clarifying the status of his resurrection (20:34–36), denouncing their hypocrisy (20:45–47), and praising a widow's offering of two small copper coins (21:1–4). After this, Jesus speaks about the destruction of the temple and says there will be trials and turbulence (21:5–19). But he assures the people that God will protect those who endure because of him (21:18–19). Lastly, he foretells the destruction of Jerusalem (21:20–24) and warns people that they must be ready for the coming of the Son of Man (21:25–38).

22:1–23:56, The Suffering and Death of Jesus

The Lukan passion narrative follows Mark. The chief priests and scribes plot to kill Jesus near the time of the Passover, "for they [are] afraid of the people" (Luke 22:2). They arrange Judas's betrayal of Jesus by agreeing to give him money. They are looking for an opportunity to capture Jesus. Then Jesus's disciples prepare the Passover meal at his request. At the table, he says to them, "I have eagerly desired to eat this Passover with you before I suffer; for I tell you, I will not eat it until it is fulfilled in the kingdom of God" (Luke 22:15–16). This saying of Jesus is unique to Luke, and Jesus says he does not eat the Passover meal because the kingdom of God is yet to come (22:16, 18). In Mark and Matthew, Jesus eats the Passover meal with his disciples (Mark 14:22–25; Mt 26:26–29). Then he institutes the Lord's Supper (Luke 22:19–20). But there is a dispute about greatness among the disciples, and Jesus tells them that the one who serves others is greater (22:27). With this advice, the disciples must be prepared for Jesus's impending trials and suffering. Peter thinks he is ready and swears this to him (Luke 22:33). But Jesus knows how weak Peter is and how he will deny Jesus three times (22:34).

Now Jesus prepares for his final battle in Jerusalem and says to his disciples, "But now, the one who has a purse must take it, and likewise a bag. And the one who has no sword must sell his cloak and buy one" (Luke 22:36). Earlier, when Jesus sent out his disciples for a mission, he told them not to take a purse, bag, or sandals (10:4). So this saying of Jesus in Luke 23:36 must be understood figuratively; he means they have to prepare for difficult times of trials due to Jesus's words and deeds about God's rule in the here and now. Buying a sword must be symbolic in the sense that they must be ready for violence; Jesus does not mean that they should be armed with swords. As seen in the arrest of Jesus (Luke 22:47–53), Jesus forbids them to use a sword and says to the chief priests and the officers of the temple police, "Have you come out with swords and clubs as if I were a bandit?" (22:52). However, the disciples' response to Jesus is interesting: "Lord, look, here are two swords" (22:38). They have misunderstood him, so Jesus responds, "It is enough" (22:38). In other words, he seems to shrug off and tells them to shut off. His point seems to say, "No time! Let's move on!"

Then Jesus goes to the Mount of Olives to pray and says to his disciples, "Pray that you may not come into the time of trial" (Luke 22:40, 46). Here, he shows no anxiety or agitation about his death, which is very different from in Mark and Matthew, where Jesus is distressed and says, "I am deeply grieved, even to death; remain here, and keep awake" (Mark 14:34; cf. Mt 26:38). Likewise, in Mark and Matthew, he prays three times because suffering and death are too hard to go through. But in Luke, Jesus's prayer at the Mount of Olives is so calm that it shows he is ready to die. After this, Jesus is arrested due to Judas's betrayal (Luke 22:47–53; cf. Mark 14:43–52; Mt 26:47–56). Then Peter denies Jesus three times (Luke 22:54–62; cf. Mark 14:66–72; Mt 26:69–75). Then Jesus is mocked, beaten by those who've held him, and taken to the Jewish council, where the chief priests and scribes are gathered. They charge him with blasphemy because the people called Jesus the Messiah and the Son of God (Luke 22:66–72). Then the council members bring Jesus to Pilate and say, "We found this man perverting our nation, forbidding us to pay taxes to the emperor, and saying that he himself is the Messiah, a king" (23:2). This accusation is mistaken because Jesus did not pervert his nation or forbid them to pay taxes to Rome, even though he has acknowledged that he is a king. Then Pilate must accuse Jesus of his political claim to a kingship. But ironically, Pilate says, "I find no basis for an accusation against this man" (Luke 23:4). This is nonsense. Then they insist and say, "He stirs up the people by teaching throughout all Judea, from Galilee where he began even to this place" (Luke 23:5). But they do not point out any specific treason he's made. To save face or maybe to feel less burdened, Pilate sends Jesus off to Herod, who is in Jerusalem by chance, because Jesus is under Herod's jurisdiction. This story is unique to Luke. In the end Herod wants to see Jesus out of curiosity, and so he questions him. But Jesus does not answer him at all. The chief priests and the scribes accuse Jesus again. Then, like Pilate, Herod sends Jesus back to Pilate to save face. All of a sudden, Luke says Pilate and Herod have become friends with each other this day; before this, they had been enemies (23:12). They use council members and other Jewish leaders in charging him and achieve their common goal of removing Jesus. Pilate's tactic is to let the Jews be responsible for the death of Jesus. So he keeps saying that he cannot find a fault with Jesus. He also saves Herod from his direct involvement in the death of Jesus, because, like him, Herod also says he's not found anything Jesus has done to deserve death (Luke 23:13–15). But people shout and want Jesus to be crucified. Then, a third time, Pilate says to them, "Why, what evil has he done? I have found in him no ground for the sentence of death; I will therefore have him flogged and then release him" (Luke 23:22). Pilate's insistence on Jesus's innocence is peculiar to Luke. In all of this, Luke implies that Jesus's death is caused by the Jews. But the story reveals that Pilate, Herod, and the religious leaders are directly involved in his death.

Simon of Cyrene carries the cross of Jesus, and many people follow him. Some women are beating their breasts and weep for him (Luke 23:26–27). Jesus says, "Daughters of Jerusalem, do not weep for me, but weep for yourselves and for your children" (23:28). He also says, "Father, forgive them; for they do not know what they are doing" (23:34). The inscription over Jesus reads, "This is the King of the Jews" (23:38), which is a political title. Initially, the Jewish leaders have charged Jesus with blasphemy, but they later change the charge to perverting the people. Two other criminals are also crucified. One of them says to Jesus, "Jesus, remember me when you come into your kingdom" (Luke 23:42). Jesus says, "Truly I tell you, today (*sēmeron*) you will be with me in Paradise" (23:43). For Luke, salvation takes effect today.

At about noon, "darkness [comes] over the whole land," and "the curtain of the temple [is] torn in two" (Luke 23:45). After this, Jesus cries aloud, "Father, into your hands I commend my spirit" (23:46). Then he dies. His last words are so calm, and he maintains imperturbability. There is no sense of despair. This image of his death in Luke differs from that in Mark, where Jesus cries despairingly, "My God, my God, why have you forsaken me?" (Mark 15:34). Then, seeing all this, a Roman centurion says, "Certainly this man was innocent" (Luke 23:47). This saying is different from Mark and Matthew, where the centurion says Jesus is truly the Son of God (Mark 15:39; Mt 27:54). But in Luke, he says that Jesus is innocent, which means he is not a Roman criminal. Then all the crowds who've gathered to see Jesus's crucifixion return home, "beating their breasts" (Luke 23:48), which is found only in Luke. Their "beating their breasts" is a sign of repentance. Luke indicates that the way to salvation is repentance.

Jesus is buried by Joseph of Arimathea, "a good and righteous man," who is a member of the council (Luke 23:50). He lays the body of Jesus "in a rock-hewn tomb where no one had ever been laid" (23:53). The women from Galilee follow and see the tomb. They return home and prepare spices and ointments (Luke 23:56).

24:1–53, The Resurrection of Jesus

On the first day of the week, the women visit the tomb and do not find the body of Jesus. Suddenly, "two men in dazzling clothes" appear to them and say, "Why do you look for the living among the dead? He is not here, but has risen" (Luke 24:5), which is found only in Luke. It reveals Luke's theology very well. Jesus is not in a tomb but lives among people in the world. This means Jesus's vision and work must be realized in today's world—in the lives of everyday people. This day (*sēmeron*) is the day of new life and resurrection. The two men remind the women of Jesus's teaching that "the Son of Man must be handed over to sinners, and be crucified, and on the third day rise again" (Luke 24:7). The women remember Jesus's words. They return to the community and tell the good news to the eleven and to others (24:8–9). These women are Mary Magdalene, Joanna, Mary the mother of James, and the other women. But only Peter believes them, runs to the tomb, and sees the linen cloth. He is amazed at what he sees.

The next scene in the resurrection narrative is also unique to Luke (24:13–35). Jesus talks with two disciples on the way to Emmaus, but they do not recognize Jesus. It is impossible for them to think of Jesus's execution because of their expectation that he would liberate Israel. But it has not happened. There is news about the empty tomb, but no one has seen him. Later, when Jesus shares bread with them, their eyes are opened. But Jesus disappears while their hearts are burning within themselves. So they return to Jerusalem and report to all gathered there what has happened on the road. Then Jesus appears to his disciples while they are talking (Luke 24:36–49), and he says, "Peace be with you" (24:36). They are terrified because they think he is a ghost. Jesus says, "Touch me and see; for a ghost does not have flesh and bones as you see that I have" (Luke 24:39). The disciples' experience with Jesus must be a real-yet-surreal one because they cannot recognize him even though he appears in flesh and bones. He eats a piece of broiled fish in their presence and explains the scripture about him. Finally, they understand the scriptures. They are given a new mission: they must proclaim "repentance and forgiveness of sins" to all nations (Luke 24:48), which is the goal of the Lukan mission strategy. They must stay in Jerusalem until they have received the Holy Spirit. After some time, Jesus ascends into heaven. But the disciples return to Jerusalem to wait for the Holy Spirit.

QUESTIONS FOR REFLECTION

1. Luke posits himself as a historian, as is hinted in Luke 1:1–4, and argues that his account is correct. Why does Luke state this, and what does he try to convey to his Christian audience or to non-Christians in the Roman world?
2. Is Luke's Gospel a politically innocuous gospel or a social gospel?
3. Is Luke's Gospel a book of legitimation for its Christian audience or a book of apology for the non-Christian people in the Roman world? The former has to do with comforting Christians so that they may feel safe in the Roman Empire. The latter is about explaining Christianity to the non-Christian world—that is, the Roman Empire.
4. There are parables unique to Luke, such as the good Samaritan, the father and two sons, and the unjust judge and widow. In what way do these parables contribute to Lukan theology? If you read them from Jesus's context, what implications can you draw from them?
5. Why do you think Luke devotes ten chapters to Jesus's journey to Jerusalem? If that journey is important, can you say in what way?
6. How does the Lukan Jesus differ from the Matthean Jesus? (Read Luke 4:16–30; Mt 10:5–6; 15:21–28). Why does Luke portray Jesus in a different way?

FURTHER READING

Bovon, François. *Luke the Theologian: Fifty-five Years of Research (1950–2005)*. 2nd ed. Waco, TX: Baylor University Press, 2006.

Brawley, Robert L. *Centering on God: Method and Message in Luke-Acts*. Louisville, KY: Westminster John Knox, 1990.

Byrne, Brendan. *The Hospital of God. A Reading of Luke's Gospel*. Collegeville, MN: Liturgical Press, 2000.

Carey, Greg. *Sinners. Jesus and His Earliest Followers*. Waco, TX: Baylor University Press, 2009.

Crowder, Stephanie B. "The Gospel of Luke." In *True to Our Native Land: An African American New Testament Commentary*, edited by Brian K. Blount, Cain H. Felder, Clarice J. Martin, and Emerson B. Powery, 158–85. Minneapolis, MN: Fortress, 2007.

González, Justo. *The Story Luke Tells: Luke's Unique Witness to the Gospel.* Grand Rapids, MI: William B. Eerdmans, 2015.

Green, Bridgett A. "'Nobody's Free until Everybody's Free': Exploring Gender and Class Injustice in a Story about Children (Luke 18: 15–17)." In *Womanist Interpretations of the Bible: Expanding the Discourse,* edited by Gay L. Byron and Vanessa Lovelace, 291–310. Atlanta, GA: Society of Biblical Literature, 2016.

Guardiola-Saenz, Leticia. "Luke: The Stories We Live By." In *Latinx Perspectives on the New Testament,* edited by Osvaldo D. Vena and Leticia A. Guardiola-Saenz, 61–82. Lanham, MD: Lexington Books, 2022.

Harrington, Daniel J. *Meeting St. Luke Today: Understanding the Man, His Mission, and His Message.* Chicago: Loyola Press, 2009.

Kim, Yung Suk. *Preaching the New Testament Again: Faith, Freedom, and Transformation.* Eugene, OR: Cascade Books, 2019.

King, Karen L. *The Gospel of Mary of Magdala: Jesus and the First Woman Apostle.* Santa Rosa, CA: Polebridge Press, 2003.

Levine, Amy-Jill, ed. *A Feminist Companion to Luke.* New York: Sheffield Academic Press, 2002.

———. *Short Stories by Jesus. The Enigmatic Parables of a Controversial Rabbi.* New York: HarperOne, 2015.

Neyrey, Jerome H., ed. *The Social World of Luke-Acts: Models for Interpretation.* Peabody, MA: Hendrickson, 1991.

Patte, Daniel. *The Challenge of Discipleship: A Critical Study of the Sermon on the Mount as Scripture.* Harrisburg, PA: Trinity Press International, 1999.

Powell, Mark A. *What Are They Saying about Luke?* Mahwah, NJ: Paulist Press, 1989.

Talbert, Charles H. *Reading Luke: A Literary and Theological Commentary on the Third Gospel.* Macon, GA: Smyth & Helwys, 2002.

Tupamahu, Ekaputra. "The Gospel of Luke." In *An Asian Introduction to the New Testament,* edited by Johnson Thomaskutty, 103–25. Minneapolis, MN: Fortress, 2022.

Ukpong, Justin. "Luke." In *Global Bible Commentary,* edited by Daniel Patte, 385–394. Nashville, TN: Abingdon Press, 2004.

NOTES

1. Douglas E. Oakman, "The Countryside in Luke-Acts," in *The Social World of Luke-Acts: Model for Interpretation,* ed. Jerome H. Neyrey (Peabody, MA: Hendrickson, 1991), 151–79. What follows in the text comes from this article.

2. See Philip Esler, *Community and Gospel in Luke-Acts: The Social and Political Motivations of Lucan Theology* (Cambridge, England: Cambridge University Press, 1989). See also, J. Andrew Cowan, *The Writings of Luke and the Jewish Roots of the Christian Way: An Examination of the Aims of the First Christian Historian in the Light of Ancient Politics, Ethnography, and Historiography* (New York: T&T Clark, 2019).

3. Troy Troftgruben, "Salvation 'Today' in Luke's Gospel," *Currents in Theology and Mission* 45, no. 4 (2018): 6–11, http://currentsjournal.org/index.php/currents/article/view/144.

Chapter 5

The Gospel of John

For a long time, since Clement of Alexandria first mentioned it at the end of the second century CE, the Gospel of John has been read as a spiritual gospel. Indeed, spiritual language permeates John's Gospel; for example, Jesus comes from heaven (John 3:31; 6:22–59), speaks of his special relationship with God (8:19; 10:30; 12:45; 14:10), promises to send the Paraclete, who is the Spirit of truth (14:16–17, 26; 15:26–27; 16:7–11), and breathes the Holy Spirit on his disciples after he is risen (20:22). But this being a spiritual gospel does not mean it is a dualistic, otherworldly gospel. The Fourth Gospel argues that Jesus came in the flesh and that this world is God's creation. So God sent his Son to save the world: "For God so loved the world that he gave his only Son, so that everyone who believes in him may not perish but may have eternal life. Indeed, God did not send the Son into the world to condemn the world, but in order that the world might be saved through him" (John 3:16–17). But later in the Johannine community, some members argued that Jesus was not a human but fully God and that he did not suffer. They were prototypes of later Gnostic Christians, who flourished in the second to third centuries CE. They thought this world is evil and the body, a prison. They eventually left the Johannine community because of their Christological conflict with other members (1 John 2:19). They are called antichrists and liars (1 John 2:22; 4:2–3; 2 John 7).

John's writing style, vocabulary, and sources differ from the Synoptic Gospels. For instance, John has long discourses, such as the farewell discourses in John 14–17 and the peculiar "I am" sayings of Jesus. John also uses ironies and metaphors frequently, including dualisms between heaven and earth and between light and darkness. John also has a distinct vocabulary, such as that seen in his references to the Paraclete (14:16–17, 26; 15:26–27; 16:7–11), the spirit of truth (14:17), and the truth to which Jesus was born to testify (18:37). While we do not know where John's literary sources came from, there are some distinct sources, such as the "I am" sayings of Jesus, the farewell discourses, and unique miracles. Unlike the Synoptic Gospels, John's Gospel does not have the following materials: parables, exorcisms, water baptism, and the temptation in the wilderness. But the above differences do not mean that John is less historical than the Synoptics. John's Gospel also reflects the historical realities of the community behind this gospel and some early Christian traditions relating to Jesus. The low Christology—namely, that Jesus is considered the Jewish human Messiah—is reflected in John 1:36–42, where some Aramaic words are translated into Greek: the title "rabbi" translates as teacher, "Messiah" as Christ, and "Cephas" as Peter. Though the Fourth Gospel does not include parables or the direct sayings of the kingdom of God, there are rich symbols/metaphors such as water, light, and bread, as well as the "I am" sayings of Jesus, which correspond to his kingdom teaching in the Synoptic Gospels. Jesus is the bread, the shepherd, the living water, the gate, the light, the way, the life, and the resurrection because he does the work of God and shows God's love. The "I am" sayings of Jesus and related metaphors communicate the kingdom of God to John's audience. Indeed, only one time does Jesus talk about the kingdom of God: Nicodemus comes and says to him, "Rabbi, we know that you are a teacher who has come from God; for no one can do these signs that you do apart from the presence of God" (John 3:2). Then Jesus answers, "Very truly, I tell you, no one can see the kingdom of God without being born from above" (3:3). "Being born from above" means birth from God or the Spirit because, later, he says again, "Very truly, I tell you, no one can enter the kingdom of God without being born of water and Spirit" (3:5). Jesus's point is that one must live by God or the Spirit; then one can live in the reign of God. Understood this way, Jesus's saying here in John is not very different from what is seen in the Synoptic Gospels, where the kingdom of God means God's reign or activity.

John's Gospel also has distinctive features. First, John portrays Jesus as one who comes from heaven, delivering "the word of God" (17:14, 17) and returning to God. In the absence of Jesus, the Paraclete will come to teach his disciples and remind them of his teaching (14.26). Second, John introduces "logos theology," as is seen in 1:14: "The Word (*logos*) became flesh and lived among us, and we have seen his glory, the glory as of a father's only son, full of grace and truth." Jesus delivers the word of God to the disciples and the world. Third, John emphasizes eternal life, which is realized in the present when one follows the way of Jesus—his exemplary life embodying God's word. Fourth, John's Gospel retains dualistic languages in 7:13, 9:22, 12:42, and 19:38, among others. In the story an excruciating tension arises between Jesus and the synagogue, which represents Judaism. But this kind of severe conflict is hard to understand in a historical context because, for example, expulsion from the synagogue did not happen during Jesus's ministry time. Fifth, John fosters universal love of God for all (3:16). Jesus's mission will continue with his disciples, so he sends them into the world to do the work of God, which is to love the world and its people. Sixth and lastly, the Johannine Jesus has come to testify to the truth, which may be the truth of God (John 18:37).

TEXTBOX 5.1 *John's Gospel at a Glance*

DATE

John was likely written around 90–100 CE. It is also called the Fourth Gospel.

AUTHOR

Traditionally, it is attributed to John, the disciple of Jesus, but the real author is unknown. We do not know who the beloved disciple is.

PLACE

There is no information about the place of composition. (Maybe it was in Rome?)

SOURCE

The Fourth Gospel differs from the Synoptic Gospels concerning source and writing style. But this does not mean that it is less historical than the others. It also contains early traditions about Jesus and historical information about the Johannine community. Possible sources include miracle stories, stories about the beloved disciple, and a farewell discourse.

AUDIENCE

The audience is a small, close-knit, and deeply spiritual community that has bitter relationships with Judaism (the synagogue).

HOW IT BEGINS

The Gospel begins with the Logos. "In the beginning" (*en arche*) in John 1:1 echoes the phrase "in the beginning" (*bereshit*) in Genesis 1:1. But actually, both of the Greek and Hebrew phrases lack a definite article that means "a certain time of the beginning." Jesus incarnates the Logos (John 1:14).

HOW IT ENDS

The Gospel ends with Jesus appearing with wounds, eating breakfast, and breathing the Holy Spirit on his disciples. The purpose of the Gospel is found at John 20:31: "But these are written so that you may come to believe that Jesus is the Messiah, the Son of God and that through believing you may have life in his name." Chapter 21 was added by the author, a member of the second-generation Johannine community. Another ending is found at John 21:25: "But there are also many other things that Jesus did; if every one of them were written down, I suppose that the world itself could not contain the books that would be written."

ESCHATOLOGY

While Mark and Matthew emphasize future eschatology, the Fourth Gospel focuses on the present eschatology ("eternal life" now), as is seen in John 3:36; 5:24; 6:47–48.

JESUS

Jesus is the Jewish Messiah, sent from heaven, who witnesses to the Father, dies a glorified death of love, and will be available spiritually to believers after his death.

DISCIPLES

They know who Jesus is and receive the Holy Spirit.

HUMAN CONDITION

People do not know God; they are spiritually dead.

TRANSFORMATION

They must know the truth of God and abide in God and Jesus.

UNIQUE CONTENT

1:1–18, The prologue: The Word became flesh
1:29, The testimony of John the Baptist: "Here is the Lamb of God who takes away the sin of the world"
2:1–11, The wedding at Cana
3:1–21, Nicodemus coming by night to Jesus
4:1–42, A Samaritan woman at Jacob's well
11:1–44, Raising of Lazarus, brother of Mary and Martha, at Bethany
13:1–20, Washing the disciples' feet
14:1–16:33, Farewell discourse
17:1–26, Jesus's long prayer

20:24–29, Resurrection appearance to Thomas
21:1–25, Epilogue: An appearance by the sea of Tiberias and the large catch of fish

UNIQUE HEALING

5:1–18, Healing of a crippled man at Pool of Beth-zatha
9:1–41, Healing of a man born blind

OUTLINE

1:1–18, Prologue
1:19–5:47, Jesus's Ministry
6:1–12:50, Jesus's Ministry Grows, Facing Opposition
13:1–17:26, Farewell Discourses
18:1–20:31, Suffering and Glory
21:1–25, Addendum

THE JOHANNINE JESUS

The Johannine Jesus comes from heaven, which means God sent his Son to save the world. Jesus does the work of God, and his work testifies that he is the Son of God. His job is to deliver the word of God to his disciples and to send them into the world so that they may continue his work through the Paraclete, who will remind them of his teaching. Likewise, the Johannine Jesus does not promise the disciples that he will come back. The only exception is found in John 14:2–4. But his promised coming is replaced by the Paraclete. He promises that the Spirit of truth will come and help the disciples after he is gone. He even says it would be better for him to go away so that the Paraclete could come in his absence. He understands that he must return to the Father once he has completed the work of God. So he says, "It is finished" (John 19:30). After the resurrection, Jesus says to Mary Magdalene, "Do not hold on to me, because I have not yet ascended to the Father. But go to my brothers and say to them, 'I am ascending to my Father and your Father, to my God and your God'" (John 20:17).

The Johannine Jesus is paralleled with Moses, as he is sent by God to deliver his people from darkness. God says to Moses, "See, I have made you like God to Pharaoh, and your brother Aaron shall be your prophet" (Ex 7:1). Moses was made like God! So, too, Jesus was made like God to the world so that he would do the work of God powerfully. But Jesus in John is more than Moses because he has come as the Son of God who takes on the cross to save people. The Johannine Jesus lays down his life for the sheep. He has come for this and never felt anguish over his suffering and death. This does not mean that he condones evil or torture. Rather, the point is that he expresses his love for the world voluntarily and takes on the risk of dying for the world to save people.

The Johannine Jesus cares for his disciples. He even has the Beloved Disciple, who has close relationships with him. He washes the disciples' feet as a ritual of love between him and them. He prays to God for them before he leaves for God. He says, "I have given them your word, and the world has hated them because they do not belong to the world, just as I do not belong to the world. *I am not asking you to take them out of the world, but I ask you to protect them from the evil one*" (John 17:14–15; emphasis added). In the farewell discourses, Jesus comforts the disciples: "Do not let your hearts be troubled. Believe in God; believe also in me" (John 14:1). He also affirms that he has shown them the way, the truth, and the life so that they may abide in him and God (14:6). He appears to the disciples three times after his rising and shows them his resurrection body—for example, one incident occurs when they have a meal together by the Sea of Tiberias (21:1–14). He even breathes the Holy Spirit on them (20:22).

DISTINCTIVE THEOLOGICAL THEMES

In the Johannine worldview, eternal life begins in the present and is a present quality of life, which is made possible through abiding in God and Jesus. It is not a life that lives after death. Rather, the point is a personal relationship with God. This eternal life is the same as resurrection in some sense, as Jesus says to Martha, "I am the resurrection and the life. Those who believe in me, even though they die, will live, and everyone who lives and believes in me will never die. Do you believe this?" (John 11:25–26). This never dying can be understood spiritually, and it begins now, through Jesus. The other important theme is the "world" (*kosmos*), which is good because it is God's creation (Gn 1). So God loves it and sends his Son to save it, not to condemn it (John 3:16–17). Yet this world is full of darkness because of humans' depravity and unwillingness to live in light. The light has come through prophets and many others, yet people resist and fall into evil acts. Now Jesus has come to testify to the truth of God and provide life and light to the dark world. But the world (people) do not accept him. Rather, it hates him and his followers. As we see here, in John's worldview, the world (*kosmos*) has a double meaning: it is the object of God's love (John 3:16), and at the same time, it hates

Jesus's word and his disciples because they do not belong to the world. The other important theme in John is the mission of Jesus. He always makes sure that he does the work of God. Father and the Spirit are with him, and his goal is to show the love of God (John 3:16) and save people in darkness. He finishes this mission as he utters, just before his death, "It is finished" (19:30). Earlier, he'd prayed to the Father for his disciples so that they could continue his work: "As you have sent me into the world, so I have sent them into the world. And for their sakes I sanctify myself, so that they also may be sanctified in truth" (John 17:18–19). Given the above emphasis on Jesus's mission, the Johannine community members must love the world even if the world hates them. In times of trials and persecution, the Holy Spirit (also known as the Paraclete or the Spirit of truth) will guide them into truth.

"I AM" SAYINGS OF JESUS

In John's Gospel, there are no parables of Jesus. But there are seven "I am" sayings of Jesus, which may be relevant in teaching the kingdom of God. These "I am" sayings from John are below:

- "I am the bread of life/living bread" (6:35–51).
- "I am the light of the world" (8:12; cf. 9:5).
- "I am the gate of the sheepfold" (10:7–9).
- "I am the good shepherd" (10:11–14).
- "I am the resurrection and the life" (11:25).
- "I am the way, the truth, and the life" (14:6).
- "I am the vine/true vine" (15:1–5).

Even if the kingdom of God is not a main phrase of the Gospel of John (except for Jesus's conversation with Nicodemus in John 3:1–11), the "I am" sayings of Jesus may be understood as teachings about the kingdom of God (God's rule or reign). The reason is that Jesus embodies God's rule through his teaching. In other words, these sayings of Jesus may be taken as the description of his work of God.[1] All these sayings are metaphorical statements confirming that Jesus embodies the word of God so that God's rule may be effective for all. In John's language, this rule of God is established/realized when one abides in Jesus, who also abides in the Father; that is, abiding in Jesus means keeping his word and teaching about God. Jesus says that a mere belief in him is not enough and those who keep Jesus's word are his disciples and will know the truth (John 8:31). Jesus is the bread because people may live by his exemplary life in which he has shown the way of God. Jesus is the light of the world because he's helped people to live in light. A man born blind recovers sight (John 9:1–41). Jesus is the gate of the sheepfold because he's guided people into the green pastures. Jesus is the good shepherd because he lays down his life for his sheep. Jesus is the resurrection and the life because, through him, his people may have good relationships with God. Jesus is the way and the life because he's discerned and embodied the word of God. In other words, his life is the way, and those who follow him will live abundantly. Jesus is the truth because he testifies to the truth of God. Jesus is the vine because people must stick to his word, his love, and his truth.

NOTABLE INTERPRETATION ISSUES

First, we may hardly know from where John obtained oral or written sources to compose the Gospel. John uses distinct sources such as the "I am" sayings of Jesus, a set of unique signs, and farewell discourses. While John's vocabulary and sources are different from the Synoptic Gospels, John also preserves the sound teaching and theology of Jesus. If we study John's Gospel with the Synoptic Gospels, we may get more of a sense of the historical Jesus while deepening our understanding of each evangelist. Second, one of the hardest issues in John has to do with the so-called high Christology. What does Jesus say of himself in the narrative? What does the narrator say about him? How should we interpret the language of incarnation in John 1:14? Should we take John 1:14 in a literal sense or a metaphorical sense? How can we understand the embodiment of the Word (Logos) through the life of Jesus? Third, likewise, how should we interpret John 14:6? Is this an exclusive statement saying that Christianity is the only true religion of salvation, or is there room for engaging with others? Fourth, how should we understand the character/figure of the disciple whom Jesus loved (the Beloved Disciple; John 13:23; 19:26; 20:2; 21:7, 20)? He appears multiple times in the story at important junctures. Is that person merely a fictive character? Or is he or she someone who is a leader of the Johannine community? Fifth, how should we understand the community behind this gospel? How can we explain the events of expulsion from the synagogue in the text? Who are the Johannine community members? What was the community's theology or mission? Sixth and lastly, the phrase "the Jews" (Ioudaios) appears many times in John (e.g., 7:13; 19:38; 20:19). Who were they? Are they a single group with a cause like the Jewish leaders and elites had? Or does the term refer to the mass of people? But the narrator of John says some Jews believed in Jesus, while others did not. Given this narration, it seems not all Jews are cast into the single category of Jews.

A CLOSE READING OF JOHN

1:1–18, Prologue

The narrator of John's Gospel begins with a unique prologue in which the keyword is the Word (Logos). It is uncertain whether the narrator is referring to Logos as being from Hellenistic philosophy, something that represents an abstract principle or foundation of all things, or as God's creation by word, found in Genesis 1:1, when he created the heavens and earth by speaking. Given the primordial phrase in Genesis 1:1, "in a certain beginning" (*en archē*, which has no definite article), John is seeming to refer to Genesis 1:1, which also has the same phrase in Hebrew, *bereshit* ("in a certain beginning," which has no definite article). In Genesis 1:1–2, the narrator of Genesis declares that once upon a time—that is, a certain time of the beginning—God created the heavens and the earth. At this time, a *ruach* of God, which means "a wind from God" or "the Spirit of God," was there with God, participating in God's creation. With this grand story of God's creation in mind, John claims that the divine Logos or the Spirit (wind) comes through Jesus so that the world/people may be full of light and life. In other words, Jesus is the Word incarnate (John 1:14), being sent by God (3:16; 6:57; 9:4). As the Son of God, he does the work of God (4:34; 6:38; 7:16), delivers the word of God to his disciples (17:8, 17), sends them into the world so that they might continue his work, lays down his life because of his love for the world (15:18–27), and returns to the Father (7:33; 16:5–11; 19:28–30). When Jesus returns to the Father, the Paraclete will come to help the disciples to keep his teaching (14:15–31; 16:5–11; 17:20). So the work of Jesus continues with his disciples through the Paraclete. They will testify to the truth of God through the Paraclete (John 17:20).

The Johannine prologue (John 1:1–18) deals with the origin of the Logos (1:1–5), its work and testimony (1:6–13), and its relationship with Jesus (1:14–18). Logos means a word, speech, or reasoning, and its verbal form is *lego*, which means "to speak."[2] Since the Logos in John 1:1 is related to God's creation in Genesis 1:1, we translate it as "the Word." John declares in a hymnic tone that, once upon a time, was the Word (Logos); the Word was with God, and the Word was God (1:1). In John 1:3, the narrator refers to God's creation by word: "All things came into being through him (the Logos)."[3] In the Word, there was life and light, which was the light of all people (1:4). And "the light shines in the darkness, and the darkness did not overtake it" (1:5). Life and light are two important themes in John's narrative. In John 1:6–13, the narrator talks about John the Baptist, who was sent by God to testify to the light. He is not the light, but the true light will come to enlighten the world. Those who accept and live by the

Word will become children of God. They are born "not of blood or of the will of the flesh or of the will of man, but of God" (John 1:13). This new birth is explained later, in Jesus's encounter with Nicodemus (3:1–11).

In John 1:14–18, at long last, the narrator introduces Jesus, the Son of God, who incarnates the Word of God. "The Word became flesh [*sarx*]" (John 1:14). One possible understanding of the incarnation is focused on Christology: God became human, who is Jesus. But an alternative interpretation looks at the embodiment language—that is, Jesus revealed who God is through his life and death, as John 1:18 implies: "No one has ever seen God. It is the only begotten Son, who is close to the Father's heart, who has made him known."[4] So one way we can explain the link between the Word and flesh is to read it metaphorically. Metaphors should not be taken literally in the sense that God became a human, Jesus. In John, Jesus uses plenty of metaphors and ironies to convey the deeper meaning of truth and life. For example, seven "I am" sayings may be also understood as metaphors, as we've seen before. When he says that if anyone does not eat his flesh, there will be no life in him or her, he does not mean it literally (John 6:52–59). With this in mind, we can understand John 1:14 ("And the Word became flesh and lived among us, and we have seen his glory, the glory as of a father's only son, full of grace and truth") as Jesus's embodiment of the divine word. The word "flesh" (*sarx*) also insinuates the frailty of Jesus, which indicates that he suffers and dies because of his testimony to the divine Word. This incarnation theology is confirmed throughout the narrative of John and goes against Gnostic Christology, which denies that Jesus came in the flesh.

TEXTBOX 5.2 **Consider and Discuss**

JESUS AND THE WORD (LOGOS)

The Word (Logos) is a central theme in the Johannine prologue (John 1:1–18). Jesus is assumed to be the Word in verses 1–13, though he is not explicitly mentioned there. But in John 1:14, there is a definitive statement that the Word became flesh. How can we understand this incarnational statement? Does it mean God became Jesus? If so, in what way? Or can it be understood as Jesus's embodiment of the Word or the Word of God?

1:19–5:47, Jesus's Ministry

The narrator talks about John the Baptist's testimony of Jesus, Jesus's calling of the first disciples, and his work through signs and teaching. First, John the Baptist appears and sets the stage for Jesus. The priests and

Levites from Jerusalem ask John, "Who are you?" (John 1:19). John says, "I am not the Messiah," and he then says, "I am the voice of one crying out in the wilderness, 'Make straight the way of the Lord'" (1:23; quote from Is 40:3). Also, he says, "I baptize with water. Among you stands one whom you do not know, the one who is coming after me; I am not worthy to untie the thong of his sandal" (John 1:26–27). The next day John sees Jesus coming toward him and says, "Here is the Lamb of God who *takes up* the sin of the world!" (1:29, 36; cf. Is 53:7). In John 1:29, the root form of the verb *airó* means "to take up" or "to remove." The New Revised Standard Version (NRSV) and the New International Version (NIV), along with many other versions of the Bible, translate the participle verb *airōn* as "who takes away" (meaning to remove), which connotes the redemptive sacrifice of Jesus; that is, Jesus is prefigured as a paschal lamb that removes the sin of the world. But an alternative translation of *airó* is "to take up," which may be understood as a love sacrifice, not as a sin offering. In fact, the word "sin" is singular in the phrase "the sin of the world," not "sins" of the world/people. The singular sense of sin may have to do with the people's / the world's not accepting Jesus as the Messiah.

Then Jesus engages the disciples of John the Baptist who follow him and says, "What are you looking for?" (John 1:37). They answer, "Rabbi, where are you staying?" (1:38). Jesus says, "Come and see" (1:39). They stay with him that day. One of these disciples is Andrew, Simon Peter's brother. Andrew finds Peter and says to him, "We have found the Messiah [translated as Christ]" (John 1:41). He brings Simon to Jesus, and Jesus calls him Cephas, which is translated as Peter (1:42). This call story in John is different from the one in the Synoptic Gospels, where Jesus calls his disciples from their fishing job at the sea of Galilee. In Luke, Jesus calls Peter from a fishing boat amid storms on the sea of Gennesaret (Luke 5:1–11). In Mark and Matthew, he simply calls his disciples, saying, "Follow me and I will make you fish for people" (Mark 1:17; Mt 4:19). But here, in John, the call story is an extended one in which Jesus and the disciples engage one another and spend time together. Also, there are step-by-step evangelizing activities that reflect the early community of John: (1) hearing John the Baptist talking about Jesus; (2) two disciples following Jesus and inquiring about him; (3) Jesus's invitation to "come and see" (John 1:39); (4) the disciples' remaining with him; (5) Andrew's invitation to his brother Simon, saying, "We have found the Messiah" (1:41); and (6) Andrew's bringing Simon to Jesus, who recognizes Simon and calls him a new name (Cephas). Aramaic words (Rabbi, Messiah, Cephas), which are translated into Greek, also reflect the early time of the community behind John's Gospel.

Then, the next day, Jesus goes to Galilee. He finds Philip and says, "Follow me" (John 1:43). Then Philip evangelizes Nathanael, saying something akin to "We have found the Messiah" (1:45). Nathanael says, "Can anything good come out of Nazareth?" (1:46). Philip says, "Come and see" (1:46). Nathanael comes to Jesus, who recognizes him and commends him, saying, "Here is truly an Israelite in whom there is no deceit!" (1:47). Nathanael responds, "Rabbi, you are the Son of God! You are the King of Israel!" (1:49). This call story of Philip and Nathanael resembles the earlier one of Andrew and Peter in that it involves step-by-step processes, such as sayings like "We have found the Messiah" and "Come and see." But the difference is the narrator does not explain how Philip is evangelized; Jesus simply asks him to follow him. Probably, Philip had already heard about Jesus from Andrew and Peter because the narrator says, "Now Philip was from Bethsaida, the city of Andrew and Peter" (John 1:44).

Jesus's public ministry starts with the wedding in Cana of Galilee, and he does the first sign (a miracle), which is turning water into wine. When the mother of Jesus realizes there is no more wine, she says something to Jesus about this. Jesus says his time has not come yet. But he listens to her and supplies the best-quality wine to the steward and guests. In the end he makes his mother, the steward, the bridegroom, and all the guests happy. Through this event Jesus reveals his glory and that his disciples believe in him (John 1:11). After this event Jesus goes to Capernaum with his mother, his brothers, and his disciples, "and they [remain] there a few days" (1:12). Jesus's family is seen as an ordinary, peaceful one, which is very different than their image in the Synoptic Gospels, where his family is hostile to him. For example, his family thinks that Jesus is mad (Mark 3:21, 31–35; Mt 12:46–50; Luke 8:19–21). Though John 7:5 says his brothers do not believe in him, there is no indication that his family has treated him in the same way as they have in the Synoptic Gospels.

Then Jesus visits Jerusalem to observe the Passover. Whereas, in the Synoptic Gospels, Jesus makes one final journey to Jerusalem, in John, he travels multiple times to Jerusalem—at least three times, as he's observed the Passover three times (John 2:13–22; 6:4; 11:55). Likewise, in John, he cleanses the temple very early in his ministry, whereas, in the Synoptics, it occurs in the last week of his ministry in Jerusalem. He drives out money changers from the temple and says, "Take these things out of here! Stop making my Father's house a marketplace!" (John 2:16). Then some Jews ask about Jesus's authority, saying, "What sign can you show us for doing this?" (2:18). Then Jesus answers, "Destroy this temple, and in three days I will raise it up" (2:19). He means it metaphorically, "speaking of the temple of his body" (2:21). The narrator says, "After he was raised from the dead, his disciples remembered that he had said this; and they believed the scripture and the word that Jesus had spoken" (2:22). The disciples in John are portrayed positively. The disciples in Mark never understand Jesus. In Luke, the risen Lord walks with two of his disciples on the way to Emmaus and explains the scripture about him. But they do not remember Jesus's teaching or understand the scripture. While Jesus is in Jerusalem during the Passover, "many [believe] in his name because they saw the signs that he was doing" (John 2:23).

Then Jesus meets Nicodemus, a leader of the Jews, who comes to Jesus by night and says, "Rabbi, we know that you are a teacher who has come from God; for no one can do these signs that you do apart from the presence of God" (John 3:2). Nicodemus is a seeker of truth. Jesus answers, "Very truly, I tell you, no one can see the kingdom of God without being born *from above* [*anōthen*]" (John 3:3; emphasis added). Jesus says that one can live in the reign of God when one is born from above (*anōthen*). The Greek adverb *anōthen* means "anew," "again," or "from above." But here, "from above" fits well because Jesus rebuts Nicodemus's understanding of being born again. Nicodemus says, "How can anyone be born after having grown old? Can one enter a second time into the mother's womb and be born?" (John 3:4). Nicodemus understood *anōthen* as "again." Then Jesus corrects him and says this new birth is born of the Spirit—that is, "born from above" means one's new life is rooted in and connected with God or the Spirit. Jesus says, "Very truly, I tell you, no one can enter the kingdom of God without being born of water and Spirit. What is born of the flesh is flesh, and what is born of the Spirit is spirit. Do not be astonished that I said to you, 'You must be born from above'" (John 3:5–7). The phrase "born of water and Spirit" connotes the water baptism at which the Spirit is present. But this new birth from above is not about water baptism. The point is whether one depends on the Spirit. Jesus further explains this new birth with a reference to the wind: "The wind blows where it chooses, and you hear the sound of it, but you do not know where it comes from or where it goes. So it is with everyone who is born of the Spirit" (John 3:8). The spiritual person must accept Jesus's testimony and follow his words of God. Therefore, "whoever believes in the Son has eternal life; whoever disobeys the Son will not see life, but must endure God's wrath" (John 3:36).

While Nicodemus does not understand Jesus's point, the Johannine community members understand it, as the narrator uses "we" sayings in John 3:11–21; for example, he says, "Very truly, I tell you, *we speak of what we know and testify to what we have seen; yet you do not receive our testimony*" (emphasis added, 3:11). The centerpiece of their testimony is summarized in John 3:16–21, which is also a synopsis of the whole narrative of John. First, the testimony is about God's initiative of love: "For God so loved the world that he gave his only Son, so that everyone who believes in him may not perish but may have eternal life" (John 3:16). The claim is this: "God did not send the Son into the world to condemn the world, but in order that the world might be saved through him" (3:17). Second, people must trust the Son of God, hear his word, and dwell in the light. Those who do evil hate the light and try to hide their evil deeds (John 3:20). Mere belief in him is not enough, as Jesus says later in John 8:31–32: "If you continue in my word, you are truly my disciples; and you will know the truth, and the truth will make you free." Third, judgment or condemnation is realized at the present. As eternal life is in the present, judgment is also in the present. Those who hear the word of God through Jesus live the new life now; others are condemned already.

> TEXTBOX 5.3 *Consider and Discuss*
>
> **NICODEMUS (JOHN 3:1–21)**
>
> Jesus says to Nicodemus, "Very truly, I tell you, no one can see the kingdom of God without being born *from above* [or *again*]" (John 3:3). The Greek adverb *anōthen* means either "from above" or "again." Nicodemus understands it as "again" and asks, "How can anyone be born after having grown old? Can one enter a second time into the mother's womb and be born?" (John 3:4). Jesus refutes him and talks about birth from above: "Very truly, I tell you, no one can enter the kingdom of God without being born of water and Spirit" (3:5). "Being born of water and Spirit" may be understood in the context of water baptism, when one receives the Spirit from above. Those who experience spiritual birth from above dwell in the rule of God. In the end the question is as follows: Which translation makes better sense, "born from above" or "born again"? Explain why one is better than the other. Or you might propose an alternative translation.

Then Jesus goes into the Judean countryside with his disciples and the baptized people. Note that he also baptizes people (John 3:22, 26). With the news that many people are going to Jesus for baptism, John the Baptist says, "I am not the Messiah" (3:28) and "He must increase, but I must decrease" (3:30). One day, Jesus learns that "the Pharisees had heard, 'Jesus is making and baptizing more disciples than John'" (4:1). Then the narrator comments, "Although it was not Jesus himself but his disciples who baptized" (4:2). But the truth is that he was baptizing people (3:22, 26). After a while, Jesus leaves Judea and goes back to Galilee. He has to go through Samaria, which is a passing region for Galilee. He comes to a Samaritan city called Sychar, near Jacob's well. He sits there by the well because he is tired out from his journey (John 4:5–6). A Samaritan woman comes to the well to draw water, and Jesus says to her, "Give me a drink" (4:7). He's initiated a conversation with her. She is startled because she does not expect that a Jew would ask her, a woman of Samaria, for a drink. Then Jesus shifts the topic to spiritual living water. He says to her, "The water that I will give will become in them a spring of water gushing up to eternal life" (John 4:14). But she still is thinking about plain water so that she may never be thirsty again (4:15). All of a sudden, he says to her, "Go, call your husband, and come back" (4:16). In the end she reveals that she does not have a husband. Then she recognizes him as a prophet and he says, "Woman, believe me, the hour is coming when you will worship the Father neither on this mountain nor in Jerusalem" (John 4:21). He also says that "God is spirit, and those who worship him must worship in spirit and truth" (4:24). Then, the woman says, "I know that Messiah [Aramaic] is coming (who is called Christ)" (4:25). Finally, Jesus reveals himself and says, "I am he, the one who is speaking to you" (4:26). When Jesus's disciples come back, the woman has left her water jar and gone back to her community, saying to the people, "Come and see a man who told me everything I have ever done! He cannot be the Messiah, can he?" (John 4:29). Because of her testimony, all her community people believe in him, saying, "It is no longer because of what you said that we believe, for we have heard for ourselves, and we know that this is truly the Savior of the world" (4:42). By contrast, the disciples of Jesus are concerned about physical food only (4:31–38). True food is to do the will of God (4:34). After two days, Jesus comes to Galilee, and, unexpectedly, "the Galileans [welcome] him since they had seen all that he had done in Jerusalem at the festival; for they too had gone to the festival" (4:45). Then Jesus comes to Cana in Galilee, where he'd made his first sign, changing the water into wine. A royal official comes to Jesus and asks him to heal his son. Jesus says, "Go; your son will live" (John 4:50). "The man [believes] the word that Jesus spoke to him and [starts] on his way" (4:50). His son is healed at the time he believes. This is the second sign that Jesus does.

Now Jesus makes a second journey to Jerusalem because there is a festival for the Jews (John 5:1). There he heals a man at a pool called Bethzatha (in Aramaic); the man had been ill for thirty-eight years. Jesus says to him, "Do you want to be made well?" (John 5:6). The man says that no one has helped him get in the pool. Jesus says, "Stand up, take your mat and walk" (John 5:8). Immediately, the man is cured and begins to walk. This healing happens on the Sabbath. The Jews accuse him, but Jesus says to them, "My Father is still working, and I also am working" (John 5:17). Then the Jews are angry and seek to kill him "because he [is] not only breaking the Sabbath, but [is] also calling God his own Father, thereby making himself equal to God" (5:18). But this accusation is an exaggeration because Jesus has never called himself equal to God. Calling God the Father is not wrong. The only debatable accusation concerns his breaking the Sabbath. Jesus's defense is that God works on the Sabbath. Whereas other Jews think that God rests on the Sabbath, Jesus insists that God works regardless of the time. Then he emphasizes that he "can do nothing on his own, but only what he sees the Father doing" (John 5:19). He also says, "Very truly, I tell you, anyone who hears my word and believes him who sent me has eternal life, and does not come under judgment, but has passed from death to life" (5:24). Here, the point is not about Jesus's authority but the congruence between Jesus's work and God's. Jesus's work is testified to by John the Baptist (John 5:32–33). But the greater testimony is God's. Jesus says, "The works that the Father has given me to complete, the very works that I am doing, testify on my behalf that the Father has sent me" (John 5:36). The Word incarnate with Jesus is confirmed in John 5:37–38: "And the Father who sent me has himself testified on my behalf. You have never heard his voice or seen his form, and you do not have his word abiding in you, because you do not believe him whom he has sent." In the end there will be consequences between those who accept the word of Jesus and those who do not; the former will have the resurrection of life, and the latter, the resurrection of condemnation (John 5:29).

6:1–12:50, Jesus's Ministry Grows and Faces Opposition

Jesus's journey of Logos gets rougher, as he vehemently engages the Jews and Jewish leaders. First, Jesus feeds the five thousand (John 6:1–15) and says he is the bread from heaven (6:22–71). He uses a boy's five barley loaves and two fish and feeds the five thousand. This is the third sign that Jesus has done for people. The next day, when the crowd is looking for him for more signs, Jesus says to them, "I am the bread of life. Whoever comes to me will never be hungry, and whoever believes in me will never be thirsty" (John 6:35). The bread of life is spiritual food for people, which is the word of God. As people need bread every day, they need the word of God every day. Jesus delivers the word of God and embodies it through his work. People may look to Jesus to know who God is. So he says, "I have come down from heaven, not to do my own will, but the will of him who sent me" (John 6:38). So eternal life begins with believing in him, as John 6:40 says, "This is indeed the will of my Father, that all who see the Son and believe in him may have eternal life, and I will raise them up on the last day." Then the Jews complain about Jesus because he's said, "I am the bread that came down from heaven" (John 6:41); "Whoever eats of this bread will live forever; and the bread that I will give for the life of the world is my flesh" (6:51); and "Those who eat my flesh and drink my blood abide in me, and I in them. Just as the living Father sent me, and I live because of the Father, so whoever eats me will live because of me" (6:56–57). The whole point here is that people may see and experience God through his sacrificial living for them. But even his disciples say, "This teaching is difficult; who can accept it?" (John 6:60). But Jesus explains eternal life: "It is the spirit that gives life; the flesh is useless. The words that I have spoken to you are spirit and life" (John 6:63). In the end, however, many disciples leave Jesus because of this difficult teaching. But the twelve remain with him.

The Gospel of John

Jesus attends the Jewish Feast of Booths (John 7:1–52). He has a hard time there because, on the one hand, the crowds misunderstand him, and on the other hand, the Jewish leaders try to kill him. They do not believe that Jesus is the Messiah and think he has a demon. At other times, the Jews are astonished at his teaching. Jesus keeps saying that he does the work of God. So he says, "Do not judge by appearances, but judge with right judgment" (John 7:24). As Jesus insists that he is the Messiah whom God has sent, people try to arrest him. The chief priests and Pharisees send temple police to arrest Jesus. Then Jesus says humorously to them, "I will be with you a little while longer, and then I am going to him who sent me. You will search for me, but you will not find me; and where I am, you cannot come" (John 7:33–34). They do not get it. Eventually, they go back to the chief priests and Pharisees without arresting him, because they've found out great things about him. Nicodemus, who earlier talked with Jesus, appears and defends him in the hearing.

Jesus continues engaging with the Jews who do not believe that he is the Messiah. He says, "I am the light of the world" (John 8:12). The Pharisees and other Jews do not believe this. Later "Jesus [says] to the Jews who had believed in him: 'If you continue in my word, you are truly my disciples; and you will know the truth, and the truth will make you free'" (John 8:31–32). Then they argue that they are already free because they are descendants of Abraham. But Jesus refutes their claim and says that they are from the devil (John 8:44). Then they say, "You are a Samaritan and have a demon" (8:48). Jesus answers them, saying that Abraham saw his day (8:56). Then they say, "You are not yet fifty years old, and have you seen Abraham?" (8:57). According to Luke, Jesus is crucified when he is about thirty years old, at the time of Emperor Tiberius. But here, how do they know that he is about fifty years old? When Jesus answers that he was before Abraham was, they are unable to tolerate any more of him, and they try to throw stones at him. But Jesus goes out of the temple.

TEXTBOX 5.4 *Consider and Discuss*

"YOU ARE FROM YOUR FATHER THE DEVIL" (JOHN 8:44)

Jesus tells the Jews who do not believe in him, "You are from your father the devil" (John 8:44). This statement is controversial. How can we understand this? Does this lead to anti-Semitism? To answer, one must consider several things. First, this devil language does not apply to all of the Jews throughout history. Second, there is a distinction between the historical Jesus and the Johannine Jesus, as he is portrayed by John. Third, using the harsh language of the devil is unacceptable even if John claims that Jesus is the Messiah, the Son of God.

Now Jesus enrages the Pharisees and others because he has, on the sabbath, healed a blind man (John 9:1–41). While the disciples think that blindness is the result of sin, Jesus does not see it that way but says that it is a chance to reveal the work of God. Then the Pharisees do not believe the blind man's healing and ask his parents about it. His parents say, "We know that this is our son, and that he was born blind; but we do not know how it is that now he sees, nor do we know who opened his eyes. Ask him; he is of age. He will speak for himself" (John 9:20–21). Then the narrator comments, "His parents said this because they were afraid of the Jews; for the Jews had already agreed that anyone who confessed Jesus to be the Messiah would be put out of the synagogue. Therefore his parents said, 'He is of age; ask him'" (John 9:22–23). The narrator's comment seem to reflect the Johannine community's experience with the synagogue, which is hardly proved either way, because while there is no external or internal evidence that the community was expelled from the synagogue, such an expulsion never happened in Jesus's time either. Jesus is free to enter the synagogue and teach there.

In this story of a blind man's healing, there is a set of contrasts between him and the Pharisees. He emphasizes what he has experienced, acknowledging his imperfect knowledge: "I do not know whether he is a sinner. One thing I do know, that though I was blind, now I see" (John 9:25). But the Pharisees are confident about their tradition and are not able to see beyond it. So they argue that God speaks to them only: "You are his disciples, but we are disciples of Moses" (John 9:28). But Jesus says the Pharisees remain blind.

Jesus continues engaging the Jews and says that he is the gate of the sheep and the good shepherd because he lays down his life for the sheep (John 10:11). This image of his death is different from that of the Markan Jesus, who is distressed about his suffering and death. He says he lays down his life voluntarily and takes it up again (John 10:17–18). The Jews are divided; some believed in him, and others think he has a demon. At the Feast of the Dedication, Jesus says, "My sheep hear my voice. I know them, and they follow me" (John 10:27) and "The Father and I are one" (10:30). Here "one" (*hen*) is a neuter noun, and Jesus is referring to their union with the common purpose, which is to love and save the world. If "one" were *heis*, a masculine noun, it could mean Jesus's equality with God. But throughout the narrative of John, he never claims that he is God. He always says he is sent by God and does the work of God. So John 10:30 must be understood as Jesus's union with God in terms of his work of God. Then "the Jews [take] up stones again to stone him" because they think that he is blaspheming God, making himself God (John 10:33). But Jesus rejects the charge of blasphemy because he does the work of God. So he says, "If I am not doing the works of my Father, then do not believe me. But if I do them, even though you do not believe me, believe the works, so that you may know and understand that the Father is in me and I am in the Father" (John 10:37–38). Then the Jews "[try] to arrest him again, but he [escapes] from their hands" (10:39).

Then, after a while, Jesus hears that Lazarus of Bethany—the village of Mary and her sister Martha—is ill (John 11:1). But he does not rush to Lazarus's house, and Lazarus dies and is placed in the tomb for four days. Jesus delays going there to show his power to raise Lazarus so that many people may believe in him. Later he meets Martha on the way to Bethany and says to her, "I am the resurrection and the life. Those who believe in me, even though they die, will live, and everyone who lives and believes in me will never die. Do you believe this?" (John 11:25–26). He assures that resurrection or eternal life is realized in the present. Being greatly disturbed, he comes to the tomb and does several things, step-by-step (John 11:38–44): (1) asking Martha to take away the stone; (2) praying to the Father; and (3) crying out with a loud voice, "Lazarus, come out!" (11:43). Martha had not believed that Jesus could raise Lazarus even though she'd earlier heard from him, "Those who believe in me, even though they die, will live" (11:25). He prays to the Father that raising Lazarus will be a sign that people may believe in him. Then he awakens Lazarus by calling his name as if he were sleeping. Soon "the dead man [comes] out, his hands and feet bound with strips of cloth and his face wrapped in a cloth" (John 11:44). Lazarus needed help! So Jesus says to others, "Unbind him, and let him go" (John 11:44). Eternal life or resurrection can be the present reality, but it goes through a step-by-step process. Because of this wonderful sign of Jesus raising Lazarus, some Jews believe in him, and yet others do not. The Pharisees convene a council to discuss what to do with Jesus. Caiaphas, the high priest, says that Jesus's death would be a good sacrifice for the nation (John 11:48–50). If Jesus's work is unchecked, many will follow him, and the Romans will destroy their nation. He also believes that Jesus's death would unite "the dispersed children of God" (John 11:52).

A few days before the Passover, Jesus comes to Bethany, the home of Lazarus. At a dinner table, Mary anoints Jesus's feet and wipes them with her hair (John 12:3; cf. Luke 7:36–50). After this, Jesus enters Jerusalem, sitting on a young donkey (John 12:12–19). His disciples understand these things after Jesus is glorified (12:16). Soon Jesus begins to speak about his death. He says he has come to this hour to die. His death is to glorify God's name (John 12:27–28). The narrator of John says that many believe in Jesus, but because of the Pharisees, "they [do] not confess it, for fear that they [will] be out of the synagogue" (12:42). This comment seems to reflect the Johannine community's experience with Judaism, which is hard to distill (9:22).[5] Then the narrator gives a summary of Jesus's ministry in John 12:44–50:

Then Jesus cried aloud: "Whoever believes in me believes not in me but in him who sent me. And whoever sees me sees him who sent me. I have come as light into the world, so that everyone who believes in me should not remain in the darkness. I do not judge anyone who hears my words and does not keep them, for I came not to judge the world, but to save the world. The one who rejects me and does not receive my word has a judge; on the last day the word that I have spoken will serve as judge, for I have not spoken on my own, but the Father who sent me has himself given me a commandment about what to say and what to speak. And I know that his commandment is eternal life. What I speak, therefore, I speak just as the Father has told me." (NRSV)

13:1–17:26, Farewell Discourses

Jesus prepares for his departure back to God and delivers his farewell discourses. In John 13:1–20, he washes the disciples' feet, which is unique to John, and asks them to do the same thing. That is a great example that they must continue when serving others in the future. After doing this, he foretells his betrayal (John 13:21–30). The narrator then introduces the disciple whom Jesus loves (the Beloved Disciple). He asks Jesus, "Lord, who is it?" (John 13:25). After revealing who will betray him, Jesus goes out and talks about his departure. He gave the disciples a new commandment that they should love one another (John 13:34–35). Then he foretells Peter's denial (13:36–38). Peter swears that he will lay down his life for Jesus. Jesus answers, "Before the cock crows, you will have denied me three times" (John 13:38).

In John 14:1–31, Jesus gives a farewell discourse. He begins, "Do not let your hearts be troubled. Believe in God, believe also in me. In my Father's house there are many dwelling places. . . . And if I go and prepare a place for you, I will come again and will take you to myself, so that where I am, there you may be also. And you know the way to the place where I am going" (John 14:1–4). Jesus comforts his disciples and assures them that they will not be orphaned, because the Paraclete will come after he departs (14:15; 15:26; 16:7, 12). So his coming back in John 14:2–4 is equivalent to the Spirit's coming. But Thomas says, "Lord, we do not know where you are going. How can we know the way?" (John 14:5). Jesus says to him, "I am the way, and the truth, and the life. No one comes to the Father except through me. If you know me, you will know my Father also. From now on you do know him and have seen him" (John 14:6–7). Again, here, Jesus assures the disciples that they may follow the way, the truth, and the life that he has shown them after he returns to the Father. The "I am" sayings in John 14:6 must be understood in the context where Jesus prepares for his departure and assures the disciples to feel secure. Because he's shown them the way of life and truth, they must remember his work. The Spirit

The Gospel of John 125

of truth also will come to help them (John 14:17). Jesus again confirms that he will not leave them orphaned, because he is coming back with the Spirit (14:18). He identifies with the Spirit and emphasizes that the Father will send the Paraclete in his name. The Paraclete will teach them everything, reminding them of all that Jesus has said to them (John 14:26).

TEXTBOX 5.5   *Consider and Discuss*

THE PARACLETE (JOHN 14:26; 15:26; CF. 14:17; 16:13)

In John there is a different name for the Spirit: the Paraclete. The role of the Paraclete is to fill in for Jesus's absence after his departure to God. The Paraclete will come and teach Jesus's disciples everything and remind them of all that Jesus taught (John 14:26). The Paraclete will also testify on behalf of Jesus (15:26). Whereas, in the Synoptic Gospels, the Son of Man is coming back in the future, in John's Gospel, Jesus does not say that the Son of Man is coming back. Rather, he is glorified as the Son of Man, which means his death is a moment of glory (John 13:31). For instance, he says, "The hour has come for the Son of Man to be glorified" (12:23). The crowd also refers to the Son of Man in this way: "We have heard from the law that the Messiah remains forever. How can you say that the Son of Man must be lifted up? Who is this Son of Man?'" (John 12:34). In John the Paraclete will come after Jesus, so there is no saying about Jesus's coming back as the Son of Man. As seen above, John's view of Jesus and the role of the Spirit is very different from that of the Synoptic Gospels. How can we explain the differences in John? In some sense, is John more realistic in dealing with Christian lives than the Synoptic Gospels are? Or is it simply a maverick Gospel?

In John 15:1–27, Jesus talks about the vine metaphor and emphasizes the importance of bearing fruit and loving one another. He is the true vine to which the disciples are connected. When the branches are connected with the vine, they may bear fruit. Here, "connection" means their keeping of Jesus's commandments, which is to participate in God's mission, as in John 3:16—that is, to love and save the world. Jesus is the vine because God has sent him to save the world. But the world is hostile to the children of God. Even if the world hates the disciples, they should not be surprised, because if they were to belong to the world, the world would love them as its own (John 15:18). But they should wait for the Paraclete, the Spirit of truth from the Father, after Jesus is gone. Jesus even says that it is to their advantage that he goes away. If he does not go away, the Paraclete will not come to them (John 16:7). The Spirit of truth will guide them "into all the truth" (16:13). Finally, Jesus, without ironies, plainly says, "I came from the Father and have come into the world;

again, I am leaving the world and am going to the Father" (16:28). Jesus encourages his disciples to stay faithful even when they face persecution, so he says, "But take courage; I have conquered the world!" (16:33). Here, "conquering the world" is a matter of interpretation. In what way has he conquered it? While there are ways of interpreting this, we should not render it as an imperialistic invasion of other cultures or religions.

In John 17:1–26, Jesus gives a long prayer for his disciples. First of all, he says to God that he has completed his work of God and that now is the time for the glory (John 17:4). He has revealed God to the world, and he says, "For *the words that you gave to me* I have given to them, and they have received them and know in truth that I came from you; and they have believed that you sent me" (emphasis added, 17:8). The words Jesus received from God and gives to his disciples might be understood as his embodiment of the Logos (the Word) in the prologue (1:14). In this sense, the Gospel of John is about the Logos and Jesus. The latter incarnates the former. The Logos came from heaven, and Jesus has completed his work of God. So he is ready to return to the Father. Jesus continues, "I have given them *your word*, and the world has hated them because they do not belong to the world, just as I do not belong to the world" (emphasis added, John 17:14). Jesus has delivered the word of God to the world that hates him and his disciples. The reason for their hatred is Jesus and his disciples do not accept the norms and ideologies of the world (i.e., the Roman Empire). In this sense, Jesus's not belonging to the world is a political statement. Likewise, John's Gospel is not otherworldly at all; rather, he participates in the world by resisting the system of the world. He even prays to the Father so that the disciples will continue to work in the world: "I am not asking you to take them out of the world, but I ask you to protect them from the evil one" (John 17:15). If Jesus were interested in the Gnostic type of salvation, then he would have asked God to take them as soon as possible so that they may not experience suffering in the world. If he were to ask that way, he would be a Gnostic Christ who paves the way to the heavenly realm, away from this transitory world. Rather, his prayer is to keep and sanctify them in the world. They have to testify to the truth of God in the world (John 17:17).

18:1–20:31, Suffering and Glory

Jesus's long journey ends up in his arrest and suffering and death. When Judas and the soldiers come to arrest Jesus, he says openly that he is the one they are looking for (John 18:5–8). Here, he says three times, "I am he" (*egō eimi*; 18:5–6, 8), which means simply "It's me." Otherwise, this saying is not associated with the divine name given in Exodus 3:14: "I am who

I am." Moments later, Peter, who is following Jesus, denies him: "I am not" (*ouk eimi*; John 18:17). Jesus is taken to the high priest and answers openly about his teaching: "I have spoken openly to the world; I have always taught in synagogues and in the temple, where all the Jews come together. I have said nothing in secret. Why do you ask me? Ask those who heard what I said to them; they know what I said" (John 18:20–21). Peter stands and warms himself in the courtyard. He denies being one who knows Jesus two more times: "I am not" (John 18:25–27). Then Jesus is brought to Pilate, who asks, "What have you done?" (18:35). Jesus answers, "My kingdom is not from this world" (18:36), which means God's kingdom is not operative like this world is. Then Pilate asks, "So you are a king?" (18:37). Jesus answers elusively, "You say that I am a king. For this I was born, and for this I came into the world, to testify to the truth. Everyone who belongs to the truth listens to my voice" (John 18:37). Pilate asks, "What is truth?" (18:38). After this, Pilate says three times that he's found no case against Jesus (18:38; 19:4, 6). Then the Jews say, "We have a law, and according to that law he ought to die because he has claimed to be the Son of God" (19:7). In fact, the Jews' charge of Jesus is ambiguous. Earlier, they'd brought Jesus to Pilate with a criminal charge of sedition (John 18:30). Now they say Jesus has blasphemed God. But calling oneself the Son of God may not necessarily constitute blasphemy, because the Son of God is an agent of God. Otherwise, Jesus has never claimed that he is God (cf. John 10:36). Rather, his point has always been that he does the work of God, who sent him. Pilate eventually allows Jesus to be crucified because the Jews shout, "If you release this man, you are no friend of the emperor. Everyone who claims to be a king sets himself against the emperor" (John 19:12). In the end Jesus is charged as a political criminal.

TEXTBOX 5.6 ***Consider and Discuss***

"TO TESTIFY TO THE TRUTH" (JOHN 18:37)

Pilate asks Jesus, "So you are a king?" (John 18:37). Jesus answers, "You say that I am a king. For this I was born, and for this I came into the world, to testify to the truth. Everyone who belongs to the truth listens to my voice" (18:37). What kind of king is Jesus thinking of? As Pilate asks him, "What is truth?" (18:38), to what truth does Jesus testify? Is it about God or Jesus or something else? How does the truth to which Jesus testifies in John 18:37 relate to that in 8:32 ("You will know the truth, and the truth will make you free") and 14:6 ("I am the way and the truth and the life")? To what extent does Jesus's testimony to the truth affect the Roman Empire?

In John 19:16b–42, the narrator talks about the crucifixion and burial of Jesus. Jesus carries the cross by himself (there is no mention of Simon of Cyrene, as in the Synoptic Gospels) and goes to Golgotha, "the Place of the Skull." The inscription, written in Hebrew, Latin, and Greek, on the cross reads, "Jesus of Nazareth, the King of the Jews" (John 19:19). Then the narrator tells a unique story about Jesus's mother. His mother; his mother's sister, Mary the wife of Clopas; and Mary Magdalene are standing near his cross (John 19:25). Jesus sees his mother and the disciple whom he loves, and he says to her, "Woman, here is your son" (19:26). He also says to the disciple, "Here is your mother" (19:27). After this, the Beloved Disciple takes care of her. Then Jesus knows that all is done now. He says, "It is finished" (John 19:30). "Then he bowed his head and gave up his spirit" (19:30). Unlike in the Synoptic Gospels, here, the last moment of his life is so calm and short. There is no lament or anguish, as seen in Matthew or Mark. There is no elaboration on Jesus's calm, as seen in Luke. The only words he says are "It is finished." Readers wonder about what has been finished by him, and to understand it, they must review all he has said and done throughout the narrative. After these things, Joseph of Arimathea, "who was a disciple of Jesus, though a secret one because of his fear of the Jews," gets permission from Pilate to remove the body of Jesus (John 19:38). Nicodemus, another secret disciple of Jesus, "who had at first come to Jesus by night," brings "a mixture of myrrh and aloes, weighing about a hundred pounds" (19:39). He is a minor character in the Gospel, yet his presence and faith are significant even though they are not perfect. No character is perfect in the Gospel. They bury the body of Jesus in a new tomb on the day of preparation.

In John 20:1–31, the narrator talks about the resurrection of Jesus and his first appearance to the disciples. Mary Magdalene comes to the tomb early on the first day of the week and finds the stone has been removed from the tomb (John 20:1). She goes to Simon Peter and the disciple whom Jesus loved, and she reports that Jesus's body was taken out. Simon and the disciple come and confirm that they cannot find Jesus's body there. Yet they do not know what it means and so go back to their homes (John 20:10). But Mary weeps outside the tomb and looks into it. She sees two angels, who then say to her, "Woman, why are you weeping?" (John 20:13). When she tells him why she's been weeping, she turns around and sees Jesus. But "she [does] not know that it [is] Jesus" (John 20:14). Jesus says to her, "Mary!" (20:16). Now Mary knows that he is Jesus, calling him "Rabbouni [Teacher]" (20:16). Jesus says to her, "Do not hold on to me, because I have not yet ascended to the Father. But go to my brothers and say to them, 'I am ascending to my Father and your Father, to my God and your God'" (John 20:17). This instruction to Mary Magdalene is unique to John. In the Synoptic Gospels, Jesus tells the visitors that he will go to meet his disciples in Galilee (Mark and Matthew) or Jerusalem (Luke). In John, Jesus says simply that he returns to the Father. When he returns, the Paraclete will come to them in his absence. Mary Magdalene shares the news with the disciples: "I have seen the Lord" (John 20:18). Nevertheless, in the evening of that day, Jesus appears to the disciples, who've been meeting with the doors locked "for fear of the Jews," which may reflect certain tensions with the synagogue (20:19), even if it does not necessarily connote the community's expulsion. Jesus says, "Peace be with you" and, later, breathes on them, saying, "Receive the Holy Spirit" (20:22). A week later, Jesus appears to Thomas, who doubted his resurrection, and shows his wounds. Thomas answers, "My Lord and my God!" (John 20:28).

Then the narrator finishes the story about Jesus, saying, "Now Jesus did many other signs in the presence of his disciples, which are not written in this book. But these are written so that you may come to believe that Jesus is the Messiah, the Son of God and that through believing you may have life in his name" (John 20:30-31). This ending is the original ending of the Gospel and matches the prologue, where the narrator introduces the Logos, whose purpose is to give life to the world.

21:1–25, Addendum

John 21:1–25 is considered an addition by the later generation of the Johannine community. Nevertheless, from that generation, this story is part of the whole and reflects their experiences after the Beloved Disciple's testimony. Jesus again appears to some disciples by the Sea of Tiberias. Peter and his friends go fishing and catch nothing. Jesus stands on the beach and asks them to cast the net to the right side of the boat (sounding like the story of Peter in Luke 5:1–11). They do not know that it is Jesus. They catch so many fish. Then suddenly, the disciple whom Jesus loved says to Peter, "It is the Lord!" (John 21:7). The Beloved Disciple is the first to notice the risen Lord. That is important to the Johannine community because he is the witness of Jesus. Jesus says to the disciples, "Bring some of the fish that you have just caught" (John 21:10). Peter finds there are 153 of them. Jesus prepares breakfast for them. None ask Jesus, "Who are you?" This is "because they knew it was the Lord" (John 20:12). This is the third time that Jesus appears to his disciples. The next scene is about Jesus and Peter. After breakfast, Jesus says to Peter, "Simon son of John, do you love me more than these?" (John 21:15). Peter answers, "'Yes, Lord; you know that I love you.' Jesus said, 'Feed my lambs'" (John 21:15). Jesus asks two more times, and Peter answers similarly. In the first two questions, Jesus uses the verb *agapaó*, and Peter answers with *phileó*. The third time, Jesus asks with *phileó*, and Peter also answers with *phileó*. Both *agapaó* and *phileó* mean "to love." But why for the third time does Jesus change the verb to *phileó* if *agapaó* is rendered superior to *phileó*, especially as *phileó* is used for friendship? It is hard to tell. They may be interchangeable with each other. But it may be possible that Jesus chose *phileó* to indicate an intimate relationship with Peter. Earlier, Peter denied Jesus three times, and now he needs to recover from those moments of failure. While it is hard to know why the narrator uses two different verbs, both *agapaó* and *phileó*, their conversation implies that Peter's future is gloomy because he also must go through the hardships/death that Jesus underwent.

The last scene in the addendum is about Jesus and the Beloved Disciple. Peter asks Jesus about the Beloved Disciple: "Lord, what about him?" (John 21:21). Jesus says, "If it is my will that he remain until I come, what is that to you? Follow me!" (John 21:22). The narrator comments the following at this point: "So the rumor spread in the community that this disciple would not die. Yet Jesus did not say to him that he would not die, but 'If it is my will that he remain until I come, what is that to you?'" (John 21:23). This comment seems to confirm that the Beloved Disciple is already dead when this story is told. The community had expected that he would not die until Jesus came back. So the narrator retells the original story of Jesus in this way. The point is that the community must continue to live with the testimony of the Beloved Disciple. So the narrator says finally, "This is the disciple who is testifying to these things and has written them, and we know that his testimony is true" (John 21:24). There is also another ending in John 20:25: "But there are also many other things that Jesus did; if every one of them were written down, I suppose that the world itself could not contain the books that would be written."

QUESTIONS FOR REFLECTION

1. John's Gospel has often been understood as a spiritual gospel. In what sense is this claim still valid, and in what sense is it problematic?
2. The Johannine prologue is markedly different from that of Matthew and Luke. Why does John begin with the phrase "In the beginning was the Word" (John 1:1)? Does John allude to Genesis 1:1–2? What is the conclusion of the prologue? What relationship is there between the prologue and the rest of the narrative?
3. Concerning the "I am" sayings of Jesus, how can we understand them? Do they support his divine identity or his work as the Son of God? If he says, "I am the way," in what sense is he the way? He also says, "No one comes to the Father except through me" (John 14:6). What does he mean? Is there room for engaging with other religions?

4. Jesus's last words in John are "It is finished" (John 19:30). What is finished in the narrative? What should be continued by his disciples?
5. In what way does John's Gospel reflect the Johannine community's relationships with the synagogue? Is this Gospel or community behind this Gospel sectarian, or does it engage with the world positively through love?
6. The dualistic images and metaphors are ingrained in the Gospel of John—for example, heaven and earth, light and darkness, and spirit and flesh. What is the purpose of having those images or metaphors in the Gospel?
7. The Gospel of John is not a dualistic gospel, because it claims that Jesus came in the flesh and that God so loved the world. Why do many readers interpret the Gospel that way?

FURTHER READING

Anderson, Paul. *The Riddles of the Fourth Gospel: An Introduction to John*. Minneapolis, MN: Fortress, 2011.

Blount, Brian K. *Then the Whisper Put on Flesh. New Testament Ethics in an African American Context*. Nashville: Abingdon Press, 2001.

Brodie, Thomas. *The Gospel According to John: A Literary and Theological Commentary*. New York: Oxford University Press, 1993.

Callahan, Allen Dwight. "The Gospel of John." In *True to Our Native Land: An African American New Testament Commentary*, edited by Brian Blount, Cain Hope Felder, Clarice J. Martin, and Emerson B. Powery, 186–212. Minneapolis, MN: Fortress, 2007.

Clark-Soles, Jaime. *Reading John for Dear Life: A Spiritual Walk with the Fourth Gospel*. Louisville, KY: Westminster John Knox, 2016.

Coloe, Mary. *Wisdom Commentary: John 1–10; John 11–21*. Collegeville, MN: Liturgical Press, 2021.

Culpepper, R. Alan. *Anatomy of the Fourth Gospel: A Study in Literary Design*. Minneapolis, MN: Fortress, 1987.

Hylen, Susan E. *Imperfect Believers: Ambiguous Characters in the Gospel of John*. Louisville, KY: Westminster John Knox, 2009.

Kim, Yung Suk. *Truth, Testimony, and Transformation: A New Reading of the "I am" Sayings of Jesus in the Fourth Gospel*. Eugen, OR: Cascade Books, 2014.

Levine, Amy-Jill, ed. *A Feminist Companion to John*. Vol. 1. New York: Sheffield Academic Press, 2003.

Lozada, Francisco, Jr. "John: The Politics of Recognition." In *Latinx Perspectives on the New Testament*, edited by Osvaldo D. Vena and Leticia A. Guardiola-Saenz, 83–102. Lanham, MD: Lexington Books, 2022.

Martyn, J. Louis. *History and Theology in the Fourth Gospel*. 3rd ed. Louisville, KY: Westminster John Knox, 2003.

O'Day, Gail R. "The Gospel of John." In *Women's Bible Commentary, Revised Edition*, edited by Carol Newsom, Sharon H. Ringe, and Jacqueline E. Lapsey, 517–30. Louisville, KY: Westminster John Knox, 2012.

Park, Kyung-mi. "John." In *Global Bible Commentary*. Edited by Daniel Patte, 401–411. Nashville, TN: Abingdon, 2004.

Reinhartz, Adele. "Judaism in the Gospel of John," *Interpretation* 63, no. 4 (2009): 382–93.

———. "The Gospel According to John," in *The Jewish Annotated New Testament*, edited by Amy-Jill Levine and Marc Zvi Brettler, 168–218. New York: Oxford University Press, 2017.

Segovia, Fernando F., ed. *"What is John?" Vol. II, Literary and Social Readings of the Fourth Gospel*. Atlanta, GA: Scholars Press, 1998.

Thomaskutty, Johnson. "The Gospel of John." In *An Asian Introduction to the New Testament*, edited by Johnson Thomaskutty, 127–56. Minneapolis, MN: Fortress, 2022.

NOTES

1. Yung Suk Kim, *Truth, Testimony, and Transformation: A New Reading of the "I Am" Sayings of Jesus in the Fourth Gospel* (Eugene, OR: Cascade Books, 2014), 28–78.

2. The Logos in John may be understood flexibly because it has various notions: word, principle, reason, thought, and so forth. It may be associated with the word of God, the word that Jesus delivers to the disciples, or the truth of God. What John's Gospel say about the Logos is the key issue of interpretation.

3. Since Logos is a masculine, singular noun, it is translated as "he/him/his" in English. But all forms of the masculine singular pronouns in John 1:1–13 do not refer to Jesus. There is no direct mention of Jesus until at least John 1:14, when the Logos is associated with flesh.

4. There are textual variants in John 1:18: (1) *ho monogenēs huios* (the only begotten son), (2) *monogenēs theos* (the begotten God), (3) *ho monogenēs theos* (the only begotten God), and (4) *ho monogenēs* (the begotten one). For more about this issue, see "Textual Criticism" in chapter 10.

5. While Louis Martyn and other scholars posit that there was the Johannine community's expulsion from the synagogue, Adele Reinhartz opposes such a theory because, essentially, there is no one such event that can be proved. See Louis Martyn, *History and Theology in the Fourth Gospel* (Louisville, KY: Westminster John Knox, 2003), 35–66. See also, Adele Reinhartz, "Judaism in the Gospel of John," *Interpretation* 63, no. 4 (2009): 382–93; Reinhartz, "The Gospel According to John," in *The Jewish Annotated New Testament*, ed. Amy-Jill Levine and Marc Zvi Brettler (New York: Oxford University Press, 2017), 197.

II

READING THE GOSPELS FROM VARIOUS PERSPECTIVES

Chapter 6

Overview of Interpretive Approaches to the Gospels

Interpretation of the Gospels is never exhaustive as long as readers engage with the text from diverse perspectives. In part 2, we see how we can read the Gospels variously, and in so doing, we use three approaches to the interpretation of the Gospels: (1) an author-centered, historical approach; 2) a text-centered, literary approach; and 3) a reader-centered, comprehensive approach. By providing a brief definition of each method or criticism, we can focus on the illustration of the methods in the remaining chapters of part 2. See below the three approaches to the interpretation of the Gospels.

TEXTBOX 6.1 *Three Approaches to the Interpretation of the Gospels*

AUTHOR-CENTERED, HISTORICAL APPROACH

Historical-critical method
Social-science criticism

TEXT-CENTERED, LITERARY APPROACH

Textual criticism
Narrative criticism

READER-CENTERED, COMPREHENSIVE APPROACH

Reader-response criticism
Feminist criticism
Womanist interpretation

> Ekklesia-centered, theological interpretation
> Jewish interpretation
> Inter(con)textual criticism
> Queer criticism
> Postcolonial criticism
> Deconstruction
> Minoritized criticism
> Disability studies
> Ecological criticism

The above three-part division is not absolute or definitive but flexible, since one criticism may overlap with other methods. This division considers the historical development of interpretive methods, beginning with the author-centered historical approach, moving toward the text-centered and reader-centered approaches. In the author-centered, historical approach, the interpretive focus is the author of the text or the history of the community behind the text. The historical-critical method, including source criticism and redaction criticism, has traditionally been concerned with the author's meaning. Social-science criticism is also put into this historical approach because its ultimate interest is a historical-social reconstruction of the text or the community, even though the text is treated as a whole seriously.

In the text-centered, literary approach, the focus is the text itself. While textual criticism seeks to discern the earlier reading of a text, narrative criticism treats the Gospels as story. Other literary approaches, such as structural criticism and rhetorical criticism, are not included in this book, not because they are trivial but because narrative criticism is most widely practiced in the study of the Gospels.

In the reader-centered, comprehensive approach, the intentional focus is on the reader who engages with the text through various critical, interpretative lenses and decides the meaning. This approach may be arbitrary if there is inadequate treatment of a text out of context, but it can be balanced, critical, and comprehensive when readers take all the factors of a text seriously, consider their context carefully, and evaluate other readings. We cover a variety of methods or perspectives in this reader-centered comprehensive approach, including disability studies, queer criticism, and Jewish interpretation.

As it might sound odd to some readers, "theological interpretation," as narrowly defined, is not covered in this book, because theological interpretation is a broad term for biblical interpretation. Most biblical criticisms are theological in a comprehensive sense. For example, narrative criticism is theological because it deals with, among other things, the narrator's theological vocabulary infused into the text. Queer criticism is also a theological interpretation because there is a queer interpretation of God or Jesus. Likewise, disability studies is a theological interpretation because there are concerns about popular theological notions about disability. Some people posit the term "theological interpretation," primarily deals with doctrine or systematic, theology-driven reasoning and reading of scripture. Such a reading has been done for so long—for almost two thousand years throughout Western churches and scholarship—and can be continued so, but it is not included in this book, which perceives biblical interpretation broadly where theological interpretation, as broadly defined, melts in biblical criticisms or perspectives to a different degree. However, ekklesia-centered, theological interpretation is included in the reader-centered, comprehensive approach because it engages the Gospels critically in context and with a focus on the ekklesia—especially on themes such as mission, discipleship, community life, and ethical teachings in the Gospels—for the contemporary church and Christians.[1]

AUTHOR-CENTERED, HISTORICAL APPROACH

Historical-Critical Method

The historical-critical method includes various historical criticisms, such as source criticism, form criticism, redaction criticism, and tradition-historical criticism. It seeks to explore the author's meaning, which is the meaning behind the text. Interpreters investigate the text to know what happened to the community behind the literature and raise historical-critical questions about the text and the community: Who wrote? To whom did they write? Why? To answer these questions, historians treat text as a means of reconstructing the history of a community. Concerning the study of the Gospels, source or form criticism is widely practiced and seeks to find literary or oral sources in the composition of the Gospel.[2] Sources include Jesus's sayings, passion, resurrection narratives, miracle stories, and other anecdotes about him. Also, the whole Gospel may be a literary source. According to the two-source hypothesis, Mark and Q (a third source used by Matthew and Luke) became sources for Matthew and Luke. In the Gospel study, source criticism leads to redaction criticism, which seeks to identify the evangelist's change with the source material and explain why the evangelist edited it. *Redaction* means "editing" sources.[3] The redactor serves as a theologian (or evangelist), not a mere collector. Readers seek to identify literary sources and explain why the evangelist changed the source material. In doing so, they try to find different theological interests in each Gospel. We can apply this criticism to the study of the Synoptic Gospels. While in Mark, Jesus's baptism appears dynamic, vivid, and straightforward, in Matthew, the narrator adds a didactic, conversational style to the text, explaining the baptism's purpose, which is to fulfill the righteousness of God. Otherwise, the baptism of Jesus is not about the forgiveness of sins or the question of who will sit higher. Luke omits some details of the baptism concerning the baptizer's name and the place of baptism. Instead, Luke emphasizes Jesus's prayer and the presence of people at his baptism. The omission of baptism details is a conundrum because Luke puts Jesus's roots in Judaism, as seen in his circumcision, the presentation of Jesus in the temple at age twelve, and his preaching at his hometown synagogue. In the end we must say that while the historical-critical method helps us understand the historical nature of the text and the community behind it, there is no guarantee that we can access the author.

Social-Science Criticism

Social-science criticism deals with the social or cultural dimensions of the text through various theories or models of social science. Social science is a broad term that covers any discipline that deals with the sociocultural aspects of human behavior, including but not limited to sociology, cultural anthropology, political science, and economics.[4] Put simply, sociology is concerned with human social life, groups, institutions, and societies. When it comes to the study of the Gospels, the focus is to examine the gospel community's social or cultural life in a society. When a community goes through hardships due to conflict with outsiders, the *sociology of knowledge* helps explain how it handles them successfully. A social canopy provides community members with a feeling of security. They are comforted and stay in the community. For example, if the Johannine community experienced separation from the synagogue, its members needed comfort and a sense of secure identity because they were uncertain about their place. Besides the sociology of knowledge, functionalism or conflict model may be another tool for interpreting the Gospels. Functionalism has a positive view of society as a harmonious body where parts serve the whole. For example, in crises, pastors or prophets help the marginalized and deliver the message of hope and restoration so that society can go in the right direction. In this regard, early Christianity is perceived as a renewal movement within Judaism.[5] The radical prophetic preaching of early Christians mitigated crises and tensions in society. In times of social turmoil, they provided security and support to society. By contrast, the conflict model views society negatively, as there are always conflicts between classes. As we see above, social-science criticism sides with the historical-critical approach since it deals with the author's meaning. But the difference is that social science focuses on the social dimensions of the text.

TEXT-CENTERED, LITERARY APPROACH

Textual Criticism

We do not have copies of the original manuscript of the New Testament. The earliest surviving New Testament Greek manuscripts come from the late fourth century CE. There are thousands of copies of the New Testament due to many textual variations.[6] Every manuscript includes mistakes, whether they are accidental or intentional. Given this reality, textual scholars seek to discover the earliest version of the text in the form of a manuscript.[7] They developed a set of criteria to discern the earlier version of the text; for example, preference goes to the earliest and most widely dispersed and trustable manuscript. Also, the more difficult reading and multiple attestations are preferred. Textual criticism is indispensable to interpreters, who must establish a secure text before interpreting. But even if we have a dependable text through textual criticism, the meaning of a text is not secured, because we must translate the text and grapple with it from critical perspectives.

Narrative Criticism

Narrative criticism seeks the meaning within the text.[8] Meaning does not depend on history, the author, or the reader. It is found somewhere in a close reading of the text. The real author does not control the meaning. Instead, the literature is sufficient for the readers who may follow the story, involving their interpretation of plot, characterization, setting, point of view, irony, and gaps. They pay attention to the storyline from beginning to end. However, the difficulty is that readers must fill in the gaps. More importantly, the point of view also affects the reader's understanding of the story. The question is by whose perspective or point of view one reads the story. One may follow the dominant narrator's point or find an alternative voice from the story. All of this means narrative criticism is wide open to diverse meaning making. Narrative criticism works well with the Gospels because they are stories about Jesus. Some critics challenge narrative criticism because some believe it does not take history seriously.

READER-CENTERED, COMPREHENSIVE APPROACH

Reader-Response Criticism

Reader-response interpretation emphasizes the reader's active role in meaning making. While in narrative criticism, the emphasis is on the story itself (the implied reader follows the implied author), in reader-response interpretation, the flesh-and-blood reader is essential to interpreting.[9] Meaning is the result of the reader's interaction with the text. So the meaning occurs in front of the text. Real readers raise critical reader-response questions to the story, looking forward, looking back, and filling in the gaps in the narrative. Reader-response criticism extends narrative interpretation because readers must read the text closely with the whole story in mind. The difference with narrative criticism is readers consciously bring their values or attitudes toward the narrative. On one hand, readers attend to the flow and content of the story. On the other, they try to fill in gaps in the story and often struggle with unbridgeable gaps. Reader-response criticism is open-ended, and its implications are varied. Because of the role of real readers, the spectrum of interpretation is more open.

Feminist Criticism

Feminist criticism challenges the androcentric interpretation of the Bible, pointing out the gendered texts and reevaluating women characters in the Bible.[10] Furthermore, feminist critics explore women's voices in the text. The text itself is androcentric, and therefore, deconstruction is necessary. Feminist scholars expose the male experience and dominant ideology in a community or society. They also point out that gender is a social construction that needs a reconfiguration based on the equality and agency of women. Gender is studied with race and class because those determinants entangle society and its members. As in the case of reader-response criticism, feminist criticism is not singularly defined, because there is a broad spectrum of feminist criticism. The Gospels present women variously; on the one hand, they are active and positive. Yet they are not called disciples. Feminist scholars reevaluate the women in the Gospels, and the historical picture of women's presence with Jesus is a matter of debate because it is unclear. In Paul's letters the reality and issue are more complex. Paul affirms women's work in the church, and their relationship with their husbands is interdependent. But in some letters, such as the Deutero-Pauline and pastoral letters, women's place in the church is limited, and they are not allowed to teach.

Womanist Interpretation

Womanist interpretation is growing among African American women scholars. It responds to feminism on the one hand and black theology on the other. While womanist theology is akin to feminism, the difference is in its emphasis on the distinctive experience of African American women, who are different from white women.[11] While black theology generally emphasizes the broad discourse of liberation theology in society, womanist theology feels that African American women or other women of color are not fully appreciated or treated equally. So womanist theologians and biblical scholars alike point out the importance of women's experiences and perspectives and read biblical texts afresh.[12] One approach womanist interpretation emphasizes is practical holism, with the goal of restoring a whole human being to a family, community, and society.

Ekklesia-Centered, Theological Interpretation

Ekklesia-centered, theological interpretation operates with two tenets: (1) the Gospels are primarily for the church and Christians, and (2) Christianity must be rooted in early Christian witnesses and Jesus's teaching found in the Gospels.[13] The Gospels are indeed the product of the evangelists or the communities that responded to the story of Jesus and lived it out in their world. In a way, the four versions of the Gospel represent the four kinds of ekklesia-centered, theological interpretation. For example, Mark addresses persecution or suffering in the community due to the Christian gospel proclamation in a harsh world, and he emphasizes the importance of the cost of discipleship, among other things. Matthew is concerned with an authentic Christian community and its tension with the Gentiles due to the community boundary, and he explores the role of faith and the church. Luke's main concern is how to form a Christian community beyond the Jewish boundary, emphasizing the social gospel without dangers from the Roman Empire. John addresses the community's need for belonging to God and Christ amid its painful separation from the mother community, the synagogue. Related theological themes in John are eternal life, love, and realized salvation. As seen above, the Gospels are the product of ekklesia-centered, theological interpretation, and they are the word of God—a valuable theological resource for the contemporary church and Christian life. With these interpretive foci, scholars and other interpreters explore theological themes such as faith, mission, good news, discipleship, and eschatology from the Gospels to deliver relevant theological and practical insights for the church and Christians.[14] Likewise, Joel Green observes, "A theological hermeneutics of Christian Scripture concerns the role of Scripture in the faith and formation of persons and ecclesial communities."[15]

Jewish Interpretation

Some scholars engage with the New Testament from the Jewish perspective so that they may learn from it for their benefit, correct Christians' misunderstandings of Judaism, and foster interfaith dialogue. Recently, a group of Jewish scholars produced *The Jewish Annotated New Testament*, which is the first-ever annotated version of the New Testament by Jews.[16] This volume includes commentary in the margins and interpretive essays covering diverse topics, including Jesus, Judaism, Jewish history, Jewish family, and messianic movements. While Jews do not share the same beliefs as Christians, the inevitable fact is Jesus was a Jew, read Hebrew scriptures, taught in the synagogue, engaged with religious leaders, and loved the everyday people. Because of this coterminous factor with Jesus, Jews and Christians may better understand themselves through Jesus. Levine puts it very well: "Much of the ethical material in the New Testament is Jewish, and much of the history presented is Jewish."[17] She goes on to say, "I think firmly that if we Jews want Christians to respect us, our practices, our beliefs, our traditions and our texts that we need to show the broader world, in particular, the Christian world, that same grace and that same courtesy."[18] For Jewish scholars, one of the gravest concerns is anti-Semitism.[19] They vehemently defend and explain their tradition and faith. Differences with Christians are a matter of debate, which must be done respectfully rather than by condemnation or judgment.

Inter(con)textual Interpretation

Inter(con)textual interpretation emphasizes the reader's context and relationship with the text. Readers take their context seriously and engage the Bible from their social location.[20] They are very conscious of their experiences, issues, and perspectives, which are in conversation with the text. While this interpretation is close to reader-response criticism, the big difference is that this criticism emphasizes the reader's context from which they engage with the text. There are multiple layers of conversations between the reader and the text: (1) the reader's context brought to the context of the text, (2) the reader's context in dialogue with the text, and (3) the reader's overall engagement with the text. With this emphasis on the reader's context, this interpretation uses a variety of other methods as long as they make sense. Minority scholars welcome this inter(con)textual interpretation because they can bring their concerns or perspectives to the text and communicate with modern readers.

Queer Criticism

Queer criticism is concerned with sexual identity as a primary object of investigation. Reading biblical texts, critics attempt to deconstruct the dominant ideology of heteronormativity about sexuality and gender.[21] They argue that queerness is a new concept that defies any definitions and that what is not normal from the dominant perspective is not abnormal, because individual queer experiences or individual identities cannot be dictated by society or any institution. Queer criticism argues that queer experience and related identities are disparate from the biblical world and that the Bible should not determine their experience or identities. Hornsby observes it this way: "The value of queer criticism is that it challenges our preconceptions about sexuality and gender, and reminds us that there are ways of understanding passages which talk about gender and sexuality other than the dominant heterosexual ones."[22]

Postcolonial Criticism

Postcolonial criticism is concerned with unequal power relations in the geopolitical arena and deals with race, imperialism, colonialism, identity, ethnicity, gender, place, and oppression.[23] This criticism operates well for the formerly colonized world in which people still struggle with the remains of a colonial legacy and its indelible marks on them. Scholars read the Bible from the perspective of these concerns, challenge the normative colonial interpretation of the texts, and explore ways to decolonize the Western legacy and seed. They reevaluate biblical texts from postcolonial perspectives, examine the empire's ideology, and challenge all sorts of abusive, exploitative, and dominant power as well as systems.

Deconstruction Interpretation

Deconstruction is not a method but a spirit or attitude toward the world, literature, and the human condition. The deconstruction spirit began with the French philosopher Jacques Derrida, who has questioned and challenged logocentrism and grand narratives that deny diversity and multiple truths or stories. Any text involves contexts and the interaction of signifiers in free play.[24] Meaning is not encoded in the text, as he says that interpretation is "a knot of negotiation" full of "different rhythms, different forces, different differential vibrations of time and rhythm."[25] Derrida coins the term *différance* to connote the double meaning of differing and deferring. The signified is not fixed once and for all, and it must be different because the signifiers are rolling forth, like the ocean. Likewise, we should delay meaning forever. Derrida differs from Saussure, who believes that even though there is no one-to-one link between the signifier and the signified, the signified comes from a web of countless relations. Meaning comes out of a self-critical, humbling spirit and involves a constant negotiation between readers, signifiers, and contexts.[26]

Minoritized Criticism

According to Tat-siong Benny Liew, "minoritized criticism of the New Testament refers generally to academic and critical interpretations of biblical texts by people of color in the United States of America, where they are often called 'minorities.'"[27] Minority scholars in marginalized communities make their voice heard in academia, "challenge racial discrimination and address issues of identity, representation, inclusion, exclusion, exploitation, oppression, and resistance, among others, both in the biblical texts that they read and in the contemporary situations that their communities face."[28] As we see here, this interpretation may go with other criticisms, such as feminist, womanist, and postcolonial interpretations. Minoritized criticism explores the neglected aspects of the text (e.g., the silenced voices) and challenges dominant text readings.[29]

Disability Studies

Disability studies is a recent development in academic study that deals with the personal or societal misunderstanding of disability and the discrimination against those who have disabilities.[30] In the Bible, disability often receives negative responses from readers because their belief operates with an either/or thinking that says healthy bodies are God's blessing, whereas disability is the result of sin. Likewise, in John 9:2, the disciples ask Jesus, "Rabbi, who sinned, this man or his parents, that he was born blind?" But Jesus answers, "Neither this man nor his parents sinned; he was born blind so that God's works might be revealed in him" (John 9:3). Jesus reverses cultural norms about disability. Indeed, the Gospels are complex concerning disability. Therefore, we must be careful in our interpreting disabilities in the text. The field of disability studies is still growing and drives some biblical scholars to probe the intersection of "human wholeness, impairment, and disability."[31] Taking an approach informed by disability studies helps readers to understand what ability or disability means in the Bible as well as in everyday life.

Ecological Criticism

Ecological criticism deals with an environmental or ecological crisis, such as climate change or exploitation of nature. Scholars read biblical texts to foster a friendly culture on Earth. It is "an ecological reading of the text from the perspective of Earth or the Earth community."[32] Ecology studies "the interrelationships among organisms and between them and all aspects, living and non-living, of their environment."[33] Ecological criticism challenges dualisms between this world and heaven and any ideologies or practices that demote nature.[34]

NOTES

1. I am deeply indebted to Michael Gorman for the term "ekklesia-centered, theological interpretation," which he suggested for this book.

2. For more about sources, see Craig A. Evans, "Source Criticism," in *Searching for Meaning: An Introduction to Interpreting the New Testament*, ed. Paula Gooder (Louisville, KY: Westminster John Knox, 2008), 28–37.

3. For more about redaction criticism, see Norman Perrin, *What Is Redaction Criticism?* (Minneapolis, MN: Fortress, 2002). See also, James D. G. Dunn, "Form Criticism," in *Searching for Meaning: An Introduction to Interpreting the New Testament*, ed. Paula Gooder (Louisville, KY: Westminster John Knox, 2008), 21–27.

4. For more about social-science criticism, see John H. Elliott, *What Is Social Scientific Criticism?* (Minneapolis, MN: Fortress, 1993). See also, Bruce J. Malina, "Social Science Criticism," in *Searching for Meaning: An Introduction to Interpreting the New Testament*, ed. Paula Gooder (Louisville, KY: Westminster John Knox, 2008), 13–20.

5. Gerd Theissen, *The Sociology of Early Palestinian Christianity* (Minneapolis, MN: Fortress, 1978).

6. For more about New Testament manuscripts, see Bruce M. Metzger and Bart D. Ehrman, *The Text of the New Testament: Its Transmission, Corruption, and Restoration* (New York: Oxford University Press, 2005).

7. For more about textual criticism, see J. Keith Elliott, "Textual Criticism," in *Searching for Meaning: An Introduction to Interpreting the New Testament*, ed. Paula Gooder (Louisville, KY: Westminster John Knox, 2008), 49–55.

8. For more about narrative criticism, see David Rhoads, Joanna Dewey, and Donald Michie, *Mark as Story: An Introduction to the Narrative of a Gospel* (Minneapolis, MN: Fortress, 2012). See also, Mark A. Powell, *What Is Narrative Criticism?* (Minneapolis, MN: Fortress, 1991); Elizabeth Struthers Malbon, "Narrative Criticism," in *Searching for Meaning: An Introduction to Interpreting the New Testament*, ed. Paula Gooder (Louisville, KY: Westminster John Knox, 2008), 80–87.

9. For more about reader-response criticism, see Robert M. Fowler, "Reader-Response Criticism," in *Searching for Meaning: An Introduction to Interpreting the New Testament*, ed. Paula Gooder (Louisville, KY: Westminster John Knox, 2008), 127–34. See also, Edgar V. McKnight, "Reader-Response Criticism," in *To Each Its Own Meaning: An Introduction to Biblical Criticisms and Their Applications*, ed. Steven L. McKenzie and Stephen R. Haynes (Louisville, KY: Westminster John Knox, 1999), 230–52; Richard N. Soulen, *Handbook of Biblical Criticism* (Louisville, KY: Westminster John Knox, 2011), 175–76.

10. For more about feminist criticism, see Elizabeth Schussler Fiorenza, *In Memory of Her: A Feminist Theological Reconstruction of Christian Origins* (New York: Crossroad, 1983). See also, Carol A. Newsom and Sharon H. Ringe, *The Women's Bible Commentary* (Louisville, KY: Westminster John Knox, 1992); Richard Soulen, "Feminist Biblical Interpretation," in *Handbook of Biblical Criticism* (Louisville, KY: Westminster John Knox, 2011), 66–68.

11. For more about womanist interpretation, see Gay L. Byron and Vanessa Lovelace, *Womanist Interpretations of the Bible* (Atlanta, GA: SBL Press, 2016). See also, Mitzi J. Smith, *Womanist Sass and Talk Back: Social (In)Justice, Intersectionality, and Biblical Interpretation* (Eugene, OR: Cascade Books, 2018); Smith, ed., *I Found God in Me: A Womanist Biblical Hermeneutics Reader* (Eugene, OR: Cascade Books, 2015).

12. For a collection of womanist readings, see Smith, ed. *I Found God in Me*.

13. I am deeply indebted to Michael Gorman for the term "ekklesia-centered, theological interpretation," which he suggested for this book.

14. Richard Hays, "Reading the Bible with Eyes of Faith: The Practice of Theological Exegesis," *Journal of Theological Interpretation* 1 (2007): 5–21. See also, Joel Green, *Seized by Truth: Reading the Bible as Scripture* (Nashville, TN: Abingdon Press, 2007); J. Todd Billings, *The Word of God for the People of God: An Entryway to the Theological Interpretation of Scripture* (Grand Rapids, MI: William B. Eerdmans, 2010).

15. Joel Green, *Practicing Theological Interpretation (Theological Explorations for the Church Catholic): Engaging Biblical Texts for Faith and Formation* (Ada, MI: Baker Academic, 2012), 15.

16. Amy-Jill Levine and Marc Zvi Brettler, eds., *The Jewish Annotated New Testament* (New York: Oxford University Press, 2017). See also, Samuel Sandmel, *A Jewish Understanding of the New Testament* (Woodstock, VT: SkyLight, 2004).

17. NPR Staff, "A Jewish Perspective on the New Testament," NPR Radio IQ, published December 24, 2011, https://www.npr.org/2011/12/24/144228636/a-jewish-perspective-on-the-new-testament.

18. NPR Staff, "A Jewish Perspective."

19. Amy-Jill Levine, "Is the New Testament Anti-Jewish?" *Bible Odyssey*, April 25, 2023, https://www.bibleodyssey.org/bible-basics/is-the-new-testament-anti-jewish.

20. For more about intercontextual interpretation, see Daniel Patte, ed. *Global Bible Commentary* (Nashville, TN: Abingdon Press, 2004). See also, Johnson Thomaskutty, ed. *An Asian Introduction to the New Testament* (Minneapolis, MN: Fortress, 2022); Yung Suk Kim, ed. *1 and 2 Corinthians*, Texts @ Contexts Series (Minneapolis, MN: Fortress, 2013).

21. For more about queer criticism, see Ken Stone, "Queer Criticism," in *New Meanings for Ancient Texts: Recent Approaches to Biblical Criticisms and Their Applications*, ed. Steven L. McKenzie and John Kaltner (Louisville, KY: Westminster John Knox, 2013), 155–76. See also, Jeremy Punt, "Queer Theory, Postcolonial Theory, and Biblical Interpretation: A Preliminary Exploration of Some Intersections," in *Bible Trouble: Queer Reading at the Boundaries of Biblical Scholarship*, ed. Teresa J. Hornsby and Ken Stone (Atlanta, GA: Society of Biblical Literature, 2011), 321–41;

Mona West and Robert Shore-Goss, eds., *The Queer Bible Commentary* (London, England: SCM Press, 2022).

22. Teresa J. Hornsby, "Queer Criticism," in *Searching for Meaning: An Introduction to Interpreting the New Testament*, ed. Paula Gooder (Louisville, KY: Westminster John Knox, 2008), 151.

23. For more about postcolonial criticism, see R. S. Sugirtharajah, "Postcolonial Criticism," in *Searching for Meaning: An Introduction to Interpreting the New Testament*, ed. Paula Gooder (Louisville, KY: Westminster John Knox, 2008), 175–83; Fernando F. Segovia and R. S. Sugirtharajah, eds., *A Postcolonial Commentary on the New Testament Writings* (New York: T&T Clark, 2007); Musa Dube, *Postcolonial Feminist Interpretation of the Bible* (St. Louis, MO: Chalice Press, 2000).

24. Jacques Derrida, "Différance," in *Margins of Philosophy*, trans. Alan Bass (Chicago: The University of Chicago Press, 1982), 1–27. See also his interview, "The Villanova Roundtable," in *Deconstruction in a Nutshell: A Conversation with Jacques Derrida*, ed. John D. Caputo (New York: Fordham University Press, 1997), 12–15.

25. Jacques Derrida, *Negotiations: Interventions and Interviews, 1971–2001* (Stanford, CA: Stanford University Press, 2002), 29.

26. For more about deconstruction or poststructuralism, see Hugh S. Pyper, "Postmodernism," in *New Meanings for Ancient Texts: Recent Approaches to Biblical Criticisms and Their Applications*, ed. Steven L. McKenzie and John Kaltner (Louisville, KY: Westminster John Knox, 2013), 117–36. See also, William A. Beardslee, "Poststructuralist Criticism," in *To Each Its Own Meaning: An Introduction to Biblical Criticisms and Their Applications*, ed. Steven L. McKenzie and Stephen R. Haynes (Louisville, KY: Westminster John Knox, 1999), 253–67; A. K. M. Adam, *What Is Postmodern Biblical Criticism?* (Minneapolis, MN: Fortress, 1995).

27. Tat-siong Benny Liew, "Minoritized Criticism of the New Testament," *Oxford Bibliographies in Biblical Studies*, accessed January 23, 2021, https://www.oxfordbibliographies.com/view/document/obo-9780195393361/obo-9780195393361-0277.xml. See also, Rodney S. Sadler, Jr., "The Place and Role of Africa and African Imagery in the Bible," in *True to Our Native Land: An African American New Testament Commentary*, ed. Brian K. Blount, Cain H. Felder, Clarice J. Martin, and Emerson B. Powery (Minneapolis, MN: Fortress, 2007), 23–30.

28. Liew, "Minoritized Criticism of the New Testament."

29. For more about minoritized criticism, see Tat-siong Benny Liew and Fernando F. Segovia, eds., *Reading Biblical Texts Together: Pursuing Minoritized Biblical Criticism* (Atlanta, GA: Society of Biblical Literature, 2022). See also, Mitzi J. Smith and Jin Young Choi, eds., *Minoritized Women Reading Race and Ethnicity: Intersectional Approaches to Constructed Identity and Early Christian Texts* (Lanham, MD: Lexington Books, 2020); Randall C. Bailey, Tat-Siong Benny Liew, and Fernando F. Segovia, eds., *They Were All Together in One Place? Toward Minority Biblical Criticism* (Atlanta, GA: Society of Biblical Literature, 2009).

30. For more about disability studies, see Candida R. Moss and Jeremy Schipper, eds., *Disability Studies and Biblical Literature* (New York: Palgrave Macmillan, 2011). See also, Sarah J. Melcher, Mikeal C. Parsons, and Amos Yong, eds., *The Bible and Disability: A Commentary* (Waco, TX: Baylor University Press, 2017); Hector Avalos, Sarah J. Melcher, and Jeremy Schipper, eds., *This Abled Body:*

Rethinking Disabilities in Biblical Studies (Atlanta, GA: Society of Biblical Literature, 2007).

31. Melcher, Parsons, and Yong, eds., *The Bible and Disability*. See also, Moss and Schipper, *Disability Studies and Biblical Literature*.

32. Norman Habel, "Ecological Criticism," in *New Meanings for Ancient Texts, Recent Approaches to Biblical Criticisms and Their Applications*, ed. Steven L. McKenzie and John Kaltner (Louisville, KY: Westminster John Knox, 2013), 39.

33. Michael Allaby, *A Dictionary of Ecology*, 2nd ed. (Oxford, England: Oxford University Press, 2003), 36.

34. For more about ecological criticism, see Habel, "Ecological Criticism," 39–58. See also, David Horrell, "Ecological Criticism," in *Searching for Meaning: An Introduction to Interpreting the New Testament*, ed. Paula Gooder (Louisville, KY: Westminster John Knox, 2008), 192–98; Norman C. Habel and V. Balabanski, eds., *The Earth Story in the New Testament* (Sheffield, England: Sheffield Academic, 2002); David Horrell, *The Bible and the Environment: Towards a Critical Ecological Biblical Theology* (New York: Routledge, 2010).

Chapter 7

The Gospel of Mark from Various Perspectives

AUTHOR-CENTERED, HISTORICAL APPROACH

Historical-Critical Method

Using the historical-critical method in the study of Mark's Gospel involves two different times and related historical, theological reconstructions: Jesus's time and Mark's time. The former is about the historical Jesus, and the latter is about Mark the evangelist. Taking an example of the messianic secret in Mark, we can explore both the historical Jesus and Mark's Christology. The messianic secret means that Jesus tries to hide his messianic identity and asks his disciples, including others who've heard his identity and the spirits or demons who've known his identity, not to tell his identity to other people (Mark 1:24; 1:40–45; 3:11–12; 7:31–37; 8:22–26; 9:2–9). Historians wonder why there is a messianic secret in Mark. William Wrede's redactional approach to Mark concludes that Mark created the messianic-secret motif to counter the claim that Jesus was not a divine Messiah in his earthly ministry. The assumption here is that Jesus himself knew his messianic identity but did not let others know about it. Wrede's conclusion is a probable hypothesis that is hard to prove. Yet the way he thinks about the historical Jesus and Mark's intention is a historical-critical method. Besides the messianic secret in Mark, we can further explore the historical Jesus and Mark's Christology. While Matthew explains why Jesus's baptism by John is necessary, Luke does not mention who baptized Jesus. But Mark is straightforward in describing Jesus's baptism by John in the Jordan. John's baptism of Jesus seems to be a puzzle for some early Christians, but Mark has preserved the tradition of Jesus's water baptism by John. If Jesus was baptized by

John, he was likely a follower/disciple of him. Later, he gathers disciples under his ministry. Even some disciples of John the Baptist follow Jesus, according to John 1:35–36. Perhaps there may have been a rivalry between John the Baptist's ministry and Jesus's ministry, as John 3:22–27 imply. From Mark's baptism story, we can infer that Jesus's ministry owes John the Baptist. Furthermore, throughout Mark, there are low Christology clues, as is seen in Jesus's limited knowledge (13:32), his manual-labor *tekton* (carpenter or stone builder; 6:3), and his humanity (10:17–18; 15:34). Likewise, Mark portrays Jesus as the suffering Son of God who provides a way of the cross as the way to God.

Further Reading

- Janice Capel Anderson and Stephen D. Moore, "Introduction: The Lives of Mark," in *Mark and Method: New Approaches in Biblical Studies*, ed. Janice Capel Anderson and Stephen D. Moore (Minneapolis, MN: Fortress, 1992), 1–8.
- Willi Marxsen, *Mark the Evangelist; Studies on the Redaction History of the Gospel* (Nashville, TN: Abingdon Press, 1969).
- Norman Perrin, *Rediscovering the Teaching of Jesus* (New York: Harper & Row, 1967).
- Norman Perrin, *What Is Redaction Criticism?* (Minneapolis, MN: Fortress, 2002).

Social-Science Criticism

We may consider various aspects of society that were playing out in the background, behind Mark ("social description"), Mark's history in society ("social history"), and the function of Mark's knowledge ("sociology of knowledge").[1] The society under the Roman Empire was run by the patron-client system, where the lower classes must serve the elites. Peasants lost their land and rebelled against the establishment of the empire. Likewise, the Markan narrative reflects the difficult times that were facing the community.[2] The Markan Jesus also goes through harsh times and feels agitated because of the upcoming trials and suffering. He is misunderstood, opposed, and arrested because of his bold proclamation of God's rule. His disciples never understand their teacher. The women who visit the tomb of Jesus are terrified when they hear the news about Jesus's resurrection. In all these challenging times, Mark's community needs special knowledge or comfort so that the community members may survive and grow. They are encouraged to live with hope for the future even when things go rough. The path to their success is the way of the cross, which leads to the resurrection. The way of Jesus leads to success, but it is a difficult way. Nevertheless, they must seek his way as indicated in Mark 10:45, which exemplifies serving the marginalized and embracing the rule of God against the rule of Rome. They must also extend their kinship to others who need hope, as Jesus advocates voluntary kinship for all, not based on blood but on God's will. In turbulent times of persecution and oppression, Mark envisions an alternative community and society rooted in God's impartial love, as has been demonstrated by Jesus.

Further Reading

- David Rhoads, "Social Criticism: Crossing Boundaries," in *Mark and Method: New Approaches in Biblical Studies*, ed. Janice Capel Anderson and Stephen D. Moore (Minneapolis, MN: Fortress, 1992), 135–61.
- Ched Myers, *Binding the Strong Man: A Political Reading of Mark's Story of Jesus* (Maryknoll, NY: Orbis Books, 2008).
- Ekkehard W. Stegemann and Wolfgang Stegemann, "Messianic Communities in the Land of Israel after 70 CE," in *The Jesus Movement: A Social History of Its First Century* (Minneapolis, MN: Fortress, 1999), 231–247.
- John H. Elliott, *What Is Social Scientific Criticism?* (Minneapolis, MN: Fortress, 1993).

TEXT-CENTERED, LITERARY APPROACH

Textual Criticism

Even since the first copy of Mark was written down, numerous manuscripts were copied and transmitted, and many of them were lost. Because of variant readings, textual scholars have decided which readings may be more viable than others. In the following we discuss some important textual matters in Mark. Readers may refer to their study Bible with textual notes or use a New Testament textual commentary for further study. First, regarding the phrase "Son of God" seen in Mark 1:1, some manuscripts lack it, but it may be the case that copyists overlooked it. Since, in the Markan narrative, the main title of Jesus is the Son of God, it is natural to have that phrase. Second, regarding Jesus's job, as is stated in Mark 6:3, the issue is whether he is "the carpenter, the son of Mary" or if he is the "son of the carpenter and of Mary." While some ancient authorities have the latter reading, the former reading appears close to the original because many early manuscripts have the former reading. The latter reading represents some copyists' Christological concerns that Jesus the Son of God must not be a carpenter himself. The fact that Jesus is a carpenter is hard to accept for some early Christians like Matthew, who says that Jesus is the carpenter's son (Mt 13:55). Matthew felt uneasy about Jesus himself being the carpenter because he is from the royal Davidic lineage. One criterion to decide which reading is better comes from the idea that a more difficult reading is preferred. Third, there are also interesting textual variants worth pointing out. In Mark 9:29, Jesus says that "this kind can come out only through prayer." While some manuscripts add "and fasting," which may be a gloss to emphasize the importance of such a practice in the early church, reliable manuscripts do not have it. Lastly, regarding the ending of Mark, the question is whether the story ends at 16:8, which is called the shorter ending of Mark, or if it extends to 16:20, the longer ending of Mark. The most ancient authorities support the ending of Mark 16:8, which sounds a bit weird to the readers since there is no fully fledged resurrection story. With this in mind, Mark 16:9–20 was added to complement the resurrection story in this Gospel, just like with Matthew or Luke.

Further Reading

- Bruce M. Metzger, *A Textual Commentary on the Greek New Testament* (Peabody, MA: Hendrickson, 2005).
- Daniel J. Harrington, *The Gospel of Matthew*, Sacra Pagina Series, vol. 1 (Collegeville, MN: Liturgical Press, 1991).
- Bruce M. Metzger and Bart D. Ehrman, *The Text of the New Testament: Its Transmission, Corruption, and Restoration* (New York: Oxford University Press, 2005).
- David C. Parker, *The Living Text of the Gospels* (New York: Cambridge University Press, 1997).

Narrative Criticism

While the implied author of Mark tells a story about Jesus, the implied reader follows the narrator. The messianic-secret motif in Mark is understood differently, depending on different approaches. In redaction criticism, the messianic secret is considered a Markan addition, which justifies Jesus's self-understanding as the Messiah. In the early Christian community, some said that Jesus never thought he was the Messiah. So Mark argues that Jesus knew it but hid it. But in narrative interpretation, the messianic secret is treated "as a plot device that calls attention to the complexity of the image of messiahship in the Markan Gospel";[3] that is, readers are invited to rethink Jesus's messianic identity. Even if people were told about his identity, their understanding would be very deficient. So not knowing is better than insufficient or wrong knowledge.

Jesus's disciples never truly understand Jesus. Peter confesses that Jesus is the Messiah, but he thinks he is a political liberator. Moreover, in the Markan narrative, Jesus's emphasis is not on his title but on God's work. So he does not want others to know about his title, because he must focus on healing and restoring people. The implied reader must come up with a better understanding of Jesus's identity by reading the whole story. Likewise, the ending of Mark at 16:8 may be a plot device that challenges readers to rethink the cost of discipleship. The good news of Jesus Christ turns out to be fearful to the women who visit the tomb. They should be joyful at the news of the resurrection. Instead, they are terrified and do not tell other disciples the good news. The implied reader must ask what caused women to be terrified enough not to tell the story of the resurrection. What if the readers were there with the women in the tomb? Would they behave differently than the women? Read in this way, the failure-like ending is a rhetorical one, which stimulates the readers to rethink their faith and discipleship.

Further Reading

- David Rhoads, Joanna Dewey, and Donald Michie, *Mark as Story: An Introduction to the Narrative of a Gospel* (Minneapolis, MN: Fortress, 2012).
- Mark Allen Powell, *What Is Narrative Criticism?* (Minneapolis, MN: Fortress, 1991).
- Elizabeth Struthers Malbon, "Narrative Criticism: How Does the Story Mean?" in *Mark and Method: New Approaches in Biblical Studies*, ed. Janice Capel Anderson and Stephen D. Moore (Minneapolis, MN: Fortress, 1992), 23–49.
- Stephen D. Moore, *Literary Criticism and the Gospels: The Theoretical Challenge* (New Haven, CT: Yale University Press, 1989).

READER-CENTERED, COMPREHENSIVE APPROACH

Reader-Response Criticism

Real readers may respond to the text by paying attention to its special features. For example, in Mark's Gospel, the adverb "immediately" (*euthys*) appears frequently—five times in 1:12–23, which signals to the reader that something important will occur right away.[4] In these verses, there is a sense of urgency and progression for Jesus's mission. In Mark 1:12, Jesus is led into the wilderness immediately. Readers expect vivid things to happen in the wilderness. The dynamic things about Jesus have happened even before his wilderness test. He is baptized "in those days" (Mark 1:9), when he comes from Nazareth of Galilee, which reminds them of the concrete, immediate context surrounding Jesus and his life in Galilee. After his baptism, Jesus is led into the wilderness right away. There is no waste of time after his baptism, because he must proclaim the kingdom of God urgently. The kingdom of God is coming now. He cannot delay it, so he must enact it through his teaching and healing. Because of the urgency of his mission, he starts preaching right after John is arrested (Mark 1:14). He does not waste time or waver on his work, which is to proclaim God's rule in the world. He declares, "Now the time is fulfilled" (Mark 1:15). In Mark 1:18, Jesus's disciples leave their nets and follow him immediately. Jesus immediately calls them (Mark 1:20). He enters the synagogue on the Sabbath immediately and teaches (1:21). He also immediately heals a man with an unclean spirit (1:23). The other adverb, "again" (*palin*), may be also interesting for real readers because this proverb makes readers look back at things that have happened before. For example, there is the use of "again" in Mark 8:1, where the feeding of the four thousand occurs. This "again" refers to the episode of the feeding of the five thousand, as seen earlier in Mark 6:30–44. Readers need to account for the relationship between the two feeding miracles by filling in the gaps. One way they can fill in the gaps is to see Jesus's compassion for the crowd. He does not stop providing for them for as long as they need. The other way is to look at the need for training disciples, who should not give up on providing for the needs of the hungry. It must be done again and again, even in the desert. As we see here, the readers' understanding may be enriched by looking backward and forward.

Further Reading

- Robert M. Fowler, "Reader-Response Criticism: Figuring Mark's Reader," in *Mark and Method: New Approaches in Biblical Studies*, ed. Janice Capel Anderson and Stephen D. Moore (Minneapolis, MN: Fortress, 1992), 50–83.
- Wolfgang Iser, "The Reading Process: A Phenomenological Approach," *New Literary History* 3 (1972): 279–99.
- Edgar V. McKnight, *Reader Perspectives on the New Testament*, Semeia 48 (Atlanta, GA: Scholars Press, 1989).
- Richard Soulen, "Reader-Response Criticism," in *Handbook of Biblical Criticism* (Louisville, KY: Westminster John Knox, 2011), 175–76.

Feminist Criticism

Feminist interpretation interrogates the text, for example, as to why Jesus calls male disciples only, even though some women have followed him faithfully from Galilee and throughout his ministry. All the male disciples flee when Jesus is arrested. The first visitors to the tomb are also women, who hear the good news of Jesus's resurrection. In a way, the true disciples of Jesus were the women. But male readers do not recognize this aspect of discipleship. Instead, they focus on the surface story of Jesus, who calls the twelve male disciples. Some feminist critics are concerned with early Christian communities that trace back to before Mark was written down, and they ask whether Mark and other canonical Gospels have preserved traditions about women's positive role in the early Christian communities. In addition to critiquing androcentric interpretation, the feminist interpretation also focuses on women characters in the narrative and empowers them. For example, an anointing woman at Bethany loves Jesus and pours expensive oil on his head (Mark 14:3–9). Then some who are gathered there criticize her because they think she's wasting the potential money that could be used for the poor. But Jesus commends her because her action prepares him for his burial. While helping the poor is important, her choice of love and care must be commended and remembered. The other woman we may consider is the Syrophoenician woman in Mark 7:24–30 (cf. Mt 15:21–28). This woman is a Gentile who has a desperate situation regarding her daughter. She gets what she wants because she has persistent faith that she and her daughter also deserve God's blessing. Lastly, feminist interpretation heeds the negative interpretation of women characters. In Mark 6:14–29, there is a horrendous story about John the Baptist's death at Herod's birthday party. Herod listens to his daughter's request that she needs John's head on a platter, which is the idea of Herodias, her mother. This story is graphically difficult to imagine. While Herodias is blamed for John's death, Herod is responsible for his death, but he is potentially absolved. This story needs a careful analysis from various critical perspectives.

Further Reading

- Janice Capel Anderson, "Feminist Criticism: The Dancing Daughter," in *Mark and Method: New Approaches in Biblical Studies*, ed. Janice Capel Anderson and Stephen D. Moore (Minneapolis, MN: Fortress, 1992), 103–34.
- Mary Ann Beavis, "Women as Models of Faith in Mark," *Biblical Theology Bulletin* 18 (1988): 3–9.

- Winsome Monro, "Women Disciples in Mark?," *Catholic Biblical Quarterly* 44 (1982): 225–41.
- Elizabeth Struthers Malbon, "Gospel of Mark," in *The Women's Bible Commentary*, ed. Carol A. Newsom and Sharon H. Ringe (Louisville, KY: Westminster John Knox, 1992), 479–92.
- Sharon H. Ringe, "A Gentile Woman's Story, Revisited: Rereading Mark 7:24–31a," in *Feminist Companion to Mark*, ed. Amy-Jill Levine (Sheffield, England: Sheffield Academic, 2001), 79–100.

Womanist Interpretation

Mitzi Smith reads the story of the Syrophoenician woman in Mark 7:24–30 from a womanist perspective. She especially employs the notion of "sass" as a way of responding to Jesus, arguing that the Syrophoenician woman embodies a resistant, bold speech of talk back in the form of *heteroglossia*—a "social diversity of speech types."[5] The importance of sass in a marginalized community and society cannot be overemphasized, because otherwise there is no other language that the marginalized people can use and speak. Mere submission to an authority or to the Lord deprives them of their human authenticity and agency. So, in the story, the Gentile woman "[goes] toe to toe with Jesus" and "counters Jesus's speech with her heteroglossia."[6] This thoroughness of her response to Jesus shows her desperate hope for the healing of her daughter. Smith puts it this way: "She engages in subversion and improvisation: (1) she speaks from her cultural context, recontextualizing and substituting Jesus's words with her sass. In her sass, *tekna* becomes *paidia*. In her sass, her people sit at the table; (2) the *paidia*, unlike the *tekna*, demonstrates compassion for the table dogs, allowing them to eat crumbs off their plates; and (3) she eliminates the language of priority."[7] The Syrophoenician woman reimagines herself and her community to be blessed no matter what. She cannot waver on her faith until she realizes that blessing. She cannot agree with a lesser position or lesser blessing. Her people are also the people of God, who must eat on the table. Until she gets what she needs, she must speak up and talk back, staying in the faith. As we see here, while womanist interpretation is akin to feminist criticism, it emphasizes the specific cultural context of African American women, including people of color, and their agency and wholeness.

Further Reading

- Gay L. Byron and Vanessa Lovelace, *Womanist Interpretations of the Bible* (Atlanta, GA: SBL Press, 2016).

- Mitzi J. Smith, *Womanist Sass and Talk Back: Social (In)Justice, Intersectionality, and Biblical Interpretation* (Eugene, OR: Cascade Books, 2018).
- Mitzi J. Smith, ed., *I Found God in Me: A Womanist Biblical Hermeneutics Reader* (Eugene, OR: Cascade Books, 2015).
- Raquel St. Clair, *Call and Consequences: A Womanist Reading of Mark's Gospel* (Minneapolis, MN: Fortress, 2008).

Ekklesia-Centered, Theological Interpretation

Interpreting the Gospel of Mark for the Black Church today, Brian Blount perceives the kingdom of God language as a sociopolitical, theological one and challenges the church to rethink the apocalyptic message of Jesus's preaching in Mark's Gospel, which invades and transforms the present world and community.[8] Blount examines not only the first-century sociopolitical world in Palestine, which was infused with satanic powers, injustices, and chaos, but also the power of Jesus's proclamation of the coming Kingdom of God, which breaks boundaries against the poor and the marginalized, shatters all human ideologies and political ideals, and embraces the radical inbreaking of God's kingdom in the present. Jesus's crucifixion is "the inevitable end of his preaching ministry," so his disciples need to take on the inevitable cost of discipleship to proclaim the kingdom of God in the present.[9] Blount's study brings practical insights into the ministry of the Black Church today. The kingdom of God in Mark's Gospel is not merely a spiritual or theological event but the power of God making an impact on the present world, where politics and religion intersect. The kingdom of God is also boundary crossing, which means God's rule permeates every sphere of human life, invades all aspects of the sociopolitical world, and removes all kinds of discrimination and injustices.[10] Likewise, today's churches and preachers must focus on Jesus's preaching of God's radical, urgent rule in the world today, rejecting any human order or political or religious ideologies. All Christians are disciples of Jesus and must bear the cost of proclaiming the gospel.

Further Reading

- Joel Green, *The Way of the Cross: Following Jesus in the Gospel of Mark* (Eugene, OR: Wipf & Stock, 2009).
- Brian K. Blount, "Jesus as Teacher: Boundary Breaking in Mark's Gospel and Today's Church," *Interpretation: A Journal of Bible and Theology* 70, no. 2 (2016): 184–93.
- David M. Rhoads, "Jesus and the Syrophoenician Woman in Mark: A Narrative-Critical Study," *Currents in Theology and Mission* 47, no. 4 (2020): 36–48.

- Amy Lindeman Allen, "Baptism and Children in Mark's Vision of the Realm of God," *Currents in Theology and Mission* 47, no. 4 (2020): 31–35.

Jewish Interpretation

Adela Yabro Collins reads the story of the death of Jesus in Mark's Gospel against the liberation-focused reading of Mark 10:45, "For the Son of Man came not to be served but to serve and to give his life a ransom for many," by Sharyn Dowd and Elizabeth Struthers Malbon,[11] who argue that "ransom (*lutron*) for many" has to do with liberating "captives of the enemies of God."[12] But Collins challenges this reading because the immediate context of the saying in Mark 10:45 does not go to the issue of power in 10:43–44, but it goes back to the death of Jesus in 10:38–39, where Jesus talks about the cup he will drink and the baptism he will be baptized. She argues, "The issue is not the oppression of the followers of Jesus and others by the tyrants and rulers of Judea and Rome. The issue is how the alternative society constituted by the followers of Jesus will organize and conduct itself."[13] Then, to support her point, Collins brings to the text a wide variety of contexts of *lutron* from the Septuagint and challenges the attempt to attribute one dominant reading to the text. For example, the singular noun *lutron* has to do with "redeeming tithes and paying compensation to a husband wronged by an adulterer (Lev 27:31; Prov 6:35)."[14] The plural noun *lutra* connotes various meanings: "the manumission of a slave; the redemption of land; the redemption of an Israelite 'sold' as a hired, resident laborer; and for the release of prisoners of war (Lev 19:20; 25:24, 51–52; Isa 45:13)."[15] The other usages of the term *lutron* include the redemption money for the owner (Ex 21:29) and the sum of money that propitiates God (Ex 30:11–26). With all these above, Collins argues *lutron* must be understood in various contexts, and it should not be fixed. It is more than the liberation reading and is linked with the death of Jesus, which also implies various things. Excluding the forgiveness of sins from his death is hardly convincing given the textual links and contexts. She concludes, "In my view, the theme of liberation from human tyrants is a minor and subtle one in Mark. The liberation from demonic powers, in contrast, is a major theme, especially in the first part of Mark (1:1–8:26). I propose, nevertheless, that we not allow major themes to obscure variety in Mark. Rather than impose a conceptual coherence pleasing to systematic thinkers in our own time, we should appreciate the richness and multi-valence of Mark's narrative."[16]

Further Reading

- Lawrence M. Wills, "The Gospel According to Mark," in *The Jewish Annotated New Testament*, ed. Amy-Jill Levine and Marc Zvi Brettler (New York: Oxford University Press, 2017), 67–106.
- Adela Yabro Collins, "Mark's Interpretation of the Death of Jesus," *Journal of Biblical Literature* 128, no. 3 (2009): 545–54.
- Sharyn Dowd and Elizabeth Struthers Malbon, "The Significance of Jesus' Death in Mark: Narrative Context and Authorial Audience," *Journal of Biblical Literature* 125, no. 2 (2006): 271–97.

Inter(con)textual Interpretation

Hisako Kinukawa reads Mark's Gospel from her Japanese context, taking issue with free market capitalism that ruins the lives of the common Japanese people as well as Japan's relations with other Asian countries. She recognizes Japan's colonial past, which has devastated many Asian countries. Also, she sees the ruin of the middle- and lower-class people in Japan due to capitalism's merciless pursuit of profits for the rich as well as American hegemony in a global economy. In this context she examines three stories in Mark, which show "the power relationships at work": the story of the Gerasene demoniac (Mark 5:1–20); the story of the Syrophoenician woman (7:24–30); and the disciples, the father and his mute-deaf son, and Jesus (9:14–29).[17] In the story of the Gerasene demoniac, she identifies the imperial powers and local elites responsible for the harsh conditions of life for the demoniac. Gerasa is a Hellenistic city prospering due to imperial control of people and commerce. Local elites also benefit from the imperial business, which protects their enterprise and exploits the powerless. The demoniac with unclean spirits symbolizes the most miserable conditions of life at the bottom of imperial greed, coupled with the local elites' exploitation. Jesus's exorcism is more than healing; it challenges and subverts abusive power structures, restoring the disabled and outcasts to their place. In the story of the Syrophoenician woman, Kinukawa also similarly analyzes the power relationships in Tyre and Galilee. Whereas Tyre is a wealthy port thriving due to imperial control of commerce and trade, Galilee represents a poor region with many peasants. Kinukawa interprets Jesus differently in the story; he denies the woman's initial request because he identifies her with the wealthy in Tyre, taking sides with the poor Galilean peasants. But the woman insists she and her child are like Galilean peasants. So Jesus allows her request. In the story of the father and his mute-deaf son, Kinukawa deals with discipleship, which needs radical faith and prayer to restore social outcasts and the disabled in society. The father never gives up on his son and cries to Jesus with the urgency of needing healing. Jesus's advice to his disciples is that they must be like the father who is desperate for his son's recovery. From all of the above stories, Kinukawa concludes the Japanese churches and Christians worldwide must recognize the complexities of power at work in society and take sides with the marginalized and voiceless. More specifically, Christians must be keenly aware of hierarchical power structures at work locally and globally, challenging such power and advocating for the marginalized at all risks. *That* is faith and discipleship.

Further Reading

- Hisako Kinukawa, "Mark," in the *Global Bible Commentary*, ed. Daniel Patte (Nashville, TN: Abingdon, 2005), 367–78.
- Edwin Jebaraj and Johnson Thomaskutty, "The Gospel of Mark," in *An Asian Introduction to the New Testament*, ed. Johnson Thomaskutty (Minneapolis, MN: Fortress, 2022), 75–101.
- Holly Joan Toensing, "'Living among the Tomb': Society, Mental Illness, and Self-Destruction in Mark 5:1–20," in *This Abled Body: Rethinking Disabilities in Biblical Studies*, ed. Hector Avalos, Sarah J. Melcher, and Jeremy Schipper (Atlanta, GA: Society of Biblical Literature, 2007), 131–43.
- Gerd Theissen, *The Gospels in Context: Social and Political History in the Synoptic Tradition*, trans. Linda M. Maloney (Minneapolis, MN: Fortress, 1991).

Queer Criticism

The normative reading of Mark's Gospel has been focused on Christology or redemption. Likewise, certain doctrines, ideologies, or identities have been privileged. But Ana Esther Padua Freire reads the Gospel from the perspective of antihegemonic low theology, which opposes the structures of capitalism and all normative descriptions of identity, be it sexual or ethnic/cultural identity.[18] While normative reading focuses on the birth, life, and death of Jesus, queer reading focuses on what appears to be abnormal or unusual in the text. One example is the presence of a queer multitude in the Gospel, which is hardly defined in one way. In Mark the crowd (*ochlos*) is a mixture of low-class people who listen to Jesus and follow him. Yet they are not close followers of Jesus. They are not a unified group with an asserted political agenda. We do not know if the crowds are the same people throughout the narrative, but they present themselves as abnormal and try to solve their individual issues because they are not united. While there is no leader for them, they're looking for answers to their unrevealed issues. Freire suggests three points through a queer reading of the multitude: First, we must "allow the queer multitude to invade the text."[19] This means our focus must be on something that discontinues traditional reading. The point is the queer multitude is not a unified group and, therefore, it rejects any categorization or description of them. But the presence and movement of a queer multitude must be recognized, and then society as a whole will be better shaped. The queer multitude is not an obstacle to Jesus's ministry. Rather, in the story, they take a part that may be small but is important. Second, we must see "the displacements caused by the multitude."[20] From the normative society's perspective, the displacements caused by the multitude are undesirable and need to be controlled, but their activity must be seen as a call for change. In other words, our focus must be more than on the displacements themselves. Rather, we must see divergent voices in them and incorporate them into a larger community. Third, and lastly, we need to "understand the multitude as a multitude of indecent Christians."[21] This means no one or no group can reject other people's ideas or wants. Even if some Christians are judged as abnormal or absurd from the mainline perspective, they bring to others some voice, challenge, or perspective on life, which will open the door for a healthier society for all.

Further Reading

- Ana Esther Padua Freire, "Mark," in *The Queer Bible Commentary*, ed. Mona West and Robert Shore-Goss (London: SCM Press, 2022), 518–32.
- Marcella Althaus-Reid, "Mark," in *The Queer Bible Commentary*, edited by Deryn Guest and Robert Goss (London: SCM Press, 2006), 517–25.
- Jeremy Punt, "Queer Theory, Postcolonial Theory, and Biblical Interpretation: A Preliminary Exploration of Some Intersections," in *Bible Trouble: Queer Reading at the Boundaries of Biblical Scholarship*, ed. Teresa J. Hornsby and Ken Stone (Atlanta, GA: Society of Biblical Literature, 2011), 321–41.

Postcolonial Criticism

Some scholars read Mark's Gospel from postcolonial perspectives, and their reading is diverse. According to Simon Samuel, there are four models of postcolonial interpretation of Mark's Gospel.[22] The first model is the most widely practiced; it is focused on essentialist postcolonial resistance, close to liberation theology.[23] Ched Myers reads Mark "as an ideological narrative, the manifesto of an early Christian discipleship community in its war of myths with the dominant social order and its political adversaries."[24] In this resistance model, Jesus represents the prophetic tradition of Israel, opposes imperial rule, and advocates for the poor and marginalized. Jesus's teaching of the kingdom of God is a direct challenge to the establishment of power in Rome and Jerusalem, including the local elites. He shatters Rome's propaganda of "peace and security" and replaces it with God's mercy and justice. He subverts the world of the empire where Rome and Jerusalem cooperate for their benefit, suppressing revolting peasants in Galilee and elsewhere in the first century CE.[25] The second model is a resistant yet colonizing discourse. On the one hand, Mark opposes imperial rule; on the other, he adopts another form of imperialism. For example, Tolbert writes, "In fact, taken as a whole, the Gospel of Mark presents what amounts to a sustained polemic against traditional social, religious, and political leadership groups by insisting on their consistently evil exercise of authority."[26] The third model is "a colonial mimetic discourse representing tyranny, boundary and might."[27] For example, Tat-Siong Liew argues that Mark reproduces new imperialism with Jesus, duplicating the colonial mimicry. He writes, "Jesus' status as God's only son and heir in Mark's Gospel seems to result in another hierarchical community structure. Despite the familial terms we have seen Mark use to describe the community of Jesus, Jesus' family, like most families on earth, is not devoid of its own pecking order."[28] He goes on to say, "Presenting an all-authoritative Jesus who will eventually annihilate all opponents and all other authorities, Mark's Utopian, or dystopian, vision, in effect, duplicates the colonial (non)choice of 'serve-or-be-destroyed.'"[29] The last model is "a colonial archive with traces of postcolonial heteroglossy."[30] For example, Jim Perkinson reads the Syrophoenician woman as the subaltern other, whom Jesus does not silence. She challenges the image of the Messiah and leads him to act for her.[31] As we see above, postcolonial criticism applies to Mark's Gospel variously.

Further Reading

- Mary Ann Tolbert, "When Resistance Becomes Repression," in *Reading from This Place*, vol. 2, ed. Fernando Segovia and Mary Ann Tolbert (Minneapolis, MN: Fortress, 1995), 331–46.
- Tat-Siong Benny Liew, "Tyranny, Boundary and Might," *Journal for the Study of the New Testament* 21, no. 73 (1999): 7–31.
- Simon Samuel, *A Postcolonial Reading of Mark's Story of Jesus* (New York: T&T Clark, 2007).
- Fernando F. Segovia and R. S. Sugirtharajah, eds., *A Postcolonial Commentary on the New Testament Writings* (New York: T&T Clark, 2007).

Deconstruction Interpretation

With the spirit of deconstruction, Mark can be read differently. For example, topics in Mark, such as discipleship or faith, would never be fully understood by anyone, and their meaning should not be decided once and for all. For example, what discipleship means in Mark should not be decided by the typical Western model of "correct knowledge" about Jesus; rather, it requires a mysterious and long process for readers seeking to know who Jesus is or what the Messiah means.[32] Often people assume that they know the truth of Jesus, and then they train other people based on this knowledge. But discipleship is action based on Jesus, whose teaching is inexhaustible. Therefore, what Jesus says or does in Mark needs to be interpreted without stopping. In the narrative of Mark, there are insurmountable signifiers that relate to Jesus. Then there are endless relationships between Jesus and all other signifiers. This means there is no central signifier that solely decides who Jesus is. Eventually, one realizes knowing Jesus is not fully obtainable. So readers must be humble and seek the endless search for meaning in context. Perhaps Jesus has known it is impossible for people to know who he is. That is why he tries to hide his messianic identity. This explanation about the messianic secret differs from Wrede's thesis that Mark created this secret to confirm that Jesus himself knew about his messianic identity but that he did not let others know about it. But from the perspective of deconstruction, the messianic secret may be read differently; that is, Jesus does not want people to misunderstand him, because knowing him takes time and people need an awakening from what they've known already. His teaching through parables is also a form of deconstruction because he subverts the world of his readers. One cannot know him merely by the information about him, but it is through the experience of him. In this context, faith means endless listening to him, wondering about God's initiative of love and justice in the world, and following him. As we see above, deconstruction is not a method but a critical attitude or spirit toward the interpretation of literature. Closure of meaning is shunned, and readers must seek to deconstruct their knowledge, or the things they know about Jesus or faith.

Further Reading

- Hugh S. Pyper, "Postmodernism," in *New Meanings for Ancient Texts: Recent Approaches to Biblical Criticisms and Their Applications*, ed. Steven L. McKenzie and John Kaltner (Louisville, KY: Westminster John Knox, 2013), 117–36.
- A. K. M. Adam, *What Is Postmodern Biblical Criticism?* (Minneapolis, MN: Fortress, 1995).

- Jin Young Choi, *Postcolonial Discipleship of Embodiment: An Asian and Asian American Feminist Reading of the Gospel of Mark* (New York: Palgrave Macmillan, 2015).
- Yung Suk Kim, *Resurrecting Jesus: The Renewal of New Testament Theology* (Eugene, OR: Cascade Books, 2015).

Minoritized Criticism

Osvaldo Vena reads Mark's Gospel from a perspective of minoritized criticism, which tackles issues facing the Latinx community "struggling to survive ethnically and emotionally in a society deeply divided on issues of race, gender identity, politics, and national and individual security, to mention just a few."[33] He explores Mark's Gospel in Roman imperial contexts and relates it to the Latinx experiences in America. Then he focuses on five themes in the Gospel: "(1) excessive use of force by the police; (2) racial profiling; (3) sense of selfhood and family; (4) division and separation of families due to the undocumented status of its members; and (5) acculturation or assimilation as a way of survival."[34] He goes into detail to investigate each theme from the Gospel and draws from them applicable insights for the marginalized. The crux of his thesis is as follows: "The inescapable reality of the cross serves not only as a model for Jesus' ministry but also for the disciples'—and the readers'—own ministry."[35] The point of the cross lies in Jesus' love of the marginalized at the risk of his life. In Mark's context of a crisis due to the Jewish-Roman war, the community members must be ready to resist imperial rules and find an alternative community as envisioned and established by Jesus. The distinctive reading of Vena includes the emphasis on discipleship rooted in Jesus, his spirit challenging evil systems, and his grand vision of a beloved community of God. While the disciples fail to understand and follow Jesus in the narrative of Mark, the implicit challenge is that true disciples must imitate Jesus. In the end, Vena hopes the marginalized communities in the US will be empowered through a Jesus-like discipleship that shares his vision, spirit, and faith. So Vena observes,

> The message for the Markan community is a powerful one: avoid the center, Jerusalem, and stick to the margins, Galilee, for it is there where the kingdom, contrary to what the Jewish revolutionaries thought, will manifest itself. And its implementation will not be through violence but through the giving of one's life, if necessary, for the sake of the Gospel, as Jesus had announced in 8:35. The community is thus encouraged to keep an attitude of nonalignment with either the Zealots or the Romans. Their allegiance is to the kingdom of God, as outlined by Jesus of Nazareth.[36]

Further Reading

- Osvaldo D. Vena, "Mark: A Disabled Gospel for a Disabled Community," in *Latinx Perspectives on the New Testament*, ed. Osvaldo D. Vena and Leticia A. Guardiola-Saenz (Lanham, MD: Lexington Books, 2022), 33–60.
- Emerson Powery, "The Gospel of Mark," in *True to Our Native Land: An African American New Testament Commentary*, ed. Brian K. Blount, Cain H. Felder, Clarice J. Martin, and Emerson B. Powery (Minneapolis, MN: Fortress, 2007), 151–57.
- Tat-siong Benny Liew and Fernando F. Segovia, eds. *Reading Biblical Texts Together: Pursuing Minoritized Biblical Criticism* (Atlanta, GA: Society of Biblical Literature, 2022).
- Jin Young Choi, *Postcolonial Discipleship of Embodiment: An Asian and Asian American Feminist Reading of the Gospel of Mark* (New York: Palgrave Macmillan, 2015).

Disability Studies

Jaime Clark-Soles reads the Gospel of Mark "through the lens of disability, with attention to understandings of disability in the ancient world, the language of affliction, questions of faith and sin, forms of healing, and the agency of the impaired person."[37] She also "examines the 'powers' in the Gospel of Mark as a form of empire and demonstrates how Jesus's action in casting out demons and unclean spirits is a disruption of the status quo at a cosmic level."[38] Confronting the common assumptions that "disability is caused by sin and that if one has enough faith, one will be healed,"[39] she distinguishes between temporarily able-bodied persons and persons with disabilities. In other words, disabilities are not a sin, and people are disabled in one way or another, especially as aging continues. She also distinguishes between cure and healing. The former is a physical recovery on an individual level, and the latter refers to "a person's experience of integration and reconciliation to self, God, and the community."[40] This means healing may not require a cure. The last distinction Clark-Soles makes is that "not all impairments cause pain and suffering."[41] For example, to a person born blind, it feels natural to live with it. Society assumes that it is not natural. There is no decisive connection between disability and sin in Mark. The exception is in Mark 2:3–12, but even here, Jesus's forgiving of sins must apply to all because no one is righteous before God. In fact, the faith of four people who carry a paralyzed man helps heal this man. Healing is a communal aspect of liberation. Then Clark-Soles analyzes two healing stories: a blind man at Bethsaida in Mark 8:22–26 and the healing of blind Bartimaeus in Mark 10:46–52. In the former, this man seems born blind, and he is brought to Jesus by others against his agreement or desires. Often, society and/or the community judges those who live with a disability as needing treatment. Blindness should not be a metaphor that renders blind people less human. In contrast, in Mark 10:46–52, the blind beggar actively seeks his healing, calling Jesus "Son of David," asking him to have mercy on him (Mark 10:47–48). He regains his sight as he has wished and becomes a disciple of Jesus. But even in this healing story, while faith is important, there are concerns, as he could have become a disciple with a disability. The important thing is how to live with a disability and contribute to society without being discriminated against. Lastly, Clark-Soles discusses the healing story of a man possessed by demons in Mark 5:1–20 and points out the problem of imperial powers coupled with the local people and communities, which made this man disabled.

Further Reading

- Jaime Clark-Soles, "Mark and Disability," *Interpretation: A Journal of Bible and Theology* 70, no. 2 (2016): 159–71.
- Louise J. Lawrence, "Exploring the Sense-Scape of the Gospel of Mark," *Journal for the Study of the New Testament* 33, no. 4 (2011): 387–97.
- Louise J. Lawrence, *Sense and Stigma in the Gospels: Depictions of Sensory-Disabled Characters* (Oxford, England: Oxford University Press, 2013).

Ecological Criticism

Jesus's agricultural parables, such as those of the sower, mustard seed, and the seed growing secretly, are ecologically friendly and deal with a rural farming culture, where people must learn how to live. In Mark 4:1–9, Jesus tells the parable of the sower from a boat on the sea because a large crowd has gathered. He uses God-given nature to talk about the kingdom of God, which must be realized in everyday life. The sower must realize all things are given by God. Even a sower is a masterpiece of God's creation. The land, seeds, birds, sun, and all things in nature are from God. There are things humans can do, and there are things they cannot do. This aspect of human limitations is best expressed in the parable of the seed growing secretly (Mark 4:26–29): "The kingdom of God is as if someone would scatter seed on the ground and would sleep and rise night and day, and the seed would sprout and grow, he does not know how. The earth produces of itself first the stalk, then the head, then the full grain in the head. But when the grain is ripe, at once he goes in with his sickle because the harvest has come." But in the parable of the sower, the emphasis is on the sower's hard work. His job is to work diligently, thanking God for all that is given. A sower goes out to sow and scatters seed as much as and as far as he can. Some fall on a path, and birds eat them up. It is natural for birds to eat them up because they need food. Some fall on rocky ground and wither away because the sun has risen, and they are scorched. Rocky ground and the sun are not bad; they are needed in God-given nature. Some seeds falling on the rocky ground is expected because of the sower's hard efforts of sowing. Still, some fall among thorns, which is hard for the seeds. But they are there as a part of the ecological environment. Thorns are not bad. The sower does not expect grain from those places. Some seeds fall on good soil and yield abundantly. Until the sower finishes sowing seeds on good soil, he should not give up, even with the hostile conditions of nature. He believes that his hard work pays off because God provides all things necessary, such as the soil, the sun, and seeds. He does not make anything for his farm. Likewise, in the parable of the mustard seed, the sower cannot make even the smallest seed. Therefore, he must be humble and honor all God-given blessings in the world. When people trust God, know their limits, and live with simplicity and open-mindedness, they are under the rule of God.

Further Reading

- Elaine Wainwright, "Healing Ointment/Healing Bodies: Gift and Identification in an Ecofeminist Reading of Mark 14:3–9," in *Exploring Ecological Hermeneutics*, ed. Norman C. Habel and Peter Trudinger (Atlanta, GA: Society of Biblical Literature, 2008), 131–40.
- Elaine Wainwright, "Part Four: An Ecological Reading of Mark's Gospel," *Tui Motu InterIslands Magazine*, May 1, 2015, https://hail.to/tui-motu-interislands-magazine/publication/430InQe/article/p9j2RGB.
- Yung Suk Kim, *Jesus's Truth: Life in Parables* (Eugene, OR: Resource, 2018).
- Susan Miller, "The Descent of Darkness over the Land: Listening to the Voice of Earth in Mark 15:33," in *Exploring Ecological Hermeneutics*, ed. Norman C. Habel and Peter Trudinger (Atlanta, GA: Society of Biblical Literature, 2008), 123–30.

NOTES

1. David Rhoades, "Social Criticism," in *Mark and Method: New Approaches in Biblical Studies*, ed. Janice Capel Anderson and Stephen D. Moore (Minneapolis, MN: Fortress, 1992), 135–61.
2. Wolfgang Stegemann, *The Social Setting of Jesus and the Gospels* (Minneapolis, MN: Fortress, 2002).
3. Elizabeth Struthers Malbon, "Narrative Criticism: How Does the Story Mean?" in *Mark and Method: New Approaches in Biblical Studies*, ed. Janice Capel Anderson and Stephen D. Moore (Minneapolis, MN: Fortress, 1992), 39–40.
4. Robert M. Fowler, "Reader-Response Criticism: Figuring Mark's Reader," in *Mark and Method: New Approaches in Biblical Studies*, ed. Janice Capel Anderson and Stephen D. Moore (Minneapolis, MN: Fortress, 1992), 58–59.
5. Mitzi J. Smith, *Womanist Sass and Talk Back: Social (In)Justice, Intersectionality, and Biblical Interpretation* (Eugene, OR: Cascade Books, 2018), 29.
6. Smith, *Womanist Sass*, 39.
7. Smith, *Womanist Sass*, 39–40.
8. Brian K. Blount, *Go Preach!: Mark's Kingdom Message and the Black Church Today (Bible & Liberation)* (Maryknoll, NY: Orbis, 1998). See also, Blount, "Jesus as Teacher: Boundary Breaking in Mark's Gospel and Today's Church," *Interpretation: A Journal of Bible and Theology* 70, no. 2 (2016): 184–93.
9. Blount, *Go Preach!*, xi. See also, Heber F. Peacock, "Discipleship in the Gospel of Mark," *Review & Expositor* 75, no. 4 (1978): 555–64; Eduard Schweizer, "The Portrayal of the Life of Faith in the Gospel of Mark," *Interpretation* 32, no. 4 (1978): 387–99.
10. Blount, *Go Preach!*, 3–31. See also, David M. Rhoads, "Jesus and the Syrophoenician Woman in Mark: A Narrative-Critical Study," *Currents in Theology and Mission* 47, no. 4 (2020): 36–48.
11. Adela Yabro Collins, "Mark's Interpretation of the Death of Jesus," *Journal of Biblical Literature* 128, no. 3 (2009): 545–54. See Sharyn Dowd and Elizabeth Struthers Malbon, "The Significance of Jesus' Death in Mark: Narrative Context and Authorial Audience," *Journal of Biblical Literature* 125, no. 2 (2006): 271–97. See also, Joel Marcus, "Crucifixion as Parodie Exaltation," *Journal of Biblical Literature* 125, no. 1 (2006): 73–87.
12. Dowd and Malbon, "The Significance of Jesus' Death in Mark," 284. They quote from Ched Myers to support their claim: "The phrase 'as a ransom (*lutron*) for many' appears to be an allusion back to 'slave' [at Mark 10:43–44]. The term referred to the price required to redeem captives or purchase freedom for indentured servants. Jesus promises then that the way of 'servanthood' has been transformed by the Human One into the way of liberation." Ched Myers, *Binding the Strong Man: A Political Reading of Mark's Story of Jesus* (Maryknoll, NY: Orbis, 1988), 279.
13. Collins, "Mark's Interpretation of the Death of Jesus," 546.
14. Collins, "Mark's Interpretation of the Death of Jesus," 546–47.
15. Collins, "Mark's Interpretation of the Death of Jesus," 547.
16. Collins, "Mark's Interpretation of the Death of Jesus," 550.

17. Hisako Kinukawa, "Mark," in *Global Bible Commentary*, ed. Daniel Patte (Nashville, TN: Abingdon Press, 2005), 367.

18. Ana Esther Padua Freire, "Mark," in *The Queer Bible Commentary*, ed. Mona West and Robert E. Shore-Goss (London: SCM Press, 2022), 518–32.

19. Freire, "Mark," 528.

20. Freire, "Mark," 528.

21. Freire, "Mark," 528.

22. Simon Samuel, *A Postcolonial Reading of Mark's Story of Jesus* (New York: T&T Clark, 2007), 76–81.

23. See Richard A. Horsley, *Jesus and Empire: The Kingdom of God and the New World Disorder* (Minneapolis, MN: Augsburg Fortress Press, 2003). See also, Myers, *Binding the Strong Man*.

24. Myers, *Binding the Strong Man*, 31.

25. David Sánchez, "Ambivalence, Mimicry, and the Ochlos in the Gospel of Mark," in *Reading Minjung Theology in the Twenty-first Century*, ed. Yung Suk Kim and Jin-ho Kim (Eugene, OR: Pickwick, 2013), 134–47.

26. Mary Ann Tolbert, "When Resistance Becomes Repression," in *Reading From This Place*, vol. 2, ed. Fernando Segovia and Mary Ann Tolbert (Minneapolis, MN: Fortress, 1995), 331–46.

27. Samuel, *A Postcolonial Reading of Mark's Story of Jesus*, 79.

28. Tat-Siong Benny Liew, "Tyranny, Boundary and Might," *Journal for the Study of the New Testament* 21, no. 73 (1999): 7–31.

29. Liew, "Tyranny, Boundary and Might," 23.

30. Samuel, *A Postcolonial Reading of Mark's Story of Jesus*, 81.

31. Jim Perkinson, "A Canaanite Word in the Logos of Christ," *Semeia* 75 (1996): 61–85.

32. See Jin Young Choi, *Postcolonial Discipleship of Embodiment: An Asian and Asian American Feminist Reading of the Gospel of Mark* (New York: Palgrave Macmillan, 2015).

33. Osvaldo D. Vena, "Mark: A Disabled Gospel for a Disabled Community," in *Latinx Perspectives on the New Testament*, ed. Osvaldo D. Vena and Leticia A. Guardiola-Saenz (Lanham, MD: Lexington Books, 2022), 33–60. For African American commentary on Mark's Gospel, see Emerson Powery, "The Gospel of Mark," in *True to Our Native Land: An African American New Testament Commentary*, ed. Brian K. Blount, Cain H. Felder, Clarice J. Martin, and Emerson B. Powery (Minneapolis, MN: Fortress, 2007), 151–57.

34. Vena, "Mark: A Disabled Gospel," 33–60.

35. Vena, "Mark: A Disabled Gospel," 36.

36. Vena, "Mark: A Disabled Gospel," 37.

37. Jaime Clark-Soles, "Mark and Disability," *Interpretation: A Journal of Bible and Theology* 70, no. 2 (2016): 159.

38. Clark-Soles, "Mark and Disability," 159.

39. Kerry H. Wynn, "Johannine Healings and Otherness of Disability," *Perspectives in Religious Studies* 34 (2007): 61–75.

40. Clark-Soles, "Mark and Disability," 160.

41. Clark-Soles, "Mark and Disability," 160.

Chapter 8

The Gospel of Matthew from Various Perspectives

AUTHOR-CENTERED, HISTORICAL APPROACH

Historical-Critical Method

Matthew uses the Markan passion narrative but adds controversial anti-Jewish statements, such as "Woe to you, scribes and Pharisees, hypocrites!" (seen seven times in Mt 23:1–36) and "His blood be on us and on our children" (27:25). Historians infer that these pungent sayings may reflect Matthew's community in conflict with formative Judaism after the fall of Jerusalem, in the post-Jewish war. Some historians think of this Matthean community as struggling with "two fronts": one, with mainline Judaism; the other, with "antinomian Gentile Christianity."[1] Matthew affirms the Jewish root of a community along with Jesus's image as the Jewish Messiah, yet he criticizes Judaism because many Jews did not accept Jesus as the Messiah, who came to fulfill the law and the prophets. But Matthew is also concerned about the arrogance of the Gentiles leading to the rejection of Judaism. According to Donald Senior, Matthew's concern was to "lose all contact with its Jewish origins and result in Christian communities that were either all Jewish or all Gentile."[2] He goes on to say, "Matthew's vision was that of an assembly or church in which both Jew and Gentile would flourish together."[3] Jesus's saying in Matthew 10:5–6 shows distinct evidence that the Matthean community has struggled with a Gentile mission: "Do not take a road leading to Gentiles, and do not enter a Samaritan town, but go rather to the lost sheep of the house of Israel." Here, Jesus prohibits his disciples from going to preach to the Gentiles, which is hardly understandable, as the overall narrative of Matthew portrays Jesus as a great teacher, healer, and prophet who says God is for all, the evil and the good (Mt 5:45). Matthew continues to ponder on if they open the Gentile mission, on what basis should it be? The Canaanite woman's encounter with Jesus in Matthew 15:21–28 shows the answer; it is through faith, which also needs interpretation. Overall, even with the above two-fronts situation for Matthew, the Canaanite woman's story is not easy to interpret, because Jesus refuses to listen to her, calling her a dog, and expressing Jewish exclusivism (Mt 15:24).

Further Reading

- Anthony Saldarini, *Matthew's Christian-Jewish Community* (Chicago: University of Chicago Press, 1994).
- Anthony Saldarini, "Reading Matthew without Anti-Semitism," in *The Gospel of Matthew in Current Study*, ed. David E. Aune (Grand Rapids, MI: William B. Eerdmans, 2001), 166–84.
- Donald Senior, "Between Two Worlds: Gentiles and Jewish Christians in Matthew's Gospel," *Catholic Biblical Quarterly* 61 (1999): 1–23.
- J. Andrew Overman, *Matthew's Gospel and Formative Judaism: The Social World of the Matthean Community* (Minneapolis, MN: Fortress, 1990).

Social-Science Criticism

Rodney Stark uses "social description" and "social history" and argues that Matthew's community thrived in Antioch, the fourth largest city of the Roman Empire, because it provided people with "new norms and new kinds of social relationships able to cope with many urgent, urban problems."[4] They must love even enemies and treat all equally (Mt 5:45). Jesus's teaching is radical and thorough, as it goes beyond traditional lines between friend and enemy. Retaliation is prohibited, and additional help is necessary for those in need (Mt 5:38–42). If one does not love one's enemy, one is not the child of God (5:43–38). People must be as perfect as God is. Jesus says, "But I say to you that if you are angry with a brother or sister, you will be liable to judgment, and if you insult a brother or sister, you will be liable to the council, and if you say, 'You fool,' you will be liable to the hell of fire" (Mt 5:22, NRSVue). All of these radical, moral teachings for the community of Matthew have contributed to the lives of many marginalized people who had personal or social crises. The mandate to love all—even enemies—is important to Matthew's community because, in this way, the community found itself secure at the edges of the Roman Empire. Others see Matthew's community as a voluntary association that goes through "stages of community growth" as well as a performing stage after that.[5] Being in the community involves formation, cohesion, regulation, and performance for a set goal. Community members gather together voluntarily for a common purpose, and they may support each other in the love of God. In times of persecution, they are bound together with the message of blessings, as seen in the Beatitudes (Mt 5:3–12).[6] They also establish community norms to maintain their lives securely in the love of God through the example of Christ. Conflict may be resolved within the community when members follow the way of Christ and forgive one another (Mt 18:15–22).

Further Reading

- Rodney Stark, "Antioch as the Social Situation for Matthew's Gospel," in *Social History of the Matthean Community*, ed. David Balch (Minneapolis, MN: Fortress, 1991), 189–210.
- Richard S. Ascough, "Matthew and Community Formation," in *The Gospel of Matthew in Current Study*, ed. David E. Aune (Grand Rapids, MI: William B. Eerdmans, 2001), 166–84.
- Bruce J. Malina, "Early Christian Groups: Using Small Group Formation Theory to explain Christian Organizations," in *Modelling Early Christianity: Social-Scientific Studies of the New Testament in Its Context*, ed. Philip F. Esler (New York: Routledge, 1995), 96–113.

TEXT-CENTERED, LITERARY APPROACH

Textual Criticism

There are a few pivotal textual variations in Matthew. Matthew 6:13 says, "And do not bring us to the time of trial, but rescue us from the evil one," to which other ancient authorities add, "For the kingdom and the power and the glory are yours forever. Amen." But this ascription that says, "For the kingdom and the power of God and the glory are yours forever. Amen" is not in "early and important representatives of the Alexandrian (ℵ B), the Western (D and most of the Old Latin), and the pre-Caesarean (f^1) types of text, as well as early patristic commentaries on the Lord's Prayer (those of Tertullian, Origen, Cyprian)."[7] Given this, the ascription may have to do with "liturgical use in the early church."[8]

In Matthew 24:36, the narrator says, "But about that day and hour no one knows, neither the angels of heaven, nor the Son, but only the Father," while other ancient authorities lack "nor the Son" for the understandable reasons of Christological concerns (for example, the later Byzantine text lacks it); that is, Jesus must know the day and hour. But the phrase is contained in "the best representatives of the Alexandrian, the Western, and the Caesarean types of text."[9]

In Matthew 27:16, the narrator says, "At that time they had a notorious prisoner, called *Jesus* Barabbas." In Matthew 27:17, he also says, "Whom do you want me to release for you, *Jesus* Barabbas or Jesus who is called the Messiah?" Other ancient authorities lack the second reference to the name Jesus. This lack is perhaps due to "reverential considerations."[10] But the best possibility is that both are named "Jesus," since the double name is attested to in "several witnesses of the Caesarean text."[11] Pilate's question with the double name sounds funny but makes sense: "Whom do you want me to release for you, *Jesus* Barabbas or *Jesus* who is called the Messiah?" (Mt 26:17).

Further Reading

- Bruce M. Metzger, *A Textual Commentary on the Greek New Testament* (New York: Hendrickson, 2005).
- David C. Parker, *Textual Scholarship and the Making of the New Testament* (New York: Oxford University Press, 2014).
- Bruce M. Metzger and Bart D. Ehrman, *The Text of the New Testament: Its Transmission, Corruption, and Restoration* (New York: Oxford University Press, 2005).
- David C. Parker, *The Living Text of the Gospels* (New York: Cambridge University Press, 1997).

Narrative Criticism

The Gospel of Matthew may be read through narrative criticism in that both story and discourse are analyzed. Jack Kingsbury puts it this way: "The story of Matthew is of the life of Jesus from conception and birth to death and resurrection. The 'discourse' of Matthew is the means whereby this story of Jesus' life is told. In simple terms, the 'story' is 'what' is told, whereas the 'discourse' is 'how' the story is told."[12] While the story involves "events, characters, and settings,"[13] the discourse has to do with the concept of the implied author, the implied reader, and what is read in a text. So flesh-and-blood readers find it very complicated, following the above story and discourse elements. This way of reading the Gospel is just like reading fiction or watching a movie. The focus is not on what happened historically but what is going on in the story world of Jesus, who conflicts with Israel, the world, and Jewish leaders. Also, readers must figure out what the implied author is trying to tell them with all the story elements. There are many related events in the story, which need to be connected and wondered about by the implied readers. There are also many different characters in the story: Jesus, the disciples, Jewish leaders, crowds, and minor characters. All of these need to be analyzed, whether they are stable or unstable. Where the story occurs involves the settings. With these elements of the story and with consideration of the implied author's intention, readers may go in several directions, appreciating the plot of a story in Matthew's Gospel. For example, they may focus on conflict scenes of Jesus with the Jewish leaders, who receive woes from him. Or they may focus on the character of the disciples, who have little faith sometimes, do not understand their teacher at other times, ask him to send a Canaanite woman away, deny him, flee from his trials and death, and yet are commissioned in the end.

Further Reading

- Jack Kingsbury, *Matthew as Story* (Philadelphia, PA: Fortress, 1988).
- Seymour Chatman, *Story and Discourse: Narrative Structure in Fiction and Film* (New York: Cornell University Press, 1978).
- Mark A. Powell, "Toward a Narrative-Critical Understanding of Matthew," *Interpretation: A Journal of Bible and Theology* 46, no. 4 (1992): 341–46.

READER-CENTERED, COMPREHENSIVE APPROACH

Reader-Response Criticism

In Matthew two Gentiles are commended for their great faith: a centurion in 8:5–13 and a Canaanite woman in 15:21–28. Since Jesus does not explain their great faith, readers wonder about the nature of their faith and ask why only two are praised for their faith. One way we can answer this question is to closely read the surrounding texts. The two Gentiles' great faith is contrasted with the disciples' little faith. In Matthew 6:30, Jesus rebukes them in his Sermon on the Mount: "But if God so clothes the grass of the field, which is alive today and tomorrow is thrown into the oven, will he not much more clothe you—you of little faith?" The disciples worry about themselves and do not seek God's rule and his righteousness. In other words, they care for themselves only. But a centurion in Matthew 8:5–13 shows great faith by caring for his servant and trusting Jesus wholeheartedly. But the disciples never fully trust Jesus or understand him. They're almost always seeking, as their ambition is to be great. Also, in Matthew 8:23–27, the disciples in the boat are terrified by the waves and call out to Jesus, "Lord, save us! We are perishing!" (Mt 8:25). Only when they are in danger do they seek Jesus. Again, they are rebuked: "Why are you afraid, you of little faith?" (Mt 8:26). In Matthew

14:28–33, Peter tries to walk on the water, but he is frightened and begins to sink. Jesus saves him and says, "You of little faith, why did you doubt?" (Mt 14:31). After this story, a Canaanite woman's story follows. While she is triply marginalized in society as a woman, a mother, and a member of a poor family with a sick daughter, she asks for her daughter's healing with unwavering faith in the Messiah. After this story, the disciples still remain the same, with little faith. In Matthew 16:8–9, Jesus rebukes his disciples for worrying about no bread: "You of little faith, why are you talking about having no bread? Do you still not perceive?" In Matthew 17:14–20, Jesus again rebukes his disciples, who cannot cast the demon out from a man with epilepsy and tells them they cannot do so because they have little faith. And in fact, this little faith is futile because it is not real faith according to Jesus's standard: "If you have faith the size of a mustard seed, you will say to this mountain, 'Move from here to there,' and it will move, and nothing will be impossible for you" (Mt 17:20). In other words, the disciples do not have faith even the size of a mustard seed. In the end, real readers are given the chance to interpret "little faith" in various places in Matthew. Is it effective, even if not perfect? Or is it futile?

Further Reading

- Mark A. Powell, *Chasing the Eastern Star: Adventures in Biblical Reader–Response Criticism* (Louisville, KY: Westminster John Knox, 2001).
- Mary Hinkle Shore, "Creation, Vocation, and Little Faith in Matthew's Gospel," *Word & World* 5 (2006): 66–72.
- Richard Edwards, "Uncertain Faith: Matthew's Portrait of the Disciples," in *Discipleship in the New Testament*, ed. Fernando Segovia (Philadelphia, PA: Fortress, 1985), 47–61.

Feminist Criticism

Matthew's Gospel as a whole may be analyzed from the feminist perspective.[14] But in particular, an individual story like the Canaanite woman's story in Matthew 15:21–28 may be examined through feminist criticism. The Canaanite woman is perceived as "a boundary-walker" who challenges Jesus and gets what she wants.[15] She comes out of her boundary and cries for mercy "as a narrative embodiment of a lament psalm."[16] Wainwright observes the following: "She does not accept the dichotomies of insider and outsider within which Jesus functions but creates a new space that is inside the house and that allows both the children and dogs to be fed within that household, both from the same table."[17] Accordingly, her role is "prophetic and transgressive."[18] In Matthew 15:21–28, she leads the story. O'Day puts it like this: "She initiates the movement of the story with her first petition, refuses to be silenced or ignored, and in the end goes away victorious, having been answered and heard by Jesus. . . . She is the life blood of this story."[19] The traditional reading of this text goes with the submissive model of discipleship in that obedience to God or Jesus is necessary under any circumstances. Here, Jesus tests the woman. But the problem of this reading ignores plain texts where Jesus denies the woman's request because of his "Israel first" theology (Mt 15:24). Earlier, in Matthew 10:5–6, Jesus has also expressed this theology when he's sent out his disciples: "Go nowhere among the Gentiles, and enter no town of the Samaritans, but go rather to the lost sheep of the house of Israel."[20] While, at the end of the story, Jesus acknowledges her faith and allows her daughter to be healed, and at the end of the narrative, he commissions the disciples to go into all nations, feminist criticism does not stop asking about Jewish exclusivism or the primacy of Judaism embedded in the text, as well as its role in the community.

Further Reading

- Elaine M. Wainwright, *Shall We Look for Another? A Feminist Rereading of the Matthean Jesus* (Maryknoll, NY: Orbis, 1998).
- Leticia Guardiola-Sáenz, "Borderless Women and Borderless Texts: A Cultural Reading of Matthew 15:21–28," *Semeia* 78, no. 1 (1997): 69–81.
- Elisabeth Schussler Fiorenza, *But She Said: Feminist Practices of Biblical Interpretation* (Boston, MA: Beacon Press, 1993).
- Amy-Jill Levine, "The Gospel of Matthew," in *Women's Bible Commentary. Revised Edition*, ed. Carol Newsom and Sharon H. Ringe (Louisville, KY: Westminster John Knox, 2012), 465–77.

Womanist Interpretation

Mitzi Smith reads the feeding miracle of Jesus in Matthew 14:13–21 from a womanist experience or perspective, which sheds new light on a biblical text.[21] She begins with her context: her mother had taught her children the importance of sharing even the smallest thing with their neighbors. Her mother lived with abject conditions of health and economics but never gave up the spirit of helping others because no African American community can live alone without others. Feeding the hungry and caring for them is good news for them. Smith's experience and her community's struggle with food, especially with children, has led her to read the feeding miracle differently, with a focus on Jesus's embodiment of the law of God's love. The Matthean Jesus fulfills the love command by feeding the most desperate souls and bodies. The crowds in the desert need healing and food due to their marginality. For them, food is not merely for physical provisions, but God is seen through the miracle. It is like heaven incarnate on earth. Likewise, Cheryl Sanders observes, "God feeds the poor in our kitchen; God's kingdom come alive on earth."[22] Jesus's compassion and justice for the helpless crowd stretch women and children, who are the most vulnerable. It should be noted that only Matthew mentions women and children in the miracle, which implies Matthew's emphasis on the marginalized (cf. Mt 25:31–46).[23] Throughout the narrative of Matthew, there is the consistent theme that one of the least must be taken care of. Through the feeding miracle, Jesus's disciples are expected to experience holistic transformation.[24] Initially, they feel they are deficient since what they have is too small to feed the multitude. They recognize their imperfection, which is a mode of thinking, "I am no one." Then they hear their teacher's instructions. This is a mode of thinking, "I am someone." With their trust in Jesus and compassion for the crowds, they see the miracle in their eyes. According to Jesus's instruction, they give the loaves to the multitudes, including women and children. There are leftovers in twelve baskets, which symbolize the abundance of God's blessing and the future feeding by the disciples. This last mode is called "I am one for others." All the above three modes of transformation are called "holistic human transformation."[25] As we see above, Jesus's miracle of feeding the five thousand is more than a story of a miracle (Mt 14:13–21). It is a very inspiring story of Jesus's ministry in which not only are the hungry fed, but they are encouraged to live with hope and love. The miracle begins with small things. It can happen in our world. Mitzi Smith sees the importance of sharing food or adequate means of living with those living in extreme poverty.

Further Reading

- Mitzi J. Smith, "'Give Them What You Have': A Womanist Reading of the Matthean Feeding Miracle (Matthew 14:13–21)," *Journal of Bible and Human Transformation* 3, no. 1 (2013): 1–22.
- Mitzi J. Smith and Michael Willett Newheart, *We Are All Witnesses: Toward Disruptive and Creative Biblical Interpretation* (Eugene, OR: Cascade Books, 2022).
- Cheryl J. Sanders, *Ministry at the Margins: The Prophetic Mission of Women, Youth and the Poor* (Downers Grove, IL: InterVarsity, 1997).
- N. Lynne Westfield, *Dear Sisters: A Womanist Practice of Hospitality* (Cleveland, OH: Pilgrim Press, 2001).

Ekklesia-Centered, Theological Interpretation

Gerald West is concerned with the theology of Matthew's Gospel and its impact on the African church, especially on local African communities of the poor and marginalized. He has led the Ujamaa Center, which has conducted a community-based contextual Bible study for more than thirty years to bring about social transformation in South Africa and the African continent.[26] Believing in the power of the gospel, committed biblical scholars have participated in leading Bible studies for them. Community gatherings around the Bible study are *ekklesia*—not a traditional type but an alternative form that responds to Matthew's witnessing of Jesus in South African contexts. The ultimate goal of the Bible study is not gaining information but participating in the power of the gospel that can change people and society. So the center is against apartheid-led biblical interpretation and "stands in the biblical-theological tradition that affirms liberation, inclusion, and transformation."[27] The center's Contextual Bible Study (CBS) incorporates the see-judge-act process and engages with both the text and context. Seeing is to consider the text in context, judging is to think about things from God's perspective, and acting involves a change in thought or action. Among other texts in Matthew's Gospel, CBS has selected Matthew 15:21–31, which features Jesus's encounter with the Canaanite woman whose daughter is tormented by a demon. In this passage, the issues are about ethnicity, disability, marginality, gender, economics, religion, and politics. The readers are also reminded of the World Health Organization's notion of equity, which is "the absence of unfair, avoidable or remediable differences among groups of people, whether those groups are defined socially, economically, demographically, or geographically or by other dimensions of inequality (e.g., sex, gender, ethnicity, disability, or sexual orientation)."[28] The notion continues: "Health is a fundamental human right. Political, economic, socio-cultural, technological, environmental, legal and institutional structures determine how power and resources are distributed, which in turn determine how people are born, live and die."[29] In the facilitation of the Bible study, the following questions are given to its participants:[30]

- Listen to a dramatic reading of Matthew 15:21–31 in different translations.
- Who are the characters in these stories, and what do we know about them? How are these two stories connected? Draw a picture or create a drama that shows the connections between these healing stories.
- Reread verses 22–24. In these verses the disciples bring their concerns about the woman to Jesus. What is it that worries the disciples about

this woman? How does Jesus respond to the disciples? What is Jesus's initial attitude to the woman?
- Reread verses 25–28. In these verses the woman engages Jesus directly, refusing to be silenced. She argues with Jesus. What is the reason Jesus gives for not healing her? What is her argument in response? How does Jesus then respond to her argument?
- Matthew connects two healing stories, that of a Canaanite woman (15:21–28) and that of the crowds (15:29–31). Reread verses 15:29–31. If we read these verses carefully, we see that many of those who were brought to Jesus for healing were not from the Jewish-Israelite community, for when they were healed, "they glorified the God of Israel" (15:31). In what ways has this foreign woman enabled other foreigners to come to Jesus for healing? In what ways has this foreign woman persuaded Jesus that his ministry of healing is for everyone, not only the Jewish-Israelite community?
- There are other similarities between the two healing stories. In both stories there are those who enable the healing of others. What is the role of those who facilitate the healing of others in these two stories?
- Who are the "disciples" in our contexts who hinder the healing of those on the margins, particularly women, children, foreigners, and those living with disability?
- What arguments should the church be making in our contexts to ensure that the available health care is made accessible to all, particularly women, children, foreigners, and those living with disability?
- Jesus acts to change the reality of the marginalized and discriminated. What actions should the church take in our contexts to ensure that the available health care is made accessible to all, particularly women, children, foreigners, and those living with disability? Be specific about what actions can be taken immediately and what actions could be taken with further planning.

Further Reading

- James P. Martin, "The Church in Matthew," *Interpretation* 29, no. 1 (1975): 41–56.
- Donald Senior, *The Gospel of Matthew: Interpreting Biblical Texts Series* (Nashville, TN: Abingdon Press), 1997.
- Stephen Barton, "Matthew's Gospel for Today," *Journal of Theology* 126, no. 1 (2023): 3–19.

Jewish Interpretation

Aaron Gale argues that Matthew's community is located in Galilee and that it must be understood within sectarian Judaism after the Jewish war. In so doing, he finds supporting evidence such as "Jewish archaeological data from the region," Matthew's parallels with Talmudic patterns, and its setting "with a formative group residing in Galilee."[31] Since Matthew's Gospel is very much Jewish, it is plausible that it was written in Galilee because the region was predominantly Jewish and flourished religiously.[32] Mark Chancey's archaeological data confirms "the region's religious inclinations with his four tests of a Jewish Galilee (lack of pig bones, limestone vessels, *mikva'ot*, synagogues, and ossuaries)."[33] Also, archaeological data show that Galilee was a fairly prosperous region, and this fact is reflected in Matthew's Gospel. For example, Matthew mentions ten thousand talents, which is a huge amount of money, in the parable of the unforgiving servant. The other example is when Matthew says, "Blessed are those who are poor in spirit" (Mt 5:3), whereas Luke says, "Blessed are those who are poor" (Luke 6:20). The other factor in supporting Galilee as a possible location of the community has to do with the rabbis' presence and engagement with the community in Galilee. Furthermore, there are strong parallels between rabbinic Jewish interpretations / Talmud and Matthean interpretations. For instance, the story in Matthew 19:16–22 may be interpreted as it is in the Talmud. In the story, a rich young man asks Jesus about how to earn eternal life. Here, the point is not that he must sell all his possessions and give them to the poor to earn salvation. Through the Talmudic thought, the point here is "simply to follow the Torah commandments and be an observant Jew."[34] The Talmud and the rabbis emphasize *tzedakah*, "righteousness" or "charity," which is "more important than all of the other commandments."[35] The last contributing evidence to Galilee being the community's location has to do with the presence/activity of other formative Jewish groups (such as proto-rabbinic ones) in Galilee following the destruction of the Second Temple. Possibly, in its conflict with them, the Matthean community might have emphasized the observance of the Torah commandments (Mt 5:17–20) because the community felt the need to prove they are the true Jews.

Further Reading

- Aaron M. Gale, "Matthew, Galilee, and the Rabbis: A Review of John Kampen, Matthew within Sectarian Judaism," *Conversations with the Biblical World* 40 (2020): 98–106.
- John Kampen, *Matthew within Sectarian Judaism* (New Haven, CT: Yale University Press, 2019).

- Amy-Jill Levine, "Matthew's Advice to a Divided Readership," in *The Gospel of Matthew in Current Study*, ed. David E. Aune (Grand Rapids, MI: William B. Eerdmans, 2001), 22–41.

Inter(con)textual Interpretation

Alejandro Duarte reads Matthew's Gospel in the social and political context of Argentina in the 1970s–1980s.[36] Addressing the military dictatorship; the exploitation of women, children, and poor people; and the killings of innocents in Argentina, he reexamines Jesus's birth story, his escape to Egypt, his return to Israel, and the massacre of infants in Matthew 2. He reads the story inter(con)textually and analyzes sociopolitical situations in ancient and contemporary contexts involving injustices caused by political ambitions and the oppression of the most vulnerable people. In ancient times and in modern-day society, the reality is cruel because injustices are too prevalent to contain. The good news from God seems too weak to defeat evil. Duarte points out the irony of the Messiah's birth and the consequence of the massacre of infants, referring to a similar case of innocent deaths in Argentina due to neoliberalism coupled with the cruel military dictatorship. He asserts that the problem is not Jesus's birth but Herod's plot and ambitious plan to keep his power by removing his future rival. In other words, the massacre of infants is not justifiable; it is morally wrong. God did not plan it either. In the narrative, Jesus is saved from the massacre because his parents take him to Egypt. Through God's grace, he is preserved and prepared for God's mission of liberating the captives. He is like a new Moses, who leads his people from oppression. So he returns to Israel to embark on the journey of liberation for them. Matthew presents Jesus as the new hope; he will comfort those who weep and advocate for justice for them. He is Emmanuel (Mt 1:23) and savior (Mt 1:21) for the marginalized, establishing an alternative community full of God's impartial love and justice. The community/church is newly formed, based on Jesus's teaching that the little ones are to be taken care of (Mt 18:12–14; 25:31–36). For this vision of a community, Matthew emphasizes discipleship, which is to follow Jesus and listen to the word of God. As we see above, for Duarte, Matthew's Gospel is not merely a historical, theological document but a contextual guide to people who need empowerment in times of chaos and injustice.

Further Reading

- Alejandro Duarte, "Matthew," in *Global Bible Commentary*, ed. Daniel Patte (Nashville, TN: Abingdon Press, 2004), 350–60.

- Warren Carter, *Matthew and the Margin: A Sociopolitical and Religious Reading* (Maryknoll, NY: Orbis, 2000).
- Richard Erickson, "Divine Injustice? Matthew's Narrative Strategy and the Slaughter of the Innocents (Matthew 2:13–23)," *Journal for the Study of the New Testament* 64 (1996): 5–27.

Queer Criticism

Thomas Bohache reads Matthew's Gospel from a queer perspective and takes on the term "queer," which "refers to all who are disempowered in a heteronormative world."[37] He forges the concept of queer: "When something is 'queer,' it is uncommon, out of the ordinary, unusual, and non-conforming to the dominant culture. One who is 'queer' may be seen as transgressive, unorthodox, radical, in-your-face or against-the-grain, because in imperialist straight society, s/he navigates in intentional opposition to a seemingly fixed current."[38] With the above queer concept, Bohache examines the Matthean genealogy in Matthew 1:1–17, which includes four women (Tamar, Rahab, Ruth, and Bathsheba) from the Hebrew Bible, as well as Mary, the mother of Jesus. The inclusion of women is unusual, given the patriarchal genealogy. Against the view that four women from the Hebrew Bible represent sinners, foreigners, or "parties to sexual liaisons that were 'unusual' for Hebrew patriarchal culture, who foreshadow Mary's abnormal conception," Bohache argues, along with Jane Schaberg, that these women are queer because they challenge patriarchal culture and find ways out of their morass.[39] Tamar secures her rights from her father-in-law Judah, who does not protect her. Rahab helps two spies sent by Joshua, who then saves her because of her courageous act. Ruth seduces and marries Boaz and secures her future with a son. Bohache states, "Each of these queer acts set the stage for the queer act that will occur in connection with Mary's pregnancy."[40] But in Matthew, Joseph does an act of queerness while Mary stays a silent character/victim. He violates the custom (cf. Dt 22:23–27) and marries her. From a normative perspective of society, he has done an unrighteous thing, because Mary betrayed him. But the text says he did a righteous thing—that is, a queer thing. Matthew hints that Joseph did not beget Jesus; he is only the husband of Mary (1:16). Jesus is born from Mary; that is queer. Bohache concludes,

> In this way, Joseph subverts heteropatriarchal expectation; he spoils the spoiled system of sexual double standards that would demand a woman's life. As a result of his queer act, Mary and Jesus are neither ostracized nor put to death, but allowed to live and prosper: God's Messiah is born because of a man who acts outside of his heteronormative role. Joseph, by not doing what his society expects of him, can be a model for queer people of faith who,

following God's directive, choose to act contrary to society's demands—by marrying illicitly, by having children in non-traditional ways, by forming intentional, non-biological families.[41]

Further Reading

- Thomas Bohache, "Matthew," in *The Queer Bible Commentary*, ed. Mona West and Robert Shore-Goss (London: SCM Press, 2022), 491–517.
- Jane Schaberg, *The Illegitimacy of Jesus: A Feminist Theological Interpretation of the Infancy Narratives* (Sheffield, England: Sheffield Phoenix Press, 2006).
- Janice Capel Anderson, "Matthew: Gender and Reading," *Semeia* 28 (1983): 3–27.

Postcolonial Criticism

Fernando Segovia argues that Matthew's Gospel is not completely anti-imperial or imperial but that it is conflicted in its relationships with the Roman Empire.[42] On the positive side, Matthew presents Jesus as the king of the Jews, who proclaims the rule of God, which is different from the rule of Rome. God's rule with justice for the marginalized breaks the rule of Rome, which does not seek justice for all people. For example, Warren Carter argues that Matthew creates an alternative vision of a community based on Jesus's work or God's rule, not Rome's rule.[43] He explores Matthew's responses and messages against the Roman Empire;[44] that is, salvation comes from Israel and Jesus, not from Rome or the emperor. The alternative vision is based on Jesus's teaching that the community's members must take his yoke, not Rome's (Mt 11:28–30). Concerning paying the tax to Rome, Matthew's strategy is nuanced yet subversive since all that belongs to God is given to God (Mt 17:24–27).[45] Jesus also confronts Pilate, who is the Roman governor, and affirms that he is the king of the Jews (27:11–26).[46] But on the negative side, Matthew includes pro-empire connotations. For example, in Matthew 8:5–13, a centurion, or a Roman military officer, is treated well and praised for his faith. The Roman centurion represents Roman hierarchy and has a sick *pais*, which has an ambiguous translation. Is *pais* a son, servant, or something else? There are clear words for a son and a slave: *huios* and *doulos*. There is also a word for a child (*tekton*). So Jennings and Liew argue that *pais* in Matthew 8:5–13 is an object of exploitation and desire, most likely in a pederasty context.[47] For his benefit and urgency, the centurion approaches Jesus and considers him as a new authority above him. He perceives human relationships as solely based on hierarchy, just as he's lived with chains of command. All this implies that Matthew accepts the status quo of the Roman Empire. Likewise, the Canaanite woman's story in Matthew 15:21–28 may be read as the Matthean community's subordination of the Gentiles; that is, the Matthean Jesus appears as the authority that benefits inferiors through their submission to faith. Similarly, Matthew 28:16–20 may be considered an imperial text that obviates geographical and cultural boundaries and subjugates others.[48]

Further Reading

- Fernando F. Segovia, "Postcolonial Criticism and the Gospel of Matthew," in *Methods for Matthew*, ed. Mark Allan Powell (New York: Cambridge University Press, 2009), 194–238.
- Warren Carter, *Matthew and Empire: Initial Explorations* (Harrisburg, PA: Trinity International, 2001), 57–90.
- Ted Jennings and Tat-Siong Benny Liew, "Mistaken Identities but Model Faith: Rereading the Centurion, the Chap, and the Christ in Matthew 8:5–13," *Journal of Biblical Literature* 123, no. 3 (2004): 467–94.
- Musa W. Dube, "'Go Therefore and Make Disciples of All Nations' (Matt 28:19a): A Postcolonial Perspective on Biblical Criticism and Pedagogy," in *Teaching the Bible: The Discourses and Politics of Biblical Pedagogy*, ed. Fernando F. Segovia and Mary A. Tolbert (Maryknoll, NY: Orbis Books, 1998), 224–46.

Deconstruction Interpretation

Deconstruction is not a method but a comprehensive spirit that defies any attempt to fix the meaning. It shows the undecidability or incompleteness of meaning due to the self-collapsing system of the literature.[49] The main reason for this undecidability is that it results from the endless web of signifiers producing numerous complexities. With this notion, we can take an example of Jesus's commissioning of the disciples from Matthew 28:16–20. Against the dominant reading that the disciples are given transparent tasks they understand and should do, the deconstruction reading posits that this text does not give them obvious central meaning. Rather, it is undecidable, or ambiguous, because there are conflicting stories, such as Jesus's prohibition for his disciples going to the Gentiles (Mt 10:5–6) and his rejection of the Canaanite woman (Mt 15:21–28). Then why, all of a sudden, does the risen Lord send his male disciples to all nations? Why does he not send female disciples? Why send them to all nations since he's prevented the disciples from going to the Gentiles and rejected the Canaanite woman's request? He asks them the following: "Obey everything that I have commanded you" (Mt 28:20). But it is hard to pinpoint what he's taught. Indeed, there are many things he's taught throughout the narrative. On the one hand, he is very much caring for the marginalized, as shown in the feeding miracle in the desert (Mt 14:13–21) and his eschatological sermon that emphasizes serving one of the least (Mt 25:31–46). On the other hand, he limits his mission to the lost sheep of the house of Israel (Mt 15:21–28; 10:5–6). Given this complexity, or ambiguity, it is hard to know Jesus's teaching in the commission. If what he's taught is unclear or complex, how can his disciples teach as they go to all nations?[50] Is his command to go to all nations imperial or inclusive of others? What kind of authority does Jesus receive? How can the disciples do their job, since they've doubted Jesus? As we see above, the deconstruction spirit raises a host of questions that challenge normative reading, which denies other possibilities of meaning. The point is not merely that there is no central meaning of a text but that one meaning should not be dominant as if it were the only possibility. The spirit of deconstruction arises due to the dominant group's hegemonic interpretation and opens the door for more inclusive, diverse, and ethical interpretation.

Further Reading

- Daniel Patte, "Reading Matthew 28:16–20 with Others: How It Deconstructs Our Western Concept of Mission," *HTS Theological Studies* 62, no. 2 (2006): 521–57.
- George Soares-Prabhu, "Two Mission Commands: An Interpretation of Matthew 28:16–20 in the Light of a Buddhist Text," *Biblical Interpretation* 2, no. 3 (1994): 264–82.
- Mitzi J. Smith and Jayachitra Lalitha, eds., *Teaching All Nations: Interrogating the Matthean Great Commission* (Minneapolis, MN: Fortress, 2014).
- William A. Beardslee, "Poststructuralist Criticism," in *To Each Its Own Meaning: An Introduction to Biblical Criticisms and Their Applications*, ed. Steven L. McKenzie and Stephen R. Haynes (Louisville, KY: Westminster John Knox, 1999), 253–67.

Minoritized Criticism

Minoritized criticism seeks to elevate the constructive voice for empowering the marginalized.[51] Jin Young Choi reads Matthew's Gospel at the intersection of ethnicity, gender, and empire.[52] In so doing, she examines Jesus's "shifting" identities in the narrative of Matthew. His identity must be understood variously because of his experience and solidarity with the marginalized. The son of God does not stay in a lofty room, teaching heavenly things without attending to the neediest in the world. Choi argues that an understanding of Jesus's identity needs to incorporate mothers' voices, such as Rachel's lament for her lost children at Ramah in the narrative (Mt 2:18; cf. Jer 31:5).[53] These mothers are the most marginalized because of their gender and children's sacrifice. They suffer and cry under the empire's control and power. Herod does not care for people, thinking only about his power. In this context of the empire and mothers' suffering, Jesus's identity must be understood; that is, he has come to empower those who are hopeless and helpless. He has come to fulfill the righteousness of God (Mt 5:17; 6:33), which is to care for the poor and marginalized. He teaches the impartial love of God for all (5:43–48). Even the enemy is loved. He teaches economic justice for all through the parable of vineyard workers (Mt 20:1–16). He also emphasizes the importance of forgiveness in the community (Mt 18:21–22). How can the son of God be indifferent to the cries of injustice? Herod's killing of innocent children at Bethlehem is reminiscent of the death of Israel's children at the time of the Babylonian captivity. Even though Jesus escapes this senseless massacre, he carries an enormous burden of grief and a duty of saving those who mourn and thirst for God's justice. He also dies on the cross and stands in solidarity with them. As we see above, minoritized criticism sheds new light on the neglected elements of the text and enlivens the marginalized because they find new voices of empowerment. Minoritized criticism often employs intersectional reading, which helps us rethink the meaning of Jesus's marginality and suffering.

Further Reading

- Jin Young Choi, "Weren't You with Jesus the Galilean? (Matt. 26:69): Diasporic Trauma and Mourning," in *Minoritized Women Reading Race and Ethnicity: Intersectional Approaches to Constructed Identity and Early Christian Texts*, ed. Mitzi J. Smith and Jin Young Choi (Lanham, MD: Lexington Books, 2020), 1–22.
- Mitzi J. Smith, "If Rachel Does Not Weep, Who Will?: A Pro-Choice Quality of Life Womanist Reading of Matthew 2," in *Currents in Theology and Mission* 49, no. 4 (2022): 5–9.
- Michael J. Brown, "The Gospel of Matthew," in *True to Our Native Land: An African American New Testament Commentary*, ed. Brian K. Blount, Cain H. Felder, Clarice J. Martin, and Emerson B. Powery (Minneapolis, MN: Fortress, 2007), 85–120.
- Gilberto A. Ruiz, "Matthew: Negotiating Tradition and Identity in Matthean and Latinx Contexts." In *Latinx Perspectives on the New Testament*, ed. Osvaldo D. Vena and Leticia A. Guardiola-Saenz (Lanham, MD: Lexington Books, 2022), 11–32.

Disability Studies

Walter Wilson examines healings of blindness in Matthew and focuses on Jesus's healing of two blind men in Matthew 9:27–31, which departs from other similar healing stories, such as those in Mark 10:46–52 (the healing of blind Bartimaeus) and Matthew 20:29–34 (two blind men by the roadside);[54] that is, in Matthew 9:27–31, "the blind men [follow] Jesus before and not after they [are] healed. In addition, their action is accompanied by several other marks of discipleship, all of which are assigned to the men before their eyes are opened; they follow Jesus into 'the house,' they acknowledge him as 'Lord,' and they confess their belief in his ability to heal them."[55] Surprisingly, the two blind men come to know Jesus even before they gain sight.[56] They call Jesus Son of David and understand he is the Messiah sent by God to bring light to his people. Not only do they perceive Jesus as the Messiah, but they follow him "without the benefit of physical sight."[57] Their experience of Jesus engenders "the power of hearing in the formation of disciples" (Mt 9:25–26; cf. 7:24; 13:3–23).[58] Wilson observes, "What is important to note is that this integrative perspective on discipleship is applied to the blind men of Matt 9:27–31 as blind men, insofar as they hear what Jesus says, understand who he is, and act in ways that express their faith in him, all without [the] benefit of sight."[59] But they do not obey Jesus's command that they should not tell anyone about the healing. The implication is that "one may be able to perceive the truth before being made whole but being made whole is itself no guarantee that one will always obey the truth."[60] Likewise, "for Matthew, physical healing is not necessarily accompanied by spiritual illumination, even in a story that involves the healing of blindness."[61] In the end, Wilson warns us that since healing stories are varied, we must read each carefully through the lens of disability.

Further Reading

- Walter T. Wilson, "Perception, Discipleship, and Revelation in the Gospel of Matthew," *Journal of Disability & Religion* 19, no. 1 (2015): 66–84.
- Mary Ann Beavis, "From the Margin to the Way: A Feminist Reading of the Story of Bartimaeus," *Journal of Feminist Studies in Religion* 14, no. 1 (1988): 19–39.
- Louise J. Lawrence, "Reading Matthew's Gospel with Deaf Culture," in *Matthew*, Texts @ Contexts series, ed. N. W. Duran and J. P. Grimshaw (Minneapolis, MN: Fortress, 2013), 155–71.
- Amos Yong, *The Bible, Disability, and the Church: A New Vision of the People of God* (Grand Rapids, MI: William B. Eerdmans, 2011).

Ecological Criticism

Matthew 6:25–33 is a part of the Sermon on the Mount. The tenor of this story is one of severe anxiety, as Jesus says, "Therefore I tell you, do not worry about your life, what you will eat or what you will drink, or about your body, what you will wear. Is not life more than food and the body more than clothing?" (Mt 6:25). The point is the excessive anxiety arises about these things, which leads to exploitation of others, natural resources, and ecological environments. Human-centered, irresponsible development does damage to God's good creation. Mother Earth now suffers and stands on the brink of its collapse due to climate change. Jesus's point is not that humans are more important than the birds of the air or the lilies of the field but that they should not worry about those basic things of what to eat or what to drink. They must realize they are part of God's creation; they must depend on God's provision and honor what God has given them. As God provides for the birds and the lilies, he also takes care of them. Jesus evokes the irenic picture of a world where the birds and the lilies exist peacefully because they do not fight against others. They simply live in the condition without fighting for more food or more space. In other words, injustices and exploitation of God-given nature result from fighting against each other to get more. The issue is not trusting God and seeking for themselves only. They have little faith and see others as competitors and treat all things in the world as objects of use. Their moral principle must be based on seeking God's rule and righteousness (Mt 6:33). This verse is a response to the issue of excessive human anxiety for the future, which will damage one's life as well as society. The solution to the problem is to seek the way of God, which means seeing others as themselves. In other words, what matters is a priority, not a dualism between faith and the world or between heaven and earth. People must follow the way of God and see the needs of others as important as their own needs. They must honor God as a creator as well as all his creatures and nature. Their lives must be centered on God's character, which is "the righteousness of God" (Mt 6:33). They must realize God cares for all beings and all things in his creation. When people adopt the attitude that they are part of God's creation and seek God's righteousness, they live peacefully with others, in harmony with ecosystems in the world. Richard Bauckham observes, "We cannot appreciate Jesus' message in this passage unless we place ourselves as creatures within God's creation, along with our fellow-creatures the birds and the wild flowers. . . . ourselves not as masters of creation entitled to exploit its resources to our heart's desire, but as participants in the community of God's creation."[62]

Further Reading

- Richard Bauckham, *The Bible and Ecology: Rediscovering the Community of Creation* (Waco, TX: Baylor University Press, 2010).
- Vicki Balabanski, "An Earth Bible Reading of the Lord's Prayer: Matthew 6:9–13," in *Readings from the Perspective of Earth*, ed. Norman C. Have (Sheffield, England: Sheffield Academic Press, 2000), 151–61.
- Elaine Wainwright, "A Transformative Struggle Towards the Divine Dream: An Ecofeminist Reading of Matthew 11," in *Readings from the Perspective of Earth*, ed. Norman C. Have (Sheffield, England: Sheffield Academic Press, 2000), 162–73.

NOTES

1. Donald Senior, "Directions in Matthean Studies," in *The Gospel of Matthew in Current Study*, ed. David E. Aune (Grand Rapids, MI: William B. Eerdmans, 2001), 19. See also, Senior, "Between Two Worlds: Gentiles and Jewish Christians in Matthew's Gospel," *Catholic Biblical Quarterly* 61 (1999): 1–23; J. Andrew Overman, *Matthew's Gospel and Formative Judaism: The Social World of the Matthean Community* (Minneapolis, MN: Fortress, 1990); Anthony J. Saldarini, *Matthew's Christian-Jewish Community* (Chicago: University of Chicago Press, 1994).
2. Senior, "Directions in Matthean Studies," 19.
3. Senior, "Directions in Matthean Studies," 19.
4. Rodney Stark, "Antioch as the Social Situation for Matthew's Gospel," in *Social History of the Matthean Community*, ed. David Balch (Minneapolis, MN: Fortress, 1991), 189–210.
5. Richard S. Ascough, "Matthew and Community Formation," in *The Gospel of Matthew in Current Study*, ed. David E. Aune (Grand Rapids, MI: William B. Eerdmans, 2001), 99. See also, Bruce J. Malina, "Early Christian Groups: Using Small Group Formation Theory to Explain Christian Organizations," in *Modelling Early Christianity: Social-Scientific Studies of the New Testament in Its Context*, ed. Philip F. Esler (New York: Routledge, 1995), 103–5.
6. Ascough, "Matthew and Community Formation," 111.
7. Bruce Metzger, *A Textual Commentary on the Greek New Testament* (New York: Hendrickson, 2005), 16–17.
8. Metzger, *A Textual Commentary on the Greek New Testament*, 17.
9. Metzger, *A Textual Commentary on the Greek New Testament*, 62.
10. Metzger, *A Textual Commentary on the Greek New Testament*, 68.
11. Metzger, *A Textual Commentary on the Greek New Testament*, 67.
12. Jack Kingsbury, *Matthew as Story* (Philadelphia, PA: Fortress, 1988), 3.
13. Seymour Chatman, *Story and Discourse: Narrative Structure in Fiction and Film* (New York: Cornell University Press, 1978), 19–27. See also, Kingsbury, *Matthew as Story*, 3.
14. Elaine A. Wainwright, *Shall We Look for Another? A Feminist Rereading of the Matthean Jesus* (Maryknoll, NY: Orbis, 1998).

15. Wainwright, *Shall We Look for Another?* See also, Leticia Guardiola-Sáenz, "Borderless Women and Borderless Texts: A Cultural Reading of Matthew 15:21–28," *Semeia* 78, no. 1 (1997): 69–81.

16. Gail R. O'Day, "Surprised by Faith: Jesus and the Canaanite Woman," *Listening* 24 (1980): 294. See also, Wainwright, *Shall We Look for Another?*, 87.

17. Wainwright, *Shall We Look for Another?*, 87–88.

18. Wainwright, *Shall We Look for Another?*, 88.

19. Gail R. O'Day, "Surprised by Faith: Jesus and the Canaanite Woman," *Listening* 24 (1980): 294. See also, Elaine Wainwright, *Shall We Look for Another?*, 87.

20. O'Day, "Surprised by Faith," 294.

21. Mitzi J. Smith, "'Give Them What You Have': A Womanist Reading of the Matthean Feeding Miracle (Matthew 14:13–21)," *Journal of Bible and Human Transformation* 3, no. 1 (2013): 1–22.

22. Cheryl J. Sanders, *Ministry at the Margins: The Prophetic Mission of Women, Youth and the Poor* (Downers Grove, IL: InterVarsity, 1997), 30.

23. Smith, "'Give Them What You Have,'" 1–22.

24. The idea of holistic transformation that involves three modes of human existence comes from Yung Suk Kim. Mitzi Smith discusses it in her writing. See Smith, "'Give Them What You Have,'" 1–22. See also, Yung Suk Kim, *A Transformative Reading of the Bible: Explorations of Holistic Human Transformation* (Eugene, OR: Cascade Books, 2013), 22–37.

25. Kim, *A Transformative Reading of the Bible*, 22–37.

26. "The Ujamaa Center at University of KwaZulu-Natal," University of Kwazulu-Natal, accessed July 21, 2023, https://srpc.ukzn.ac.za/research-units-centres/ujamaa.

27. Gerald O. West, "Mobilizing Matthew among the Marginalized: Thirty Years of Community-Based Bible Study in South Africa," *Currents in Theology and Mission* 49, no. 4 (2022): 27–34.

28. Tedros Adhanom Ghebreyesus, "Health Is a Fundamental Human Right," World Health Organization, published December 10, 2017, https://www.who.int/news-room/commentaries/detail/health-is-a-fundamental-human-right.

29. Ghebreyesus, "Health Is a Fundamental Human Right."

30. West, "Mobilizing Matthew among the Marginalized," 29–30.

31. Aaron M. Gale, "Matthew, Galilee, and the Rabbis: A Review of John Kampen, Matthew within Sectarian Judaism," *Conversations with the Biblical World* 40 (2020): 100. See also, Gale, *Redefining Ancient Borders: The Jewish Scribal Framework of Matthew's Gospel* (New York: T&T Clark, 2005); John Kampen, *Matthew within Sectarian Judaism* (New Haven, CT: Yale University Press, 2019), 6.

32. Gale, "Matthew, Galilee, and the Rabbis," 100.

33. Gale, "Matthew, Galilee, and the Rabbis," 101. See also, Mark A. Chancey, "How Jewish Was Jesus' Galilee?" *Biblical Archaeology Review* 33 (2007): 50.

34. Gale, "Matthew, Galilee, and the Rabbis," 105.

35. Gale, "Matthew, Galilee, and the Rabbis," 104.

36. Alejandro Duarte, "Matthew," in *Global Bible Commentary*, ed. Daniel Patte (Nashville, TN: Abingdon Press, 2004), 350–60.

37. Thomas Bohache, "Matthew," in *The Queer Bible Commentary*, ed. Mona West and Robert Shore-Goss (London: SCM Press, 2022), 491–517.

38. Bohache, "Matthew," 495.
39. Bohache, "Matthew," 497.
40. Bohache, "Matthew," 497.
41. Bohache, "Matthew," 498.
42. Fernando F. Segovia, "Postcolonial Criticism and the Gospel of Matthew," in *Methods for Matthew*, ed. Mark Allan Powell (New York: Cambridge University Press, 2009), 194–238.
43. Warren Carter, *Matthew and Empire: Initial Explorations* (Harrisburg, PA: Trinity International, 2001), 57–90.
44. Carter, *Matthew and Empire*, 57–107.
45. Carter, *Matthew and Empire*, 130–44.
46. Carter, *Matthew and Empire*, 145–68.
47. Ted Jennings and Tat-Siong Benny Liew, "Mistaken Identities but Model Faith: Rereading the Centurion, the Chap, and the Christ in Matthew 8:5–13," *Journal of Biblical Literature* 123, no. 3 (2004): 467–94.
48. Musa W. Dube, "'Go Therefore and Make Disciples of All Nations' (Matt 28:19a): A Postcolonial Perspective on Biblical Criticism and Pedagogy," in *Teaching the Bible: The Discourses and Politics of Biblical Pedagogy*, ed. Fernando F. Segovia and Mary A. Tolbert (Maryknoll, NY: Orbis Books, 1998), 224–46.
49. Jacques Derrida, "Différance," in *Margins of Philosophy*, trans. Alan Bass (Chicago: The University of Chicago Press, 1982), 3–27. See also his interview, "The Villanova Roundtable," in *Deconstruction in a Nutshell: A Conversation with Jacques Derrida*, ed. John D. Caputo (New York: Fordham University Press, 1997), 12–15.
50. George Soares-Prabhu, "Two Mission Commands: An Interpretation of Matthew 28:16–20 in the Light of a Buddhist Text," *Biblical Interpretation* 2, no. 3 (1994): 264–82.
51. See Michael J. Brown, "The Gospel of Matthew," in *True to Our Native Land: An African American New Testament Commentary*, ed. Brian K. Blount, Cain H. Felder, Clarice J. Martin, and Emerson B. Powery (Minneapolis, MN: Fortress, 2007), 85–120. See also Rodney S. Sadler Jr., "The Place and Role of Africa and African Imagery in the Bible," in *True to Our Native Land*, 23–30.
52. Jin Young Choi, "Weren't You with Jesus the Galilean? (Matt. 26:69): Diasporic Trauma and Mourning," in *Minoritized Women Reading Race and Ethnicity: Intersectional Approaches to Constructed Identity and Early Christian Texts*, ed. Mitzi J. Smith and Jin Young Choi (Lanham, MD: Lexington Books, 2020), 1–22.
53. Choi, "Weren't You with Jesus the Galilean?"
54. Walter T. Wilson, "Perception, Discipleship, and Revelation in the Gospel of Matthew," *Journal of Disability & Religion* 19, no. 1 (2015): 66–84.
55. Wilson, "Perception, Discipleship, and Revelation," 79.
56. Wilson, "Perception, Discipleship, and Revelation," 79. See also, Mary Ann Beavis, "From the Margin to the Way: A Feminist Reading of the Story of Bartimaeus," *Journal of Feminist Studies in Religion* 14, no. 1 (1988): 19–39; S. M. Olyan, *Disability in the Hebrew Bible: Interpreting Mental and Physical Differences* (Cambridge, England: Cambridge University Press, 2008), 9.
57. Wilson, "Perception, Discipleship, and Revelation," 79.
58. Wilson, "Perception, Discipleship, and Revelation," 79.

59. Wilson, "Perception, Discipleship, and Revelation," 79–80.
60. Wilson, "Perception, Discipleship, and Revelation," 80.
61. Wilson, "Perception, Discipleship, and Revelation," 80.
62. Richard Bauckham, *The Bible and Ecology: Rediscovering the Community of Creation* (Waco, TX: Baylor University Press, 2010), 75.

Chapter 9

The Gospel of Luke from Various Perspectives

AUTHOR-CENTERED, HISTORICAL APPROACH

Historical-Critical Method

Redaction criticism helps find Luke's edited materials by comparing them with Mark or Matthew, depending on the source Luke used (Mark or Q). Luke uses the same sources for the story of the baptism of Jesus (Luke 3:21–22) as were used for Mark 1:9–11, though Luke freely edits it, adding and omitting materials. For example, Luke does not say who has baptized Jesus or where it's happened. He does not even mention where Jesus comes from. Perhaps Luke intends to portray Jesus as the savior of the world and chooses not to include details about Jewish geography and the baptizer's name, because he is the Messiah for the whole world. Luke also adds the presence of all the people at the baptism, which reflects down-to-earth perspectives on the mission. For example, at the crucifixion of Jesus, the crowds respond to Jesus's death by beating their breasts, which means repentance. Luke also adds Jesus's prayer during his baptism. In the parable of the widow and judge, Luke also emphasizes the importance of prayer, even though the parable proper is not about prayer but justice. Besides, the Holy Spirit descends on Jesus "in a *bodily form* like a dove" (Luke 3:22), which also signals the importance of the world and people in the present, expressed in the language of "today" (*sēmeron*) throughout the narrative. Today is the day of salvation and that the Holy Spirit works with the community. All the above redactional details reflect Luke's context and theological agenda that the focus is on the savior of the world as well as down-to-earth perspectives on ministry, the mission today, and importance of prayer. The other example of redaction criticism comes from Pilate's and a centurion's response to Jesus. Pilate three times insists that he cannot find fault with Jesus. A centurion also says that Jesus is innocent. Luke thinks Jesus is not a political criminal. One last example of redaction criticism comes from the parable of the lost sheep shared between Matthew and Luke. Two versions of a parable in Matthew 18:10–14 and Luke 15:4–7 represent two different foci by the evangelists. While the two versions are similar, the most striking difference has to do with the shepherd's reason for being overjoyed. In Matthew he is pleased because the one who was led astray has returned. So Jesus says, "So it is not the will of your Father in heaven that *one of these little ones* should be lost" (Mt 18:14). But in Luke, the shepherd is happy because he's found his sheep that was lost (Luke 15:6). So Jesus says, "Just so, I tell you, there will be more joy in heaven over one sinner who repents than over ninety-nine righteous persons who need no repentance" (15:7). Luke emphasizes the repentance and return of a sinner (the lost).

Further Reading

- C. K. Barrett, *Luke the Historian in Recent Study* (Eugene, OR: Wipf & Stock, 2009).
- Joseph A. Fitzmyer, *Luke the Theologian: Aspects of His Teaching* (Mahwah, NJ: Paulist Press, 1989).
- Mark A. Powell, *What Are They Saying about Luke?* (Mahwah, NJ: Paulist Press, 1989).
- Craig Keener, *The Historical Jesus of the Gospels* (Grand Rapids, MI: Eerdmans, 2012).

Social-Science Criticism

Early Christian communities were a millenarian movement, and they expected the return of the Lord within their lifetime or soon after that. But about fifty to sixty years had passed after Jesus's death before Luke wrote his Gospel. The delay of the Parousia may have caused tensions or cognitive dissonance among the Lukan community members.[1] Cognitive dissonance theory applies to a person's or a community's conflict between belief and reality. In this dire moment, the community finds a way out of the quagmire called cognitive dissonance. Likewise, the Lukan community has found a way out of the irreconcilable psychological conflict by focusing on the ministry for today. Instead of waiting for the coming of the Lord, they reorient their energy to saving people in the present. Throughout the narrative, Luke emphasizes "today" (*sēmeron*). Today a savior is born in the city of David (Luke 2:11). Today the scripture has been fulfilled in people's hearing (4:21). Jesus says to Zacchaeus, "Today salvation has come to this house, because he, too, is a son of Abraham. For the Son of Man came to seek out and to save the lost" (Luke 19:9–10). He also says to one of the thieves, "Truly I tell you, today you will be with me in paradise." Lukan Jesus also confirms the importance of God's reign today in Luke 17:20–21: "The kingdom of God is not coming with things that can be observed, nor will they say, 'Look, here it is!' or 'There it is!' For, in fact, the kingdom of God is among you." The Lukan community members do not have to worry about tomorrow or Parousia, because today is the day of salvation.[2] With this renewed mission strategy, the community feels secure and focuses on its present ministry through the Spirit. But today's focus in Luke comes with a blunt sword: Luke's hesitance to challenge Roman imperial rule directly, as hinted at by Pilate's and a Roman centurion's view that Jesus is innocent—which means he is not a political criminal from Rome's perspective (Luke 23:1–25, 47).

Further Reading

- John Gager, *Kingdom and Community: The Social World of Early Christianity* (Upper Saddle River, NJ: Prentice Hall, 1975).
- Douglas E. Oakman, "The Countryside in Luke-Acts," in *The Social World of Luke-Acts: Models for Interpretation*, ed. Jerome H. Neyrey (Peabody, MA: Hendrickson, 1991), 151–80.
- Vernon K. Robbins, "The Social Location of the Implied Author of Luke-Acts," in *The Social World of Luke-Acts: Models for Interpretation*, ed. Jerome H. Neyrey (Peabody, MA: Hendrickson, 1991), 305–32.

TEXT-CENTERED, LITERARY APPROACH

Textual Criticism

In the following we will explore a few textual variations found in Luke. In Luke 3:22, it says, "You are my Son, the Beloved; with you I am well pleased," while other ancient authorities read, "You are my Son, today I have begotten you," which is derived from Psalm 2:7. The earliest codices—Sinaiticus, Alexandrinus, and Vaticanus—witness the former. The oldest papyrus fragment, papyrus 4 (P4), also attests to this reading. Otherwise, the latter is attested to by Codex Bezae and the majority of the Old Latin witnesses, including quotes by Justin Martyr, Clement of Alexandria, and Augustine. While there is no consensus on which reading is closer to the original, the majority view prefers the former reading ("You are my Son, the Beloved; with you I am well pleased" [found in Luke 3:22]) because of the quality of the manuscripts. However, considering the development of Christology, we are led to conclude the Adoptionist Christology seems earlier than otherwise, as early Christians most likely believed that Jesus was adopted as the Son of God (cf. Rom 1:4).[3]

In Luke 10:1, the issue is whether Jesus has appointed seventy missionaries or seventy-two. Manuscript traditions vary between these two differences.[4] It is hard to tell which reading is better. In Luke 11:2, there are textual variants. The text in the NRSV has the following: "Father, hallowed be your name. Your kingdom come" (Luke 11:2). Other ancient authorities read, "Our Father in heaven" instead of "Father," most likely to borrow it from the Lord's Prayer in Matthew 6:9. Likewise, other ancient authorities add the following in Luke 11:2: "Your will be done, on earth as in heaven"; this is to be consistent with the Matthean form (Mt 6:10). In the NRSV, verses 43–44 of chapter 22 in Luke are included within double square brackets, which means these verses are considered a later addition: "[[43 Then an angel from heaven appeared to him and gave him strength. 44 In his anguish he prayed more earnestly, and his sweat became like great drops of blood falling down on the ground]]." In Luke 23:38, the mention of the three languages in the inscription seems a later addition, which may have been taken from John 19:20. Lastly, in Luke 24:52, it says, "And they *worshiped him, and* returned to Jerusalem with great joy" (NRSV), other ancient authorities lack the phrase "worshiped him," and given the manuscript's evidence, it is hard to tell which reading is better.

Further Reading

- Bruce M. Metzger, *A Textual Commentary on the Greek New Testament* (Peabody, MA: Hendrickson Publishers, 2005).
- Luke T. Johnson, *The Gospel of Luke*, Sacra Pagina Series, vol. 3 (Collegeville, MN: Liturgical Press, 1991).
- David C. Parker, *Textual Scholarship and the Making of the New Testament* (New York: Oxford University Press, 2014).
- Bruce M. Metzger and Bart D. Ehrman, *The Text of the New Testament: Its Transmission, Corruption, and Restoration* (New York: Oxford University Press, 2005).

Narrative Criticism

Implied readers follow what the implied author tells. The Lukan narrative is complex and long, and there are ironies and gaps that they must fill in to understand the story. In particular, Luke's story is distinguished from other narratives, such as Mark's or Matthew's, because the narrator takes almost eleven chapters (9:51–19:27) to describe Jesus's tedious journey to Jerusalem. While Mark has three chapters (8:31–10:52), Matthew has only two chapters (19:1–20:4). Jesus's journey to Jerusalem begins with the episode of people in a Samaritan village who refuse to accept him (Luke 9:51–56). James and John ask him to consume the Samaritan people with fire. But Jesus rebukes his disciples and goes to another village. Jesus's long journey ends with the parable of the ten pounds (Luke 19:11–27), which encourages the disciples to do their best in proclaiming the good news everywhere, including to the Samaritans. Between the beginning and the end of his journey to Jerusalem, Jesus prepares the disciples for the mission. He sends the seventy-two people to the mission (Luke 10:1–12), utters woes to unrepentant cities (10:13–16), teaches the importance of prayer (11:1–13), heals the sick (13:10–17), and teaches people through parables, many of which are unique to Luke: the good Samaritan (10:25–37), the rich fool (12:13–21), the lost parable series (ch. 15), the dishonest manager (16:1–9), the rich man and Lazarus (16:19–31), the widow and the unjust judge (18:1–8), and the Pharisee and the tax collector (18:9–14). All these unique parables support the Lukan emphasis on the charity gospel through the down-to-earth perspective. Jesus's encountering Zacchaeus reaches the apex of Jesus's teaching before he reaches Jerusalem (Luke 19:1–10). Zacchaeus repents, and his household is saved today. He was lost and is found, like the younger son in the parable of the lost son (Luke 15:11–32). Jesus's saying in Luke 19:9–10 shows the Lukan mission of saving the lost: "Today salvation has come to this house, because he, too, is a son of Abraham. For the Son of Man came to seek out and to save the lost." It seems the narrator presents the double entendre that while Jesus must go to Jerusalem soon, it is delayed because he still has lots of things to do outside of Jerusalem—that is, saving the lost. Jerusalem is his final destination, but it is not the goal of life. His ministry begins today and will be done tomorrow, and eventually, he will suffer and die. But until then, he must focus on his work today. In his lament over Jerusalem, he says to some Pharisees, "'Listen, I am casting out demons and performing cures *today and tomorrow, and on the third day* I finish my work. Yet *today, tomorrow, and the next day* I must be on my way, because it is impossible for a prophet to be killed outside of Jerusalem'" (Luke 13:32–33; emphasis added).

Further Reading

- Joel Green, *The Theology of the Gospel of Luke* (New York: Cambridge University Press, 1993).
- Robert C. Tannehill, *The Narrative Unity of Luke-Acts: A Literary Interpretation, Vol. 1: The Gospel According to Luke* (Philadelphia, PA: Augsburg Fortress, 1991).
- Monique Cuany, "'Today, Salvation has Come to this House': God's Salvation of God's People in Luke's Gospel," *Currents in Theology and Mission* 45, no. 4 (2018): 12–17.

- David H. Gill, "Observations on the Lukan Travel Narrative and Some Related Passages," *Harvard Theological Review* 63, no. 2 (1970): 199–221.

READER-CENTERED, COMPREHENSIVE APPROACH

Reader-Response Criticism

Readers may ask many critical, imaginative questions about Luke 5:1–11 because this episode involves complexities and dynamics around Jesus's teaching, fishing, and calling of Peter. First, Jesus stands beside Lake Gennesaret for an unknown reason. They may delve into the story and ponder Jesus's place and emotions. Why does Jesus stand beside the Lake of Gennesaret? Second, the crowds looks for Jesus to hear the word of God. What kind of word of God do they want or need? Third, Jesus takes Peter's boat and asks him "to put out a little way from the shore" (Luke 5:3). Why does Jesus pick out Peter's boat among the two available boats? Why does Jesus teach from the boat, and what does he teach since the crowds are wanting to hear the word of God? Fourth, Jesus says to Peter after teaching, "Put out into the deep water and let down your nets for a catch" (Luke 5:4). Why does he say the deep water? Peter hesitates but obeys Jesus. Then Peter and his fellows catch so many fish. But so many fish get him in trouble, as his boat is sinking. Why is there an irony of there being too many fish, or success amid a sinking boat? Fifth, Peter suddenly falls down at Jesus's knees and says, "Go away from me, Lord, for I am a sinful man!" (Luke 5:8). Why does he say he is a sinner? What sins does he confess? What has he done wrong? He needs Jesus in the day of trouble, but he asks him to go away. Why? Jesus says, "Do not be afraid; from now on you will be catching people" (Luke 5:10). Why does he say "from now on" at no other times? What causes him to call Peter? What lesson is there to learn in the comparison between Peter's fishing experience and his new vocation of catching people? How will catching people be done? Sixth and lastly, Peter and his fellows leave everything and follow Jesus. What is everything they've left? Is leaving everything a condition to follow Jesus?

Further Reading

- Jon L. Berquist, "Luke 5:1–11," *Interpretation* 58, no. 1 (2004): 62–64.
- Edgar V. McKnight, "Reader-Response Criticism," in *To Each Its Own Meaning: Biblical Criticisms and Their Applications*, ed. Steven L.

McKenzie and Stephen R. Haynes (Louisville, TN: Westminster John Knox, 1999), 230–52.
- Stephen D. Moore, *Literary Criticism and the Gospels: The Theoretical Challenge* (New Haven, CT: Yale University Press, 1989).

Feminist Criticism

Luke includes more women than in other Gospels. For example, we have Mary and Martha's story in Luke 10:38–42, which is unique to Luke. Martha welcomes Jesus into her home, and her sister Mary listens to Jesus at his feet. Martha asks Jesus, "Lord, do you not care that my sister has left me to do all the work by myself? Tell her then to help me" (Luke 10:40). Jesus says, "Martha, Martha, you are worried and distracted by many things; there is need of only one thing. Mary has chosen the better part, which will not be taken away from her" (Luke 10:41–42). Jesus's point is that Martha is worried too much since one can choose what to do first. Mary has chosen a better part for herself by hearing the word of God. Otherwise, Jesus does not mean Martha's work is unnecessary or worthless. Mary's choice of "the better part" implies her relationship with God. So far, the point is well-taken. But is she a disciple of Jesus? Some readers are suspicious about women's roles here because, ultimately, in the whole narrative of Luke, women are not recognized as disciples of Jesus. They follow Jesus from Galilee to Golgotha but are never called his disciples. In the feeding of the five thousand, women are not included in the number of feeding. In the story of Mary and Martha, women's agency is a matter of debate. Here, the prevalent image of women still seems a submissive one because their role is limited.[5] A similar picture of women is also seen in the parable of the widow and the unjust judge (Luke 18:1–8), where Luke underscores the importance of prayer, even though the parable proper is not about prayer but the woman's persistent faith in seeking justice. The importance of prayer is stated in Luke 18:1: "Then Jesus told them a parable about their need to pray always and not to lose heart." Luke uses the original parable about justice for women to emphasize the importance of prayer. So Barbara Reid observes that the Lukan use of this parable ends up taming women by encouraging them to be a model of prayer, not a model of justice seeking.[6]

Further Reading

- Barbara E. Reid and Shelly Matthews, *Wisdom Commentary: Luke 1–9 (Vol 1); Luke 10–24 (Vol 2)* (Collegeville, MN: Liturgical Press, 2021).
- Veronica Koperski, "Women and Discipleship in Luke 10:38–42 and Acts 6:1–7: The Literary Context of Luke-Acts," in *A Feminist*

Companion to Luke, ed. Amy-Jill Levine (New York: Sheffield Academic, 2002), 161–96.
- Charles Cosgrove, "A Woman's Unbound Hair in the Greco-Roman World, with Special Reference to the Story of the 'Sinful Woman' in Luke 7:36–50," *Journal of Biblical Literature* 124, no. 4 (2005): 675–92.
- Barbara E. Reid, "'Do You See this Woman?' Luke 7:36–50 as a Paradigm for Feminist Hermeneutics," *Biblical Research* 40 (1995): 37–49.

Womanist Criticism

While the womanist interpretation is not a monolithic one, one possible reading comes from a theme of hospitality in Luke.[7] Jesus heals the sick and provides food for the hungry. The Lukan beatitudes convey the importance of care and hospitality with one another in the community: "Blessed are you who are poor, for yours is the kingdom of God"; "Blessed are you who are hungry now, for you will be filled"; "Blessed are you who weep now, for you will laugh" (Luke 6:20–21). The poor, the hungry, and those who weep now are the most marginalized people, and they need food, shelter, and restoration in the present. In the reign of God, they must be blessed, fed, and satisfied. The blessing should happen *today* in the Lukan world. It should not be postponed until tomorrow. The other example of womanist reading comes from the parable of the widow and the unjust judge (Luke 18:1–8). In the traditional reading, the widow's faith and prayer are emphasized. But from a womanist perspective with African American experience, it becomes evident that the widow wants justice or vengeance, challenging all sorts of stereotypes of women.[8] The last example of womanist reading is from Jesus's healing of a crippled woman (Luke 13:10–17). Mitzi Smith raises specific, contextual, womanist questions from her justice framework.[9] A few of them are as follows: "How does a mother's chronic illness impact her children and her as a mother? How do individuals and communities, including churches, react to mothers suffering from chronic illnesses? Are Black mothers disproportionately impacted and how or why?"[10] As we see here, she is concerned with injustices around the disabled body and its impact on their children. Jesus refutes the leader of the synagogue who challenges him: "You hypocrites! Does not each of you on the Sabbath untie his ox or his donkey from the manger and lead it to water? And ought not this woman, a daughter of Abraham whom Satan bound for eighteen long years, be set free from this bondage on the Sabbath day?" (Luke 13:15–16).

Further Reading

- Mitzi J. Smith, "Centering Social Justice in Biblical Interpretation: The Woman with a Chronic Illness That Challenged Her Posture (Luke 13:10–17)," in *We Are All Witnesses: Toward Disruptive and Creative Biblical Interpretation* (Eugene, OR: Cascade Books, 2023), 64–85.
- Febbie Dickerson, *Luke, Widows, Judges, and Stereotypes: Womanist Readings of Scripture* (Minneapolis, MN: Fortress, 2019).
- Mitzi J. Smith and Yung Suk Kim, "The Gospel of Luke," in *Toward Decentering the New Testament* (Eugene, OR: Cascade Books, 2018), 139–60.

Ekklesia-Centered, Theological Interpretation

Troy Troftgruben communicates the significance of "today" (*sēmeron*) in Luke's Gospel with contemporary Christians and the church by examining the role of this word in the narrative. The word appears in the following, among other, places: "To you is born today in the city of David a Savior, who is the Messiah, the Lord" (Luke 2:11); "Today this scripture has been fulfilled in your hearing" (4:21); "Today salvation has come to this house, because he, too, is a son of Abraham" (19:9); and "Truly I tell you, today you will be with me in paradise" (23:43). Troftgruben argues that "today" in Luke's Gospel is more than an eschatological shift from future to present or about the importance of discipleship. In traditional scholarship, "today" in Luke's Gospel is considered a resolution to the delay of Parousia in the Lukan community, reorienting the members to work today instead of waiting for future salvation. But, according to Troftgruben, "today" in Luke's Gospel has the transformative power of God revealed in Jesus, who welcomes and transforms people through his healing, exorcism, and teaching. He states, "'Today' is the sphere of salvation—it is the time frame when God's saving activity takes shape."[11] "Today" applies to all people and places throughout history and culture; namely, God's salvation is the present. The narrator performs the story of Jesus as if it were happening "today" and envisions God's saving activity for his audiences. In this way, the "today" language in Luke's Gospel is not merely descriptive about God's salvation but performative in the sense that his audiences may participate in God's salvation through Jesus. Donald Juel observes, "As is the case with other art forms, the gospel must be experienced; study prepares hearers to listen for themes, for invention, for irony and surprise."[12] Accordingly, readers of the gospel are encouraged to join in God's work today, which is based on Jesus's earthly ministry—the whole of his ministry "from his birth ([Luke] 2:11) to his death (23:43), from the start of his public ministry (4:21; cf. 5:26;

13:16) to his arrival among tax collectors and 'sinners' (19:9)—not merely his death (the cross)."[13] In Luke salvation is not a single dimension or aspect but "a multi-dimensional reality that entails healing, forgiveness, life, restoration, redemption, and social reversal."[14] Read this way, the "today" language continues to appeal to modern readers, Christians, and the church. François Bovon also observes, "The *sēmeron* becomes 'today' for each hearer and reader to the extent that they rightly understand the proclamation."[15] Troftgruben's interpretation of "today" in Luke's Gospel challenges contemporary churches and Christians to participate in God's reign today so that the world/people may experience salvation today.

Further Reading

- Ralph Martin, "Salvation and Discipleship in Luke's Gospel," *Interpretation* 30, no. 4 (1976): 366–80.
- Matthew L. Skinner, "Looking High and Low for Salvation in Luke," *Currents in Theology and Mission* 45, no. 4 (2018): 6–11.
- Luis Menéndez-Antuña, "Black Lives Matter and Gospel Hermeneutics: Political Life and Social Death in the Gospel of Luke," *Currents in Theology and Mission* 45, no. 4 (2018): 29–34.
- John T. Carroll, "Bodies Restored, Communities Fractured? Luke and Salvation Revisited," *Currents in Theology and Mission* 45, no. 4 (2018): 18–22.

Jewish Interpretation

Amy-Jill Levine reads the Gospel of Luke from a Jewish perspective and argues that "Luke renders Jewish practice and belief, outside of Jesus' interpretation, as relegated to the past, insignificant: corrupt, or co-opted by Jesus and his followers."[16] Acknowledging the mixed views of Luke, this scholar holds views of the Gospel such as "[it is] one of the most pro-Jewish and the most anti-Jewish writing in the New Testament,"[17] and she presents her own Jewish reading of Luke and examines "Luke's presentation of Jewish religious markers: circumcision, temple worship, sacred space (Jerusalem, synagogues) and sacred time (Sabbath), Scripture, and myth."[18] Luke "begins by depicting the land of Israel, Jerusalem, and the temple as replete with righteous Jews, whose piety stands over and against Rome, the site of profane power."[19] Zechariah, the priest, and his wife Elizabeth are "righteous before God, living blamelessly according to all the commandments and regulations of the Lord" (Luke 1:6). Jerusalem is called "the city of David" (2:11). Joseph's membership is in the house of David (1:27). But soon, the "sacred quality of Israel, Jerusalem, and the temple is gradually eroded."[20] Simeon, the devout priest, fades out (Luke

1:8–20). The crowds no longer come to the temple (7:29). The Pharisees and the lawyers are seen as rejecting "the purpose of God for themselves because they had refused to be baptized by John" (7:30).[21] For Luke, Jerusalem is no longer the holy city. It is the city where the prophets are killed (Luke 13:34); the temple is cleansed by Jesus (19:45–46); and the chief priests, the officers of the temple police, and the elders have cooperated with Judah (22:52). In the story of Luke, the last person to be circumcised is Jesus, and his baptism demarcates a new ministry focused on the Gentiles. Even his genealogy is connected with Adam, the son of God (Luke 3:38), as opposed to the son of Abraham and David, like in Matthew's genealogy. Jesus's preaching in his hometown synagogue alarms his village people because he does not affirm the traditional Jewish beliefs (4:16–30). Levine observes, "The synagogue becomes identified not as the locus of Torah and sanctity, but as the site of violence and rejection."[22] Her conclusion is as follows: "For Luke's Gospel, the 'Jewish religion' consists of a bankrupt and soon to be defunct temple, synagogues of violence, leaders who pervert the tradition, and halakhic practices that lack scriptural warrant or that prove either misguided or irrelevant."[23] In the end, she argues that "surely divine mercy is broader than at least this reading of the Third Gospel suggests."[24]

Further Reading

- Amy-Jill Levine, "Luke and the Jewish Religion," *Interpretation: A Journal of Theology and Bible* 68, no. 4 (2014): 389–402.
- Amy-Jill Levine and Ben Witherington III, *The Gospel of Luke (New Cambridge Bible Commentary)* (New York: Cambridge University Press, 2018).
- Joseph B. Tyson, *Luke-Acts and the Jewish People: Eight Critical Perspectives* (Philadelphia, PA: Augsburg Fortress, 1988).
- Lloyd Gaston, "Anti-Judaism and the Passion Narrative in Luke and Acts," in *Anti-Judaism in Early Christianity*, ed. Feter Richardson with David Granskou (Waterloo, Ontario: Wilfrid Laurier University Press, 1986), 127–53.

Inter(con)textual Interpretation

Justin Ukpong reads Luke's Gospel from an anticolonial, Nigerian perspective. In doing so, he takes on two strategies.[25] On the one hand, he challenges Western missionaries in the nineteenth century who, having taken the side of the colonialists, considered African culture inferior and its people as dwelling in darkness. They did not confront or oppose colonial oppression and exploitation against Africans, because they believed they brought the light of Christ to them. But they ended up suppressing African culture, educating people through Western style, and prohibiting African instruments in the church. On the other hand, Ukpong makes contextual comments on select passages in Luke, challenging Luke's innocuous gospel for the Gentiles that accepts the status quo of the Roman Empire. He argues Luke is more interested in spreading the gospel than justice. To focus on the Gentile mission, Luke needs support from the empire so that the gospel might appeal to Roman elites. Because of this concern, Luke's message is blunt and portrays Rome as politically correct. For example, Luke refers to Roman political figures, such as Caesar Augustus and Caesar Tiberias, to imply that Jesus is a good fit for the empire (2:1; 3:1–2). Ukpong also points out that the exorcized Gerasene, who "sat at Jesus's feet (8:35) in an act of discipleship," is not considered a disciple, because he is a Gentile.[26] He also takes on the case of Pontius Pilate, who insists that he cannot find fault with Jesus, which means Jesus is not a criminal from the perspective of Rome (23:1–25). In other words, Luke suggests that Jesus's death is because the Jews do not understand their Messiah correctly. In the end, Ukpong concludes, "Contemporary missionary efforts must take note of these inadequacies in Luke's missionary theology to avoid the mistakes of the past."[27] His inter(con)textual reading illustrates the importance of both contexts: the reader's context and the historical context of Luke.

Further Reading

- Justin Ukpong, "Luke," in *Global Bible Commentary*, ed. Daniel Patte (Nashville, TN: Abingdon Press, 2004), 385–94.
- Ekaputra Tupamahu, "The Gospel of Luke," in *An Asian Introduction to the New Testament*, ed. Johnson Thomaskutty (Minneapolis, MN: Fortress, 2022), 103–25.
- Raj Nadella, *Dialogue Not Dogma: Many Voices in the Gospel of Luke* (New York: T&T Clark, 2011).

Queer Criticism

Robert Shore-Goss focuses on the queer reading of Jesus, who "is out of place with the empire and the nationalist priestly party of the temple and some of their Pharisee surrogates."[28] Halvor Moxnes also uses the term "queer" this way and describes "the unsettling quality" of Jesus;[29] that is, Jesus's ministry of kin-dom is "queer in the sense it questions identities and blurs distinctions."[30] In Luke, Jesus embraces sinners, prostitutes, and other social outcasts, eating with them and celebrating God's presence amongst them. In this way Jesus "destabilizes the symbolic cultural world and Jewish exclusive purity maps, turning it inside-out and transgressing social boundaries to create a queer utopia, the kin-dom of God."[31] Jesus's proclamation of the reign of God debunks dominant apocalyptic theology that emphasizes the future completion of the messianic kingdom. God's rule invades everywhere and transgresses gender roles, class distinctions, and social determinants. So Shore-Goss observes, "Jesus' notion of the reign of God is a queer symbol, turning upside down and inside out some nationalistic and exclusive theological additions to make them more universal and Jewish challenges the political interests of inclusive."[32] Similarly, Joerg Rieger emphasizes "'a contrast society' in which the God Jesus does not rule from the top down—conveniently located in heaven or other high places—but is at work on the ground, in the formation of alternative communities whose way of life does not aim at overpowering others but at inviting them into shared relations of power. The politics of Jesus functions, thus, not via coercion but attraction."[33] In Luke 6:27–36, Jesus's transgressive teaching and ethics are well summarized. His main points are as follows: "Love your enemies" (Luke 6:27); "Do to others as you would have them do to you" (6:31); and "Be merciful, just as your Father is merciful" (6:36). Jesus does not pursue the way of imperial coercion, but embraces "a compassionate path of attraction."[34] He also embodies God's love "within a society colonized by the Romans and surrogates that [have] produced suffering, trauma, the loss of land through indebtedness, debt slavery, and poverty."[35]

Further Reading

- Robert E. Shore-Goss, "Luke," in *The Queer Bible Commentary*, ed. Mona West and Robert E. Shore-Goss (London: SCM Press, 2022), 533–59.
- Halvor Moxnes, *Putting Jesus in His Place: A Radical Vision of Household and Kingdom* (Louisville, KY: Westminster John Knox, 2003).
- Joerg Rieger, *Jesus vs. Caesar: For People Tired of Serving the Wrong God* (Nashville, TN: Abingdon Press, 2018).

Postcolonial Criticism

Like other Gospels, Luke receives mixed evaluations from postcolonial critics. Luke contains both the positive, anti-imperial voices and the mimicking, condoning stance on the Roman Empire. Regarding the former, the Lukan Jesus promotes social justice for the poor people, as seen in Luke 4:16–30. His prophetic message for the marginalized goes against the imperial politics that ignores them. Likewise, the parables unique to Luke, such as the parables of the rich fool, good Samaritan, rich man and Lazarus, Pharisee and tax collector, and widow and the unjust judge, undergird Jesus's prophetic message for social justice. Luke's beatitudes also highlight the importance of caring for those who are poor now, hungry now, and weep now (Luke 6:20–23). Then, unlike in Matthew, what immediately follows are the "four woes," through which the rich are criticized. Mary's Song of Praise in Luke 1:46–55 also opposes imperial propaganda and privilege regarding power and wealth. But on the other hand, Luke contains empire-friendly gestures and connotations. For example, Luke portrays Jesus not as a political criminal but as an innocent prophet whose death is driven by the Jews. Luke wants to convey to the Roman world that Jesus is a good savior, not a dangerous revolutionary. He emphasizes Jesus's connection with Judaism to appeal to the Roman world because anything new is suspicious. Jesus grew up in Jewish tradition (Luke 2:21–40) and frequents the synagogue on the Sabbath day (4:16–30). Luke does not seem to challenge Rome or its imperial system. For example, Luke's beatitudes lack a beatitude about the inheritance of the land, which is the basis of the elites' wealth; this opposes Matthew 5:5, which says that the meek will inherit the earth. In Luke the rich or powerful can share what they have with the poor, but their source of income is not questioned (cf. Luke 16:19–31). With the empire-friendly gospel, Luke portrays Gentiles as dwelling in darkness and the object of evangelization, while ignoring their traditions and cultures.[36] Luke's dealing with the Gentiles is subtle. Luke seems open and inclusive of the Gentiles, as Jesus is connected with son of Adam. Yet the Lukan genealogy is not radical enough to include Gentiles or women, as opposed to Matthew's genealogy.

Further Reading

- Jeffrey L. Staley, "Postcolonial Reflections on Reading Luke-Acts from Cabo San Lucas and Other Places," in *Literary Encounters with the Reign of God*, ed. Sharon Ringe and Paul Kim (Harrisburg, PA: Trinity Press International, 2003), 422–45.
- Yong Sung Ahn, *The Reign of God and Rome in Luke's Passion Narrative: An East Asian Global Perspective* (Leiden, The Netherlands: Brill, 2006).
- Virginia Burrus, "The Gospel of Luke," in *A Postcolonial Commentary on the New Testament Writings*, ed. Ferdinando F. Segovia and R. S. Sugirtharajah (New York: T&T Clark, 2009), 133–55.

Deconstruction Interpretation

The reading of deconstruction rejects a single meaning or determinacy of the meaning because, according to Derrida, the meaning must be different depending on contexts and is deferred for later times. The main reason for different and deferred meanings is that numerous signifiers are working not cohesively but conflictingly. With this notion of deconstruction, we can take an example of "truth" in the Gospel of Luke. As is the case with other Gospels, Luke does not give us a single truth about God or Jesus or the world, even though he insinuates his objectivity in the preface: "I too decided, after investigating everything carefully from the very first, to write an orderly account for you, most excellent Theophilus, so that *you may know the truth* concerning the things about which you have been instructed" (1:3-4). He argues that he is an objective historian and theologian who is meticulous about the source material and is eager to deliver the truth to others. But, in fact, there are many voices or conflicting views in Luke.[37] While Luke presents a certain truth he wants to communicate to the audience, the definition of truth is ambiguous, and people understand it differently. Regardless of Luke's intention, which is also hard to understand, the truth is not encoded in the text. It is only investigated and discussed endlessly by the reader. So the readers can ask, Whose truth do we pick up? Do we have to follow the politically innocuous gospel? Does the truth have to do with spreading the gospel without political changes? Or is the truth more about God's love of Gentiles? Does the truth have to do with Jesus's prophetic message and justice? As we see above, the merit of deconstruction is not to find an objective meaning but to challenge normative, dominant readings so that readers may see different meanings that stand in solidarity with the marginalized and foster justice-minded communities.

Further Reading

- Raj Nadella, *Dialogue Not Dogma: Many Voices in the Gospel of Luke* (New York: T&T Clark, 2012).
- James M. Dawsey, *The Lucan Voice: Confusion and Irony in the Gospel of Luke* (Macon, GA: Mercer University Press, 1980).
- A. K. M. Adam, *Faithful Interpretation: Reading the Bible in a Postmodern World* (Minneapolis, MN: Fortress, 2006).
- Robert Detweiler, ed., *Semeia 23: Derrida and Biblical Studies* (Atlanta, GA: Society of Biblical Literature, 1982).

Minoritized Criticism

Mary Foskett reads Luke 7:36-50 from the perspective of an Asian American female scholar and tackles racism against Asian Americans, especially against Asian women.[38] This passage is about a woman called a sinner who anoints Jesus with ointment at Simon the Pharisee's house dinner. Foskett brings to the text intersectional analysis covering racial sexual stereotypes in America, hegemonic interpretations of readers, and multiple layers of biblical texts. She painfully addresses the anti-Asian American hate crimes that have been fast rising since the COVID-19 global pandemic, including the 2021 Atlanta Spa Shooting that claimed the lives of eight people, six of whom were Asian women—who are most vulnerable in society and are marginalized due to their race, gender, and class. The young shooter targeted them because of their race, marginality, and gender. With this multilayered context involving racism, sexism, and the dominant culture's fetishizing of these unprotected women, Foskett reads Luke 7:36–50 and argues that the dominant interpretation labeling the anointing woman as a sex-related sinner is misguided, because the woman's gestures, such as bathing Jesus's feet with her tears and drying them with her hair, does not evince her identity.[39] In the text, Simon the Pharisee calls her a sinner, but it is unclear what his notion of a sinner is. He judges her as a worthless woman-sinner who is not fit for his house, where he is having dinner with Jesus. But Jesus praises her act of love, that she has anointed him with ointment. In the end her faith saves her, and she recovers from the stigma of being a sinner because Jesus forgives her sins. What is forgiven is her sins, whatever they are. It does not point to sex work or any particular thing. Therefore, if she is a sinner, Simon is also a sinner, as no humans are perfect. Foskett expertly shows biblical interpretation is never simple; it must analyze multiple dimensions of a text, the reader's hegemonic mindset, and the contemporary context. She argues biblical interpretation needs intersectional analysis including a social, cultural, and political environment that incubates racial profiling or sexual stereotyping because, in the end, biblical interpretation must serve the public, especially the most marginalized.

Further Reading

- Mary F. Foskett, "An Initial Reading of Luke 7:36–50: Anti-Asian Hate and Intersectional Interpretation," *The Bible & Critical Theory* 17, no. 1 (2021): 46–54.
- Charles Cosgrove, "A Woman's Unbound Hair in the Greco-Roman World, with Special Reference to the Story of the 'Sinful Woman' in Luke 7:36–50," *Journal of Biblical Literature* 124, no. 4 (2005): 675–92.
- Barbara E. Reid, "'Do You See this Woman?' Luke 7:36–50 as a Paradigm for Feminist Hermeneutics," *Biblical Research* 40 (1995): 37–49.
- Stephanie B. Crowder, "The Gospel of Luke," in *True to Our Native Land: An African American New Testament Commentary*, ed. Brian K. Blount, Cain H. Felder, Clarice J. Martin, and Emerson B. Powery (Minneapolis, MN: Fortress, 2007), 158–85.

Disability Studies

Mikeal Parsons is concerned with "Luke's physical description of Zacchaeus as 'short in stature,'" which is not given much attention in scholarly literature.[40] For example, Joseph Fitzmyer states, "The reference is a mere physical description of the man. We are not to conclude from the episode that Zacchaeus finds real 'stature' through the welcome extended him by Jesus."[41] But Parsons reads Luke's physical description of Zacchaeus's stature in Luke 19:3 "in light of the 'physiognomic consciousness' that permeated the ancient world and the rhetorical practice of using physical abnormalities, such as shortness, to ridicule one's adversary."[42] During Luke's time, "it was commonplace to associate outer physical characteristics with inner qualities."[43] In late antiquity, philosophers, astrologers, and physicians were interested in widely practiced physiognomies.[44] When Luke's audience initially heard of Zacchaeus's shortness, they might have considered him ridiculous and belittled him because people judge one by appearance. So smallness in stature conveys notions of "smallness in spirit," "a small-minded person," or a person with "low self-expectations and greediness."[45] He becomes a preferred target of ridicule from the public because he is short and rich, as he is a chief tax collector. Even his name is an irony since it means "innocent" or "pure."[46] Seen in this way, the phrase "short in stature" in Luke 19:3 must be understood in light of socially and culturally driven ridicule or stigma, as is conveyed in Luke 19:7, where Jesus goes to Zacchaeus's house: "All who saw it began to grumble and said, 'He has gone to be the guest of one who is a sinner.'" They may have thought that "Zacchaeus is a sinner not only because he cheated people in his role as a chief tax collector (as most commentators observe), but also because his physical smallness may have been regarded as the result of sin."[47] Despite his short stature, low self-esteem, and the crowd's ridicule, Zacchaeus is eager to see Jesus and climbs a sycamore tree. After Jesus sees him, Zacchaeus immediately changes his mind, which is repentance, and commits to living righteously. Then Jesus says, "Today salvation has come to this house, because he, too, is a son of Abraham" (Luke 19:9). Here, Luke subverts the normative view of ridicule based on physical appearance or social status. Parsons observes well that "the stranglehold of physiognomic determinacy is broken, and the ridicule is turned against itself. Just because Zacchaeus is small in stature does not mean he must be small in spirit. Just because he is pathologically short does not mean he is to be excluded from the family of God."[48]

Further Reading

- Mikeal C. Parsons, "'Short in Stature': Luke's Physical Description of Zacchaeus," *New Testament Studies* 47 (2001): 50–57.

- Tamsyn Barton, *Power and Knowledge: Astrology, Physiognomies and Medicine under the Roman Empire* (Ann Arbor, MI: University of Michigan, 1994).
- Luke T. Johnson, *The Literary Function of Possessions in Luke-Acts* (Missoula, MT: Scholars Press, 1977).
- Joel Green, *The Gospel of Luke* (Grand Rapids, MI: William B. Eerdmans, 1997).

Ecological Criticism

The Lord's Prayer in Luke 11:1–4 involves ecological insights that are applicable to us. First, we should remember God is our creator and protector, which includes his protecting all things and creatures in God's creation. Calling God a Father does not mean he is a masculine father. God is beyond any image or name. The point is that God is holy and cares for his creation. Jesus teaches that we must call on and trust God, who provides for us and wants us to live in a righteous relationship with him and in harmony with all other human beings and ecological environments. The first line in the Lord's Prayer is not a mere address to God but our theological, ecological preamble undergirding our attitude toward God, the world, fellow human beings, and all things in God's creation. Second, Jesus asks us to pray, "May your kingdom come" (Luke 11:2). God's kingdom or his rule covers and permeates all spheres of human life, including creatures and ecological environments and all things in his creation. God's reign is in the here and now. So we should check our desires and consider all others in God's creation as precious. Third, we pray, "Give us each day our daily bread" (Luke 11:3). Each day is a gift from God, and we can breathe in and out every moment. But tomorrow is not ours. So we need daily bread, not too much or too little. If one stores too much in one's warehouse and does not share it with others, they will lack and perish. Ecologically friendly life begins with simple-yet-satisfactory life every day. Fourth, we also need to pray, "Forgive us our sins, for we ourselves forgive everyone indebted to us" (Luke 11:4). In this prayer we must include the ecological sins we commit to Earth. Humans are not the centers of God's creation but copartners with other creatures and resources in God's creation. Lastly, we must pray, "Do not bring us to the time of trial" (Luke 11:4). This prayer must be for all of us, all of humanity, because we are reaching a tipping point where we cannot return to what we used to take for granted.

Further Reading

- Michael Trainor, "'And on Earth, Peace . . .' (Luke 2:14): Luke's Perspectives on the Earth," in *Readings from the Perspective of Earth*, ed. Norman C. Habel (Sheffield, England: Sheffield Academic Press, 2000), 174–93.
- Vicki Balabanski, "An Earth Bible Reading of the Lord's Prayer: Matthew 6:9–13," in *Readings from the Perspective of Earth*, ed. Norman C. Habel (Sheffield, England: Sheffield Academic Press, 2000), 151–61.
- Elaine Wainwright, "Our Daily Bread—Luke 11:1–4," *Tui Motu InterIslands Magazine*, June 30, 2019, https://hail.to/tui-motu-inter islands-magazine/publication/430InQe/article/3NI7p9o.

NOTES

1. John Gager, *Kingdom and Community: The Social World of Early Christianity* (Upper Saddle River, NJ: Prentice Hall, 1975).

2. Ironically, even with this emphasis on today, Luke seems to tone down the radicalness of Jesus's mission, which is to challenge the system of the Roman Empire. Overall, Luke emphasizes sharing ethics (charity gospel) without directly challenging Rome. See Douglas E. Oakman, "The Countryside in Luke-Acts," in *The Social World of Luke-Acts: Models for Interpretation*, ed. Jerome H. Neyrey (Peabody, MA: Hendrickson, 1991), 174.

3. Bart Ehrman, *The Orthodox Corruption of Scripture: The Effect of Early Christological Controversies on the Text of the New Testament* (Oxford, England: Oxford University Press, 2011).

4. Bruce Metzger, *A Textual Commentary on the Greek New Testament* (Peabody, MA: Hendrickson, 2005), 150–51.

5. Amy-Jill Levine, ed. *A Feminist Companion to Luke* (New York: Sheffield Academic Press, 2002).

6. Barbara E. Reid, *Parables for Preachers: Year C* (Collegeville, MN: Liturgical Press, 1999), 227–36.

7. Mitzi J. Smith and Yung Suk Kim, *Toward Decentering the New Testament: A Reintroduction* (Eugene, OR: Cascade Books, 2018), 150.

8. Febbie Dickerson, *Luke, Widows, Judges, and Stereotypes: Womanist Readings of Scripture* (Minneapolis, MN: Fortress, 2019).

9. Mitzi J. Smith, "Centering Social Justice in Biblical Interpretation: The Woman with a Chronic Illness That Challenged Her Posture (Luke 13:10–17)," in *We Are All Witnesses: Toward Disruptive and Creative Biblical Interpretation* (Eugene, OR: Cascade Books, 2023), 64–85.

10. Smith, "Centering Social Justice in Biblical Interpretation," 67.

11. Troy M. Troftgruben, "Salvation 'Today' in Luke's Gospel," *Currents in Theology and Mission* 45, no. 4 (2018): 6–11.

12. Donald Juel, "A Disquieting Silence: The Matter of the Ending," in *The Ending of Mark and the Ends of God*, ed. Beverly Roberts Gaventa and Patrick D. Miller (Louisville, KY: Westminster John Knox, 2005), 4.

13. Juel, "A Disquieting Silence," 9.

14. Juel, "A Disquieting Silence," 9.

15. François Bovon, *Luke 1: A Commentary on the Gospel of Luke 1:1–9:50* (Minneapolis, MN: Fortress, 2002), 154.

16. Amy-Jill Levine, "Luke and the Jewish Religion," *Interpretation: A Journal of Theology and Bible* 68, no. 4 (2014): 389.

17. This is quoted in Levine's article. The original source is from Lloyd Gaston, "Anti-Judaism and the Passion Narrative in Luke and Acts," in *Anti-Judaism in Early Christianity*, ed. Feter Richardson with David Granskou, vol. 1 (Waterloo, Ontario: Wilfrid Laurier University Press, 1986), 153.

18. Levine, "Luke and the Jewish Religion," 389.

19. Levine, "Luke and the Jewish Religion," 393.

20. Levine, "Luke and the Jewish Religion," 393.

21. Levine, "Luke and the Jewish Religion," 393.

22. Levine, "Luke and the Jewish Religion," 399.

23. Levine, "Luke and the Jewish Religion," 399.

24. Levine, "Luke and the Jewish Religion," 402.

25. Justin Ukpong, "Luke," in *Global Bible Commentary*, ed. Daniel Patte (Nashville, TN: Abingdon Press, 2004), 385–94.

26. Ukpong, "Luke," 390.

27. Ukpong, "Luke," 393.

28. Robert E. Shore-Goss, "Luke," in *The Queer Bible Commentary*, ed. Mona West and Robert E. Shore-Goss (London: SCM Press, 2022), 533–59.

29. Halvor Moxnes, *Putting Jesus in His Place: A Radical Vision of Household and Kingdom* (Louisville, KY: Westminster John Knox, 2003), 6.

30. Moxnes, *Putting Jesus in His Place*, 113.

31. Shore-Goss, "Luke," 533.

32. Shore-Goss, "Luke," 539.

33. Joerg Rieger, *Jesus vs. Caesar: For People Tired of Serving the Wrong God* (Nashville, TN: Abingdon Press, 2018), 51.

34. Shore-Goss, "Luke," 539.

35. Shore-Goss, "Luke," 539.

36. Ukpong, "Luke," 385–394.

37. Raj Nadella, *Dialogue Not Dogma: Many Voices in the Gospel of Luke* (New York: T&T Clark, 2012).

38. Mary F. Foskett, "An Initial Reading of Luke 7:36–50: Anti-Asian Hate and Intersectional Interpretation," *The Bible & Critical Theory* 17, no. 1 (2021): 46–54. See also, Stephanie B. Crowder, "The Gospel of Luke," in *True to Our Native Land: An African American New Testament Commentary*, ed. Brian K. Blount, Cain H. Felder, Clarice J. Martin, and Emerson B. Powery (Minneapolis, MN: Fortress, 2007), 158–85.

39. Foskett, "An Initial Reading of Luke," 53.

40. Mikeal C. Parsons, "'Short in Stature': Luke's Physical Description of Zacchaeus," *New Testament Studies* 47 (2001): 50–57.

41. Joseph A. Fitzmyer, *The Gospel According to Luke (X–XXIV)* (Garden City, NY: Doubleday, 1985), 1223.
42. Parsons, "'Short in Stature,'" 50.
43. Parsons, "'Short in Stature,'" 51.
44. Parsons, "'Short in Stature,'" 51.
45. Parsons, "'Short in Stature,'" 53.
46. Parsons, "'Short in Stature,'" 54.
47. Parsons, "'Short in Stature,'" 55.
48. Parsons, "'Short in Stature,'" 56.

Chapter 10

The Gospel of John from Various Perspectives

AUTHOR-CENTERED, HISTORICAL APPROACH

Historical-Critical Method

Some interpreters are interested in exploring the historical community behind the Gospel. With this interest, they read John's Gospel as a historical reference and seek the meaning behind the text. Louis Martyn argues that John's Gospel reflects a "two-level drama": one with Jesus's story; the other, with John's community experience.[1] John's Gospel is a story about Jesus, but it is also about John's community. For example, there are references to the community's "fear of the Jews" (John 7:13; 19:38; 20:19) and "being put out of the synagogue" (9:22; 12:42; 16:2). Historians argue that there is no evidence that followers of Jesus were expelled from the synagogue during Jesus's time. Only in the late first century may such expulsion have happened because the Jewish Prayer Book condemning Christians existed by that time. Given this, the above references to "fear of the Jews" or "expulsion from the synagogue" reflect the Johannine community's separation/expulsion from the synagogue during the late first century CE. Jesus's calling of the disciples in John 1:35–51 also reflects the Johannine community's early evangelization activities. Unlike the authors of the Synoptic Gospels, John details evangelization activity in the larger community. For example, Andrew's saying, "We have found the Messiah" (John 1:41) and Philip's saying, "Come and see" (1:46) reflect the Johannine evangelization activity. With the above information, historians have developed three stages of the development of the Johannine community: (1) existence within the synagogue, (2) separation/expulsion from the synagogue, and (3) after the separation.[2] The early evangelization activity of the community belongs to the first stage. References to "fear of the Jews" and "expulsion from the synagogue" reflect the second stage. John's antagonistic language against the Jews and his superior position to salvation reflect the third stage. Even though it is hard to reconstruct all these stages, it is worth pondering the community behind John's Gospel because we may understand the literature better. While many historians think the Johannine community is sectarian, it is not always clear that it is sectarian, because there are messages about God's love of the world (John 3:16; chs. 14–17). We may read the Fourth Gospel and the Johannine community as a community of love and transformation, as Jesus sent the disciples into the world so that they may continue to do the work of God as Jesus had done (17:14–19).[3]

Further Reading

- Louis Martyn, *History and Theology in the Fourth Gospel*, 3rd ed. (Louisville, KY: Westminster John Knox, 2003).
- Bart Ehrman, *The New Testament: A Historical Introduction to the Early Christian Writings*, 6th ed. (New York: Oxford University Press, 2016).
- Paul Anderson, *The Riddles of the Fourth Gospel: An Introduction to John* (Minneapolis, MN: Fortress, 2011).

Social-Science Criticism

The sociology of knowledge deals with a sectarian community that needs a protection canopy because of the crisis moments and the experiences of isolation. Applying this model of sociology of knowledge to John's Gospel and the Johannine community, Wayne Meeks argues that the Johannine community seeks a social canopy and legitimation because of the instability caused by the split. He observes, "One of the primary functions of the book, therefore, must have been to provide a reinforcement for the community's social identity, which appears to have been largely negative. It provides a symbolic universe which gave religious legitimacy, a theodicy, to the group's actual isolation from the larger society."[4] Initially, Johannine believers were part of the synagogue and told other Jews that Jesus was the Messiah. However, their evangelization activity was rough and not accepted. As a result, they were separated from the synagogue. This expulsion experience is reflected in the following words: "fear of the Jews" (John 7:13; 19:38; 20:19) and "being put out of the synagogue" (9:22; 12:42; 16:2). In this situation, there is a great need to assure the members that they are safe and in the right place. They are children of God and the light of the world. Others in the synagogue have dwelt in darkness. Jesus's comforting language in John 14 may be a social canopy for the community. Community members must feel confident in their place because Jesus is the way, the truth, and the life. In the farewell discourse, Jesus talks several times about the Advocate whom the Father will send to the disciples (14:16, 26; 15:26; 16:7). The members do not have to worry about their future, because the Advocate will remind them of Jesus's teaching. They will not be orphaned, because the spirit of Jesus will be with them. In Jesus's long prayer, he asks God to "protect them from the evil one" (John 17:15) and to "sanctify them in the truth" (17:17).

Further Reading

- Wayne A. Meeks, "The Man from Heaven in Johannine Sectarianism," *Journal of Biblical Literature* 91, no. 1 (1972): 44–72.
- Bruce J. Malina and Richard L. Rohrbaugh, *Social-Science Commentary on the Gospel of John* (Minneapolis, MN: Fortress, 1998).
- Bruce J. Malina, "John's: The Maverick Christian Group the Evidence of Sociolinguistics," *Biblical Theology Bulletin* 24, no. 4 (1994): 167–82.
- John Ashton, *Studying John: Approaches to the Fourth Gospel* (New York: Oxford University Press, 1994).

TEXT-CENTERED, LITERARY APPROACH

Textual Criticism

There are textual variants in John 1:18: (1) *ho monogenēs huios* (the only begotten son), (2) *monogenēs theos* (the begotten God), (3) *ho monogenēs theos* (the only begotten God), and (4) *ho monogenēs* (the begotten one). The NRSV has John 1:18 as follows: "No one has ever seen God. It is *God the only Son*, who is close to the Father's heart, who has made him known" (emphasis added). Which one is the best? While it is not easy to decide, the phrase "the only begotten son" (*ho monogenēs huios*), which is the first option, is preferred because it goes well with John 3:16: "For God so loved the world that he gave *his only Son*, so that everyone who believes in him may not perish but may have eternal life" (emphasis added). It is also congruent with John 3:18: "Those who believe in him are not condemned; but those who do not believe are condemned already, because they have not believed in the name of *the only Son of God*" (emphasis added). This form of the phrase "the begotten Son" also fits the Johannine theological teaching that Jesus embodies the Logos (John 1:14). God sent his Son to save the world (3:16). In John, Jesus emphasizes that he is sent by God (6:57; 9:4) to do the work of God (4:34; 6:38; 7:16). He delivers the word of God to his disciples (17:8, 17) and sends them into the world to do the same thing (17:18). When he finishes his work, he returns to the Father (7:33; 16:5–11; 17:20). The other critical textual issue in John is that the most ancient manuscripts lack John 7:53–8:11, which implies that this text may not be part of the original. The main reason for thinking this is this passage does not fit into John's vocabulary.[5] Lastly, we can review translation options for some Greek words. In John 3:3, there is the Greek adverb *anōthen*, which means "again" or "from above." Readers must decide which meaning Jesus connotes. The latter must be preferred, given Jesus's emphasis on spiritual birth from above—that is, from God. In several places in John (14:16, 26; 15:26; 16:7), there is *paraklētos*, which is translated variously: "Advocate" (NRSV/NIV), "Comforter" (American Standard Version), "Helper" (New American Standard Bible), or "Companion" (Common English Bible).

Further Reading

- Bart D. Ehrman, *Misquoting Jesus: The Story Behind Who Changed the Bible and Why* (New York: HarperOne, 2005).
- Bruce Metzger, *A Textual Commentary on the Greek New Testament* (Peabody, MA: Hendrickson, 2005).
- Bruce M. Metzger and Bart D. Ehrman, *The Text of the New Testament: Its Transmission, Corruption, and Restoration* (New York: Oxford University Press, 2005).

Narrative Criticism

The narrator does not specify the identity of the disciple whom Jesus loved. Why does the narrator tell the story this way? Does the narrator know who that person is? Is the Beloved Disciple a leader of the Johannine community? Is the Beloved Disciple a woman leader of the community, such as Mary Magdalene? Or is this character only a fictive, mysterious figure in the story? We explore what the narrator may be implying. In John 13:21–30, Peter could ask Jesus directly who the betrayer would be, but he finds the disciple whom Jesus loves and "[motions] to him to ask Jesus" (13:23). The narrator implies that the Beloved Disciple has a special relationship with Jesus. In John 19:26–27, the Beloved Disciple stands beside Jesus's mother. Jesus sees them and says first to his mother, "Woman, here is your son" (19:26). Then he says to the disciple, "Here is your mother" (19:27). The narrator says that "from that hour the disciple [takes] her into his own home" (19:27). Jesus trusts the disciple and asks him to take care of his mother. Though the narrator does not say the Beloved Disciple is a woman, it is possible, as all who are standing near the cross of Jesus are women (John 19:25). In John 20:2–10, Peter and the Beloved Disciple run to the tomb because of Mary Magdalene's report. The Beloved Disciple comes earlier than Peter, but it is Peter who goes into the tomb. Then the Beloved Disciple also enters the tomb and sees and believes. The narrator implies that the beloved disciple is the last person who checks in the tomb and testifies to the truth after Peter is gone. This implication is seen clearly in the addendum (John 21:20–24). In John 21:7, at the Sea of Tiberias, the Beloved Disciple first notices the risen Lord and says to Peter, "It is the Lord!" The narrator indicates that the testimony of the Beloved Disciples is historical first, and it can be trusted. In John 21:20–23, there are conversations between Peter and Jesus, and the topic is about the Beloved Disciple. The narrator implies that the Johannine community believes that the Beloved Disciple will not die before Jesus comes back. But the reality is that he also dies. So the narrator explains that Jesus did not mean that the disciple would not die but that that Peter should not worry about the Beloved Disciple. Finally, in John 21:24, the narrator says the Beloved Disciple is trusted and that the community must go on with his testimony to the truth.

Further Reading

- Mark W. G. Stibbe, *John as Storyteller: Narrative Criticism and the Fourth Gospel* (Cambridge, England: Cambridge University Press, 1992).
- R. Alan Culpepper, *The Gospel and Letters of John* (Nashville, TN: Abingdon Press, 1998).
- M. C. de Boer, "Narrative Criticism, Historical Criticism, and the Gospel of John," *Journal for the Study of the New Testament* 15, no. 47 (1992): 35–48.

READER-CENTERED, COMPREHENSIVE APPROACH

Reader-Response Criticism

We may raise reader-response questions to the resurrection appearances and wonder about the deeper meaning of the text. Answers to those questions vary, but the point is not to find the answers but the process—to raise questions and ponder them without concluding. In John 20:19–29 and 21:1–14, the risen Lord appears to his disciples three times. First, he visits the disciples, who are afraid of the Jews, in a closed room and says, "Peace be with you" (John 20:19). They rejoice when they see the Lord because he shows them his hands and sides. With one more time of the same greeting, "Peace be with you," he says, "as the Father has sent me, so I send you" (John 20:21). Then he gives them the Spirit by breathing on them, asking them to forgive others. This first appearance is enough to complete the postresurrection scene because it is like a final commissioning of them. Why is the first scene not enough for them? Now Jesus appears to the disciples for the second time to show his wounds to Thomas, who was not with them earlier. Seeing his sides, Thomas believes in the resurrection and says, "My Lord and my God" (John 20:28). What does he mean by this? Then Jesus says that believing without seeing is more blessed. Why is it so? Other disciples have seen this scene and may have felt more confident in him. But this scene is not the last one. Why does Jesus appear one last time to the disciples by the Sea of Tiberias again? This last scene is like a short movie, which brings vivid and picturesque scenes of the disciples fishing, finding the Lord, and eating breakfast. When the disciples catch nothing, Jesus stands on the beach, but they cannot recognize him. Why? Are the two times' appearances not enough? He asks them to cast the net to the right side of the boat. They do it without hesitation. Why? With so many fish caught, the Beloved Disciple says to Peter, "It is the Lord" (John 21:7). How does he notice the risen Lord? Why is it not Peter? On hearing the news of finding the Lord, Peter jumps into the sea. Why does he act that way while other disciples come in the boat? At the shore, Jesus prepares breakfast and asks them to eat it. But "now none of the disciples [dare] to ask him, 'Who are you?' because they [know] it [is] the Lord" (John 21:12). How do they know? Because it is the third time they've seen him? Or is it because of the food prepared by Jesus? Or do they remember things from his ministry with them? Why is the Sea of Tiberias significant to the resurrection scenes?

Further Reading

- Susan E. Hylen, *Imperfect Believers: Ambiguous Characters in the Gospel of John* (Louisville, KY: Westminster John Knox, 2009).
- David J. Hawkin, "The Function of the Beloved Disciple Motif in the Johannine Redaction," *Laval Théologique et Philosophique* 33 (1977): 135–50.
- Richard Bauckham, "The Beloved Disciple as Ideal Author," *Journal for the Study of the New Testament* 49 (1993): 21–44.
- James H. Charlesworth, *The Beloved Disciple: Whose Witness Validates the Gospel of John?* (Valley Forge, PA: Trinity Press International, 1995).

Feminist Criticism

The story of Jesus's encounter with a Samaritan woman in John 4:1–42 is so complex a text that scholars may understand it variously. Some read the Samaritan woman as a model of faith. For example, Paul Anderson states, "In general, the treatment of women in John is more elevated than in Matthew. In John, the Samaritan woman becomes a follower of Jesus and even an 'apostle to the Samaritans' (Jn. 4:7–42)."[6] Similarly, Jerome Neyrey also states about the woman that "she represents the quintessential deviant (non-Jew, unclean, shameless, even sinner); but in her transformation, she exemplifies the radical inclusivity of Jesus' circle."[7] In this view she engages Jesus positively, and Jesus breaks cultural taboos. Through a long conversation, she recognizes that he is the Messiah and shares the news with her community. In a way she becomes a true disciple of Jesus. Some feminist critics go along with this line. For example, Luise Schottroff argues that Jesus is not judgmental about the Samaritan woman's past and that she liberates herself in conversation with him.[8] Mary D'Angelo also has the similar view that Jesus does not ask for the woman's repentance; therefore, she states, "The text imputes neither sin nor shame to the woman."[9] But Meredith Warren reads the story differently, pointing out Jesus's revealing of the woman's past "as a tactic to convince her of his identity through his knowledge of her life";[10] that is, Warren problematizes Jesus's "slut-shaming" as she observes the following: "Slut-shaming is a cultural phenomenon that is as contemporary as it is long-lived; it is a pervasive feature of both recent and ancient times. Slut-shaming is a means of restricting women's sexual activity by using a woman's sexual history, reputation, or activity to discredit her."[11] She continues: "Recognizing slut-shaming in biblical accounts and in scholarly assessments of biblical texts is important because it reveals the scaffolding supporting systemic sexism in biblical texts as well as in the guild."[12] From this above perspective, Warren concludes that the passage is not a call for the inclusion of women or Samaritans. Rather, it perpetuates "the tendency known as slut-shaming, a tactic frequently employed to denigrate women and police their sexualities."[13]

Further Reading

- Meredith Warren, "Five Husbands: Slut-Shaming the Samaritan Woman," *The Bible & Critical Theory* 17, no. 2 (2021): 51–70.
- Angela N. Parker, "'And the Word Became . . . Gossip?': Unhinging the Samaritan Woman in the Age of #MeToo," *Review & Expositor* 117, no. 2 (2020): 259–71.
- Surekha Nelavala, "Jesus Asks the Samaritan Woman for a Drink: A Dalit Feminist Reading of John 4," *Lectio Difficilior* 1 (2007): 1–25.
- Victor H. Matthews, "Conversation and Identity: Jesus and the Samaritan Woman," *Biblical Theology Bulletin* 40, no. 4 (2010): 215–26.

Womanist Interpretation

Womanist interpreters read the Samaritan woman in John 4:1–42 differently because of their perspectives. The diversity of reading is possible because of their choices about contextual issues, textual focus, and theological lens.[14] Mitzi Smith reads this story as a story of hospitality between Jesus and the woman;[15] that is, hospitality in this story is mutual, not a unilateral route from Jesus to the woman. The traditional reading focuses on either Jesus or the woman. But Smith's focus is mutuality between Jesus and the woman. This idea of co-humanity is essential to womanist interpretation, which views humanity and the world from the perspective of mutual solidarity or wholeness. In it there is not a hierarchy but a circle of dance-like sharing. Both need hospitality in a strange world. Jesus is tired out from his tireless journey and is thirsty. He asks for a drink of water, which is life for him. In return, Jesus offers what he has: "living water" (John 4:10); that is, he delivers the truth of God to her and explains that all people, regardless of ethnicity or gender, may worship God in spirit and truth. Jesus and the woman find a way to survive and live abundantly in a harsh world under Roman imperialism. Then Mitzi Smith relates the significance of mutual help or solidarity to the water crisis in Flint, Michigan, where the marginalized have been unable to afford the rising cost of water. Privatization of water is unacceptable, because it is given free. Water is a human right. Jesus provides water freely, and it should not be an expensive commodity for the marginalized. As we see here, a biblical text is not simply about the past but today. Smith's reading through the lens of mutuality and care for each other is a prime example of womanist interpretation.

Further Reading

- Mitzi J. Smith, *Womanist Sass and Talk Back: Social (In)Justice, Intersectionality, and Biblical Interpretation* (Eugene, OR: Cascade Books, 2018).
- Teresa Okura, "Jesus and the Samaritan Woman (John 4:1–42) in Africa," *Theological Studies* 70 (2009): 401–18.
- Yung Suk Kim, *Truth, Testimony, and Transformation: A New Reading of the "I Am" Sayings of Jesus in the Fourth Gospel* (Eugene, OR: Cascade Books, 2014).
- Raquel St. Clair, "Womanist Biblical Interpretation," in *True to Our Native Land: An African American New Testament Commentary*, ed. Brian K. Blount, Cain H. Felder, Clarice J. Martin, and Emerson B. Powery (Minneapolis, MN: Fortress Press, 2007), 54–62.

Ekklesia-Centered, Theological Interpretation

R. Alan Culpepper surveys the history of Johannine scholarship, covering the 1950s through the 2000s, and reclaims John's Gospel as "the church's gospel," which encourages and challenges the contemporary Christians and the church to respond to the Johannine church's witnesses to the love of God manifested by Jesus.[16] In the 1950s–1960s, the emphasis was a theological approach, which explored Johannine theology featuring realized eschatology and dogmatic orthodoxy as distinguished from other gospels. In the 1970s–1980s, the focus was a historical approach led by J. Louis Martyn, who wrote a monumental book, *History and Theology in the Fourth Gospel*, where he explored a two-level drama in the narrative: one from the story of Jesus; the other, from the story of the Johannine community. For example, according to Martyn, John 9:22 reflects an entwined story: "His parents said this because they were afraid of the Jews, for the Jews had already agreed that anyone who confessed Jesus to be the Messiah would be put out of the synagogue." In this verse there is an anachronistic aspect in that there was no expulsion of followers of Jesus during his ministry. But late in the first century, such a thing could have happened in the Johannine community. Martyn suggests three plausible stages of the community: "1) an early period in which the messianic group existed within the community of the synagogue; 2) a middle period in which part of the group became a separate community reacting to the traumas of excommunication from the synagogue and martyrdom; and 3) a late period in which the community was solidifying its social and theological identity."[17] In the 1990s–2000s, the scholarly approach moved to a literary one, examining the story itself closely and showing the larger landscape of the Gospel, featuring both the theology and the church within the Gospel. For instance, Mary Coloe argues that Christology and the nature of the church are inseparable and that the church in John's Gospel radically differs from that of the traditional religious institution or gathering. The new community is built on the believers' faith and experience of divine love as revealed in Jesus. So the church means such symbolic yet realistic gatherings based on God's love and manifested in Jesus's love, and the symbol of "many mansions in his father's house" is not "a future place in heaven but the preparation of a place for abiding and indwelling here and now through his death and resurrection."[18] Culpepper gives more examples of John's design for the church in the passion narrative, farewell discourses, and resurrection narratives. Jesus dies the death of love for the church, extended to all people, and emphasizes service to others by washing the disciples' feet. He sends the disciples into the world so that they may do the work as he has done. He also ensures that the Paraclete comes to help them in his absence. Culpepper concludes the following:[19]

> The function of the biblical text is to preserve and continually renew the foundational stories of God's redemptive acts in history, the gospel of Jesus Christ, and the founding vision of the church. The calling of biblical interpreters is to read its stories perceptively in our ever-changing contexts. The calling of the church, in turn, is to be faithful to the biblical stories, preaching their good news, and challenging the community to represent ever more fully God's redemptive purposes in our midst. When at their best, therefore, the church supports biblical scholarship, and biblical scholarship nurtures the church.

Further Reading

- J. Louis Martyn, *History and Theology in the Fourth Gospel*, 3rd ed. (Louisville, KY: Westminster John Knox, 2003).
- Mary L. Coloe, *Dwelling in the Household of God: Johannine Ecclesiology and Spirituality* (Collegeville, MN: Liturgical Press, 2007).
- Richard Bauckham, *Gospel of Glory: Major Themes in Johannine Theology* (Ada, MI: Baker Academic, 2015).
- Herman Ridderbos, *The Gospel According to John: A Theological Commentary* (Grand Rapids, MI: William B. Eerdmans, 2018).

Jewish Interpretation

Reading John's Gospel from a Jewish perspective, Adele Reinhartz "describes both the positive and negative elements of John's portrayal of Jews and Judaism, and suggests some ways that twenty-first-century readers might come to terms with this problematic issue."[20] Regarding the positive elements, she points out John's recognition of Jesus's Jewishness and context—for example, the story's setting "in Galilee (2:1), Judea (2:13), and Samaria (4:1) during Caiaphas' time as high priest."[21] John includes the following Jewish practices: "ritual handwashing (2:6), blessing of the bread before a meal (6:11), the Sabbath (e.g., 5:9), and festivals, such as the Passover (2:13; 6:4; 12:1), the Feast of Tabernacles (7:2), and the Feast of Dedication (Hanukkah; 10:22)."[22] Jesus is called rabbi, which is a Jewish title, and his disciples are also Jewish. In addition, John's Gospel includes "an exalted vision of the cosmic harmony between God and humankind as mediated by the Divine Word."[23] Nevertheless, John "includes numerous hostile statements that condemn the Jews and place them outside the sphere of salvation that John's Jesus promises to humankind."[24] So Reinhartz is concerned about John's Gospel that "vilifies nonbelievers and identifies them with a historical group, 'the Jews,' in a manner that contributed significantly to Christian anti-Semitism for many centuries."[25] Focusing on the term *hoi ioudaioi*, which is often translated as "the Jews" and appears seventy times in the Gospel, she evaluates various options for understanding this term and, in the end, throws doubt on any attempt to smooth out the term's negative connotations in the Gospel because, regardless of the individual usage of the term in context, its negative rhetorical impact is prevalent throughout the narrative. For example, "the Jews" (*hoi ioudaioi*) try to kill Jesus (John 5:18), arrest him (7:30, 44–52; cf. 8:59, 9:49–52, 10:31), and call out for his crucifixion (19:15). Reinhartz points out not only the above negative image of the Jews but also that of the Fourth Gospel's overarching, cosmological storyline that demotes Jews and Judaism because Jesus is the truth coming from heaven. All who do not accept him dwell in darkness, and the Jews are called "children of the devil" (John 8:44). In this view, inevitably, there are binary oppositions "such as light/darkness, life/death, above/below, and from God/not from God. Another set describes opposing activities, such as believing/disbelieving, accepting/rejecting, doing good/doing evil, and loving/hating."[26] In this worldview there is no hope for the Jews and Judaism. In the end Reinhartz asks, "Is there really only one path to God, only one way to be in covenantal relationship with God?"[27] She answers,

> My own answer to this question, as a Jewish reader of the Gospel of John, is no. One has only to look around to see that there are many ways to live a good life, a life of integrity and morality. No single faith can satisfy the needs of all, and, indeed, for some, the absence of faith may be the best answer. An engaged reading of John would therefore challenge the gospel as follows: In order for you to be a child of God, is it necessary that I, or anyone else, be a child of the devil?[28]

Further Reading

- Adele Reinhartz, "Judaism in the Gospel of John," *Interpretation* 63, no. 4 (2009): 382–93.
- Adele Reinhartz, "The Gospel According to John," in *The Jewish Annotated New Testament*, ed. Amy-Jill Levine and Marc Zvi Brettler (New York: Oxford University Press, 2017), 168–218.
- Steven T. Katz, "Issues in the Separation of Judaism and Christianity after 70 C.E: A Reconsideration," *Journal of Biblical Literature* 103, no. 1 (1984): 43–76.

Inter(con)textual Interpretation

Kyung-mi Park reads John's Gospel in the Korean context where people suffer due to sharp income disparity in a competitive, capitalistic economy. She addresses "the disintegration of the vision of life—the inner world or symbolic world—that people suffer in our time of globalization."[29] People, including those foreigners/outsiders who came to find work in Korea, lose a sense of belonging and hope for the future. They are deprived of life energy and despondent in the labor market. In this context she focuses on authentic spirituality in John's Gospel and examines the Johannine community's disintegration/separation from the synagogue, which has caused community members great pain and loss of identity. While the issues and experiences in Korea differ from those of the Johannine community, an experience of disintegration or a lack of sense in life is similar. So there is a way John's Gospel may help boost weary souls in Korea. Park discusses how John's Gospel has helped re-form and strengthen the Johannine community members who've felt abandoned and hopeless. The Spirit empowers them to go through difficult times, and eternal life is realized in the here and now. They feel a sense of oneness through the Spirit, Jesus's teaching of love, and God's abiding with them. They are not orphaned, because the Paraclete is with them and reminds them of Jesus's love and teaching. The Spirit is here with them, and they live a heavenly love in the present and amid all chaos. They are born from above, from the Spirit and the love of God. When they are led by the Spirit, they find meaning in life, loving others, and overcoming the hatred and obstacles against them. Park argues that the Fourth Gospel is not the otherworldly gospel, but "it demands that people rush into the world that refuses them and hates them, and wrestle with this world to reform it."[30] As seen above, her reading is inter(con)textual in two ways—dealing with multilayered texts and contexts combining Jesus's teaching and the Johannine community's experience, as well as discussing two disparate contexts (John's and Korea's), resulting in contextually proper insights into modern-day life.

Further Reading

- Kyung-mi Park, "John," in *Global Bible Commentary*, ed. Daniel Patte (Nashville, TN: Abingdon Press, 2004), 401–11.
- Petros Vassiliadis, "John in an Orthodox Perspective," in *Global Bible Commentary*, ed. Daniel Patte (Nashville, TN: Abingdon Press, 2004), 412–18.
- Johnson Thomaskutty, "The Gospel of John," in *An Asian Introduction to the New Testament*, ed. Johnson Thomaskutty (Minneapolis, MN: Fortress, 2022), 127–56.

Queer Criticism

We see two examples of queer-criticism reading in John from Robert Shore-Goss.[31] First, he emphasizes "the carnal word: queer fluidity," which means Jesus embodies God—the most sensational, queer event.[32] Johannine Christianity begins with the queer idea that divine wisdom takes the form of human flesh. Likewise, Rosemary Haughton observes, "Christianity is, far more than any other, a physical religion, which is one reason why many spiritually minded people find it gross and fleshly and try to refine and 'spiritualize' it. But it is inescapably 'fleshly,' being founded in the human flesh of . . . Christ."[33] Spiritualizing Jesus and his work is misleading because, from a queer perspective, by doing so, queer theology is lost. Indeed, God's revelation through the human flesh is "the queerest of all the Gospels."[34] Second, the Beloved Disciple in John's Gospel is one of the most debated topics. The unavoidable fact in the Gospel is his intimacy with Jesus (John 13:23). He is physically and spiritually close to him and talks much with him privately. He seems the best witness to Jesus and is given authority to the gospel and his community. He stands out as a special, favorite disciple and is Jesus's beloved. This person could be Lazarus, as his identity is unknown and mysterious. Shore-Goss suggests there are homoerotic relationships between Jesus and the Beloved Disciple. Likewise, Dale Martin observes, "For those unable to imagine anything erotic going on here, just consider what people would think if we took the 'beloved disciple' to be a woman (as has been imagined by heterosexuals); in that case, most people wouldn't be able to resist the consequent erotic imaginings. Jesus is certainly not a normal man not even a 'normal' gay man. He ends up again looking very singular very queer."[35] Similarly, Ted Jennings states, "Perhaps one day, even those steeped in the Christian story can read with open eyes the story of Jesus and the man he loved."[36]

Further Reading

- Robert E. Shore-Goss, "John," in *The Queer Bible Commentary*, ed. Mona West and Robert E. Shore-Goss (London: SCM Press, 2022), 560–85.
- Ted Jennings, *The Man Jesus Loved: Homoerotic Narratives from the New Testament* (Cleveland, OH: Pilgrim Press, 2003).
- Tat-siong Benny Liew, "Queering Closets and Perverting Desires: Cross-Examining John's Engendering and Transgendering Word across Different Worlds," in *They Were All Together in One Place? Toward Minority Biblical Criticism*, ed. Randall C. Bailey, Tat-Siong

Benny Liew, and Fernando F. Segovia (Atlanta, GA: Society of Biblical Literature, 2009), 251–88.
- Dale Martin, *Sex and the Single Savior* (Louisville, KY: Westminster John Knox, 2006).

Postcolonial Criticism

From a postcolonial perspective, Jesus's encounter with a Samaritan woman in John 4 is seen negatively, because Jesus travels to a foreign territory, Samaria, and converts her from her religion and culture. This activity of Jesus is compared to the Western missionaries' going to foreign countries to conquer them with the gospel. From this perspective, what Jesus did leads to a colonial drive.[37] Indeed, not only this story but the whole narrative of John consistently registers the voice of colonial drive. For example, the Johannine Jesus comes from above and delivers the Word to the world. He incarnates God, and he is "the way, the truth, and the life"; no one comes to God except through him (John 14:6). The high Christology in John with Jesus's "I am" sayings undergirds John's colonial push to the world. In the story of a Samaritan woman, it takes a long time until Jesus is able to accomplish his colonial drive. Along the way he proves himself more knowledgeable and provides her with information about true religion. She is very active, engaging Jesus actively. Nevertheless, she is not named. Unlike a Jewish man, Nicodemus, seen in John 3, she is anonymous, which implies her marginality and invisibility in the narrative. In the end she becomes a colonial object through Jesus's superior position about religion and culture. She mimics the colonial subject—in this case, Jesus—by following his action.[38] Accepting the colonizer's message with confidence, she becomes a representative of the community, eager to share the gospel she's heard with her community people. But on the other hand, from the perspective of the Roman Empire, Jesus is also colonized. Adele Reinhartz points out Jesus's double status as both the colonizer and the one who is colonized.[39] Similarly, the Samaritan woman mimics a colonial subject (Jesus) while she is doubly marginalized by the Roman Empire and John's Jesus. Here we see the complexity of the Roman imperial realities that affect the colonized people.

Further Reading

- Musa Dube, "Reading for Decolonization (John 4:1–42)," *Semeia* 75 (1996): 37–59.
- Adele Reinhartz, "The Colonizer as Colonized, in *John and Postcolonialism: Travel, Space and Power*, ed. Musa W. Dube and Jeffrey L. Stanley (Sheffield, England: Sheffield Academic Press, 2005), 169–92.

- Sung Uk Lim, "Speak My Name: Anti-colonial Mimicry and the Samaritan Woman in John 4:1–42," *Union Seminary Quarterly Review* 62, no. 3–4 (2010): 35–51.

Deconstruction Interpretation

In the Fourth Gospel, "truth" is a big word and is used more than twenty times. Deconstruction challenges the normative reading of the truth in John's Gospel not only because there is a diversity of notions of the truth but also because all signifiers in the Gospel make endless possibilities of meaning making. What is the truth in the Gospel of John? Is there one truth in John that we can understand? John the Baptist testifies to the truth (John 5:33), which is ambiguous. It can be about Jesus or the truth of God. Jesus says the word of God is truth (John 17:17). How does the word of God relate to the truth? Is the word of God identical to the Logos in the prologue? If so, then how are we to understand John 1:14 ("The Word became flesh")? Does this mean God became human or that the invisible God became known through the flesh? How is Jesus the truth (John 14:6)? Does this mean Jesus is the truth in the sense that people must accept him as the savior—that is, does it mean he is the only way to salvation, as he says, "No one comes to the Father except through me" (John 14:6)? Or does it mean that he embodies the truth of God? Here, still, we have to ask what truth of God he embodies. At the trial of Jesus, Pilate asks, "What is truth?" (John 18:37). Jesus says he was born to testify to the truth (18:37). What is this truth to which he testifies? Is it the truth of God? If so, then what is the truth of God? It may be God's love of the world (John 3:16). It may be God's sending of his Son to the world. It may be God's justice for all people. It can be many things, and it is not fixed. The Advocate is the Spirit of truth, which will guide the disciples into all the truth (John 16:13; cf. 14:17, 26; 15:26; 16:7). What truth does the Advocate convey to the disciples? Is it about Jesus or God? The Fourth Gospel says the Beloved Disciple's testimony is true (John 21:24). Who is the Beloved Disciple, and how can we know his testimony is true? As we see above, deconstruction is not a method but a way of raising critical, self-critical, and ethical questions: by challenging the dominant orthodoxy that subjugates the minority voices.

Further Reading

- A. K. M. Adam, *Faithful Interpretation: Reading the Bible in a Postmodern World* (Minneapolis, MN: Fortress, 2006).
- David Jobling, Tina Pippin, and Ronald Schleifer, eds., *The Postmodern Bible Reader* (Oxford, England: Wiley-Blackwell, 2001).

- The Bible and Culture Collective, *The Postmodern Bible* (New Haven, CT: Yale University Press, 1995).

Minoritized Criticism

Minoritized criticism examines John's Gospel from the perspective of race and ethnicity.[40] Is John's Gospel helpful in addressing the diversity of race and ethnicity? This is the question Andrew Benko asks in his work.[41] With concerns about racism in America, he examines John's Gospel through race and ethnicity—that is, what does the Gospel say about race and ethnicity? In answering this question, he investigates John's portrayal of Galileans, Samaritans, and Judeans and concludes that John does not recognize the characteristics or distinctiveness of each ethnic group. Instead, John is interested in the cosmological-racial groups; one descended from God and the other descended from the devil. Benko observes, "John consistently downplays the significance of various markers of earthly race, such as one's descent, and instead champions a new layer of racialized identity."[42] In John, the followers of Jesus are honored as children of God, and they are united with themselves. Otherwise, there is a clear boundary between those who are included as children of God and those who are condemned as children of the devil. John's kinship is "an affirmation of consubstantial unity, of shared essence, derived from their membership in the same people."[43] Benko concludes that John is not so helpful in embracing the diversity of people and their ethnicity, because John has no interest in the earthly level of ethnic or racial identity. On the other hand, Stewart Penwell sees the positive aspect of ethnicity in John's Gospel because Jesus involves two ethnic labels: Jew and Samaritan. Jesus crosses the territorial boundary between Samaria and Judea to engage the people there.[44] For Penwell, Jesus's dual labeling in John serves as a paradigmatic model for ethnic inclusivity. While Penwell's study is limited to Jews and Samaritans, Benko's approach is broad, applying race category carefully to ancient contexts and texts.

Further Reading

- Andrew Benko, *Race in John's Gospel: Toward an Ethnos-Conscious Approach* (Lanham, MD: Lexington, 2019).
- Stewart Penwell, *Jesus the Samaritan: Ethnic Labeling in the Gospel of John* (Boston, MA: Brill, 2019).
- Rudolfo Estrada, *A Pneumatology of Race in the Gospel of John* (Eugene, OR: Pickwick, 2019).
- Allen Dwight Callahan, "The Gospel of John," in *True to Our Native Land: An African American New Testament Commentary*, ed. Brian

Blount, Cain Hope Felder, Clarice J. Martin, and Emerson B. Powery (Minneapolis, MN: Fortress, 2007), 186–212.

Disability Studies

Kerry Wynn reads healings in the Fourth Gospel through the lens of disability.[45] In so doing, she focuses on the two seemingly puzzling stories of John 5:1–18 (the man at Bethesda who has been ill for thirty-eight years) and John 9 (the man of Siloam born blind). In the former, the man has become accustomed to the pool and wants to be healed; that is, he believes his disability is unacceptable and problematic, which means he accepts society's norm. So he desperately needs a cure (John 5:6). However, when he is asked about who has healed him, he does not know. This implies that he is not interested in the healer. Later Jesus finds him and says, "See, you have been made well! Do not sin any more, so that nothing worse happens to you" (John 5:14). This saying seems puzzling because Jesus links disability to sin. But he does not mean that sin is the cause of disability. Wynn explores John 5:14, stating that the man at Bethesda accepts society's norm that disability is abnormal and that his sole want is a cure. So when Jesus later finds him, he is concerned that the man might fall to sin. In other words, Jesus warns him that he must live righteously (cf. John 13:27; Gn 4:7). The implication is that the cure does not necessarily lead to transformation. On the other hand, the healing story in John 9 is different from in John 5. The man at the pool of Siloam was born blind and feels natural about it. He does not seek a cure. He is active in his begging and lives without problems, from his perspective. When the disciples ask by whose sin he became blind, Jesus clearly says it is by nobody's sin. He was born blind "so that God's works might be revealed in him" (John 9:3). The disability is not caused by sin. When the blind man's neighbors ask him about his identity, he repeatedly says, "I am he" (John 9:9). He is the same person, "blind or sighted."[46] After his healing, he knows who healed him and testifies to others objectively, without pretending to know too much. He simply states what has happened to him (John 9:25). Soon he meets Jesus again and believes in him, not because of his healing but because of his desperate faith in seeking to understand him. While he never has thought of his disability as a sin, his healing has helped him to encounter the "otherness" of Jesus. In John 9, disability is not caused by sin, and healing is not the result of faith.

Further Reading

- Kerry H. Wynn, "Johannine Healings and Otherness of Disability," *Perspectives in Religious Studies* 34 (2007): 61–75.

- Jaime Clark-Soles, "John, First-Third John, and Revelation," in *The Bible and Disability: A Commentary*, edited by Sarah J. Melcher, Mikeal C. Parson, and Amos Yong (Waco, TX: Baylor University Press, 2017), 333–78.
- Colleen Grant, "Reinterpreting the Healing Narratives," in *Human Disability and the Service of God*, ed. Nancy L. Eiesland and Don E. Saliers (Nashville, TN: Abingdon Press, 1998), 72–87.

Ecological Criticism

We can read the Fourth Gospel from an ecological perspective because the Johannine worldview undergirds the protection of this world, all creatures, and ecological environments.[47] The Johannine worldview does not support or encourage dualisms between heaven and earth, between the Word and the world, or between the body and the spirit. God so loved the world and sent his only Son (John 3:16). God is embodied in the world through Jesus, the Son of God, who delivers the divine Logos to the world. In all these, the premise is that this world is God's good creation, and God's will is to be done in the here and now. John 1:1 refers to God's good creation in Genesis 1: "In the beginning" God created the heavens and the earth by word. So this world and all creatures and things in it reflect God and are sacred (1:3). He was pleased with what he made each day. John is aware of the creation story and his audience also knows it. John reimagines God's good creation through the Logos, which is Jesus, who restores humanity and all things and creatures back to God's good creation full of life and light (John 1:4–5). So God sent his Son, Jesus. While the world is still evil and dark, it can be recovered through Jesus's work. As God sent Jesus into the world, Jesus sent his disciples into the world to do the same work of him. Jesus's mission is not to condemn the world but to save it. Jesus's mission is to let people trust God and love the world as is. If they understand God's love of the world, they must protect God's creation with all efforts. They must love God's creatures and ecological environments as much as they love other people. In that world, as is seen in the feeding miracle (John 6:51–58), people are fed enough, and there will be no waste, because the leftovers are collected for the future. Saving resources for others or for the future is crucial in dealing with the shortage of food. In the contemporary world, food waste is beyond belief.

Further Reading

- Margaret Daly-Denton, *John: An Earth Bible Commentary: Supposing Him to Be the Gardener* (London: T&T Clark, 2019).

- Susan Miller, "I Came That They May Have Life, and Have It Abundantly" (John 10:10): An Ecological Reading of John's Gospel," *The Expository Times* 124, no. 2 (2012): 64–71.
- Elaine Wainwright, "Bread of Life for the World: John 3:16–18; John 6:51–58," *Tui Motu InterIslands Magazine*, May 31, 2020, https://hail.to/tui-motu-interislands-magazine/publication/430InQe/article/46vIvtJ.
- Yung Suk Kim, *Truth, Testimony, and Transformation: A New Reading of the "I Am" Sayings of Jesus in the Fourth Gospel* (Eugene, OR: Cascade Books, 2014).

NOTES

1. Louis Martyn, *History and Theology in the Fourth Gospel*, 3rd ed. (Louisville, KY: Westminster John Knox, 2003), 35–66.
2. Bart Ehrman, *The New Testament: A Historical Introduction to the Early Christian Writings*, 6th ed. (New York: Oxford University Press, 2016), 186–88.
3. Yung Suk Kim, *Truth, Testimony, and Transformation: A New Reading of the "I Am" Sayings of Jesus in the Fourth Gospel* (Eugene, OR: Cascade Books, 2014).
4. Wayne A. Meeks, "The Man from Heaven in Johannine Sectarianism," *Journal of Biblical Literature* 91, no. 1 (1972): 70.
5. Bart Ehrman, *Misquoting Jesus: The Story Behind Who Changed the Bible and Why* (New York: HarperCollins, 2005), 65.
6. Paul Anderson, *The Christology of the Fourth Gospel: Its Unity and Disunity in the Light of John 6* (Tübingen, Germany: Mohr Siebeck, 1996), 236.
7. Jerome H. Neyrey, "What's Wrong with This Picture? John 4, Cultural Stereotypes of Women, and Public and Private Space," in *The Feminist Companion to John*, vol. 1, ed. Amy-Jill Levine (Sheffield, England: Sheffield Academic, 2003), 98–125.
8. Luise Schottroff, "Die Samaritanerin am Brunnen (Joh 4)," in *Auf Israel Hören: Sozialgeschichtliche Bibelauslegung*, ed. Renate Jost, Rainer Kessler, and Christoph M. Raisig (Lucerne, Switzerland: Edition Exodus, 1992), 115–32. See also, Stephen D. Moore, "Are There Impurities in the Living Water That the Johannine Jesus Dispenses? Deconstruction, Feminism, and the Samaritan Woman," in *The Feminist Companion to John*, vol. 1, ed. Amy-Jill Levine (Sheffield, England: Sheffield Academic, 2003), 78–97.
9. Mary Rose D'Angelo, "(Re)presentations of Women in the Gospels: John and Mark," in *Women and Christian Origins*, ed. Ross Shepard Kraemer and Mary Rose D'Angelo (Oxford, England: Oxford University Press, 1999), 129–49.
10. Meredith Warren, "Five Husbands: Slut-Shaming the Samaritan Woman," *The Bible & Critical Theory* 17, no. 2 (2021): 56.
11. Warren, "Five Husbands," 55.
12. Warren, "Five Husbands," 55.
13. Warren, "Five Husbands," 51.

14. See Yung Suk Kim, *Biblical Interpretation: Theory, Process, and Criteria* (Eugene, OR: Pickwick, 2013).

15. Mitzi J. Smith, *Womanist Sass and Talk Back: Social (In)Justice, Intersectionality, and Biblical Interpretation* (Eugene, OR: Cascade Books, 2018), 7–27. See also, Mitzi J. Smith and Yung Suk Kim, *Toward Decentering the New Testament: A Reintroduction* (Eugene, OR: Cascade Books, 2018), 61–66.

16. R. Alan Culpepper, "The Quest for the Church in the Gospel of John," *Interpretation* 63, no. 4 (2009): 341–54.

17. Culpepper, "The Quest for the Church," 344. See also, J. Louis Martyn, *History and Theology in the Fourth Gospel*, 3rd ed. (Louisville, KY: Westminster John Knox, 2003), 145–67.

18. Culpepper, "The Quest for the Church," 349. See also, Mary L. Coloe, *Dwelling in the Household of God: Johannine Ecclesiology and Spirituality* (Collegeville, MN: Liturgical Press, 2007). See also, her book, *God Dwells with Us: Temple Symbolism in the Fourth Gospel* (Collegeville, MN: Liturgical Press, 2001).

19. Culpepper, "The Quest for the Church," 354.

20. Adele Reinhartz, "Judaism in the Gospel of John," *Interpretation* 63, no. 4 (2009): 382.

21. Reinhartz, "Judaism in the Gospel of John," 382.

22. Reinhartz, "Judaism in the Gospel of John," 382.

23. Reinhartz, "Judaism in the Gospel of John," 382.

24. Reinhartz, "Judaism in the Gospel of John," 383.

25. Reinhartz, "Judaism in the Gospel of John," 383.

26. Reinhartz, "Judaism in the Gospel of John," 386.

27. Reinhartz, "Judaism in the Gospel of John," 392.

28. Reinhartz, "Judaism in the Gospel of John," 392.

29. Kyung-mi Park, "John," in *Global Bible Commentary*, ed. Daniel Patte (Nashville, TN: Abingdon Press, 2004), 401.

30. Park, "John," 401.

31. Robert E. Shore-Goss, "John," in *The Queer Bible Commentary*, ed. Mona West and Robert E. Shore-Goss (London: SCM Press, 2022), 560–85.

32. Shore-Goss, "John," 560–85.

33. Rosemary Haughton, *Beginning Life in Christ* (Westminster, MD: Newman Press, 1969), 38.

34. Shore-Goss, "John," 563.

35. Dale Martin, *Sex and the Single Savior* (Louisville, KY: Westminster John Knox, 2006), 100.

36. Ted Jennings, *The Man Jesus Loved: Homoerotic Narratives from the New Testament* (Cleveland, OH: Pilgrim Press, 2003), 91.

37. Musa Dube and Jeffrey Staley, eds. *John and Postcolonialism: Travel, Space, and Power* (New York: Continuum, an imprint of Sheffield Academic Press, 2002). See also, Musa Dube, "Reading for Decolonization (John 4:1–42)," *Semeia* 75 (1996): 37–59.

38. Sung Uk Lim, "Speak My Name: Anti-colonial Mimicry and the Samaritan Woman in John 4:1–42," *Union Seminary Quarterly Review* 62, no. 3–4 (2010): 35–51.

39. Adele Reinhartz, "The Colonizer as Colonized," in *John and Postcolonialism: Travel, Space and Power*, ed. Musa W. Dube and Jeffrey L. Stanley (Sheffield, England: Sheffield Academic Press, 2005), 169–92.

40. See Allen Dwight Callahan, "The Gospel of John," in *True to Our Native Land: An African American New Testament Commentary*, ed. Brian Blount, Cain Hope Felder, Clarice J. Martin, and Emerson B. Powery (Minneapolis, MN: Fortress, 2007), 186–212.

41. Andrew Benko, *Race in John's Gospel: Toward an Ethnos-Conscious Approach* (Lanham, MD: Lexington, 2019).

42. Benko, *Race in John's Gospel*, 205.

43. Benko, *Race in John's Gospel*, 183.

44. Stewart Penwell, *Jesus the Samaritan: Ethnic Labeling in the Gospel of John* (Boston, MA: Brill, 2019).

45. Kerry H. Wynn, "Johannine Healings and Otherness of Disability," *Perspectives in Religious Studies* 34 (2007): 61–75.

46. Wynn, "Johannine Healings and Otherness of Disability," 68.

47. This point about Johannine worldview comes from Yung Suk Kim's ongoing research project concerning the Fourth Gospel and its impact on ecology.

Chapter 11

Conclusion

I have come full circle now and want to reiterate what I wrote in the introduction—the importance of a solid historical, literary introduction to and various readings of the Gospels. One of the primary goals of this book is to encourage readers/students to read the Gospels closely and diversely. On the one hand, this book covers various introductory matters about the Gospels, including the following sections: "Gospel at a Glance," "Distinctive Theological Themes," the portrayals of Jesus and the parables, and "Notable Interpretation Issues." On the other hand, it deals with comprehensive interpretive methods, or perspectives, ranging from a historical-critical approach to a postmodern one to ecological reading. With a variety of interpretive perspectives or tools in hand, readers can not only deepen their close reading of the Gospels but can also expand it to deal with complexities in the text. Following the story of Jesus closely, readers may raise critical contextual questions about the text and ponder on interpretive issues on every page of the story because the Gospels are not merely ancient stories of Jesus or early Christian communities, but they are continuously engaged by contemporary readers.

To be sure, various readings of the Gospels are embedded in the stories of Jesus, which involve three dimensions of the story: (1) the story of Jesus in his context, (2) the story of Jesus interpreted by the evangelists, and (3) the story of Jesus told by the evangelists that continues to be retold by contemporary readers. Along the spectrum of these multiple layers of the story of Jesus, readers can ask many questions, be they historical, literary, or reader-driven. In a way we can say true biblical interpretation begins with engaging questions.

More crucially, various readings of the Gospels are possible because of the reader's choices: contextual choices, textual choices, and theological or hermeneutical choices.[1] Contextual choices have to do with the readers' social location, experience, and perspective.[2] Because of their distinctive experiences or perspectives, they might focus on different aspects of the text or on different issues. For example, readers in the previously colonized countries may read the Samaritan woman's encounter with Jesus in John 4:1–42 differently because they are concerned about colonial rule, which ruined their cultures, lives, and dignity. Textual choices have to do with textual methods—that is, how to treat the text. One might render it as a historical product (historical-critical methods), as a literary medium (literary approaches), or as mirrors that reflect the readers (reader-focused readings). Lastly, theological or hermeneutical choices have to do with the readers' focus on a particular concept of theological vocabulary. For example, the meaning of Jesus's death as atonement is not self-evident, because it can be construed in several ways. Therefore, readers must decide and check specific aspects of atonement to make sense of the text. For example, one can understand the view of Jesus's death as a moral sacrifice in that his death results from his proclamation of the gospel of God, which challenges the political ideology of the Roman Empire.

While we can celebrate the diversity of interpretations, the reality is that not *all* readings are equally helpful or valid. The question is in how we can evaluate them. So in this conclusion, on the one hand, we revisit the importance of various readings of the Gospels, and on the other hand, we address some concerns about solid interpretation. The sections of this conclusion are, in order, as follows: (1) "The Importance of Various Readings of the Gospels," (2) "Criteria for Solid Interpretation," and (3) "Readers' Critical, Imaginative Role."

THE IMPORTANCE OF VARIOUS READINGS OF THE GOSPELS

Why do we need various readings of the Gospels? I propose at least three reasons for them. First, the Gospels are entangled with multiple layers, starting with Jesus's own time and story; moving to the evangelists' layers; and then ending with the real readers' contextual, critical engaging with Jesus's and the evangelists' stories. Imagine how many readings we can make because of the complex nature of the Gospels as we see here. All of this means no one reading or one perspective can cover the whole spectrum of the Gospels. One of the biggest challenges in reading the Gospels is reductionism, or determinism (in that the meaning is fixed rather than open-ended).[3] If we take the example of phrase "the kingdom of God," how should we understand this vocabulary? What does Jesus

Conclusion 241

mean? What do the evangelists (Mark, Matthew, Luke, and John) mean? How should we, as modern readers, understand it? Each of these meaning dimensions defies fixation because meaning is flexible or open-ended. For Jesus and/or the evangelists, the kingdom of God may have meant various things: the realized eschatology (John's Gospel), the work of the Holy Spirit in the present (Luke's Gospel), the radical intervention of God's rule in the future (Mark's Gospel or Matthew's Gospel), or God's rule or activity in the present, in the progression, and in the future (perhaps close to the historical Jesus's understanding). Besides, readers may interpret this vocabulary in their own context, dealing with all spheres of human life.

Second, we need various readings of the Gospels because the Gospels themselves reflect the complexities in human life in first-century Palestine under the Roman Empire, where Jesus was born, raised, and worked for the cause of the good news of God. He was a poor Galilean Jew who dealt with all spheres of human life, including personal crises, family/community instability, religious politics, and, perhaps most importantly, the Roman Empire. How can we cover such breadth or spectrums of the story of Jesus and/or early Christian communities with a few readings? So we can engage with the Gospels as we deal with many issues in our world. While some readers need insights into their lives, in terms of new wisdom focused on the simple life, others may need empowerment in their lives and be looking for such power in the Gospels.

Third and lastly, we need to reread familiar texts or stories of Jesus in a new, challenging way. For example, traditionally, the Canaanite woman's encounter with Jesus in Matthew 15:21–28 has been read with a focus on Christological salvation in which submissive faith is absolutely necessary. For so long, Jesus's demeanor has been explained away or justified for various reasons. But in the text, Jesus clearly has rejected her request of healing for her daughter, not once but three times: one time with silence (Mt 15:23), one time with exclusive salvation theology (Mt 15:24), and one time with verbal humiliation by calling her a dog (Mt 15:26). How can we read the Canaanite woman's encounter with Jesus in Matthew 15:21–28? Is there good news? If there is any, what kind of good news is it? How can we relate the Matthean Jesus as portrayed here with the historical Jesus? Why, then, does Matthew portray Jesus this way? What is Matthew's purpose or strategy that he hopes to achieve in this story? Why do Jesus and his disciples behave in such mean ways? What kind of faith does she have? Is it faith in God, in Jesus, or in something else? In the end does Jesus change his mind? What is it that he's changed? Is it his view of the mission? Questions ensue endlessly. Another question is how to rediscover women's role or discipleship in the Gospel stories. While it is hard to uncover many aspects of their work and their relationships with

Jesus, because the Gospels do not reveal a lot about women's activities, we should vigilantly explore the significance of women's work and their role in the early Christian movement. For example, Susan Hylen endeavors to unravel popular assumptions about women in the New Testament world and helps us understand their positive, influential works.[4] So our interpretive gauge must extend to cover women's contributions to the community and society.

CRITERIA FOR SOLID INTERPRETATION

While there are no definite criteria for solid interpretation on which we may all agree, it is important to talk about them because, otherwise, we may fall into the traps of relativism. We must understand that one's interpretation affects others'.[5] I propose three tests for solid interpretation. First, we must go through historical and literary tests in the sense that we must honor the historical or literary contexts of the Gospels. Even if we are not clear on the complete aspects of such contexts, we can always be mindful of ancient contexts. For example, if someone portrays Jesus as a separatist Jew who's rejected Judaism, that reading hardly passes, because the canonical Gospels affirm Jesus's rootedness in Judaism. Also, socially or culturally speaking, Jesus's identity with Judaism makes better sense because, in first-century Palestine, a group of messiah figures had connected with some sense of Judaism even though their understanding of religion or the law may have differed from each other. Jesus did not lead a separatist movement, like, for instance, the sectarian Essenes had done.

Second, we must pass the perspective or ideological tests because not all ideas or perspectives are good or beneficial to others. Some people may read Jesus as an authority figure, the powerful Son of God who can do anything. Using this interpretation, they may manipulate other people in the name of Jesus. Their perspective or ideology is self-serving. Others might employ the ideology of otherworldly salvation when they interpret the kingdom of God. Such a perspective, while not implausible, may not well present the teaching of Jesus, who advocated for the marginalized and social outcasts. So we must test every interpretation because it is human construction. No one is exempt from this test.

Third and last, we must test the service or benefits of a particular reading and ask who is helped or benefited, as well as who is excluded. Any divisive reading or dominant reading for particular groups must be considered suspicious. For example, if anyone rejects women's leadership roles in the church or its greater mission work by reading Matthew 28:16–20, where Jesus commissions male disciples only, that reading must be problematic, as the text does not utter such a prohibition against women discipleship. Moreover, from the narrative, we know that the women followers of Jesus are more faithful and sincere than the male disciples, who all flee from the crucifixion of Jesus. Even if there were a preference for male discipleship in the text, eventually, it will be the readers' job to decide on such a view.

READERS' CRITICAL, IMAGINATIVE ROLE

In the end the most important part of biblical interpretation or reading of the Gospels rests on the readers, who must read the text closely, critically, and contextually. Whichever methods they use, their interpretation does not merely depend on methods but on their choices, as we have seen before. While we must be careful about our presupposition, the goal of interpretation is not to move away from selfhood or one's social location or concern but to engage with the text from various perspectives. Whether one decides to dig deeper into the text from a historical perspective, search for meaning within the text, or respond to the text variously, the fact remains that without readers, there would be no meaning. Applying the same method to the text does not result in the same interpretation, because, after all, readers are different. Ultimately, readers make choices about interpretation and must be held accountable for their interpretation.

Since there is no neutral interpretation (one that does not need a test), our job is not merely to read something neutrally or transcendentally but to engage with it seriously, reading "ourselves" in the world and tackling issues we face today, locally and globally. In this sense, biblical interpretation is about or for today's world because, while we engage with the text and the past, we do not live for the past but in the present; namely, "our narrative of the past and our imagined future narrative impact on our every moment."[6] Stephen Crites also writes, "Only the present exists, but it exists only in these tensed modalities."[7] He continues, "They are inseparably joined in the present itself. Only from the standpoint of the present experience could one speak of the past and future. The three modalities are correlative to one another in every moment of experience."[8] In the end, various levels of the story in the Gospels affect the readers who engage with them diversely from their narratives.[9] According to Jocelyn Bryan, "we are living narratives," which means we can communicate with narratives of the Gospels from our stories, and vice versa.[10] While we cannot change the past, we can reshape our world today. We can also change the course of the future by reimagining ourselves in the present.

Critical questions are essential to interpretation. We can ask about anything, including about ourselves. We need an attitude of humility, realizing our limitedness in knowledge or understanding. More often than not, I hear people saying, "As the Bible says." Strictly speaking, it does not say. Even if it speaks, it speaks with multiple meanings. Rather than saying, "The Bible says," it would be better to say, "I have read this part, and my interpretation is this." Otherwise, people may kill or destroy others in the name of the Bible or God. We should avoid all forms of Biblicism (idolatry of the Bible) and naive interpretations supporting one's ego or ideology. We should not worship the Bible but honor it by interpreting it carefully, critically, contextually, and faithfully.

Before closing, including a few words about my vocation might be helpful. As a professor, I am not merely interested in knowledge of the past but also in today's world. The Gospel narratives reflect us and speak to us. Then we need to respond to them variously. I want the Gospels to be read closely and variously so that they may touch on our contemporary issues and lives as widely as possible, including the socioeconomic discrepancies, the political arena, personal identity, cultural communal crisis, mental health challenges, and climate crisis, among others. I am not saying the Gospels provide needed solutions to our problems. But the point is that we need to revisit the stories of Jesus from our modern-day context and tell our stories in response to them.

As such, interpretation of the Gospels or the stories of Jesus cannot be dominated or domesticated by one group or school. All readers can interpret them carefully from their context and discern what is good. In doing so, we must avoid Biblicism in all our efforts. The Gospels are neither a weapon that tramples other religions or cultures nor the knowledge books that subsume all other books. The Gospels are ongoing stories inviting us to read them through *our* stories. The purpose is never to be triumphant over others but to better understand and respond to the good news that Jesus and the early Christian communities proclaimed.

NOTES

1. See Cristina Grenholm and Daniel Patte, "Overture: Reception, Critical Interpretations, and Scriptural Criticism," in *Reading Israel in Romans: Legitimacy and Plausibility of Divergent Interpretations*, vol. 1, ed. Cristina Grenholm and Daniel Patte (Harrisburg, PA: Trinity International Press, 2000), 1–54.

2. Yung Suk Kim, *Biblical Interpretation: Theory, Process, and Criteria* (Eugene, OR: Pickwick, 2013), 25–44.

3. See Jacques Derrida, "Différance," in *Margins of Philosophy*, trans. Alan Bass (Chicago: The University of Chicago Press, 1982), 3–27.

4. For example, Susan Hylen has written books about New Testament women and their significance: *Women in the New Testament World* (New York: Oxford Uni-

versity Press, 2019); *Finding Phoebe: What New Testament Women Were Really Like* (Grand Rapids, MI: William B. Eerdmans, 2023).

5. I have articulated a set of criteria for solid biblical interpretation elsewhere. See Yung Suk Kim, *Biblical Interpretation*, 45–57. For me, the best interpretation is the one that engages the text in balanced ways, drawing a sense of meaning closely from the text, promoting diversity and solidarity.

6. Jocelyn Bryan, "Narrative, Meaning Making, and Mental Health," in *The Bible and Mental Health: Towards a Biblical Theology of Mental Health*, ed. Christopher C. H. Cook and Isabelle Hamley (London, SCM Press: 2020), 4.

7. See Stephen Crites, "The Narrative Quality of Experience," *The Journal of the American Academy of Religion* 39 (1971): 291–311.

8. Crites, "The Narrative Quality of Experience," 291–311.

9. Jerome Bruner, "Life as Narrative," *Social Research* 54, no. 1 (1987): 11–32.

10. Jocelyn Bryan, *Human Being: Insights from Psychology and the Christian Faith* (London: SCM Press, 2016), 44, 51–74.

Bibliography

Adam, A. K. M. *Faithful Interpretation: Reading the Bible in a Postmodern World*. Minneapolis, MN: Fortress, 2006.

———. *What Is Postmodern Biblical Criticism?* Minneapolis, MN: Fortress, 1995.

Ahn, Yong Sung. *The Reign of God and Rome in Luke's Passion Narrative: An East Asian Global Perspective*. Leiden, The Netherlands: Brill, 2006.

Allaby, Michael. *A Dictionary of Ecology*. 2nd ed. Oxford, England: Oxford University Press, 2003.

Allen, Amy Lindeman. "Baptism and Children in Mark's Vision of the Realm of God." *Currents in Theology and Mission* 47, no. 4 (2020): 31–35.

Althaus-Reid, Marcella. "Mark." In *The Queer Bible Commentary*, edited by Deryn Guest and Robert Goss, 517–25. London: SCM Press, 2006.

Anderson, Janice Capel. "Feminist Criticism: The Dancing Daughter." In *Mark and Method: New Approaches in Biblical Studies*, edited by Janice Capel Anderson and Stephen D. Moore, 103–34. Minneapolis, MN: Fortress, 1992.

———. "Matthew: Gender and Reading." *Semeia* 28 (1983): 3–27.

Anderson, Janice Capel, and Stephen D. Moore. "Introduction: The Lives of Mark." In *Mark and Method: New Approaches in Biblical Studies*, edited by Janice Capel Anderson and Stephen D. Moore, 1–8. Minneapolis, MN: Fortress, 1992.

Anderson, Paul. *The Christology of the Fourth Gospel: Its Unity and Disunity in the Light of John 6*. Tübingen, Germany: Mohr Siebeck, 1996.

———. *The Riddles of the Fourth Gospel: An Introduction to John*. Minneapolis, MN: Fortress, 2011.

Ascough, Richard. "Matthew and Community Formation." In *The Gospel of Matthew in Current Study*, edited by David E. Aune, 96–126. Grand Rapids, MI: William B. Eerdmans, 2001.

Ashton, John. *Studying John: Approaches to the Fourth Gospel*. New York: Oxford University Press, 1994.

Aune, David E, ed. *The Gospel of Matthew in Current Study: Studies in Memory of William G. Thompson, S. J.* Grand Rapids, MI: William B. Eerdmans, 2001.

Avalos, Hector, Sarah J. Melcher, and Jeremy Schipper, eds. *This Abled Body: Rethinking Disabilities in Biblical Studies.* Atlanta, GA: Society of Biblical Literature, 2007.

Bailey, Randall, Tat-Siong Benny Liew, and Fernando F. Segovia, eds. *They Were All Together in One Place? Toward Minority Biblical Criticism.* Atlanta, GA: Society of Biblical Literature, 2009.

Balabanski, Vicki. "An Earth Bible Reading of the Lord's Prayer: Matthew 6:9–13." In *Readings from the Perspective of Earth,* edited by Norman C. Have, 151–61. Sheffield, England: Sheffield Academic Press, 2000.

Barrett, C. K. *Luke the Historian in Recent Study.* Eugene, OR: Wipf & Stock, 2009.

Barton, Stephen. "Matthew's Gospel for Today," *Journal of Theology* 126, no. 1 (2023): 3–19.

Barton, Tamsyn. *Power and Knowledge: Astrology, Physiognomies and Medicine under the Roman Empire.* Ann Arbor, MI: University of Michigan, 1994.

Bauckham, Richard. *Gospel of Glory: Major Themes in Johannine Theology.* Ada, MI: Baker Academic, 2015.

———. "The Beloved Disciple as Ideal Author." *Journal for the Study of the New Testament* 49 (1993): 21–44.

———. *The Bible and Ecology: Rediscovering the Community of Creation.* Waco, TX: Baylor University Press, 2010.

Beardslee, William A. "Poststructuralist Criticism." In *To Each Its Own Meaning: An Introduction to Biblical Criticisms and Their Applications,* edited by Steven L. McKenzie and Stephen R. Haynes, 253–67. Louisville, KY: Westminster John Knox, 1999.

Beavis, Mary Ann. "From the Margin to the Way: A Feminist Reading of the Story of Bartimaeus." *Journal of Feminist Studies in Religion* 14, no. 1 (1988): 19–39.

———. "Women as Models of Faith in Mark." *Biblical Theology Bulletin* 18 (1988): 3–9.

Benko, Andrew. *Race in John's Gospel: Toward an Ethnos-Conscious Approach.* Lanham, MD: Lexington, 2019.

Berquist, Jon L. "Luke 5:1–11." *Interpretation* 58, no. 1 (2004): 62–64.

The Bible and Culture Collective. *The Postmodern Bible.* New Haven, CT: Yale University Press, 1995.

Billings, J. Todd. *The Word of God for the People of God: An Entryway to the Theological Interpretation of Scripture.* Grand Rapids, MI: William B. Eerdmans, 2010.

Black, C. Clifton. *Mark's Gospel: History, Theology, Interpretation.* Grand Rapids, MI: William B. Eerdmans, 2023.

Blount, Brian. *Go Preach!: Mark's Kingdom Message and the Black Church Today (Bible & Liberation).* Maryknoll, NY: Orbis, 1998.

———. "Jesus as Teacher: Boundary Breaking in Mark's Gospel and Today's Church." *Interpretation: A Journal of Bible and Theology* 70, no. 2 (2016): 184–93.

———. *Then the Whisper Put on Flesh. New Testament Ethics in an African American Context.* Nashville: Abingdon Press, 2001.

Bohache, Thomas. "Matthew." In *The Queer Bible Commentary,* edited by Mona West and Robert Shore-Goss, 491–517. London: SCM Press, 2022.

Borg, Marcus. *Jesus: The Life, Teaching, and Relevance of a Religious Revolutionary.* New York: HarperCollins, 2015.

Bovon, François. *Luke 1: A Commentary on the Gospel of Luke 1:1–9:50.* Minneapolis, MN: Fortress, 2002.

———. *Luke the Theologian: Fifty-five Years of Research (1950–2005).* 2nd ed. Waco, TX: Baylor University Press, 2006.

———. *The Last Days of Jesus.* Louisville, KY: Westminster John Knox, 2006.

Boyarin, Daniel. "The Sovereignty of the Son of Man: Reading Mark 2." In *The Interface of Orality and Writing: Speaking, Seeing, Writing in the Shaping of New Genres*, edited by Annette Weissenrieder and Robert B. Coote, 353–62. Tübingen, Germany: Mohr Siebeck, 2010.

Brawley, Robert L. *Centering on God: Method and Message in Luke-Acts.* Louisville, KY: Westminster John Knox, 1990.

Brodie, Thomas. *The Gospel According to John: A Literary and Theological Commentary.* New York: Oxford University Press, 1993.

Brown, Michael J. "The Gospel of Matthew." In *True to Our Native Land: An African American New Testament Commentary*, edited by Brian K. Blount, Cain H. Felder, Clarice J. Martin, and Emerson B. Powery, 85–120. Minneapolis, MN: Fortress, 2007.

Bruner, Jerome. "Life as Narrative." *Social Research* 54, no. 1 (1987): 11–32.

Bryan, Jocelyn. *Human Being: Insights from Psychology and the Christian Faith.* London: SCM Press, 2016.

———. "Narrative, Meaning Making, and Mental Health." In *The Bible and Mental Health: Towards a Biblical Theology of Mental Health*, edited by Christopher C. H. Cook and Isabelle Hamley, 3–33. London, SCM Press: 2020.

Burrus, Virginia. "The Gospel of Luke." In *A Postcolonial Commentary on the New Testament Writings*, edited by Ferdinando F. Segovia and R. S. Sugirtharajah, 133–55. New York: T&T Clark, 2009.

Byrne, Brendan. *The Hospital of God. A Reading of Luke's Gospel.* Collegeville, MN: Liturgical Press, 2000.

Byron, Gay L., and Vanessa Lovelace. *Womanist Interpretations of the Bible.* Atlanta, GA: SBL Press, 2016.

Callahan, Allen Dwight. "The Gospel of John." In *True to Our Native Land: An African American New Testament Commentary*, edited by Brian Blount, Cain H. Felder, Clarice J. Martin, and Emerson B. Powery, 186–212. Minneapolis, MN: Fortress, 2007.

Carey, Greg. *Sinners. Jesus and His Earliest Followers.* Waco, TX: Baylor University Press, 2009.

Carroll, John T. "Bodies Restored, Communities Fractured? Luke and Salvation Revisited." *Currents in Theology and Mission* 45, no. 4 (2018): 18–22.

Carter, Warren. *Matthew and Empire: Initial Explorations.* Harrisburg, PA: Trinity International, 2001.

———. *Matthew and the Margin: A Sociopolitical and Religious Reading.* Maryknoll, NY: Orbis, 2000.

———. *Matthew: Storyteller, Interpreter, Evangelist.* 2nd ed. Peabody, MA: Hendrickson, 2004.

———. "Postcolonial Biblical Criticism." In *New Meanings for Ancient Texts: Recent Approaches to Biblical Criticisms and Their Applications*, edited by Steven L. McKenzie and John Kaltner, 97–116. Louisville, KY: Westminster John Knox, 2013.

Cartlidge, David, and David Dungan. *Documents and Images for the Study of the Gospels*. Minneapolis, MN: Fortress, 2015.

Chancey, Mark A. "How Jewish Was Jesus' Galilee?" *Biblical Archaeology Review* 33 (2007): 42–50.

Charlesworth, James H. *The Beloved Disciple: Whose Witness Validates the Gospel of John?* Valley Forge, PA: Trinity Press International, 1995.

Chatman, Seymour. *Story and Discourse: Narrative Structure in Fiction and Film*. New York: Cornell University Press, 1978.

Cho, Jae Hyung. "The Gospel of Matthew." In *An Asian Introduction to the New Testament*, edited by Johnson Thomaskutty, 47–73. Minneapolis, MN: Fortress, 2022.

Choi, Jin Young. *Postcolonial Discipleship of Embodiment: An Asian and Asian American Feminist Reading of the Gospel of Mark*. New York: Palgrave Macmillan, 2015.

———. "Weren't You with Jesus the Galilean? (Matt. 26:69): Diasporic Trauma and Mourning." In *Minoritized Women Reading Race and Ethnicity: Intersectional Approaches to Constructed Identity and Early Christian Texts*, edited by Mitzi J. Smith and Jin Young Choi, 1–22. Lanham, MD: Lexington Books, 2020.

Clark-Soles, Jaime. "John, First-Third John, and Revelation." In *The Bible and Disability: A Commentary*, edited by Sarah J. Melcher, Mikeal C. Parson, and Amos Yong, 333–78. Waco, TX: Baylor University Press, 2017.

———. "Mark and Disability." *Interpretation: A Journal of Bible and Theology* 70, no. 2 (2016): 159–71.

———. *Reading John for Dear Life: A Spiritual Walk with the Fourth Gospel*. Louisville, KY: Westminster John Knox, 2016.

Collins, Adela Yabro. *Mark: A Commentary*. Minneapolis, MN: Fortress, 2007.

———. "Mark's Interpretation of the Death of Jesus." *Journal of Biblical Literature* 128, no. 3 (2009): 545–54.

Coloe, Mary. *Dwelling in the Household of God: Johannine Ecclesiology and Spirituality*. Collegeville, MN: Liturgical Press, 2007.

———. *God Dwells with Us: Temple Symbolism in the Fourth Gospel*. Collegeville, MN: Liturgical Press, 2001.

———. *Wisdom Commentary: John 1–10; John 11–21*. Collegeville, MN: Liturgical Press, 2021.

Cosgrove, Charles. "A Woman's Unbound Hair in the Greco-Roman World, with Special Reference to the Story of the 'Sinful Woman' in Luke 7:36–50." *Journal of Biblical Literature* 124, no. 4 (2005): 675–92.

Cowan, J. Andrew. *The Writings of Luke and the Jewish Roots of the Christian Way: An Examination of the Aims of the First Christian Historian in the Light of Ancient Politics, Ethnography, and Historiography*. New York: T&T Clark, 2019.

Crites, Stephen. "The Narrative Quality of Experience." *The Journal of the American Academy of Religion* 39 (1971): 291–311.

Crowder, Stephanie B. "The Gospel of Luke." In *True to Our Native Land: An African American New Testament Commentary*, edited by Brian K. Blount, Cain H.

Felder, Clarice J. Martin, and Emerson B. Powery, 158–85. Minneapolis, MN: Fortress, 2007.

Cuany, Monique. "'Today, Salvation has Come to this House': God's Salvation of God's People in Luke's Gospel." *Currents in Theology and Mission* 45, no. 4 (2018): 12–17.

Culpepper, R. Alan. *Anatomy of the Fourth Gospel: A Study in Literary Design*. Minneapolis, MN: Fortress, 1987.

———. *Matthew: A Commentary*. Louisville, KY: Westminster John Knox, 2022.

———. *The Gospel and Letters of John*. Nashville, TN: Abingdon Press, 1998.

———. "The Quest for the Church in the Gospel of John." *Interpretation* 63, no. 4 (2009): 341–54.

Daly-Denton, Margaret. *John: An Earth Bible Commentary: Supposing Him to Be the Gardener*. London: T&T Clark, 2019.

D'Angelo, Mary Rose. "(Re)presentations of Women in the Gospels: John and Mark." In *Women and Christian Origins*, edited by Ross Shepard Kraemer and Mary Rose D'Angelo, 129–49. Oxford, England: Oxford University Press, 1999.

Dawsey, James M. *The Lucan Voice: Confusion and Irony in the Gospel of Luke*. Macon, GA: Mercer University Press, 1980.

de Boer, M. C. "Narrative Criticism, Historical Criticism, and the Gospel of John." *Journal for the Study of the New Testament* 15, no. 47 (1992): 35–48.

Derrida, Jacques. "Différance." In *Margins of Philosophy*, translated by Alan Bass, 3–27. Chicago: The University of Chicago Press, 1982.

———. *Negotiations: Interventions and Interviews, 1971–2001*. Stanford, CA: Stanford University Press, 2002.

———. "The Villanova Roundtable." In *Deconstruction in a Nutshell: A Conversation with Jacques Derrida*, edited by John D. Caputo, 12–15. New York: Fordham University Press, 1997.

Detweiler, Robert, ed. *Semeia 23: Derrida and Biblical Studies*. Atlanta, GA: Society of Biblical Literature, 1982.

Dewey, Joanna. *Markan Public Debate: Literary Technique, Concentric Structure, and Theology in Mark 2:1–3:6*. Chico, CA: Scholar's Press, 1980.

Dickerson, Febbie. *Luke, Widows, Judges, and Stereotypes: Womanist Readings of Scripture*. Minneapolis, MN: Fortress, 2019.

Dowd, Sharyn, and Elizabeth Struthers Malbon. "The Significance of Jesus' Death in Mark: Narrative Context and Authorial Audience." *Journal of Biblical Literature* 125, no. 2 (2006): 271–97.

Duarte, Alejandro. "Matthew." In *Global Bible Commentary*, edited by Daniel Patte, 350–60. Nashville, TN: Abingdon Press, 2004.

Dube, Musa. "'Go Therefore and Make Disciples of All Nations' (Matt 28:19a): A Postcolonial Perspective on Biblical Criticism and Pedagogy." In *Teaching the Bible: The Discourses and Politics of Biblical Pedagogy*, edited by Fernando F. Segovia and Mary A. Tolbert, 224–46. Maryknoll, NY: Orbis Books, 1998.

———. "Mark's Healing Stories in an AIDS Context." In *Global Bible Commentary*, edited by Daniel Patte, 379–384. Nashville, TN: Abingdon Press, 2005.

———. *Postcolonial Feminist Interpretation of the Bible*. St. Louis, MO: Chalice Press, 2000.

———. "Reading for Decolonization (John 4:1–42)." *Semeia* 75 (1996): 37–59.

Dube, Musa, and Jeffrey Staley, eds. *John and Postcolonialism: Travel, Space, and Power*. New York: Continuum, an imprint of Sheffield Academic Press, 2002.

Dunn, James D. G. "Form Criticism." In *Searching for Meaning: An Introduction to Interpreting the New Testament*, edited by Paula Gooder, 21–27. Louisville, KY: Westminster John Knox, 2008.

"Early Christian Writings." Early Christian Writings.com. Accessed May 23, 2023. https://www.earlychristianwritings.com.

Edwards, Richard. "Uncertain Faith: Matthew's Portrait of the Disciples." In *Discipleship in the New Testament*, edited by Fernando Segovia, 47–61. Philadelphia, PA: Fortress, 1985.

Ehrman, Bart. *Misquoting Jesus: The Story Behind Who Changed the Bible and Why*. New York: HarperCollins, 2005.

———. *The New Testament: A Historical Introduction to the Early Christian Writings*. 6th edition. New York: Oxford University Press, 2016.

———. *The Orthodox Corruption of Scripture: The Effect of Early Christological Controversies on the Text of the New Testament*. Oxford, England: Oxford University Press, 2011.

Elder, Nicholas. "The Synoptic Gospels as the Mixed Media." *Biblical Research* 64 (2019): 42–66.

Elliott, J. Keith. "Textual Criticism." In *Searching for Meaning: An Introduction to Interpreting the New Testament*, edited by Paula Gooder, 49–55. Louisville, KY: Westminster John Knox, 2008.

Elliott, John H. *What Is Social Scientific Criticism?* Minneapolis, MN: Fortress, 1993.

Erickson, Richard. "Divine Injustice? Matthew's Narrative Strategy and the Slaughter of the Innocents (Matthew 2:13–23)." *Journal for the Study of the New Testament* 64 (1996): 5–27.

Esler, Philip. *Community and Gospel in Luke-Acts: The Social and Political Motivations of Lucan Theology*. Cambridge, England: Cambridge University Press, 1989.

Estrada, Rudolfo. *A Pneumatology of Race in the Gospel of John*. Eugene, OR: Pickwick, 2019.

Evans, Craig A. "Source Criticism." In *Searching for Meaning: An Introduction to Interpreting the New Testament*, edited by Paula Gooder, 28–37. Louisville, KY: Westminster John Knox, 2008.

Fiorenza, Elizabeth Schussler. *But She Said: Feminist Practices of Biblical Interpretation*. Boston, MA: Beacon Press, 1993.

———. *In Memory of Her: A Feminist Theological Reconstruction of Christian Origins*. New York: Crossroad, 1983.

Fitzmyer, Joseph A. *Luke the Theologian: Aspects of His Teaching*. Mahwah, NJ: Paulist Press, 1989.

———. *The Gospel According to Luke (X–XXIV)*. Garden City, NY: Doubleday, 1985.

Foskett, Mary F. "An Initial Reading of Luke 7:36–50: Anti-Asian Hate and Intersectional Interpretation." *The Bible & Critical Theory* 17, no. 1 (2021): 46–54.

Fowler, Robert. "Reader-Response Criticism: Figuring Mark's Reader." In *Mark and Method: New Approaches in Biblical Studies*, edited by Janice Capel Anderson and Stephen D. Moore, 50–83. Minneapolis, MN: Fortress, 1992.

———. "Reader-Response Criticism." In *Searching for Meaning: An Introduction to Interpreting the New Testament*, edited by Paula Gooder, 127–34. Louisville, KY: Westminster John Knox, 2008.

France, R. T. *The Gospel of Mark*. Grand Rapids, MI: William B. Eerdmans, 2014.

Freire, Ana Esther Padua. "Mark." In *The Queer Bible Commentary*, edited by Mona West and Robert E. Shore-Goss, 518–32. London: SCM Press, 2022.

Funk, Robert, Bernard Brandon Scott, and James Butts, *The Parables of Jesus: Red Letter Edition, The Jesus Seminar*. Sonoma, CA: Polebridge, 1988.

Gager, John. *Kingdom and Community: The Social World of Early Christianity*. Upper Saddle River, NJ: Prentice Hall, 1975.

Gale, Aaron M. "Matthew, Galilee, and the Rabbis: A Review of John Kampen, Matthew within Sectarian Judaism." *Conversations with the Biblical World* 40 (2020): 98–106.

———. *Redefining Ancient Borders: The Jewish Scribal Framework of Matthew's Gospel*. New York: T&T Clark, 2005.

———. "The Gospel According to Matthew." In *The Jewish Annotated New Testament*, edited by Amy-Jill Levine and Marc Zvi Brettler, 9–66. New York: Oxford University Press, 2017.

Gaston, Lloyd. "Anti-Judaism and the Passion Narrative in Luke and Acts." In *Anti-Judaism in Early Christianity*, Vol. 1, edited by Feter Richardson with David Granskou, 127–53. Waterloo, Ontario: Wilfrid Laurier University Press, 1986.

Gench, Frances Taylor. *Wisdom in the Christology of Matthew*. Lanham, MD: University Press of America, 1997.

Ghebreyesus, Tedros Adhanom. "Health Is a Fundamental Human Right." World Health Organization. Published December 10, 2017, https://www.who.int/news-room/commentaries/detail/health-is-a-fundamental-human-right.

Gill, David H. "Observations on the Lukan Travel Narrative and Some Related Passages." *Harvard Theological Review* 63, no. 2 (1970): 199–221.

Glancy, Jennifer A. *Slavery in Early Christianity*. Minneapolis, MN: Fortress, 2006.

González, Justo. *The Story Luke Tells: Luke's Unique Witness to the Gospel*. Grand Rapids, MI: William B. Eerdmans, 2015.

Grant, Colleen. "Reinterpreting the Healing Narratives." In *Human Disability and the Service of God*, edited by Nancy L. Eiesland and Don E. Saliers, 72–87. Nashville, TN: Abingdon Press, 1998.

Green, Bridgett A. "'Nobody's Free until Everybody's Free': Exploring Gender and Class Injustice in a Story about Children (Luke 18: 15–17)." In *Womanist Interpretations of the Bible: Expanding the Discourse*, edited by Gay L. Byron and Vanessa Lovelace, 291–310. Atlanta, GA: Society of Biblical Literature, 2016.

Green, Joel. *Practicing Theological Interpretation (Theological Explorations for the Church Catholic): Engaging Biblical Texts for Faith and Formation*. Ada, MI: Baker Academic, 2012.

———. *Seized by Truth: Reading the Bible as Scripture*. Nashville, TN: Abingdon Press, 2007.

———. *The Gospel of Luke*. Grand Rapids, MI: William B. Eerdmans, 1997.

———. *The Theology of the Gospel of Luke*. New York: Cambridge University Press, 1993.

———. *The Way of the Cross: Following Jesus in the Gospel of Mark*. Eugene, OR: Wipf & Stock, 2009.

Grenholm, Cristina, and Daniel Patte. "Overture: Reception, Critical Interpretations, and Scriptural Criticism." In *Reading Israel in Romans: Legitimacy and Plausibility of Divergent Interpretations*, vol. 1, edited by Cristina Grenholm and Daniel Patte, 1–54. Harrisburg, PA: Trinity International Press, 2000.

Guardiola-Sáenz, Leticia. "Borderless Women and Borderless Texts: A Cultural Reading of Matthew 15:21–28." *Semeia* 78, no. 1 (1997): 69–81.

———. "Luke: The Stories We Live By." In *Latinx Perspectives on the New Testament*, edited by Osvaldo D. Vena and Leticia A. Guardiola-Saenz, 61–82. Lanham, MD: Lexington Books, 2022.

Habel, Norman. "Ecological Criticism." In *New Meanings for Ancient Texts: Recent Approaches to Biblical Criticisms and Their Applications*, edited by Steven L. McKenzie and John Kaltner, 39–58. Louisville, KY: Westminster John Knox, 2013.

———, ed. *Readings from the Perspective of Earth*. Sheffield, England: Sheffield Academic Press, 2000.

———. "The Challenge of Ecojustice Readings for Christian Theology." *Pacifica* 13, no. 2 (2000): 125–41.

Habel, Norman C., and V. Balabanski, eds. *The Earth Story in the New Testament*. Sheffield, UK: Sheffield Academic, 2002.

Hanson, K. C. "The Galilean Fishing Economy and the Jesus Tradition." *Biblical Theology Bulletin* 27, no. 3 (1997): 99–111.

Harrington, Daniel J. *Meeting St. Luke Today: Understanding the Man, His Mission, and His Message*. Chicago: Loyola Press, 2009.

———. *The Gospel of Matthew*. Sacra Pagina Series. Vol. 1. Collegeville, MN: Liturgical Press, 1991.

Haughton, Rosemary. *Beginning Life in Christ*. Westminster, MD: Newman Press, 1969.

Hawkin, David J. "The Function of the Beloved Disciple Motif in the Johannine Redaction." *Laval Théologique et Philosophique* 33 (1977): 135–50.

Hays, Richard. "Reading the Bible with Eyes of Faith: The Practice of Theological Exegesis." *Journal of Theological Interpretation* 1 (2007): 5–21.

"Historical Jesus Theories." Early Christian Writings. Accessed July 15, 2023. https://www.earlychristianwritings.com/theories.html

Hornsby, Teresa J. "Queer Criticism." In *Searching for Meaning: An Introduction to Interpreting the New Testament*, edited by Paula Gooder, 144–51. Louisville, KY: Westminster John Knox, 2008.

Horrell, David. "Ecological Criticism." In *Searching for Meaning: An Introduction to Interpreting the New Testament*, edited by Paula Gooder, 192–98. Louisville, KY: Westminster John Knox, 2008.

———. *The Bible and the Environment: Towards a Critical Ecological Biblical Theology*. New York: Routledge, 2010.

Horsley, Richard. *Hearing the Whole Story: The Politics of Plot in Mark's Gospel*. Louisville, KY: Westminster John Knox, 2001.

———. *Jesus and Empire: The Kingdom of God and the New World Disorder*. Minneapolis, MN: Augsburg Fortress Press, 2003.

Hylen, Susan E. *Finding Phoebe: What New Testament Women Were Really Like*. Grand Rapids, MI: William B. Eerdmans, 2023.

———. *Imperfect Believers: Ambiguous Characters in the Gospel of John*. Louisville, KY: Westminster John Knox, 2009.

———. *Women in the New Testament World*. New York: Oxford University Press, 2019.

Iser, Wolfgang. "The Reading Process: A Phenomenological Approach." *New Literary History* 3 (1972): 279–99.

Jennings, Ted. *The Man Jesus Loved: Homoerotic Narratives from the New Testament*. Cleveland, OH: Pilgrim Press, 2003.

Jennings, Ted, and Tat-Siong Benny Liew. "Mistaken Identities but Model Faith: Rereading the Centurion, the Chap, and the Christ in Matthew 8:5–13." *Journal of Biblical Literature* 123, no. 3 (2004): 467–94.

Jobling, David, Tina Pippin, and Ronald Schleifer, eds. *The Postmodern Bible Reader*. Oxford, England: Wiley-Blackwell, 2001.

Johnson, Luke T. *The Gospel of Luke*. Sacra Pagina Series. Vol. 3. Collegeville, MN: Liturgical Press, 1991.

———. *The Literary Function of Possessions in Luke-Acts*. Missoula, MT: Scholars Press, 1977.

Juel, Donald. "A Disquieting Silence: The Matter of the Ending." In *The Ending of Mark and the Ends of God*, edited by Beverly Roberts Gaventa and Patrick D. Miller, 1–14. Louisville, KY: Westminster John Knox, 2005.Kampen, John. *Matthew within Sectarian Judaism*. New Haven, CT: Yale University Press, 2019.

Katz, Steven T. "Issues in the Separation of Judaism and Christianity after 70 C.E: A Reconsideration." *Journal of Biblical Literature* 103, no. 1 (1984): 43–76.

Keener, Craig. *The Historical Jesus of the Gospels*. Grand Rapids, MI: Eerdmans, 2012.

Kim, Yung Suk, ed. *1 and 2 Corinthians*. Texts @ Contexts Series. Minneapolis, MN: Fortress, 2013.

———. *A Transformative Reading of the Bible: Explorations of Holistic Human Transformation*. Eugene, OR: Cascade Books, 2013.

———. *Biblical Interpretation: Theory, Process, and Criteria*. Eugene, OR: Pickwick, 2013.

———. *How to Read Paul: A Brief Introduction to His Theology, Writings, and World*. Minneapolis, MN: Fortress, 2021.

———. *Jesus's Truth: Life in Parables*. Eugene, OR: Resource, 2018.

———. *Preaching the New Testament Again: Faith, Freedom, and Transformation*. Eugene, OR: Cascade Books, 2019.

———. *Resurrecting Jesus: The Renewal of New Testament Theology*. Eugene, OR: Cascade Books, 2015.

———. *Truth, Testimony, and Transformation: A New Reading of the "I Am" Sayings of Jesus in the Fourth Gospel*. Eugene, OR: Cascade Books, 2014.

King, Karen L. *The Gospel of Mary of Magdala: Jesus and the First Woman Apostle*. Santa Rosa, CA: Polebridge Press, 2003.

Kingsbury, Jack. *Matthew as Story*. Philadelphia, PA: Fortress, 1988.

Kinukawa, Hisako. "Luke." In *Global Bible Commentary*, edited by Daniel Patte, 367–378. Nashville, TN: Abingdon Press, 2005.

———. "Mark." In *Global Bible Commentary*, edited by Daniel Patte, 367–78. Nashville, TN: Abingdon Press, 2005.
Koperski, Veronica. "Women and Discipleship in Luke 10:38–42 and Acts 6:1–7: The Literary Context of Luke-Acts." In *A Feminist Companion to Luke*, edited by Amy-Jill Levine, 161–96. New York: Sheffield Academic, 2002.
Lawrence, Louise J. "Exploring the Sense-Scape of the Gospel of Mark." *Journal for the Study of the New Testament* 33, no. 4 (2011): 387–97.
———. "Reading Matthew's Gospel with Deaf Culture." In *Matthew*, Texts @ Contexts series, edited by N. W. Duran and J. P. Grimshaw, 155–71. Minneapolis, MN: Fortress, 2013.
———. *Sense and Stigma in the Gospels: Depictions of Sensory-Disabled Characters*. Oxford, UK: Oxford University Press, 2013.
Lee, Dorothy. "Matthew's Gospel and Judaism." Jewish Christian Relations. Accessed May 23, 2023. https://www.jcrelations.net/article/matthews-gospel-and-judaism.html.
Levine, Amy-Jill, ed. *A Feminist Companion to John*. Vol. 1. New York: Sheffield Academic Press, 2003.
———. *A Feminist Companion to Luke*. New York: Sheffield Academic Press, 2002.
———. *A Feminist Companion to Mark*. Sheffield, England: Sheffield Academic Press, 2001.
———. *A Feminist Companion to Matthew*. Sheffield, England: Sheffield Academic Press, 1998.
———. "Is the New Testament Anti-Jewish?" *Bible Odyssey*. April 25, 2023. https://www.bibleodyssey.org/bible-basics/is-the-new-testament-anti-jewish.
———. "Luke and the Jewish Religion." *Interpretation: A Journal of Theology and Bible* 68, no. 4 (2014): 389–402.
———. "Matthew's Advice to a Divided Readership." In *The Gospel of Matthew in Current Study*, edited by David E. Aune, 22–41. Grand Rapids, MI: William B. Eerdmans, 2001.
———. *Short Stories by Jesus. The Enigmatic Parables of a Controversial Rabbi*. New York: HarperOne, 2015.
———. "The Gospel of Matthew." In *Women's Bible Commentary. Revised Edition*, edited by Carol Newsom and Sharon H. Ringe, 465–77. Louisville, KY: Westminster John Knox, 2012.
Levine, Amy-Jill, and Ben Witherington III, *The Gospel of Luke (New Cambridge Bible Commentary)*. New York: Cambridge University Press, 2018.
Levine, Amy-Jill, and Marc Zvi Brettler, eds. *The Jewish Annotated New Testament*. New York: Oxford University Press, 2017.
Liew, Tat-siong Benny. "Minoritized Criticism of the New Testament." *Oxford Bibliographies in Biblical Studies*. Accessed January 23, 2021. https://www.oxfordbibliographies.com/view/document/obo-9780195393361/obo-9780195393361-0277.xml.
———. *Politics of Parousia: Reading Mark Inter(con)textually*. Brill, 1999.
———. "Queering Closets and Perverting Desires: Cross-Examining John's Engendering and Transgendering Word across Different Worlds." In *They Were All Together in One Place? Toward Minority Biblical Criticism*, edited by

Randall C. Bailey, Tat-Siong Benny Liew, and Fernando F. Segovia, 251–88. Atlanta, GA: Society of Biblical Literature, 2009.

———. "Tyranny, Boundary and Might." *Journal for the Study of the New Testament* 21, no. 73 (1999): 7–31.

Liew, Tat-siong Benny, and Fernando F. Segovia, eds. *Reading Biblical Texts Together: Pursuing Minoritized Biblical Criticism*. Atlanta, GA: Society of Biblical Literature, 2022.

Lim, Sung Uk. "Speak My Name: Anti-colonial Mimicry and the Samaritan Woman in John 4:1–42." *Union Seminary Quarterly Review* 62, no. 3–4 (2010): 35–51.

Lozada, Francisco, Jr. "John: The Politics of Recognition." In *Latinx Perspectives on the New Testament*, edited by Osvaldo D. Vena and Leticia A. Guardiola-Saenz, 83–102. Lanham, MD: Lexington Books, 2022.

Luz, Ulrich. *The Theology of the Gospel of Matthew*. Cambridge, England: Cambridge University Press, 1995.

Malbon, Elizabeth Struthers. "Gospel of Mark." In *The Women's Bible Commentary*, edited by Carol A. Newsom and Sharon H. Ringe, 479–92. Louisville, KY: Westminster John Knox, 1992.

———. *Hearing Mark: A Listener's Guide*. Harrisburg, PA: Trinity Press International, 2002.

———. "Narrative Criticism: How Does the Story Mean?" In *Mark and Method: New Approaches in Biblical Studies*, edited by Janice Capel Anderson and Stephen D. Moore, 23–49. Minneapolis, MN: Fortress, 1992.

———. "Narrative Criticism." In *Searching for Meaning: An Introduction to Interpreting the New Testament*, edited by Paula Gooder, 80–87. Louisville, KY: Westminster John Knox, 2008.

Malina, Bruce J. "Early Christian Groups: Using Small Group Formation Theory to Explain Christian Organizations." In *Modelling Early Christianity: Social-Scientific Studies of the New Testament in Its Context*, edited by Philip F. Esler, 96–113. New York: Routledge, 1995.

———. "John's: The Maverick Christian Group the Evidence of Sociolinguistics." *Biblical Theology Bulletin* 24, no. 4 (1994): 167–82.

———. "Social Science Criticism." In *Searching for Meaning: An Introduction to Interpreting the New Testament*, edited by Paula Gooder, 13–20. Louisville, KY: Westminster John Knox, 2008.

Malina, Bruce J., and Richard L. Rohrbaugh. *Social-Science Commentary on the Gospel of John*. Minneapolis, MN: Fortress, 1998.

Marcus, Joel. "Crucifixion as Parodic Exaltation." *Journal of Biblical Literature* 125, no. 1 (2006): 73–87.

———. *Mark 1–8*. New Haven, CT: Yale University Press, 2002.

———. *Mark 8–16*. New Haven, CT: Yale University Press, 2009.

———. *The Way of the Lord: Christological Exegesis of the Old Testament in the Gospel of Mark*. Louisville, KY: Westminster John Knox, 1992.

Martin, Dale. *Sex and the Single Savior*. Louisville, KY: Westminster John Knox, 2006.

Martin, James P. "The Church in Matthew." *Interpretation* 29, no. 1 (1975): 41–56.

Martin, Ralph. "Salvation and Discipleship in Luke's Gospel," *Interpretation* 30, no. 4 (1976): 366–80.
Martyn, J. Louis. *History and Theology in the Fourth Gospel*. 3rd ed. Louisville, KY: Westminster John Knox, 2003.
Marxsen, Willi. *Mark the Evangelist; Studies on the Redaction History of the Gospel*. Nashville, TN: Abingdon Press, 1969.
Matthews, Victor H. "Conversation and Identity: Jesus and the Samaritan Woman," *Biblical Theology Bulletin* 40, no. 4 (2010): 215–26.
McKnight, Edgar V. *Reader Perspectives on the New Testament*. Semeia 48. Atlanta, GA: Scholars Press, 1989.
———. "Reader-Response Criticism." In *To Each Its Own Meaning: An Introduction to Biblical Criticisms and Their Applications*, edited by Steven L. McKenzie and Stephen R. Haynes, 230–52. Louisville, KY: Westminster John Knox, 1999.
Meeks, Wayne A. "The Man from Heaven in Johannine Sectarianism." *Journal of Biblical Literature* 91, no. 1 (1972): 44–72.
Melcher, Sarah J., Mikeal C. Parsons, and Amos Yong, eds. *The Bible and Disability: A Commentary*. Waco, TX: Baylor University Press, 2017.
Menéndez-Antuña, Luis. "Black Lives Matter and Gospel Hermeneutics: Political Life and Social Death in the Gospel of Luke." *Currents in Theology and Mission* 45, no. 4 (2018): 29–34.
Metzger, Bruce. *A Textual Commentary on the Greek New Testament*. Peabody, MA: Hendrickson, 2005.
Metzger, Bruce M., and Bart D. Ehrman. *The Text of the New Testament: Its Transmission, Corruption, and Restoration*. New York: Oxford University Press, 2005.
Miller, Susan. "I Came That They May Have Life, and Have It Abundantly" (John 10:10): An Ecological Reading of John's Gospel." *The Expository Times* 124, no. 2 (2012): 64–71.
———. "The Descent of Darkness over the Land: Listening to the Voice of Earth in Mark 15:33." In *Exploring Ecological Hermeneutics*, edited by Norman C. Habel and Peter Trudinger, 123–30. Atlanta, GA: Society of Biblical Literature, 2008.
Monro, Winsome. "Women Disciples in Mark?" *Catholic Biblical Quarterly* 44 (1982): 225–41.
Moore, Stephen D. "Are There Impurities in the Living Water That the Johannine Jesus Dispenses? Deconstruction, Feminism, and the Samaritan Woman." In *The Feminist Companion to John*, vol. 1, edited by Amy-Jill Levine, 78–97. Sheffield, England: Sheffield Academic, 2003.
Moore, Stephen D. *Literary Criticism and the Gospels: The Theoretical Challenge*. New Haven, CT: Yale University Press, 1989.
Moss, Candida R., and Jeremy Schipper, eds. *Disability Studies and Biblical Literature*. New York: Palgrave Macmillan, 2011.
Moxnes, Halvor. *Putting Jesus in His Place: A Radical Vision of Household and Kingdom*. Louisville, KY: Westminster John Knox, 2003.
Myers, Ched. *Binding the Strong Man: A Political Reading of Mark's Story of Jesus*. Maryknoll, NY: Orbis, 1988.
Nadella, Raj. *Dialogue Not Dogma: Many Voices in the Gospel of Luke*. New York: T&T Clark, 2011.

Nelavala, Surekha. "Jesus Asks the Samaritan Woman for a Drink: A Dalit Feminist Reading of John 4," *Lectio Difficilior* 1 (2007): 1–25.
Newsom, Carol A., and Sharon H. Ringe. *The Women's Bible Commentary*. Louisville, KY: Westminster John Knox, 1992.
Neyrey, Jerome H., ed. *The Social World of Luke-Acts: Models for Interpretation*. Peabody, MA: Hendrickson, 1991.
Neyrey, Jerome H. "What's Wrong with This Picture? John 4, Cultural Stereotypes of Women, and Public and Private Space." In *The Feminist Companion to John*, vol. 1, edited by Amy-Jill Levine, 98–125. Sheffield, England: Sheffield Academic, 2003.
NPR Staff. "A Jewish Perspective on the New Testament." NPR Radio IQ. Published December 24, 2011. https://www.npr.org/2011/12/24/144228636/a-jewish-perspective-on-the-new-testament.
Oakman, Douglas. "The Countryside in Luke-Acts." In *The Social World of Luke-Acts: Models for Interpretation*, edited by Jerome H. Neyrey, 151–179. Peabody, MA: Hendrickson, 1991.
O'Day, Gail R. "Surprised by Faith: Jesus and the Canaanite Woman." *Listening* 24 (1980): 290–301.
———. "The Gospel of John." In *Women's Bible Commentary, Revised Edition*, edited by Carol Newsom, Sharon H. Ringe, and Jacqueline E. Lapsey, 517–30. Louisville, KY: Westminster John Knox, 2012.
Okura, Teresa. "Jesus and the Samaritan Woman (John 4:1–42) in Africa." *Theological Studies* 70 (2009): 401–18.
Olyan, S. M. *Disability in the Hebrew Bible: Interpreting Mental and Physical Differences*. Cambridge, England: Cambridge University Press, 2008.
Overman, J. Andrew. *Church and Community in Crisis: The Gospel According to Matthew*. Harrisburg, PA: Trinity Press International, 1996.
———. *Matthew's Gospel and Formative Judaism: The Social World of the Matthean Community*. Minneapolis, MN: Fortress, 1990.
Park, Kyung-mi. "John." In *Global Bible Commentary*, edited by Daniel Patte, 401–11. Nashville, TN: Abingdon Press, 2004.
Parker, Angela N. "'And the Word Became . . . Gossip?': Unhinging the Samaritan Woman in the Age of #MeToo," *Review & Expositor* 117, no. 2 (2020): 259–71.
Parker, David C. *Textual Scholarship and the Making of the New Testament*. New York: Oxford University Press, 2014.
———. *The Living Text of the Gospels*. New York: Cambridge University Press, 1997.
Parsons, Mikeal C. "'Short in Stature': Luke's Physical Description of Zacchaeus." *New Testament Studies* 47 (2001): 50–57.
Patte, Daniel, ed. *Global Bible Commentary*. Nashville, TN: Abingdon Press, 2004.
———. "Reading Matthew 28:16–20 with Others: How It Deconstructs Our Western Concept of Mission." *HTS Theological Studies* 62, no. 2 (2006): 521–57.
———. *The Challenge of Discipleship: A Critical Study of the Sermon on the Mount as Scripture*. Harrisburg, PA: Trinity Press International, 1999.
Peacock, Heber F. "Discipleship in the Gospel of Mark." *Review & Expositor* 75, no. 4 (1978): 555–64.

Penwell, Stewart. *Jesus the Samaritan: Ethnic Labeling in the Gospel of John*. Boston, MA: Brill, 2019.

Perkinson, Jim. "A Canaanite Word in the Logos of Christ," *Semeia* 75 (1996): 61–85.

Perrin, Norman. *Rediscovering the Teaching of Jesus* (New York: Harper & Row, 1967).

———. *What Is Redaction Criticism?* Minneapolis, MN: Fortress, 2002.

Plato. *Plato's Phaedo*. Oxford, England: Clarendon Press, 1911.

Powell, Mark A. *Chasing the Eastern Star: Adventures in Biblical Reader–Response Criticism*. Louisville, KY: Westminster John Knox, 2001.

———. *God with Us: A Pastoral Theology of Matthew's Gospel*. Minneapolis, MN: Fortress, 1995.

———. "Toward a Narrative-Critical Understanding of Matthew." *Interpretation: A Journal of Bible and Theology* 46, no. 4 (1992): 341–46.

———. *What Are They Saying about Luke?* Mahwah, NJ: Paulist Press, 1989.

———. *What Is Narrative Criticism?* Minneapolis, MN: Fortress, 1991.

Powery, Emerson. "The Gospel of Mark." In *True to Our Native Land: An African American New Testament Commentary*, edited by Brian K. Blount, Cain H. Felder, Clarice J. Martin, and Emerson B. Powery, 151–57. Minneapolis, MN: Fortress, 2007.

Punt, Jeremy. "Queer Theory, Postcolonial Theory, and Biblical Interpretation: A Preliminary Exploration of Some Intersections." In *Bible Trouble: Queer Reading at the Boundaries of Biblical Scholarship*, edited by Teresa J. Hornsby and Ken Stone, 321–41. Atlanta, GA: Society of Biblical Literature, 2011.

Pyper, Hugh S. "Postmodernism." In *New Meanings for Ancient Texts: Recent Approaches to Biblical Criticisms and Their Applications*, edited by Steven L. McKenzie and John Kaltner, 117–36. Louisville, KY: Westminster John Knox, 2013.

Reid, Barbara. "'Do You See this Woman?' Luke 7:36–50 as a Paradigm for Feminist Hermeneutics." *Biblical Research* 40 (1995): 37–49.

———. *The Gospel According to Matthew*. Vol. 1. New Collegeville Bible Commentary. Collegeville, MN: Liturgical Press, 2005.

———. *Parables for Preachers: Year C*. Collegeville, MN: Liturgical Press, 1999.

Reid, Barbara E., and Shelly Matthews. *Wisdom Commentary: Luke 1–9 (Vol 1); Luke 10–24 (Vol 2)*. Collegeville, MN: Liturgical Press, 2021.

Reinhartz, Adele. "Judaism in the Gospel of John." *Interpretation* 63, no. 4 (2009): 382–93.

———. "The Colonizer as Colonized." In *John and Postcolonialism: Travel, Space and Power*, edited by Musa W. Dube and Jeffrey L. Stanley, 169–92. Sheffield, England: Sheffield Academic Press, 2005.

———. "The Gospel According to John." In *The Jewish Annotated New Testament*, edited by Amy-Jill Levine and Marc Zvi Brettler, 168–218. New York: Oxford University Press, 2017.

Rhoads, David. "Jesus and the Syrophoenician Woman in Mark: A Narrative-Critical Study." *Currents in Theology and Mission* 47, no. 4 (2020): 36–48.

———. "Social Criticism: Crossing Boundaries." In *Mark and Method: New Approaches in Biblical Studies*, ed. Janice Capel Anderson and Stephen D. Moore, 135–61. Minneapolis, MN: Fortress, 1992.

Rhoads, David, Joanna Dewey, and Donald Michie. *Mark as Story: An Introduction to the Narrative of a Gospel*. Minneapolis, MN: Fortress, 2012.
Rieger, Joerg. *Jesus vs. Caesar: For People Tired of Serving the Wrong God*. Nashville, TN: Abingdon Press, 2018.
Ringe, Sharon H. "A Gentile Woman's Story, Revisited: Rereading Mark 7:24–31a." In *Feminist Companion to Mark*, edited by Amy-Jill Levine, 79–100. Sheffield, England: Sheffield Academic, 2001.
Robbins, Vernon K. "The Social Location of the Implied Author of Luke-Acts." In *The Social World of Luke-Acts: Models for Interpretation*, edited by Jerome H. Neyrey, 305–32. Peabody, MA: Hendrickson, 1991.
Roberts, Alexander, ed. "Irenaeus: Against Heresies." The Gnostic Society Library. Accessed February 23, 2021. http://gnosis.org/library/advh1.htm.
Ruiz, Gilberto A. "Matthew: Negotiating Tradition and Identity in Matthean and Latinx Contexts." In *Latinx Perspectives on the New Testament*, edited by Osvaldo D. Vena and Leticia A. Guardiola-Saenz, 11–32. Lanham, MD: Lexington Books, 2022.
Sadler, Rodney S., Jr. "The Place and Role of Africa and African Imagery in the Bible." In *True to Our Native Land: An African American New Testament Commentary*, edited by Brian K. Blount, Cain H. Felder, Clarice J. Martin, and Emerson B. Powery, 23–30. Minneapolis, MN: Fortress, 2007.
St. Clair, Raquel. *Call and Consequences: A Womanist Reading of Mark*. Minneapolis, MN: Fortress, 2008.
———. "Womanist Biblical Interpretation." In *True to Our Native Land: An African American New Testament Commentary*, edited by Brian K. Blount, Cain H. Felder, Clarice J. Martin, and Emerson B. Powery, 54–62. Minneapolis, MN: Fortress Press, 2007.
Saldarini, Anthony. *Matthew's Christian-Jewish Community*. Chicago: University of ChicagoPress, 1994.
———. "Reading Matthew without Anti-Semitism." In *The Gospel of Matthew in Current Study*, edited by David E. Aune, 166–84. Grand Rapids, MI: William B. Eerdmans, 2001.
Samuel, Simon. *A Postcolonial Reading of Mark's Story of Jesus*. New York: T&T Clark, 2007.
Sánchez, David Arthur. "Ambivalence, Mimicry, and the Ochlos in the Gospel of Mark." In *Reading Minjung Theology in the Twenty-first Century*, edited by Yung Suk Kim and Jin-ho Kim, 134–47. Eugene, OR: Pickwick, 2013.
Sanders, Cheryl J. *Ministry at the Margins: The Prophetic Mission of Women, Youth and the Poor*. Downers Grove, IL: InterVarsity, 1997.
Sandmel, Samuel. *A Jewish Understanding of the New Testament*. Woodstock, VT: SkyLight, 2004.
Schaberg, Jane. *The Illegitimacy of Jesus: A Feminist Theological Interpretation of the Infancy Narratives*. Sheffield, England: Sheffield Phoenix Press, 2006.
Schottroff, Luise. "Die Samaritanerin am Brunnen (Joh 4)." In *Auf Israel Hören: Sozialgeschichtliche Bibelauslegung*, edited by Renate Jost, Rainer Kessler, and Christoph M. Raisig, 115–32. Lucerne, Switzerland: Edition Exodus, 1992.
Schweizer, Eduard. "The Portrayal of the Life of Faith in the Gospel of Mark." *Interpretation* 32, no. 4 (1978): 387–99.

Segovia, Fernando F. "Postcolonial Criticism and the Gospel of Matthew." In *Methods for Matthew*, edited by Mark Allan Powell, 194–238. New York: Cambridge University Press, 2009.

———, ed. *"What is John?" Vol. II, Literary and Social Readings of the Fourth Gospel*. Atlanta, GA: Scholars Press, 1998.

Segovia, Fernando F., and R. S. Sugirtharajah, eds. *A Postcolonial Commentary on the New Testament Writings*. New York: T&T Clark, 2007.

Senior, Donald. "Between Two Worlds: Gentiles and Jewish Christians in Matthew's Gospel." *Catholic Biblical Quarterly* 61 (1999): 1–23.

———. "Directions in Matthean Studies." In *The Gospel of Matthew in Current Study*, edited by David E. Aune, 5–21. Grand Rapids, MI: William B. Eerdmans, 2001.

———. *The Gospel of Matthew: Interpreting Biblical Texts Series* (Nashville, TN: Abingdon Press), 1997.

———. *What Are They Saying about Matthew?* Mahwah, NJ: Paulist Press, 1996.

Shore, Mary Hinkle. "Creation, Vocation, and Little Faith in Matthew's Gospel." *Word & World* 5 (2006): 66–72.

Shore-Goss, Robert E. "John." In *The Queer Bible Commentary*, edited by Mona West and Robert E. Shore-Goss, 560–85. London: SCM Press, 2022.

———. "Luke." In *The Queer Bible Commentary*, edited by Mona West and Robert E. Shore-Goss, 533–59. London: SCM Press, 2022.

Skinner, Matthew L. "Looking High and Low for Salvation in Luke." *Currents in Theology and Mission* 45, no. 4 (2018): 6–11.

Smith, Mitzi J. "Centering Social Justice in Biblical Interpretation: The Woman with a Chronic Illness That Challenged Her Posture (Luke 13:10–17)." In *We Are All Witnesses: Toward Disruptive and Creative Biblical Interpretation*, 64–85. Eugene, OR: Cascade Books, 2023.

———. "'Give Them What You Have': A Womanist Reading of the Matthean Feeding Miracle (Matthew 14:13–21)." *Journal of Bible and Human Transformation* 3, no. 1 (2013): 1–22.

———, ed. *I Found God in Me: A Womanist Biblical Hermeneutics Reader*. Eugene, OR: Cascade Books, 2015.

———. "If Rachel Does Not Weep, Who Will?: A Pro-Choice Quality of Life Womanist Reading of Matthew 2," in *Currents in Theology and Mission* 49, no. 4 (2022): 5–9.

———. *Womanist Sass and Talk Back: Social (In)Justice, Intersectionality, and Biblical Interpretation*. Eugene, OR: Cascade Books, 2018.

Smith, Mitzi J., and Jayachitra Lalitha, eds. *Teaching All Nations: Interrogating the Matthean Great Commission*. Minneapolis, MN: Fortress, 2014.

Smith, Mitzi J., and Jin Young Choi, eds. *Minoritized Women Reading Race and Ethnicity: Intersectional Approaches to Constructed Identity and Early Christian Texts*. Lanham, MD: Lexington Books, 2020.

Smith, Mitzi J., and Michael Willett Newheart. *We Are All Witnesses: Toward Disruptive and Creative Biblical Interpretation*. Eugene, OR: Cascade Books, 2022.

Smith, Mitzi J., and Yung Suk Kim. "The Gospel of Luke," in *Toward Decentering the New Testament*. Eugene, OR: Cascade Books, 2018.

———. *Toward Decentering the New Testament: A Reintroduction.* Eugene, OR: Cascade Books, 2018.

Soares-Prabhu, George. "Two Mission Commands: An Interpretation of Matthew 28:16–20 in the Light of a Buddhist Text." *Biblical Interpretation* 2, no. 3 (1994): 264–82.

Soulen, Richard. *Defining Jesus: The Earthly, the Biblical, the Historical, and the Real Jesus, and How Not to Confuse Them.* Eugene, OR: Cascade Books, 2015.

———. "Feminist Biblical Interpretation." In *Handbook of Biblical Criticism,* 66–68. Louisville, KY: Westminster John Knox, 2011.

———. *Handbook of Biblical Criticism.* Louisville, KY: Westminster John Knox, 2011.

———. "Reader-Response Criticism." In *Handbook of Biblical Criticism.* Louisville, KY: Westminster John Knox, 2011.

Staley, Jeffrey L. "Postcolonial Reflections on Reading Luke-Acts from Cabo San Lucas and Other Places." In *Literary Encounters with the Reign of God,* edited by Sharon Ringe and Paul Kim, 422–45. Harrisburg, PA: Trinity Press International, 2003.

Stark, Rodney. "Antioch as the Social Situation for Matthew's Gospel." In *Social History of the Matthean Community,* edited by David Balch, 189–210. Minneapolis, MN: Fortress, 1991.

Stegemann, Ekkehard W., and Wolfgang Stegemann. "Messianic Communities in the Land of Israel after 70 CE." In *The Jesus Movement: A Social History of Its First Century,* 231–47. Minneapolis, MN: Fortress, 1999.

Stegemann, Wolfgang. *The Social Setting of Jesus and the Gospels.* Minneapolis, MN: Fortress, 2002.

Stibbe, Mark W. G. *John as Storyteller: Narrative Criticism and the Fourth Gospel.* Cambridge, England: Cambridge University Press, 1992.

Stock, Augustine. *The Method and Message of Mark.* Wilmington, DE: Michael Glazier, 1989.

Stone, Ken. "Queer Criticism." In *New Meanings for Ancient Texts: Recent Approaches to Biblical Criticisms and Their Applications,* edited by Steven L. McKenzie and John Kaltner, 155–76. Louisville, KY: Westminster John Knox, 2013.

Sugirtharajah, R. S. "Postcolonial Criticism." In *Searching for Meaning: An Introduction to Interpreting the New Testament,* edited by Paula Gooder, 175–83. Louisville, KY: Westminster John Knox, 2008.

Talbert, Charles H. *Reading Luke: A Literary and Theological Commentary on the Third Gospel.* Macon, GA: Smyth & Helwys, 2002.

Tannehill, Robert C. *The Narrative Unity of Luke-Acts: A Literary Interpretation, Vol. 1: The Gospel According to Luke.* Philadelphia, PA: Augsburg Fortress, 1991.

Theissen, Gerd. *The Gospels in Context: Social and Political History in the Synoptic Tradition.* Translated by Linda M. Maloney. Minneapolis, MN: Fortress, 1991.

———. *The Sociology of Early Palestinian Christianity.* Minneapolis, MN: Fortress, 1978.

Thomaskutty, Johnson, ed. *An Asian Introduction to the New Testament.* Minneapolis, MN: Fortress, 2022.

———. "The Gospel of John." In *An Asian Introduction to the New Testament*, edited by Johnson Thomaskutty, 127–56. Minneapolis, MN: Fortress, 2022.

Toensing, Holly Joan. "'Living among the Tomb': Society, Mental Illness, and Self-Destruction in Mark 5:1–20." In *This Abled Body: Rethinking Disabilities in Biblical Studies*, edited by Hector Avalos, Sarah J. Melcher, and Jeremy Schipper, 131–43. Atlanta, GA: Society of Biblical Literature, 2007.

Tolbert, Mary Ann. "When Resistance Becomes Repression." In *Reading from This Place*, Vol. 2, edited by Fernando Segovia and Mary Ann Tolbert, 331–46. Minneapolis, MN: Fortress, 1995.

Trainor, Michael. "'And on Earth, Peace . . .' (Luke 2:14): Luke's Perspectives on the Earth." In *Readings from the Perspective of Earth*, edited by Norman C. Habel, 174–93. Sheffield, England: Sheffield Academic Press, 2000.

Troftgruben, Troy. "Salvation 'Today' in Luke's Gospel." *Currents in Theology and Mission* 45, no. 4 (2018): 6–11.

Tupamahu, Ekaputra. "The Gospel of Luke." In *An Asian Introduction to the New Testament*, edited by Johnson Thomaskutty, 103–25. Minneapolis, MN: Fortress, 2022.

Tyson, Joseph B. *Luke-Acts and the Jewish People: Eight Critical Perspectives*. Philadelphia, PA: Augsburg Fortress, 1988.

"The Ujamaa Center at University of KwaZulu-Natal." University of Kwazulu-Natal. Accessed July 21, 2023. https://srpc.ukzn.ac.za/research-units-centres/ujamaa.

Ukpong, Justin. "Luke." In *Global Bible Commentary*, edited by Daniel Patte, 385–94. Nashville, TN: Abingdon Press, 2004.

Vassiliadis, Petros. "John in an Orthodox Perspective." In *Global Bible Commentary*, edited by Daniel Patte, 412–18. Nashville, TN: Abingdon Press, 2004.

Vena, Osvaldo D. "Mark: A Disabled Gospel for a Disabled Community." In *Latinx Perspectiveson the New Testament*, edited by Osvaldo D. Vena and Leticia A. Guardiola-Saenz, 33–60. Lanham, MD: Lexington Books, 2022.

Wainwright, Elaine. "A Transformative Struggle Towards the Divine Dream: An Ecofeminist Reading of Matthew 11." In *Readings from the Perspective of Earth*, edited by Norman C. Have, 162–73. Sheffield, England: Sheffield Academic Press, 2000.

———. "Bread of Life for the World: John 3:16–18; John 6:51–58." *Tui Motu InterIslands Magazine*, May 31, 2020. https://hail.to/tui-motu-interislands-magazine/publication/430InQe/article/46vIvtJ.

———. "Healing Ointment/Healing Bodies: Gift and Identification in an Ecofeminist Reading of Mark 14:3–9." In *Exploring Ecological Hermeneutics*, edited by Norman C. Habel and Peter Trudinger, 131–40. Atlanta, GA: Society of Biblical Literature, 2008.

———. "Our Daily Bread—Luke 11:1–4." *Tui Motu InterIslands Magazine*, June 30, 2019. https://hail.to/tui-motu-interislands-magazine/publication/430InQe/article/3NI7p9o.

———. "Part Four: An Ecological Reading of Mark's Gospel." *Tui Motu InterIslands Magazine*, May 1, 2015. https://hail.to/tui-motu-interislands-magazine/publication/430InQe/article/p9j2RGB.

———. *Shall We Look for Another? A Feminist Rereading of the Matthean Jesus.* Maryknoll, NY: Orbis, 1998.
Warren, Meredith. "Five Husbands: Slut-Shaming the Samaritan Woman." *The Bible & Critical Theory* 17, no. 2 (2021): 51–70.
West, Gerald O. "Mobilizing Matthew among the Marginalized: Thirty Years of Community-Based Bible Study in South Africa." *Currents in Theology and Mission* 49, no. 4 (2022): 27–34.
West, Mona, and Robert Shore-Goss, eds. *The Queer Bible Commentary.* London: SCM Press, 2022.
Westfield, N. Lynne. *Dear Sisters: A Womanist Practice of Hospitality.* Cleveland, OH: Pilgrim Press, 2001.
Wills, Lawrence. "The Gospel According to Mark." In *The Jewish Annotated New Testament,* edited by Amy-Jill Levine and Marc Zvi Brettler, 67–106. New York: Oxford University Press, 2017.
Wilson, Walter, T. "Perception, Discipleship, and Revelation in the Gospel of Matthew." *Journal of Disability & Religion* 19, no. 1 (2015): 66–84.
Wynn, Kerry H. "Johannine Healings and Otherness of Disability." *Perspectives in Religious Studies* 34 (2007): 61–75.
Yong, Amos. *The Bible, Disability, and the Church: A New Vision of the People of God.* Grand Rapids, MI: William B. Eerdmans, 2011.

Index

Abraham, 98, 121, 197, 199, 203, 205, 211; "daughter of," 95, 202; genealogy from, 47, 49, 52, 54, 76, 79, 88; God and, 30
Acts of Pilate (150–255 CE), 6
Acts of the Apostles, 80
Adam, 76, 77, 78, 79, 88
addendum, John 21:1–25, 129–30
Adoptionist Christology, 198
adultery, 10, 34, 58, 59
Aeneid (Virgil), 4–5
African Americans, 141, 156, 177, 202
African culture, 205–6
Alexandrinus, codex, 197
almsgiving, 59
Anderson, Paul, 223
Andrew, 56, 90, 217
Andronicus, 23
angels, 53–54, 71, 83–85, 198
"Anti-Judaism and the Passion Narrative in Luke and Acts" (Gaston), 214n17
anti-Semitism, 121, 142, 227
Apocryphon of James, 5
archaeological data, Jewish, 181
Argentina, 182
Asian Americans, 209–10
Atlanta Spa Shooting (2021), 210

audience: John, 107; Luke, 77; Mark, 23; Matthew, 47
Augustus (63 BCE–14 CE), 4–5, 77, 85, 86, 206
author: John, 107; Luke, 77; Mark, 22; Matthew, 46; Peter, 6
author-centered, historical approach: to gospel interpretation, 135, 137–39; historical-critical method, 137–38, 149–50, 171–72, 195–96, 217–18; John, 217–19; Luke, 195–97; Mark, 149–51; Matthew, 171–73; social-science criticism, 138–39, 150–51, 172–73, 196–97, 218–19

banquets, 37, 48, 51, 79, 96
baptism: of Jesus, 7, 17, 21, 29–30, 63, 149–50; water, 17, 21, 29–30, 63, 106, 115, 117, 149
Barabbas, 39, 174
Bartimaeus, 35, 165, 166
basileia tou theou (God's reign), 8, 31
Bathsheba, 52–53, 54
Bauckham, Richard, 189
beatitudes: Luke, 75, 90, 202, 208; Matthew 5:1–12, 48, 56, 173; in Matthew and Luke, *57–58*, 90
belief (faith, *pistis*), 31, 34

Beloved Disciple, 110, 128; with risen Lord, 129, 221, 222; testimony of, 130, 221, 231; unknown identity of, 107, 220–21, 229, 231
Benko, Andrew, 232
Bethlehem, 7, 49, 53–54, 85–86, 187
Bezae, codex, 197
Biblicism, 244
biography, gospels as, 4, 23
birth narratives, 6, 28, 45, 47, 84
Black Church, 157
black theology, 141
blind man of Bethsaida: "I see people, but they look like trees, walking," Mark 8:22–26, 24, 31, 32, 165–66
blindness: Bartimaeus, 35, 165, 166; healing of, 188
Blount, Brian, 157
Boanerges, sons of thunder (Mark 3:17), 24
Bohache, Thomas, 183–84
Bovon, François, 204
Boyarin, Daniel, 43n2
Bryan, Jocelyn, 243

carpenter or stone builder (*tekton*), 7, 150
Carter, Warren, 184
CBS (Contextual Bible Study), 179
Chancey, Mark, 181
child (*tekton*), 184
Choi, Jin Young, 186–87
Christianity, Judaism and, 86, 138, 142, 171
Christian Protestant denominations, 12
Christology, 106, 198, 225; John, 112, 114, 230; Mark, 43n2, 149–50, 160; Matthew, 51
circumcision, 80, 86, 138, 204, 205
Clark-Soles, Jaime, 165–66
class, 95, 140, 159–60, 207, 210
Clement of Alexandria (second century CE), 6, 105, 197
climate change, 12, 144–45, 189, 244
close readings: defined, 3; John, 113–30; Luke, 83–103; Mark, 28–41; Matthew, 52–72

codices, 197
coins, 37, 79, 83, 99
Collins, Adela Yabro, 158
Coloe, Mary, 225
community (*ekklesia*), 12, 46
community instructions (Matthew 18:1–35), 46, 67
conflict model, 138, 139
Confucius, 73n2
content, unique: John, 108–9; Luke, 78; Mark, 24; Matthew, 48
Contextual Bible Study (CBS), 179
COVID-19, 210
crimes: hate, 210; treason, 39
Crites, Stephen, 243
crucifixion, 28, 36, 70, 128, 157; crowd at, 71, 80, 87, 102, 195, 227, 243; with trials and last supper, Mark 14:1–15:47, 38–40; women at, 71, 83, 87
Culpepper, R. Alan, 225–26
Cyril (fourth century CE), 6

D'Angelo, Mary, 223
date: John, 14, 107; Luke, 14, 77; Mark, 14, 22; Matthew, 14, 46
"daughter of Abraham," 95, 202
deaf and dumb man, "Ephphatha, be opened," Mark 7:34, 24
deconstruction interpretation: John, 231–32; Luke, 208–9; Mark, 163–64; Matthew, 185–86; reader-centered, comprehensive approach, 143–44, 163–64, 185–86, 208–9, 231–32
The Deeds of the Divine Augustus (Res Gestae Divi Augusti), 5
demoniacs, 32, 60–61, 67, 159, 166
Derrida, Jacques, 143, 208–9
Deuteronomy 6:5, 37
Deutero-Pauline, 34, 140
Dialogue of the Savior, 5
Didache, 46–47
différance, 143
disability studies: John, 233–34; Luke, 211–12; Mark, 165–66; Matthew, 188; reader-centered,

comprehensive approach, 144, 165–66, 188, 211–12, 233–34
disciples, 90; in Galilee, 7, 22–23; gender and, 52; as illiterate, 13; in Jerusalem, 7; John, 108; of John the Baptist, 115, 150; Luke, 78; Mark, 24; Mary, 5–6; Matthew, 5, 47; Matthew 4:18–22, Jesus's call of the first, 56; Nicodemus as secret, 128; with prayer, 95, 100; washing feet of, 108, 225; women, 242–43. *See also* Beloved Disciple; *specific disciples*
divorce, 34, 58–59, 67–68, 97
Dowd, Sharyn, 158, 168n12
Duarte, Alejandro, 182
Dube, Musa, 185, 230

Ebionites, Gospel of (100–160 CE), 6
ecological criticism: John, 234–35; Luke, 212–13; Mark, 166–67; Matthew, 189–90; reader-centered, comprehensive approach, 144–45, 166–67, 189–90, 212–13, 234–35
Egypt, 5, 53–54, 72, 86, 182
ekklesia (community), 12, 46
ekklesia-centered, theological interpretation, 145n1; John, 225–26; Luke, 203–4; Mark, 157–58; Matthew, 179–80; reader-centered, comprehensive approach, 137, 141, 157–58, 179–80, 203–4, 225–26
Elder, Nicholas, 43n3
Eleazar, 40
Elijah, 30, 32, 33, 76, 80, 89, 93
Elizabeth (mother of John the Baptist), 83–84, 204
Epiphanius, 6
Episcopal Church, 12
eschatology: John, 108; Luke, 78, 81; Mark, 23; Matthew, 47; Matthew 24:1–25:46 and sermon on, 70
ethnicity, 81, 143, 179, 186, 224, 232
Eusebius, 22, 77
Evangelical Lutheran Church, 12
evangelists, 7, 14, 26–27, 112, 137, 141, 196, 239–41; gospels as story of Jesus and, 12–13; gospels with significance of Jesus reflected upon by, 9–12
excessive use of force, by police, 164
exorcism, 8, 106, 159, 203, 206

faith (belief, *pistis*), 31, 34
family, sense of selfhood and, 164
farewell discourses, John, 105–7, 108, 110, 112, 124–26, 219, 225
fasting, 59–60, 61, 86, 90, 152
feminist criticism: John, 222–23; Luke, 201–2; Mark, 155–56; Matthew, 176–77; reader-centered, comprehensive approach, 140, 155–56, 176–77, 201–2, 222–23
fig tree, 36, 38, 69–70, 79
Fitzmyer, Joseph, 211
Flint, Michigan, 224
fool, 79, 95, 172, 199, 207
"For the Son of Man came not to be served but to serve, and to give his life a ransom for many" (Mark 10:45), 36
"For those who want to save their life will lose it, and those who lose their life for my sake, and for the sake of the gospel, will save it" (Mark 8:34–35), 24, 32
"For those who want to save their life will lose it, and those who lose their life for my sake, and for the sake of the gospel, will save it" (Matthew 16:24–25), 66
Foskett, Mary, 209, 210
fragmentary gospels, 6
Freire, Ana Esther Padua, 160–61
friends, 79, 95, 96, 101, 127, 129–30, 172

Gabriel (angel), 83–84
Gale, Aaron, 181
Galilee: disciples in, 7, 22–23; Luke 4:14–9:50, ministry of Jesus in, 88–93
Gaston, Lloyd, 214n17
gender, 95, 143, 186, 224; disciples and, 52; with Herod and massacre

of infants, 49, 53, 54, 182, 187; with race and class, 140, 210
genealogy: Abraham, 47, 49, 52, 54, 76, 79, 88; of Jesus, 28, 45, 52–53, 54, 78, 79, 88; queer, 53
Genesis, 34, 84, 107, 113, 130, 234
genre, 4, 23
glory, 27, 35, 99, 106, 116, 125, 173; John 18:1–20:31, suffering and, 126–29; Luke 2:14 "Glory to God in the highest heaven, and on earth peace among those whom he favors!," 85
Gnostic gospels, 5–6, 14
God: Abraham and, 30; Luke 2:14, "Glory to God in the highest heaven, and on earth peace among those whom he favors!," 85; Mark 15:34, "My God, my God, why have you forsaken me?," 40; Paul on power of, 207. *See also* kingdom of God
God's reign (*basileia tou theou*), 8, 31
golden rule, 49, 60
good Samaritan, 81–82, 94, 103, 199, 207
"the good news of Jesus Christ" (Mark 1:1), 25, 28, 43n8
Gorman, Michael, 145n1
gospels: as biography, 4, 23; criteria for solid interpretation, 242–43; with critical, imaginative role of readers, 243–44; defined, 4–6; how to read, 7–13; importance of various readings of, 240–42; types of, 5–6, 13–14. *See also specific gospels*
gospels, how to read: as story of evangelists reflecting on significance of Jesus, 9–12; as story of Jesus, 7–9; as story of Jesus and evangelists for contemporary readers, 12–13
gospels, interpretive approaches to: author-centered, historical, 135, 137–39; reader-centered, comprehensive, 135–36, 140–45; text-centered, literary, 135, 139; three approaches, 135–36

gospels, types of: Infancy, 6; narrative, 5, 13–14; other fragmentary, 6; passion, 6; sayings, 5–6
Green, Joel, 141

hate crimes, 210
Haughton, Rosemary, 229
healing: of blindness, 188; of many people, Matthew 8:1–9:38, 60–61
healings, unique: John, 109; Luke, 79; Mark, 24, 32
Hebrews (80–150 CE), Gospel of, 6
Herod (King), 56, 85, 87, 91, 155; with death of Jesus, 86, 96, 101; with massacre of infants, 49, 53, 54, 182, 187
Hillel (Rabbi), 49, 60
"His blood be on us and on our children" (Matthew 27:25), 71
historical-critical method: author-centered, historical approach, 137–38, 149–50, 171–72, 195–96, 217–18; John, 217–18; Luke, 195–96; Mark, 149–50; Matthew, 171–72
History and Theology in the Fourth Gospel (Martyn), 225
hoi ioudaioi ("the Jews"), 227
holistic transformation, 178, 191n24
human condition, 143; John, 108; Luke, 78; Mark, 24; Matthew, 48
Hylen, Susan, 242, 244n4
hypocrites, 52, 63, 69–70, 95, 171, 202

"I am" sayings, of Jesus, 111–12
illiterate, disciples as, 13
Infancy Gospels, 6
infancy narratives, 5, 22, 41, 52–54, 76, 77, 83
inter(con)textual interpretation: John, 227–28; Luke, 205–6; Mark, 159–60; Matthew, 182–83; reader-centered, comprehensive approach, 142, 159–60, 182–83, 205–6, 227–28
interpretation issues: John, 112; Luke, 82–83; Mark, 27–28; Matthew, 51–52

Index

Isaiah, 30, 55; 56:7, 36; 40:3, 29, 87; 42:1–4, 64; 7:14, 49, 53; 6:8, 84; 61:1–2, 75, 82, 88, 89; 29:13, 66

James (140–170 CE), 56, 90; Infancy Gospel, 6; Jesus and, 5, 38, 66, 69
Japan, 159–60
Jennings, Ted, 184, 229
Jerusalem: disciples in, 7; Luke 19:28–21:38, Jesus's teaching in, 99; Mark 11:1–13:37, ministry in, 36–38; Matthew 21:1–23:39, Jesus confronts leaders and enters, 69–70. *See also* Jesus on the way to Jerusalem
Jesus: baptism of, 7, 17, 21, 29–30, 63, 149–50; birth of, 6; and Elijah, 32, 33; genealogy of, 28, 45, 52–53, 54, 78, 79, 88; gospels as story of, 7–9; gospels as story of evangelists and, 12–13; gospels as story of evangelists reflecting on significance of, 9–12; Herod with death of, 86, 96, 101; "I am" sayings of, 111–12; identity of, 32; James and, 5, 38, 66, 69; Jerusalem and teaching of, 99; Jewishness of, 226; Johannine, 9, 11, 109–10; John and, 38, 108; John the Baptist and, 7, 25, 27, 29–30, 32, 46, 63, 65, 149–50; Lukan, 9, 11, 25, 46, 75–76, 79–80, 89, 197; Luke 1:5–2:52, birth and childhood of, 84–86; Luke 4:16–30, preaching on Gentile preference, 89; Luke and, 10–11, 40–41, 78, 213n2; Mark 1:1, "the good news of," 25, 28, 43n8; Mark 1:15, initial preaching of, 8, 26, 30–31, 55, 154; Markan, 9, 25, 37, 150; Mark and, 9–10, 23; Matthean, 9, 33, 46, 49–50, 76; Matthew 4:18–22, call of first disciples, 56; Matthew 8:1–9:38, heals many people, 60–61; Matthew 13:54–17:27, continues with mission and foretells death and resurrection, 64–67; Matthew 15:21–28, Canaanite Woman and, 19, 49–50, 51, 65, 81, 172, 176–77, 241; Matthew 21:1–23:39, enters Jerusalem and confronts leaders, 69–70; Matthew and, 10, 47; with messianic identity, 28, 149, 152, 163; Moses and, 33, 49; as new Moses, 45, 47, 58, 182; Peter and, 5, 28, 32, 38–39, 40; Pilate and, 39, 40, 70, 71, 76, 80, 100–101, 127, 184, 196, 206, 231; Q and, 5, 23; with radical mission, 213n2; "The Significance of Jesus' Death in Mark," 168n12; suffering and death of, 99–102; suffering of, 9–10, 23; walking on water, 65–66; which, 8–9; the Word and, 107, 114, 126, 132nn2–3. *See also* ministry of Jesus; resurrection, of Jesus

Jesus, transmission of story of: redaction criticism, 16–19; Synoptic problem, 14; two-source hypothesis, 14–15; what is Q?, 15–16

Jesus on the way to Jerusalem: Luke 9:51–19:27, 93–99; Mark 8:27–10:52, 32–36; Mark 10:45, "For the Son of Man came not to be served but to serve, and to give his life a ransom for many," 36; Matthew 19:1–20:34, continues to teach, 67–69; multiple aspects of faith, 34

Jewish interpretation: John, 226–27; Luke, 204–5; Mark, 158–59; Matthew, 181–82; reader-centered, comprehensive approach, 142, 158–59, 181–82, 204–5, 226–27

Jewishness, of Jesus, 226
Jewish Prayer Book, 217
The Jewish Annotated New Testament, 142
"the Jews" (*hoi ioudaioi*), 227
Joanna, 78, 91, 102
Johannine Jesus, 9, 11, 109–10
John, close reading of: 8:44, "You are from your father the devil," 121; 18:1–20:31, suffering and glory, 126–29; 18:37, "to testify to the truth," 127; 14:26; 15:26; CF.

14:17; 16:13, the Paraclete, 105–6, 109, 113, 124–25, 129, 226, 228; 1:1–18 prologue, 113–14; 1:19–5:47, ministry of Jesus, 114–20; questions for reflection, 130–31; 6:1–12:50, ministry of Jesus grows and faces opposition, 120–24; 13:1–17:26, farewell discourses, 124–26; 3:1–21, Nicodemus, 108, 118; 21:1–25, addendum, 129–30; the Word and Jesus, 114, 132nn2–3

John, Gospel from various perspectives: author-centered, historical approach, 217–19; deconstruction interpretation, 231–32; disability studies, 233–34; ecological criticism, 234–35; ekklesia-centered, theological interpretation, 225–26; feminist criticism, 222–23; historical-critical method, 217–18; inter(con)textual interpretation, 227–28; Jewish interpretation, 226–27; minoritized criticism, 232–33; narrative criticism, 220–21; postcolonial criticism, 230–31; queer criticism, 229–30; reader-centered, comprehensive approach, 221–35; reader-response criticism, 221–22; social-science criticism, 218–19; text-centered, literary approach, 219–21; textual criticism, 219–20; womanist interpretation, 224

John, Gospel of: audience, 107; author, 107; Christology in, 112, 114, 230; Christology with church in, 225; close reading, 113–30; date, 14, 107; disciples, 108; eschatology, 108; farewell discourses, 105–7, 108, 110, 112, 124–26, 219, 225; how it begins, 107; how it ends, 107–8; human condition, 108; "I am" sayings of Jesus, 111–12; interpretation issues, 112; Jesus, 108; Johannine Jesus, 9, 11, 109–10; 1:18, 114, 132n4, 219; outline, 109; place, 107; source, 105–6, 107; as spiritual, 105; theological themes, 110–11; transformation, 108; with "two-level drama," 217, 225; unique content, 108–9; unique healings, 109; writing style and vocabulary, 105–6

John the Baptist, 54, 83–84, 93, 113–14, 118, 120, 231; death of, 65, 155; disciples of, 115, 150; Herod and, 155; Jesus and, 7, 25, 27, 29–30, 32, 46, 63, 65, 149–50; proclamation and ministry of, 86, 87

Joseph (father of Jesus), 53, 54, 86

Joseph of Arimathea, 40, 41, 71, 102, 128

Judah (130–170 CE), Gospel of, 6

Judaism, Christianity and, 86, 138, 142, 171

Judas, 5–6, 48, 70, 90, 99–100, 126

judge, widow and unjust, 79, 80–83, 97, 103, 195, 199, 201–2, 208

Juel, Donald, 203

kairos (time), 8, 30–31

Kim, Yung Suk, 191n24, 237n47

kin-dom, 206, 207

kingdom of God: Luke 17:20–21, 98; Mark 1:15, "The time is fulfilled, and the kingdom of God has come near," 24, 26, 30–31; Mark 4:11, "To you has been given the secret of the kingdom of God," 24

Kingsbury, Jack, 174

Kinukawa, Hisako, 159–60

Koine Greek, 21

Korea, 227–28

laborers in the vineyard, parable, 45, 48, 51, 61, 64, 68, 187

language, spiritual, 105

last judgment: sheep and goats (Matthew 25:31–46), 48

Latinx community, 164

lawyers, 93–95, 205

Lazarus, 108, 229; Mary of Bethany and, 91, 123; rich man and, 75, 79, 82, 97, 199, 207–8

lepers, 31, 60, 63, 76, 79, 80, 89–91

letters, 4, 34, 46, 140
Levine, Amy-Jill, 142, 204, 214n17
Leviticus 19:18, 37
LGBT people, 12
Liew, Tat-siong Benny, 144, 162, 184
The Life of Aristotle (Andronicus), 23
The Life of Moses (Philo), 23
The Lives the Roman Emperors (Plutarch), 4
The Lives the Twelve Caesars (Suetonius), 4
living water, 33, 62, 106, 118–19, 224
Logos (the Word), 107–8, 113–14, 120, 126, 132nn2–3
Luke, 6, 7; infancy narrative in, 5, 22, 76, 77, 83; Jesus and, 10–11, 40–41, 78, 213n2
Luke, close reading of: 15:11–32, parable of father and two sons, 10–11, 79, 82, 97, 103, 199; 4:14–9:50, Jesus with ministry in Galilee, 88–93; 4:16–30, Jesus's preaching on Gentile preference, 89; 9:51–19:27, Jesus on the way to Jerusalem, 93–99; 19:28–21:38, Jesus's teaching in Jerusalem, 99; 1:1–4, preface, 83; 1:5–2:52, birth and childhood of Jesus, 84–86; 1:5–2:52, preparation for ministry of Jesus, 86–88; 17:20–21, kingdom of God, 98; 10:25–37, good Samaritan, 81–82; "today," 22, 76, 88, 98–99, 101–2, 195–96, 203–4; 24:1–53, resurrection of Jesus, 102–3; 22:1–23:56, suffering and death of Jesus, 99–102
Luke, Gospel from various perspectives: author-centered, historical approach, 195–97; deconstruction interpretation, 208–9; disability studies, 211–12; ecological criticism, 212–13; ekklesia-centered, theological interpretation, 203–4; feminist criticism, 201–2; historical-critical method, 195–96; inter(con)textual interpretation, 205–6; Jewish interpretation, 204–5;

minoritized criticism, 209–10; narrative criticism, 198–200; postcolonial criticism, 207–8; queer criticism, 206–7; reader-centered, comprehensive approach, 200–213; reader-response criticism, 200–201; social-science criticism, 196–97; text-centered, literary approach, 197–200; textual criticism, 197–98; womanist interpretation, 202–3
Luke, Gospel of: audience, 77; author, 77; beatitudes in Matthew and, 57–58, 90; close reading, 83–103; date, 14, 77; disciples, 78; eschatology, 78, 81; how it begins, 77; how it ends, 77; human condition, 78; interpretation issues, 82–83; Jesus, 78; Lukan Jesus, 9, 11, 25, 46, 75–76, 79–80, 89, 197; Mark and, 14, 21, 45, 47; 1:46–55, Mary's Magnificat, 75, 80, 84; outline, 79; parables, 10–11, 79, 81–82, 96–97; place, 77; Q and, 5, 14, 15, 47, 77, 81; questions for reflection, 103; 6:20–23, beatitudes, 75, 90, 202, 208; source, 77; synoptic, 14; theological themes, 80–81; transformation, 78; 2:14 "Glory to God in the highest heaven, and on earth peace among those whom he favors!," 85; two-source hypothesis and, 14–17, 137; unique content, 78; unique healings, 79
lutron (ransom), 158, 168n12

Maccabean Revolt, 40
Magnificat, Mary with, 75, 80, 84
Malachi 3:1, 29, 87
Malbon, Elizabeth Struthers, 158, 168n12
Marcus, Joel, 43n2
Mark: Jesus and, 9–10; Peter and, 22; "The Significance of Jesus' Death in Mark," 168n12; as theologian, 7
Mark, close reading of: 8:27–10:52, Jesus on the way to Jerusalem, 32–36; 11:1–13:37, ministry in

Jerusalem, 36–38; 15:34, "My God, my God, why have you forsaken me?," 40; 14:1–15:47, passion narrative: last supper, trials, and crucifixion, 38–40; 1:1, "the good news of Jesus Christ," 25, 28, 43n8; 1:1–13 prologue, 28–30; 1:14–8:26, public ministry, 30–32; 1:15, initial preaching of Jesus, 26; 16:1–8, resurrection of Jesus, 40–41; 10:45, "For the Son of Man came not to be served but to serve, and to give his life a ransom for many," 36

Mark, Gospel from various perspectives: author-centered, historical approach, 149–51; deconstruction interpretation, 163–64; disability studies, 165–66; ecological criticism, 166–67; ekklesia-centered, theological interpretation, 157–58; feminist criticism, 155–56; historical-critical method, 149–50; inter(con)textual interpretation, 159–60; Jewish interpretation, 158–59; minoritized criticism, 164–65; narrative criticism, 152–53; postcolonial criticism, 161–62; queer criticism, 160–61; reader-centered, comprehensive approach, 153–67; reader-response criticism, 153–54; social-science criticism, 150–51; text-centered, literary approach, 151–53; textual criticism, 151–52; womanist interpretation, 156–57

Mark, Gospel of: audience, 23; author, 22; Christology in, 43n2, 149–50, 160; close reading of, 28–41; date, 14, 22; disciples, 24; 8:22–26, blind man of Bethsaida: "I see people, but they look like trees, walking," 24, 31, 32, 165–66; 8:34–35, "For those who want to save their life will lose it, and those who lose their life for my sake, and for the sake of the gospel, will save it," 24, 32; eschatology, 23; 4:11, "To you has been given the secret of the kingdom of God," 24; 14:51, The young man left the linen cloth and ran away naked, 24; genre, 23; at a glance, 22–24; how it begins, 23; how it ends, 22, 23, 43n5; human condition, 24; influence, 14, 21, 45, 47; interpretation issues, 27–28; Jesus, 23; Markan Jesus, 9, 25, 37, 150; messianic secret in, 22, 149, 152, 163; 1:15, "The time is fulfilled, and the kingdom of God has come near," 24, 26, 30–31; oral proclamation and, 43n3; outline, 24; parables, 24, 26–27, 32, 37, 64, 81; place, 22–23; priority theory, 21; questions for reflection, 41; 7:24–30 compared to Matthew 15:21–28, *18*; 7:34, deaf and dumb man, "Ephphatha, be opened," 24; source, 23; synoptic, 14; 10:32–34, resurrection of Jesus, 35; theological themes, 25–26; 3:17, Boanerges, sons of thunder, 24; transformation, 24; 2:27–28, "The Sabbath was made for humans," 24; unique content, 24; unique healings, 24, 32

Markan Jesus, 9, 25, 37, 150
Martha, 78, 94, 108, 110, 123, 201
Martin, Dale, 229
Martyn, J. Louis, 132n5, 217, 225
Mary (mother of Jesus), 54, 64, 86, 151; conception of, 6, 53; genealogy from, 52; Magnificat, 75, 80, 84; with resurrection of Jesus, 40–41
Mary (120–180 CE), Gospel of, 5–6
Mary Magdalene, 40–41, 71, 78, 102, 109, 128–29, 220–21
Mary of Bethany, 91, 123
Matthean Jesus, 9, 33, 46, 49–50, 76
Matthew: Jesus and, 10; as tax collector, 46, 61; as theologian, 7
Matthew, close reading of: 8:1–9:38, Jesus heals many people, 60–61; 18:1–35, fourth discourse, community instructions, 46, 67; 11:1–12:50, Jesus's ministry

continues while opposition arises, 63–64; 15:21–28, Jesus and the Canaanite Woman, 19, 49–50, 51, 65, 81, 172, 176–77, 241; 5:1–7:29, first discourse, Sermon on the Mount, 56–60; 4:18–22, Jesus's call of the first disciples, 56; genealogy of Jesus, 54; 19:1–20:34, Jesus continues to teach on the way to Jerusalem, 67–69; 1:1–2:23, infancy narrative, 22, 52–54; 10:1–10:42, second discourse, missionary instructions, 61–62; 10:42, "one of these little ones," 62; 13:1–53, third discourse, collections of parables, 64; 13:54–17:27, Jesus continues with his mission and foretells his death and resurrection, 64–67; 3:1–4:25, ministry of Jesus, 54–56; 20:1–16, vineyard laborers, 68; 28:1–20, resurrection of Jesus, 71–72; 24:1–25:46, fifth discourse, sermon on eschatology, 70; 21:1–23:39, Jesus enters Jerusalem and confronts leaders, 69–70; 27:25, "His blood be on us and on our children," 71; 26:1–27:66, passion narrative, 70–71

Matthew, Gospel from various perspectives: author-centered, historical approach, 171–73; deconstruction interpretation, 185–86; disability studies, 188; ecological criticism, 189–90; ekklesia-centered, theological interpretation, 179–80; feminist criticism, 176–77; historical-critical method, 171–72; inter(con)textual interpretation, 182–83; Jewish interpretation, 181–82; minoritized criticism, 186–87; narrative criticism, 174–75; postcolonial criticism, 184–85; queer criticism, 183–84; reader-centered, comprehensive approach, 175–90; reader-response criticism, 175–76; social-science criticism, 172–73; text-centered, literary approach, 173–75; textual criticism, 173–74; womanist interpretation, 177–78

Matthew, Gospel of: audience, 47; author, 46; beatitudes in Luke and, *57–58*, 90; birth narrative, 6, 47, 84; Christology in, 51; close reading of, 52–72; date, 14, 46; disciples, 5, 47; eschatology, 47; 15:21–28 compared to Mark 7:24–30, *18*; 5:1–12, beatitudes, 48, 56, 173; 14:28–33, Peter on the water, 48, 66, 176; at a glance, 46–48; how it begins, 47; how it ends, 47; human condition, 48; interpretation issues, 51–52; Jesus and, 47; Mark and, 14, 21, 45; Matthean Jesus, 9, 33, 46, 49–50, 76; outline, 48–49; parables, 43n7, 48, 50–51, 64; place, 46–47; Q and, 5, 14, 15, 45; questions for reflection, 72–73; 16:16–19, Peter's confession at Caesarea Philippi: "I will build my church on the rock," 48; 16:24–25, "For those who want to save their life will lose it, and those who lose their life for my sake, and for the sake of the gospel, will save it," 66; source, 47; synoptic, 14; theological themes, 50; transformation, 48; 25:31–46, last judgment: sheep and goats, 48; 27:3–10, death of Judas, 48; 2:6, 7; two-source hypothesis and, 14–17, 137; unique content, 48

Meeks, Wayne, 218

messianic identity, Jesus with, 28, 149, 152, 163

messianic secret, in Mark, 22, 149, 152, 163

metanoia (repentance), 4, 29, 31

Micah 5:2, 7

ministry, of John the Baptist, 86, 87

ministry of Jesus, 45, 81; John 1:19–5:47, 114–20; John 6:1–12:50, grows and faces opposition, 120–24; Luke 3:1–4:13, preparation for, 86–88; Luke 4:14–9:50, in Galilee, 88–93; Mark 1:14–8:26, public, 30–32; Mark

11:1–13:37, in Jerusalem, 36–38;
Matthew 3:1–4:25, 54–56; Matthew
11:1–12:50, opposition arises, 63–64
minoritized criticism: John, 232–33;
Luke, 209–10; Mark, 164–65;
Matthew, 186–87; reader-centered,
comprehensive approach, 144,
164–65, 186–87, 209–10, 232–33
missionary instructions (Matthew
10:1–10:42), 61–62
Moses, 34, 109–10; birth story, 49;
Jesus and, 33, 49; Jesus as new, 45,
47, 58, 182; *The Life of Moses*, 23; on
Mount Sinai, 30
Moxnes, Halvor, 206
mustard seed parable, 24, 26–27, 32,
64, 81, 96, 166–67, 176; with field as
cultivated place, 50
Myers, Ched, 161–62, 168n12
"My God, my God, why have you
forsaken me?" (Mark 15:34), 40

Nag Hammadi, Egypt, 5
narrative criticism: John, 220–21; Luke,
198–200; Mark, 152–53; Matthew,
174–75; text-centered, literary
approach, 139, 152–53, 174–75,
198–200, 220–21
narrative Gospels, 5, 13–14
Nazareth, 7, 21, 29–30, 54, 78, 84, 86,
88, 116, 154
Nazoreans (100–160 CE), Gospel of, 6
Nero (Emperor), 23
New International Version (NIV), 115
New Revised Standard Version
(NRSV), 115, 198, 219
Neyrey, Jerome, 223
Nicodemus, 106, 114, 117, 121, 230; as
author of Gospel of Peter, 6; John
3:1–21, 108, 118; as secret disciple of
Jesus, 128
Nigeria, 205
NIV (New International Version), 115
NRSV (New Revised Standard
Version), 115, 198, 219

O'Day, Gail, 176–77
"one of these little ones" (Matthew
10:42), 62
oral traditions, 9, 13–14, 21, 23, 43n2
Origen (third century CE), 6

P4 (papyrus 4), 197
Palestine, 9, 23, 157, 241–42
papyrus 4 (P4), 197
parables: of father and two sons,
10–11, 79, 82, 97, 103, 199; laborers
in vineyard, 45, 48, 51, 61, 64,
68, 187; Luke, 10–11, 79, 81–82,
96–97; Mark, 24, 26–27, 32, 37, 64,
81; Matthew, 43n7, 48, 50–51, 64;
mustard seed, 24, 26–27, 32, 50, 64,
81, 96, 166–67, 176; rich man and
Lazarus, 75, 79, 82, 97, 199; seed
growing secretly, 24, 26–27, 32, 166;
sower, 24, 26–27, 32, 64, 81, 91–92,
166; talents, 48, 50, 51, 70; of tenant,
24, 36–37, 82; ten bridesmaids,
48, 51, 70; Thomas, 5; treasure
and pearl, 48, 51, 64; unforgiving
servant, 45–46, 48, 50–51, 59, 64,
67, 181; wedding banquet, 48, 51,
96; weeds and wheat, 43n7, 48, 50,
51, 64
the Paraclete, John, 105–6, 109, 113,
124–25, 129, 226, 228
Park, Kyung-mi, 227–28
Parousia, 22, 50–51, 76–77, 78, 98,
196–97, 203
Parsons, Mikeal, 211
passion gospels, 6
passion narratives: Mark 14:1–15:47,
last supper, trials and crucifixion,
38–40; Mark 15:34, "My God, my
God, why have you forsaken me?,"
40; Matthew 26:1–27:66, 70–71
Passover meal, 7, 38, 70, 99
pastoral letters, 34, 140
patron-client system, 4, 75, 150
Paul: letters of, 4, 140; on power of
God, 207

Penwell, Stewart, 232
Perkinson, Jim, 162
Peter, 10; confession at Caesarea Philippi: "I will build my church on the rock," Matthew 16:16–19, 48; Jesus and, 5, 28, 32, 38–39, 40; Mark and, 22; on water, Mathew 14:28–33, 48, 66, 176
Peter (70–160 CE), Gospel of, with passion narrative, 6
Pharisees, 37, 47, 49, 61, 71, 91, 96, 121; criticism of, 87; fasting and, 90; as hypocrites, 52, 69–70, 95, 171; lawyers and, 95, 205; purity laws and, 66; with Sabbath, 63–64; Simon the Pharisee, 209, 210; tax collectors and, 79, 80, 97, 199, 208
Philip (180–250 CE), Gospel of, 5–6, 217
Philo, 23
physiognomic consciousness, 211
Pilate (150–255 CE), 11, 87, 174; Acts of, 6; Herod and, 101; Jesus and, 39, 40, 70, 71, 76, 80, 100–101, 127, 184, 196, 206, 231
pistis (belief, faith), 31, 34
place: John, 107; Luke, 77; Mark, 22–23; Matthew, 46–47
Plutarch, 4
police, 100, 121, 164, 205, 223
postcolonial criticism: John, 230–31; Luke, 207–8; Mark, 161–62; Matthew, 184–85; reader-centered, comprehensive approach, 143, 161–62, 184–85, 207–8, 230–31
prayer, disciples with, 95, 100
preaching: Luke 4:16–30, Gentile preference, 89; Mark 1:15, Jesus with initial, 8, 26, 30–31, 55, 154
preface (Luke 1:1–4), 83
Presbyterian Church, 12
priority theory, Markan, 21
privatization, of water, 224
prologue: John 1:1–18, 113–14; Mark 1:1–13, 28–30
prophecy, 7, 53, 85
proverbs, 5, 154
purity laws, 66

Q: contents of, *15–16*; defined, 14–15; Jesus and, 5, 23; Luke and, 5, 14, 15, 47, 77, 81; Matthew and, 5, 14, 15, 45; two-source hypothesis and, 14–15, 137
queer, genealogy, 53
queer criticism: John, 229–30; Luke, 206–7; Mark, 160–61; Matthew, 183–84; reader-centered, comprehensive approach, 143, 160–61, 183–84, 206–7, 229–30; as theological interpretation, 137

race, 140, 143, 210, 232
Rachel, 54, 187
racial profiling, 164
racism, 209, 210, 232
Rahab, 52–53, 54, 183
ransom (*lutron*), 158, 168n12
reader-centered, comprehensive approach: deconstruction interpretation, 143–44, 163–64, 185–86, 208–9, 231–32; disability studies, 144, 165–66, 188, 211–12, 233–34; ecological criticism, 144–45, 166–67, 189–90, 234–35; ekklesia-centered, theological interpretation, 137, 141, 157–58, 179–80, 203–4, 225–26; feminist criticism, 140, 155–56, 176–77, 201–2, 222–23; to gospel interpretation, 135–36; inter(con)textual interpretation, 142, 159–60, 182–83, 205–6, 227–28; Jewish interpretation, 142, 158–59, 181–82, 204–5, 226–27; John, 221–35; Luke, 200–213; Mark, 153–67; Matthew, 175–90; minoritized criticism, 144, 164–65, 186–87, 209–10, 232–33; postcolonial criticism, 143, 161–62, 184–85, 207–8, 230–31; queer criticism, 143, 160–61, 183–84, 206–7, 229–30; reader-response criticism, 140, 153–54, 175–76, 200–201, 221–22; womanist interpretation, 141, 156–57, 177–78, 202–3, 224
reader-response criticism: John, 221–22; Luke, 200–201; Mark, 153–54;

Matthew, 175–76; reader-centered, comprehensive approach, 140, 153–54, 175–76, 200–201, 221–22
readers: gospels as story of Jesus and evangelists for contemporary, 12–13; gospels with critical, imaginative role of, 243–44
redaction criticism, 12, 14; examples, 195–96; historical-critical method and, 136, 137, 195; messianic secret and, 152; transmission of story of Jesus and, 16–19
Reformation, 12
Reid, Barbara, 201
Reinhartz, Adele, 132n5, 226, 227, 230
repentance (*metanoia*), 4, 29, 31
Res Gestae Divi Augusti (The Deeds of the Divine Augustus), 5
resurrection, of Jesus, 150; Luke 24:1–53, 102–3; Mark 10:32–34, 35; Mark 16:1–8, 40–41; Matthew 13:54–17:27, foretelling of death and, 64–67; Matthew 28:1–20, 71–72
rich man and Lazarus parable, 75, 79, 82, 97, 199
Rieger, Joerg, 207
Ruth, 52, 53, 54, 183

"The Sabbath was made for humans" (Mark 2:27–28), 24
Sadducees, 37, 54, 87
Samaritan, good, 81–82, 94, 103, 199, 207
Sanders, Cheryl, 178
"sass," 156
Satan, 30, 32, 55, 95, 157, 202
Saussure, Ferdinand de, 143–44
sayings gospels, 5–6
Schaberg, Jane, 183
Schottroff, Luise, 223
seed growing secretly, parable of, 24, 26–27, 32, 166
Segovia, Fernando, 184
selfhood, sense of family and, 164
sēmeron ("today"), in Luke, 22, 76, 88, 98–99, 101–2, 195–96, 203–4
Senior, Donald, 171

Septuagint, 53, 158
sermon on eschatology (Matthew 24:1–25:46), 70
Sermon on the Mount (Matthew 5:1–7:29), 45–46, 49, 56–60, 175, 189
sexism, 210, 223
sexuality, gender and, 143
sexual stereotyping, 210
Shore-Goss, Robert, 206, 207, 229
"The Significance of Jesus' Death in Mark" (Dowd and Malbon), 168n12
Simon of Cyrene, 39, 41, 101, 128
Simon Peter, 56, 83, 115, 128
Simon the Pharisee, 209, 210
Sinaiticus, codex, 197
slaves, 35–37, 158, 168n12, 184, 207
slut-shaming, 223
Smith, Mitzi, 156, 177, 191n24, 202, 224
social-science criticism: author-centered, historical approach, 138–39, 150–51, 172–73, 196–97, 218–19; John, 218–19; Luke, 196–97; Mark, 150–51; Matthew, 172–73
sociology of knowledge, 138, 218
Socrates, 40
sons: father and two, 10–11, 79, 82, 97, 103, 199; of thunder, Mark 3:17, 24
source: John, 105–6, 107; Luke, 77; Mark, 23; Matthew, 47
source criticism, historical-critical method and, 136, 137
South Africa, 179
sower, parable of, 24, 26–27, 32, 64, 81, 91–92, 166
spiritual language, 105
Stark, Rodney, 172
steward, 79, 91, 116
Suetonius, 4
suffering: of Jesus, 9–10, 23; John 18:1–20:31, glory and, 126–29; Luke 22:1–23:56, Jesus with death and, 99–102
supper, last (Mark 14:1–15:47), 38–40
Susanna, 78, 91
Synoptic problem, transmission of story of Jesus, 14
Syria, 22–23, 46, 56, 85, 89

Syriac manuscript, 6
Syrophoenician woman, 32, 65, 155–56, 159, 162

talents parable, 48, 50, 51, 70
Tamar, 52–53, 54, 183
tax collectors, 76, 87, 204; Matthew as, 46, 61; Pharisees and, 79, 80, 82, 97, 199, 208; Zacchaeus as, 10, 80–81, 98, 211
tekton (carpenter or stone builder), 7, 150
tekton (child), 184
tenant, parable of, 24, 36–37, 82
ten bridesmaids parable, 48, 51, 70
"to testify to the truth" (John 18:37), 127
text-centered, literary approach: to gospel interpretation, 135; John, 219–21; Luke, 197–200; Mark, 151–53; Matthew, 173–75; narrative criticism, 139, 152–53, 174–75, 198–200, 220–21; textual criticism, 139, 151–52, 173–74, 197–98, 219–20
textual criticism: John, 219–20; Luke, 197–98; Mark, 151–52; Matthew, 173–74; text-centered, literary approach, 139, 151–52, 173–74, 197–98, 219–20
theological interpretation, queer criticism as, 137. *See also* ekklesia-centered, theological interpretation
theological themes: John, 110–11; Luke, 80–81; Mark, 25–26; Matthew, 50
Theophilus, 83, 209
Thomas, 90, 124, 129, 222
Thomas, Gospel of, 5, 6, 15
Tiberius (Emperor), 56, 86, 121, 206
time (*kairos*), 8, 30–31
"The time is fulfilled, and the kingdom of God has come near" (Mark 1:15), 24, 26, 30–31
"today" (*sēmeron*), in Luke, 22, 76, 88, 98–99, 101–2, 195–96, 203–4
Tolbert, Mary Ann, 162

"To you has been given the secret of the kingdom of God" (Mark 4:11), 24
transformation: holistic, 178, 191n24; John, 108; Luke, 78; Mark, 24; Matthew, 48
treasure and pearl parable, 48, 51, 64
Troftgruben, Troy, 203, 204
"two-level drama," 217, 225
two-source hypothesis, 14–17, 137

Ujamaa Center, 179
Ukpong, Justin, 205–6
undocumented status, of family members, 164
unforgiving servant parable, 45–46, 48, 50–51, 64, 67, 181

Vaticanus, codex, 197
Vena, Osvaldo, 164
Virgil, 4–5

Warren, Meredith, 223
water, 89, 95, 200, 202; baptism, 17, 21, 29–30, 63, 106, 115, 117, 149; Jesus walking on, 65–66; living, 33, 62, 106, 118–19, 224; Matthew 14:28–33, Peter on, 48, 66, 176; privatization of, 224; into wine, 116, 119
weddings: banquet parable, 48, 51, 96; at Cana, 108, 116
weeds and the wheat parable, 43n7, 48, 50, 51, 64
West, Gerald, 179
widows, 76, 86, 89; with coin offerings, 37, 83, 99; at Nain, 90; with unjust judge, 79, 80–83, 97, 103, 195, 199, 201–2, 208
Wilson, Walter, 188
wine, water into, 116, 119
womanist interpretation: John, 224; Luke, 202–3; Mark, 156–57; Matthew, 177–78; reader-centered, comprehensive approach, 141, 156–57, 177–78, 202–3, 224
women: African Americans, 141, 156; Asian American, 210; at crucifixion,

71, 83, 87; disciples, 242–43; identity of Beloved Disciple, 220; slut-shaming of, 223. *See also* widows

the Word (Logos), 107–8, 113–14, 120, 126, 132nn2–3

World Health Organization, 179

Wrede, William, 149, 163

Wynn, Kerry, 233

"You are from your father the devil" (John 8:44), 121

The young man left the linen cloth and ran away naked (Mark 14:51), 24

Zacchaeus, 10, 77–78, 80–81, 98, 196–97, 199, 211

Zechariah, 69, 83, 84–85, 204

About the Author

Yung Suk Kim (PhD, Vanderbilt University) is professor of New Testament and Early Christianity at the Samuel DeWitt Proctor School of Theology at Virginia Union University. He has authored eighteen books in the areas of biblical interpretation, Pauline studies, and the Gospels, including *Monotheism, Biblical Traditions, and Race Relations* (2022); *How to Read Paul* (2021); and *Resurrecting Jesus* (2015). He has coauthored *Toward Decentering the New Testament* (2018) with Mitzi Smith. He has also edited *Paul's Gospel, Empire, Race, and Ethnicity* (2023); *1 and 2 Corinthians* (2013); and *Reading Minjung Theology in the Twenty-First Century* (2013). He serves as a member of the Bible Translation and Utilization Committee (BTU) to assist in the Bible-publishing activities of the National Council of Churches (NCC).

www.ingramcontent.com/pod-product-compliance
Lightning Source LLC
Chambersburg PA
CBHW031431160426
43195CB00010BB/685